Mining Amazon Web Services: Building Applications with the Amazon API

RENEWALS 458-4574
DATE DUE

AU

WITHDRAWN
UTSA Libraries

John Paul Mueller

Mining Amazon® Web Services: Building Applications with the Amazon API

Sybex

San Francisco · London

Associate Publisher: Joel Fugazzotto
Acquisitions and Developmental Editor: Tom Cirtin
Production Editor: Leslie E.H. Light
Technical Editor: Greg Guntle
Copyeditor: Cheryl Hauser
Compositor: Happenstance Type-O-Rama
Graphic Illustrator: Happenstance Type-O-Rama
Proofreaders: Laurie O'Connell and Nancy Riddiough
Indexer: Lynnzee Elze
Cover Design and Illustration: Richard Miller, Calyx Design

Copyright © 2004 SYBEX Inc., 1151 Marina Village Parkway, Alameda, CA 94501. World rights reserved. The author created reusable code in this publication expressly for reuse by readers. Sybex grants readers limited permission to reuse the code found in this publication or its accompanying CD-ROM so long as the author is attributed in any application containing the reusable code and the code itself is never distributed, posted online by electronic transmission, sold, or commercially exploited as a stand-alone product. Aside from this specific exception concerning reusable code, no part of this publication may be stored in a retrieval system, transmitted, or reproduced in any way, including but not limited to photocopy, photograph, magnetic, or other record, without the prior agreement and written permission of the publisher.

Library of Congress Card Number: 2003115258

ISBN: 0-7821-4307-5

SYBEX and the SYBEX logo are either registered trademarks or trademarks of SYBEX Inc. in the United States and/or other countries. Screen reproductions produced with PaintShop Pro.

Internet screen shots using Microsoft Internet Explorer reprinted by permission from Microsoft Corporation.

Openwave and the Openwave logo are trademarks of Openwave Systems Inc. All rights reserved.

TRADEMARKS: SYBEX has attempted throughout this book to distinguish proprietary trademarks from descriptive terms by following the capitalization style used by the manufacturer.

The author and publisher have made their best efforts to prepare this book, and the content is based upon final release software whenever possible. Portions of the manuscript may be based upon pre-release versions supplied by software manufacturer(s). The author and the publisher make no representation or warranties of any kind with regard to the completeness or accuracy of the contents herein and accept no liability of any kind including but not limited to performance, merchantability, fitness for any particular purpose, or any losses or damages of any kind caused or alleged to be caused directly or indirectly from this book.

Manufactured in the United States of America

10 9 8 7 6 5 4 3 2 1

SOFTWARE LICENSE AGREEMENT: TERMS AND CONDITIONS

The media and/or any online materials accompanying this book that are available now or in the future contain programs and/or text files (the "Software") to be used in connection with the book. SYBEX hereby grants to you a license to use the Software, subject to the terms that follow. Your purchase, acceptance, or use of the Software will constitute your acceptance of such terms.

The Software compilation is the property of SYBEX unless otherwise indicated and is protected by copyright to SYBEX or other copyright owner(s) as indicated in the media files (the "Owner(s)"). You are hereby granted a single-user license to use the Software for your personal, noncommercial use only. You may not reproduce, sell, distribute, publish, circulate, or commercially exploit the Software, or any portion thereof, without the written consent of SYBEX and the specific copyright owner(s) of any component software included on this media.

In the event that the Software or components include specific license requirements or end-user agreements, statements of condition, disclaimers, limitations or warranties ("End-User License"), those End-User Licenses supersede the terms and conditions herein as to that particular Software component. Your purchase, acceptance, or use of the Software will constitute your acceptance of such End-User Licenses.

By purchase, use or acceptance of the Software you further agree to comply with all export laws and regulations of the United States as such laws and regulations may exist from time to time.

Reusable Code in This Book

The author created reusable code in this publication expressly for reuse by readers. Sybex grants readers limited permission to reuse the code found in this publication, its accompanying CD-ROM or available for download from our website so long as the author(s) are attributed in any application containing the reusable code and the code itself is never distributed, posted online by electronic transmission, sold, or commercially exploited as a stand-alone product.

Software Support

Components of the supplemental Software and any offers associated with them may be supported by the specific Owner(s) of that material, but they are not supported by SYBEX. Information regarding any available support may be obtained from the Owner(s) using the information provided in the appropriate read.me files or listed elsewhere on the media.

Should the manufacturer(s) or other Owner(s) cease to offer support or decline to honor any offer, SYBEX bears no responsibility. This notice concerning support for the Software is provided for your information only. SYBEX is not the agent or principal of the Owner(s), and SYBEX is in no way responsible for providing any support for the Software, nor is it liable or responsible for any support provided, or not provided, by the Owner(s).

Warranty

SYBEX warrants the enclosed media to be free of physical defects for a period of ninety (90) days after purchase. The Software is not available from SYBEX in any other form or media than that enclosed herein or posted to www.sybex.com. If you discover a defect in the media during this warranty period, you may obtain a replacement of identical format at no charge by sending the defective media, postage prepaid, with proof of purchase to:

SYBEX Inc.
Product Support Department
1151 Marina Village Parkway
Alameda, CA 94501
Web: `http://www.sybex.com`

After the 90-day period, you can obtain replacement media of identical format by sending us the defective disk, proof of purchase, and a check or money order for $10, payable to SYBEX.

Disclaimer

SYBEX makes no warranty or representation, either expressed or implied, with respect to the Software or its contents, quality, performance, merchantability, or fitness for a particular purpose. In no event will SYBEX, its distributors, or dealers be liable to you or any other party for direct, indirect, special, incidental, consequential, or other damages arising out of the use of or inability to use the Software or its contents even if advised of the possibility of such damage. In the event that the Software includes an online update feature, SYBEX further disclaims any obligation to provide this feature for any specific duration other than the initial posting.

The exclusion of implied warranties is not permitted by some states. Therefore, the above exclusion may not apply to you. This warranty provides you with specific legal rights; there may be other rights that you may have that vary from state to state. The pricing of the book with the Software by SYBEX reflects the allocation of risk and limitations on liability contained in this agreement of Terms and Conditions.

Shareware Distribution

This Software may contain various programs that are distributed as shareware. Copyright laws apply to both shareware and ordinary commercial software, and the copyright Owner(s) retains all rights. If you try a shareware program and continue using it, you are expected to register it. Individual programs differ on details of trial periods, registration, and payment. Please observe the requirements stated in appropriate files.

Copy Protection

The Software in whole or in part may or may not be copy-protected or encrypted. However, in all cases, reselling or redistributing these files without authorization is expressly forbidden except as specifically provided for by the Owner(s) therein.

Foreword

SOAP and XML-based web services are changing the way that applications and Web sites are designed and built. For years, the information processing industry has been trying to build a robust and easy-to-use way to build networked applications by assembling loosely coupled component parts. Earlier efforts such as DCOM, CORBA, and RMI represented the first steps in this direction. These efforts, while respectable in their prime, must now take a backseat to portable and easy-to-use protocols such as SOAP and XML over HTTP (also known as "REST").

It is now possible to build a rich and powerful application by picking and choosing from an array of web services. Developers no longer need to pay attention to the programming language used to implement the service, the physical location of the service, the details of the internal data representation, or the type or brand of the computer running the service. Needless to say, this is a tremendous step forward. Developers can focus on what they want to build without worrying about many mundane implementation details. Service providers can upgrade and enhance their services without creating incompatibilities. The future looks bright!

The features and functionality offered through Amazon Web Services and outlined in this book are among the more powerful public web services available as of this writing. The thousands of developers who download our SDK each month show that we've torn down the walls between the developers and our product data, and paved the way for innovation.

The book in your hands will help you to join the wave of innovation being fueled by Amazon Web Services. John is a gifted writer, and he has written a remarkable book. Going far beyond simply how to accomplish a certain task, the book tells you why you would want to do it, and even what the consequences are of doing so. Each chapter in the book will patiently yet forcefully push you toward the next level of understanding. The slope of this "ramp" is gentle, but it is ever present. As you finish each chapter, you will be surprised to see just how far John has brought you. In an area as new and dynamic as this one, the latest information can often be found online; you will find plenty of links to the latest and greatest developments. John addresses many issues that are far too often left as unstated assumptions in other texts. No matter what your language or platform of choice, you will find a lot to like in this book.

Now, it's your turn. Read the book, learn all about Amazon Web Services, and create something really cool!

—Jeff Barr

Amazon.com
October 2003

Acknowledgments

Thanks to my wife, Rebecca, for working with me to get this book completed. I really don't know what I would have done without her help in researching and compiling some of the information that appears in this book. She also did a fine job of proofreading my rough draft and page proofing the result.

Russ Mullen deserves thanks for his technical edit of this book. He greatly added to the accuracy and depth of the material you see here. Russ is always providing me with great URLs for new products and ideas. I also appreciated his hard work in testing endless versions of applications and providing input for my ideas. This book is technically challenging in that it relies on a number of programming languages, new and evolving technology, and several new products. Russ met the challenge with an efficiency that few other people could match.

A number of people read all or part of this book to help me refine the approach and to test the examples on a number of systems. These unpaid volunteers helped in ways too numerous to mention here. I especially appreciate the efforts of Eva Beattie and Dennis Boyer who read the entire book and selflessly devoted themselves to this project. Osvaldo Téllez Almirall provided extensive input on international issues, making the book much better suited to international needs as a result. Richard Ward also helped with ideas and concepts, along with several other people who asked that I not directly mention their names.

Several vendors also helped with this book. The staff at Amazon has been very helpful—answering my many questions about their service. Some of the support staff at Microsoft helped in answering questions about interfacing Visual Studio to Amazon Web Services. I appreciate the efforts of Simon Fell in working with PocketSOAP.

Matt Wagner, my agent, deserves credit for helping me get the contract in the first place and taking care of all the details that most authors don't really consider. I always appreciate his help. It's good to know that someone wants to help.

Finally, I would like to thank Tom Cirtin, Leslie Light, Cheryl Hauser, and the rest of the editorial and production staff at Sybex for their assistance in bringing this book to print. It's always nice to work with such a great group of professionals and I very much appreciate the friendship we have built over the last two books. I especially appreciate the efforts of Maureen Forys and the staff at Happenstance Type-O-Rama, who provided the great design for this book.

Contents at a Glance

Appendixes

Contents

Introduction

The unicorn is a mythical beast that has attracted the attention and imagination of many people. Unicorns are magical and many people read stories that include them as agents of good. Likewise, until recently, Web services were a mythical beast that programmers only imagined might work eventually. Developers read about Web services and fantasized about their potential. The magic of Web services is that you can combine resources from multiple companies, even if those companies have no idea that you exist. Web services are agents of good—helping developers meet incredibly tight programming schedules. Amazon Web Services is unique in that it's a Web service offering that actually works as advertised. This book is your gateway to the magic that Amazon Web Services can add to your applications. Amazon Web Services isn't just about books, it's about a vast array of products. This Web service doesn't just let you buy products, it helps you research products in new ways and help realize their full potential.

Welcome to a New World

I wrote this book because I believe in the potential of Web services to improve applications everywhere. Web services have the potential to improve data sharing—an event that has always signaled a renaissance in the human condition. Consider, for a moment, the impact of the printing press and the first public newspapers. These technologies helped improve communication and other innovations followed because more people could discuss things in more ways. This book helps you discover Amazon Web Services as a communication method.

Amazon Web Services is a perfect example of how Web services can improve communication. You now have the input of thousands of people at your fingertips. No longer do you have to rely on vendor brochures to tell you about a product, you can learn about a product through the comments of other people—people who have actually bought and purchased the product. However, Amazon Web Services helps you go further. Unlike a static review you could find anywhere, the electronic nature of Amazon Web Services lets you perform analysis and really study a product before you do something with it (and that doesn't necessarily mean buying it).

Each of the sellers on Amazon also has a profile and you can use Amazon Web Services to learn more about that seller. You can consider how well a vendor meets buyer needs and whether the low cost of a product will mean an absence of service after the sale. The ability to choose is a primary human need—Amazon Web Services enhances your ability to choose wisely.

Lest you think that this book is entirely devoted to buying, selling, analyzing, and dissecting both vendors and products, I've also included a few unique uses for Amazon Web Services. For example, you can create a shopping list from Amazon Web Services that you can download to a cellular telephone to use as you shop. When you think about it, this use of Amazon Web Services is just another form of communication.

Obviously, I'll spend time filling in all the gaps. For example, you'll find a checklist for the Amazon Web Services licensing agreement in Appendix B. Using this simple tool helps you ensure that you follow all of the Amazon guidelines and makes your application development experience better.

Unlike the unicorn, Amazon Web Services is real and it's ready to make your life easier. For better or worse, now that Amazon Web Services has arrived and proven its usefulness, we all live in a new world where communication takes yet another form.

Who Should Read This Book?

I've designed this book to meet the needs of anyone who wants to use Amazon Web Services. You might be a corporate developer or a storeowner running a small business who needs an Internet presence. Depending on your needs, you won't use every part of the book, but you'll find that most parts have something to offer. No matter who you are, make sure you read Chapters 1 through 4. Chapters 5 through 8 are language specific, so choose a language and read the appropriate chapter (more if you're multilingual). Chapter 9 helps anyone who wants to write an application for mobile devices. Finally, Chapters 10 through 12 will help people who want to go a little further in the development process. In short, the book has something for everyone, but you might not need to read everything.

Some people have noted that a one-size-fits-all approach generally doesn't work. I realized this early on and made a few assumptions about your skills. You need to know something about computers—you can't pick up this book as a complete novice and expect to learn something. This book is packed with resources—many of which you'll need to locate on the Internet and read. I've assumed that you're motivated to learn what Amazon Web Services can do for you and will use these resources to augment the information that I've provided. That said, all of the examples include complete explanations, so you don't have to worry that this book is incomplete. In fact, you'll find many instances where the information provided doesn't appear anywhere else.

It's possible to use this book without much programming knowledge, but you'll get a lot more out of it if you do know how to program at least a little. I've included a few examples, such as the "Using a Browser Example" in Chapter 2 for people who don't program much (or at all). The VBA examples in Chapter 5 are very easy and might be the best choice if your programming skills are weak.

You won't find any information on using the programming language of your choice in this book—this book concentrates on Amazon Web Services solutions of all types. In fact, I'll suggest several additional books you might want to try in addition to this book if you don't have the required background. Consequently, you won't want to look at this book until you've already learned to use the programming language of your choice.

Tools Required

I've made some assumptions while writing the application programming examples in this book. During the writing of this book, I used a Windows 2000 server and two Windows XP workstations (along with other devices). I also tested many of the examples using Windows 9*x*. One of the book readers was kind enough to check as many examples as possible on a Linux setup. I even tried a few of the examples on a NetWare setup. The test machines included SQL Server and MySQL. I also created Web server setups using Internet Information Server (IIS) and Apache. The test base was as broad as I could make it, but it wasn't possible for me to test every combination of machine and software.

I tested all of the examples in this book using the most current version of the appropriate language product. In most cases, I tell you which language version I used as part of the example description. I don't guarantee that the example will work with any older versions of the product, nor did I test using educational versions of products. Given the relative simplicity of Amazon Web Services, however, I'm certain that most examples will work with any newer version of the supported language.

All of the desktop and Web application examples will work on a single machine, but I tested any database application on a two-machine setup as well to ensure you could place the database on another machine. The mobile device applications are all tested using an actual device, but I also tested them using an emulator. Chapter 9 tells you how to work with emulators and presents a number of emulators you might try when writing your application.

About the Author

John Mueller is a freelance author and technical editor. He has writing in his blood, having produced 61 books and over 300 articles to date. The topics range from networking to artificial intelligence and from database management to heads down programming. Some of his current books include several C# developer guides, an accessible programming guide, a book on .NET security, and several Windows XP user guides. His technical editing skills have helped over 32 authors refine the content of their manuscripts. John has provided technical editing services to both *Data Based Advisor* and *Coast Compute* magazines. He's also contributed articles to magazines like *InformIT, SQL Server Professional, Visual C++ Developer, Hard Core Visual Basic*, and *Visual Basic Developer*. He's currently the editor of the .NET electronic newsletter for Pinnacle Publishing (`http://www.freeenewsletters.com/`).

When John isn't working at the computer, you can find him in his workshop. He's an avid woodworker and candle maker. On any given afternoon, you can find him working at a lathe or putting the finishing touches on a bookcase. He also likes making glycerin soap, which comes in handy for gift baskets. You can reach John on the Internet at `JMueller@mwt.net`. John is also setting up a Web site at: `http://www.mwt.net/~jmueller/`, feel free to look and make suggestions on how he can improve it. One of his current projects is creating book FAQ sheets that should help you find the book information you need much faster.

Part I

Discovering Amazon Web Services

Chapter 1

Understanding Web Services | Working with Amazon Web Services | Using Amazon Web Services to Your Advantage

Learning about Amazon Web Services

Getting the Amazon Web Services Kit | Installing the Kit on a Machine | Considering the Setup of the Development System

You might have already heard quite a bit about Amazon Web Services without really understanding what the phrase means. Amazon is an amazing company. Unlike many companies that created an online presence and are no longer in business, Amazon is still around today and thriving. In fact, the company's owner, Jeff Bezos, was recently quoted as saying the Amazon Services subsidiary (the one that provides your online experience among other things) might eventually become their main business (see the InfoWorld article at `http://www.infoworld.com/article/03/06/10/HNamazondives_1.html?business` for details). Given all that Amazon is doing, it's easy to understand how all of these new services could become confusing even to seasoned professionals.

This chapter helps you understand what Amazon Web Services can do for you and how it fits within your business or research plans. It also discusses what you need to know in order to best use Amazon Web Services for your particular needs. Although you might think that Amazon Web Services is only good for people who want to act as associates and sell goods through their Web site, Amazon Web Services is capable of performing myriad other interesting tasks. For example, many individuals use Amazon Web Services as a means for performing research without ever engaging in buying or selling products.

Once the chapter gets past the basic concepts behind the Amazon Web Service, it demonstrates how to obtain the required resources and set them up on your machine. For example, you need both the Amazon Web Services Kit and a developer token to perform basic tasks. In fact, the chapter describes setup scenarios that you should consider to make your machine better reflect what the user of the Web site, document, or application you build will see. Some situations might require you to set up a system that also includes alternative devices such as a Personal Digital Assistant (PDA). In short, when you complete this chapter, you'll have a copy of the Amazon Web Services Kit installed on a machine configured to meet specific requirements.

Understanding Amazon Web Service

Whenever a new technology appears on the scene, it's important to compare it with other technologies you might have used in the past. The comparison process often helps you decide how this new technology differs from what you used in the past and reduces problems caused by hype. The media might try to convince you that a new product or service is something completely different, when in fact it's merely an update of an existing technology. Currently, there's a lot of hype about Web services that makes them sound like something new and very complex. This section of the chapter defines Web services generally, examines Amazon Web Services specifically, and compares this technology to older technologies. What you'll find might surprise you because Web services are really a new implementation of an old technique.

What Is a Web Service?

You can look at a Web service from a number of perspectives. The easiest way to view a Web service is as a means of obtaining access to information. Essentially, you ask the server for information and the server returns that information in some form. The request and the returned information normally appear in eXtensible Markup Language (XML) form. Using XML preserves the meaning behind the information, regardless of the diversity of the platforms involved, so that you receive not only the information, but understand the context in which the information is used. The "Understanding XML Basics" section of Chapter 3 tells you more about XML. All you need to know now is that you receive information in XML format.

> **▶ NOTE**
>
> Don't confuse *new* with *useful*. Web services are very useful because they add new functionality to an existing idea that has worked for a long time. They're also new in that they use a different process from other technologies. However, the technology itself builds on other techniques that you have already used in some way. In sum, the implementation is new, the process is useful, but the technique is the same one you've used in the past.

From an Amazon Web Services perspective, you request information on one or more products, vendors, or other search criteria. The request defines the kind of information you want to know and how detailed that information will be. Amazon Web Services returns the information you request (when available) in a standardized format.

A Web service also performs some type of useful work. The useful work might be something as simple as interpreting your request, calculating the answer, and sending the result back. In the case of the Amazon Web Service, the Web service accepts your request (normally some search criteria), interacts with the database through a search engine to obtain the information you requested, and sends the information back to you. You can also perform other tasks using the Amazon Web Service, such as making a purchase or selling goods to others. The rest of the book shows how to perform all of these tasks.

The final consideration for a Web service (at least from the Web service user perspective) is that it executes on the remote machine, not on your machine. In short, this means you're using resources on that other machine with the permission of the machine's owner. The remote machine can set requirements for using the Web service, as well as require you to perform specific setup and security checks as part of your request. In the case of the Amazon Web Service, you need to obtain this permission by requesting it as part of the Amazon Web Services Kit download process. The "Getting a Developer Token" section of this chapter tells how to obtain the required permission and what this permission means to you.

> **▶ TIP**
>
> You may find that Amazon Web Services is so indispensable that you'll want to work with Web services from other vendors. For example, Microsoft supports the MapPoint Web Service (`http://www.microsoft.com/mappoint/net/`). In time, standards organizations will set up directories of these Web services that you can access with ease. In the meantime, you can search for companies that offer Web services using the Web Services Finder page at `http://www.15seconds.com/WebService/`. Some people have problems using the Web Services Finder. In some cases, you'll need to use a specialty Web service list such as the one at `http://www.flash-db.com/services/`.

How Do Web Services Work?

Many people fear new technology because they don't understand how it works, and many of those who do know how it works enjoy the mystique of knowledge too much to share it with anyone else. Web services are actually quite easy to understand if you look at them in a way that relates the task to everyday occurrences. For example, you might compare the operation of a Web service to making a withdrawal at the bank—the process really is the same. The one thing to remember is that the process a Web service uses to perform a task is always the same. No matter what technology you use to make a request or receive a response, the steps are still the same. Here are the steps that most Web services, including the Amazon Web Service, use to complete a transaction.

1. *The client discovers the Web service.* During the act of discovery, the client might do things like download a file that tells how to interact with the Web service. This step is the same as someone walking into the bank. The person knows the bank exists and the bank teller might have noticed the person. The bank posts the rules for making a withdrawal or the teller might help a first-time banker understand the rules.

> **▶ NOTE**
>
> Amazon's database *schema* specifies the format of the information. A schema defines the organization of information in a database. You can learn more about the format of the data in the "Previewing the Amazon Database" section of Chapter 3.

2. *The client makes a request based on the rules delivered during the discovery phase.* The rules might specify that the request has to appear in a certain form and the client must provide specific data. This step is the same as the person walking up to the teller's window with a withdrawal request. The request must contain the person's account number, the amount they wish to withdraw, and other identifying information. The bank specifies the format of the request and the information it must contain.
3. *The server might ask the client for credentials depending on the openness of the Web service.* Amazon Web Services is public but still requires that you supply a developer token as identification. This step is the same as the bank teller asking you for a driver's license or other form of identification before honoring your withdrawal request.
4. *The Web service performs the work required to honor your request.* In most cases, the Web service accesses a database for information, it could enter an order, and it might even provide some level of formatting. Amazon Web Services performs a number of tasks depending on the request you make. The easiest request is a product search. This step equates to the bank teller getting the money from the drawer and counting it.
5. *The Web service sends the data to the client.* The content of the information depends on the Web service. Amazon Web Services provides data in a very specific format based on the content of the associated database and the nature of the request. This step equates to the teller handing the person their money. In general, the teller orders the money in a specific way and counts it out to the person, rather than simply handing the money over.
6. *The client logs out of the Web service or the Web service disconnects the client after some period of inactivity.* This step equates to the person leaving the bank, money in hand. If the person doesn't leave the bank (they just hang out in the lobby), you can be sure that someone will ask them to leave.
7. *The client does something with the data it receives.* In many cases, it formats the data and presents it on screen for the user. This step equates to the person spending the money they receive from the bank.

You can add any amount of complexity needed to the individual steps, but these seven steps define the process every Web server follows. When you break a Web service down into these seven steps, the process that used to appear as magic suddenly becomes quite doable. Chapters 5 through 9 are essentially options you can use to perform these seven steps using different technologies. This book explores the seven steps using various languages and platforms—Amazon Web Services makes information available to just about anyone who needs it. However, it's important to remember that everything comes down to a client making a request and the Web server returning data.

Considering the Usage Requirements

There's no free lunch. Some people would have you believe that the Web service does everything for you and that the client does nothing at all. However, the client interacts with the Web service, which means the client must possess some intelligence to perform the task. To use a Web service, you must understand the usage requirements.

From a client perspective, the type of device you use to access the Web service determines the access speed, as well as what you can do with the data once you receive it. Although a PDA such as the Pocket PC can access Amazon Web Services just fine, most people wouldn't want to use it to place orders. About the best you can hope for is to search for individual products or to perform other kinds of simple research. On the other hand, a desktop or laptop machine has all of the processing power, screen real estate, and functionality to perform any task. Amazon Web Services hasn't changed, but the capability of the client has.

> **▶ NOTE**
>
> This book discusses a number of mobile devices. The Pocket PC provides additional functionality and features that make it a better target for some types of applications than devices such as the Palm. On the other hand, most Palm devices are much easier to carry and cost less than the Pocket PC. This book examines the entire range of mobile devices to ensure you understand the limitations of using a specific device to access Amazon Web Services. I'm not saying one device is better than another—simply that one device works better than the other for a given application.

Amazon Web Services also has some usage requirements and these requirements might change the way that you use your client. For example, according to the license agreement (see Appendix B for details) you can't make more than one request per second. In addition, you can't send a file larger than 20KB to Amazon Web Services. Some requests let you supply information to Amazon, so it's possible to exceed the size limitation. These two limitations ensure the Amazon servers won't become overloaded, but they also mean you must provide some type of monitoring in your application to prevent abuse of the licensing terms.

Amazon is interested in protecting its intellectual property. A Web service is essentially a borrowed resource—you're using information supplied by someone else with resources on the remote server. Consequently, you'll find some restrictions on what you can do with the data that Amazon supplies through its Web service. Although you can display the data in any format desired, you can't take credit for the data or modify it (except to shorten it as necessary). You also have to display any

> **▶ WARNING**
>
> If you violate the licensing terms, Amazon Web Services simply denies your request. In addition, you might receive a message from Amazon requesting that you adhere to the terms of usage for the Web service.

copyright or other notices provided with the data. These provisions ensure that someone viewing the data you obtain from Amazon sees the same information that they'll find on the Amazon site.

Old data is a problem. The sales rank for a book might change or Amazon could change the price of a product. Consequently, when using Amazon Web Services you must guarantee that you'll refresh the data every 24 hours when you don't provide prices or availability, or every hour when you do. The licensing agreement provides an email address you can use to request changes to this policy. Data update requirements become a problem when you choose to store the data locally, rather than obtain it from Amazon each time. Developers will store the data locally to obtain a performance benefit—it takes less time to use the local copy of a product description than to request it from Amazon. Obviously, this particular requirement won't be a problem for most Pocket PC users because local storage is at a premium, but it's something you do need to consider for every other environment.

Discovering Uses for Amazon Web Service

The main reason to use Amazon Web Services is to gain personal, company, or monetary benefit. Many people view Amazon Web Services as a way to earn extra money by becoming an associate. However, there are other ways to use this Web service and many of them don't involve an exchange of money. Although this book will provide a lot of examples on how to leverage Amazon Web Services on a Web site or as part of an application to act as an associate, you'll also see other examples that show other uses. (See the "Developing a Shopping Cart Application" section in Chapter 12 for an in-depth explanation of how to develop a Web application that allows users to buy and sell products from Amazon through your Web site.)

Using Overviews and Details

No matter what you plan to do with Amazon, you need to know how to search for the products and services you want. It might be tempting to say that you could use the search engine interface provided by Amazon to perform this task, but the Amazon display is somewhat limiting in that you need to perform several searches to obtain the information you want in most cases. For example, suppose you want to find a book on working with exotic fish. To ensure the book contains information on tetras, you need to look through the table of contents for each book. Although the search engine provides this information, getting to it online can be cumbersome because you have to look up all of the available books that discuss exotic fish, select an individual book from the list, locate the table of contents, review the table of contents one page at a time, and hope that you find what you need. If the first book doesn't contain the information you need, you must perform the same process with the second and subsequent books. This search process could take all day.

Using an application to hunt down the information for you is much simpler. A program that relies on Amazon Web Services can download all of the books that discuss exotic fish, including the table of contents for each book. (Not every publisher supplies a table of contents for online viewing, so you might not be able to perform this search on every book.) The program can then do the searching for you. Your program would only display the books that actually mention tetras in the table of contents.

Searching for information on tetras is one example of a far more complex process, but it gives you a good understanding of how you can use custom search programs to your benefit. In this case, the custom program saves substantial time, lets you locate the precise book you need quickly, and still garners a sale for Amazon. It is the perfect example of how Web services can pay off for everyone involved. Amazon could never design a search engine interface that meets such specific needs—the developers at Amazon have to create a search engine interface that works for the majority of people who visit the site. In sum, a generic search engine can serve most needs, but it might not be the most efficient choice for everyone.

> **▶ NOTE**
>
> The licensing agreement you see when you sign up for an Amazon Web Services developer token includes a number of other requirements for using the Web service. For example, you must create a link back to the Amazon site for every Amazon product you display on your Web site, even if you derive this information from the Amazon data in some way that isn't apparent. Make sure you understand these requirements before you begin a project. Appendix B can also help you create a checklist for your application that ensures compliance with the requirements.

Amazon doesn't require you to know specific product names or any specifics for that matter. Searching for information lets you refine the criteria for locating specific products. You can specify searches using any of the criteria in the following list (Amazon might add other criteria in a future update).

Amazon Standard Item Number (ASIN) Amazon assigns a unique number to every product in their stock called an ASIN. You can use the ASIN, if you know it, to obtain information about a specific book. For books, Amazon uses the ISBN number without any punctuation the book publisher might provide. For example, an ISBN of 0-7821-4134-X becomes an ASIN of 078214134X. The correlation isn't always direct, but you can learn more about the ASIN topic essentials in the kit at `\AmazonWebServices\API Guide\search_asin_isbn.htm`.

Browse Identification Number A browse identification number (Browse ID) lets you search by product classification. For example, you might want to find bargain books. In this case, you'd use the Browse ID of 45. Likewise, technical books have a Browse ID of 173507. You'll find a list of common Browse IDs in the kit at `/AmazonWebServices/API Guide/common_modes.htm`.

> **▶ TIP**
>
> Some people think that the only product that Amazon sells is books. However, you can buy many products through Amazon, including products from other vendors such as Toys"R"Us. For more information on the Toys"R"Us connection, check the BusinessWeek story at `http://www.businessweek.com/2000/00_43/b3704050.htm`. Another good place to look for information is the World Trade magazine article at `http://www.worldtrademag.com/CDA/ArticleInformation/coverstory/BNPCoverStoryItem/0,3481,89675,00.html`. (Note that you might have to sign up as a subscriber to access the World Trade magazine article.) The bottom line is that you should become familiar with all of the products you can obtain through Amazon to ensure you make maximum benefit of its Web service offering.

Keyword The term keyword is somewhat misleading. A keyword can be anything from the ISBN of a book to the author's name. When searching for a CD, you can choose the artist's name. You can also select movies by genre or products by type. Any information that relates back to the product in some way can appear as a keyword. Obviously, some keywords work better than others, so you need to experiment a little to determine which keywords work best. In addition, you might find that you need to filter the information you receive to ensure you display just the products you want. You can learn more about the essentials of keyword searches in the kit at `/AmazonWebServices/API Guide/search_keywords.htm`.

Listmania® ID Amazon is very much customer driven. This way of doing business appears in every aspect of the online experience from the customer reviews to the use of the Listmania feature. Listmania is a collection of customer classifications. For example, you might find a category called best DVD or most thrilling adventure. You must actually search online to discover the Listmania ID numbers because Amazon doesn't provide a list of them in the kit. The number appears as part of the URL for the Listmania search. Figure 1.1 shows a typical example of a Listmania entry. Notice that the URL includes the number 19J6Y001ZYYD3. This is the Listmania ID. You can learn more about this search type in the kit at `/AmazonWebServices/API Guide/search_listmania.htm`.

Wish List A wish list search works very much the same as a Listmania ID search. The big difference is that someone registers wish items in a registry. Knowing the Wishlist ID lets you access this list and buy products for that person based on the entries. This is a great option to make birthdays or other special events easier to handle. You can learn more about wish list searches by looking in the kit at `/AmazonWebServices/API Guide/search_wishlist.htm`.

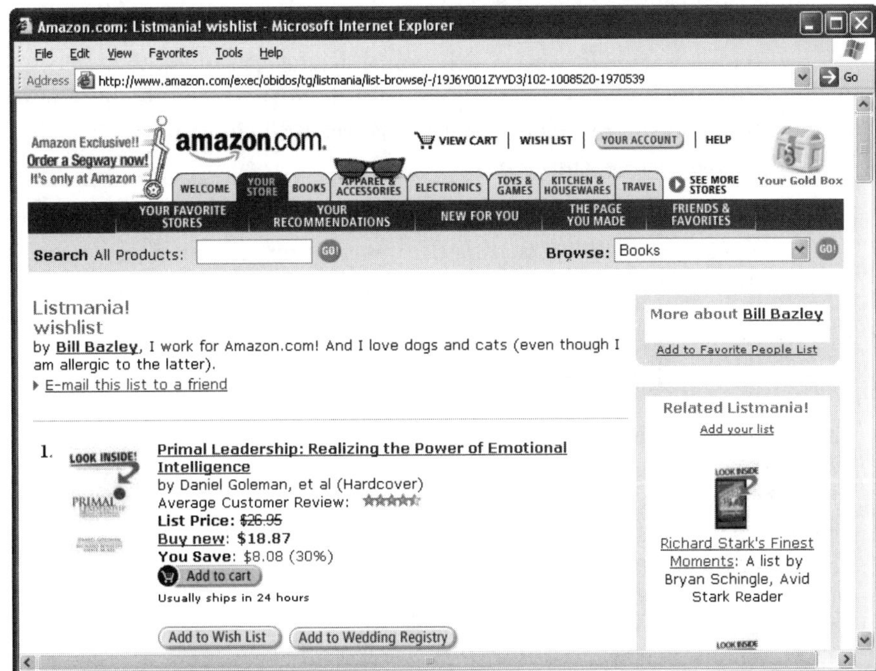

FIGURE 1.1: Use Listmania ID numbers to access specific product collections.

Now that you have a better idea of why you would want to build a custom search engine, it's time to discuss specific kinds of searches. The following sections describe three kinds of searches that you might want to perform. This list simply contains suggestions. As you become more knowledgeable about the Amazon database structure, you'll discover other kinds of searches that meet your specific needs.

Locating Books

Many people will begin their Amazon Web Services experience by looking for books because they're most familiar with that part of Amazon. You can perform searches using any of the four techniques listed at the introduction to this section. In addition to these standard techniques, you can also use a number of techniques specifically suited to meet the needs of book searches. The following list describes each of these searches.

Author Many people like to search by author name because they have read other works by that author and wish to find something new. When using the browser interface to the Amazon search engine, you can specify the author name as a keyword. However, the advanced search shown in Figure 1.2 lets you enter the author name as a specific item, which usually produces better results because the search engine understands the search type better. (You can find the advanced search page at `http://www.amazon.com/exec/obidos/ats-query-page/`.) Fortunately, the Amazon Web Services interface lets you specify author as a separate item as well as long as you specify the search type as a book. You can learn more about this kind of search by looking in the kit at `/AmazonWebServices/API Guide/search_author.htm`.

International Standard Book Number (ISBN) Like the author search, you can specify an ISBN (including the punctuation) as part of a keyword search. When you want to locate a specific book, use the ASIN search method described earlier. However, you can actually obtain better results for all books that include this ISBN as part of the descriptive data if you use a keyword search. For example, you might find that you need to perform a keyword search when you want to locate a set of books, rather than a single book. You can learn more about the ISBN option by looking in the kit at `/AmazonWebServices/API Guide/search_asin_isbn.htm`.

> **▶ TIP**
>
> This list is by no means complete. I often experiment with the online engine to see what search methods are practical and what results they produce. For example, the keyword category covers a lot of ground because you can use practically anything for a keyword. However, not all keywords work equally well. For example, entering an author's full name in the search box might not yield all of the books that are available for that author. (Some authors only use their first and last name.) On the other hand, entering just the author's last name may yield too many results. I find that specifying just the first and last name provides satisfactory results in most cases.

Power Search You might have noticed that Figure 1.2 includes more than just the author name and ISBN. Amazon Web Services lets you supply other input values for books using the power search technique. This technique only works with books and not with any other product type (including third party products). A power search can include the following keywords: Title, Subject, Author, Keyword, ISBN, Publisher, Language, and Publication. You can learn more about power searches by looking in the kit at `/AmazonWebServices/API Guide/search_power.htm`.

Locating Other Products

Amazon is directly involved in providing access for third parties, both large and small. For example, you can locate and purchase toys from Toys"R"Us and music from CDNOW through Amazon. (In fact, the `http://www.cdnow.com` URL redirects your browser to `http://www.amazon.com/exec/obidos/tg/browse/-/3023481/`.) You can even build a Web service application to handle the task. Likewise, you can find movies, music, dishes, apparel, and a long list of other items. Look at `http://www.amazon.com/exec/obidos/subst/home/all-stores.html/` for a complete list of stores that Amazon currently works with.

FIGURE 1.2:

The advanced search lets you locate books based on specific input.

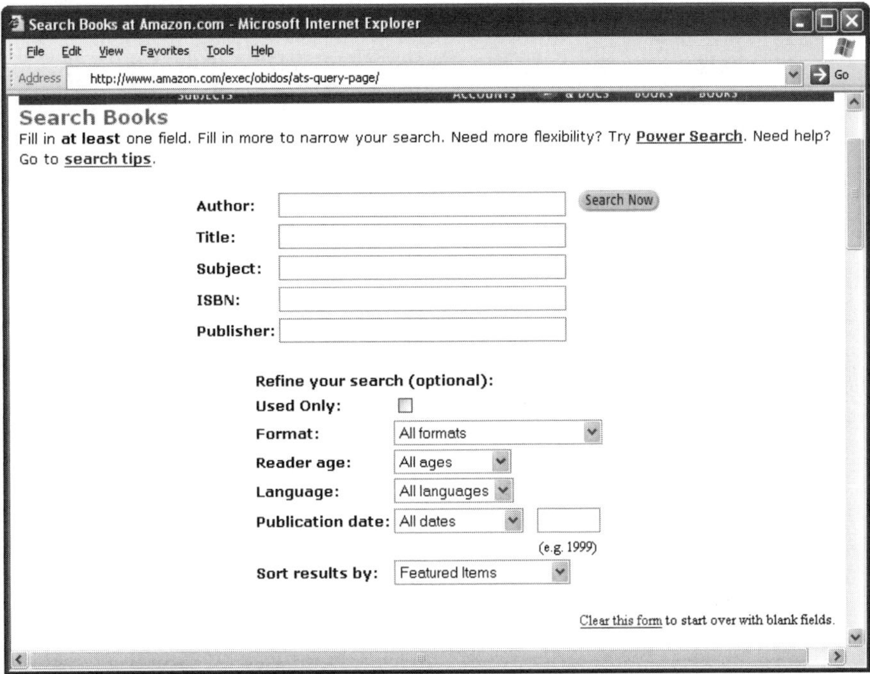

Although you can't find these items using a power search, Amazon Web Services does make them available through other means. For example, you can search for movies by the actor, actress, or director. The following list describes some of the searches you can perform.

Actor/Actress Generally, you'll use this kind of search to locate a favorite movie. The search doesn't work with non-movie searches because the Web service assumes you'll use a keyword search for other types of actor/actress searches (such as locating a book). You can learn more about actor/actress searches by looking in the kit at `/AmazonWebServices/API Guide/search_actor.htm`.

Artist/Musician An artist/musician search helps you locate music. You can't use this search to perform tasks such as locating a famous painting because the Web service doesn't view an artist in that way. If you need to

> **NOTE**
>
> A few of the searches in the "Locating Other Products" section also apply to books. For example, you can perform similarities and UPC searches on books. As Amazon improves their Web service, you'll find additional crossover between product categories. When you have doubts about the usefulness of a search, try it and see what results you get.

find an artist (the kind that paints or creates some other form of physical art), then you need to perform a keyword search. You can learn more about artist/musician searches by looking in the kit at `/AmazonWebServices/API Guide/search_artist.htm`.

Director As with the actor/actress search, this search type relates to movies. You can learn more about director searches by looking in the kit at `/AmazonWebServices/API Guide/search_director.htm`.

Exchange Every third party product offered by Amazon has an exchange identifier. This identifier works much like the Browse ID and Listmania ID mentioned earlier in the chapter. Amazon doesn't provide an Exchange ID list, so you need to perform a search to find the one you need. The Exchange ID appears as part of the URL when you see the word "exchange" in the URL as well. For example, in the URL: `http://s1.amazon.com/exec/varzea/ts/exchange-glance/Y01Y4980982Y9866305/`, Y01Y4980982Y9866305 is the Exchange ID. You can learn more about Exchange ID searches by looking in the kit at `/AmazonWebServices/API Guide/search_exchanges.htm`.

Manufacturer Manufacturer searches help you find a particular product vendor. For example, you might only want to learn about products from Sony. The problem with the manufacturer search is that it doesn't rely on an identifier—it uses a string that contains the manufacturer name. This type of search requires that you know the manufacturer name as Amazon recorded it in their database and assumes Amazon recorded the manufacturer name the same for every product. In many cases, popular manufacturers will require you to perform several searches using the variants of the vendor name. Of course, using a Web service application lets you automate the process instead of entering the information manually in a search form online. You can learn more about manufacturer searches by looking in the kit at `/AmazonWebServices/API Guide/search_manufacturer.htm`.

Marketplace A marketplace search is on the same order as a power search—except that it concentrates on products, instead of books. Like a power search, a marketplace search lets you perform very exacting research on Amazon. Figure 1.3 shows the online version of the marketplace search (`http://s1.amazon.com/exec/varzea/subst/search/fixed-search.html`). As a developer, you can use any of the following parameters as your search criteria: Keyword-Search, Browse-ID, Zipcode, Area-ID, Geo, Rank, and Index. The Area ID parameter identifies the country. Appendix C contains a complete list of Area ID values. You combine the Area ID with a Geo value to specify the location of the shipper or the recipient. The Rank property defines the sort order of the returned values. The Index property determines whether you receive marketplace or ZShop entries. You can learn more about marketplace searches by looking in the kit at `/AmazonWebServices/API Guide/search_marketplace.htm`.

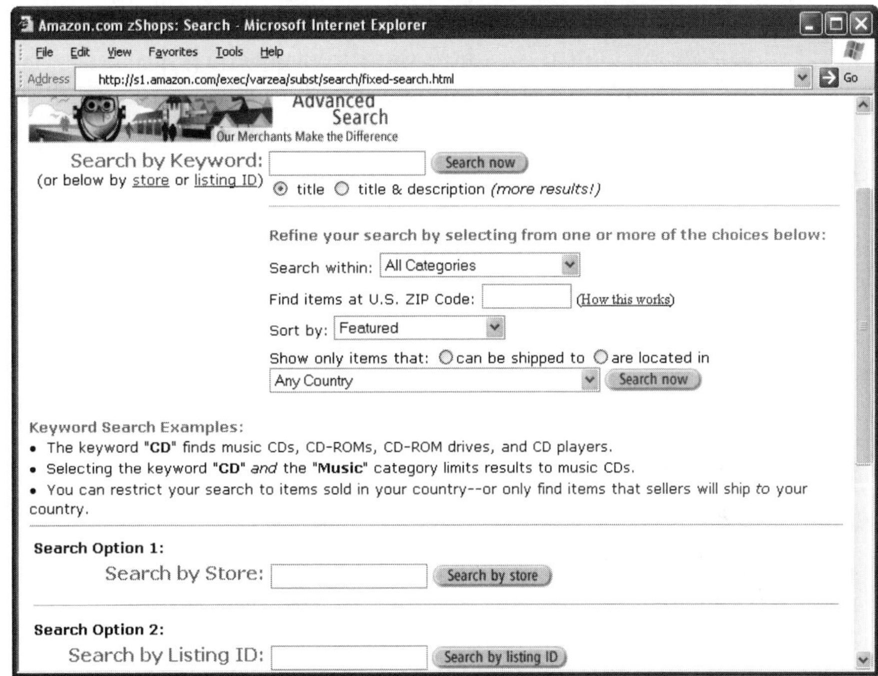

FIGURE 1.3: Use a marketplace search to provide exacting product search criteria.

Seller Profile You don't have to accept that a vendor has a spotless record. When you find a product you like online, you can use the Seller ID returned by that search to locate seller profile information. This information includes a cumulative rating and seller statistics such as nickname. The profile also includes individual comments and the number of sales the seller lost. Think of the seller profile as a sort of online Better Business Bureau (BBB). You can learn more about seller profile searches by looking in the kit at `/AmazonWebServices/API Guide/search_seller_profiles.htm`.

Similarities Many of the products you see on Amazon have a "Customers who bought this item also bought" or "Customers who shopped for this item also shopped for these items" entry. These entries tell you about similarities between the current product and the list of products that follow the entry. After you find a primary product that interests you, you can use the ASIN from that product to perform a similarities search. Unfortunately, this isn't a smart search. While two books might contain XML in the title, they might not be true replacements. This is one case where Amazon can make recommendations, but you have to exercise caution in make the selection. You can learn more about similarities searches by looking in the kit at `/AmazonWebServices/API Guide/search_similarities.htm`.

Third Party Every third party vendor that works with Amazon has a Seller ID. You obtain this ID by looking for a product sold by that person. The Seller ID appears as part of the URL in the same way that the Exchange ID (explained earlier in this section) does. You can learn more about third party searches by looking in the kit at `/AmazonWebServices/API Guide/search_third_party.htm`.

Universal Product Code (UPC) Just about every product imaginable includes a UPC symbol today. Scanning the symbol enters the UPC in a computer or special scanning device. You can use the UPC to look for items on Amazon. According to the documentation, this option currently works only for music CDs, but testing shows that it does work for other items (albeit, inconsistently). Look for Amazon to allow UPC searches for other product categories in the near future. You can learn more about UPC searches by looking in the kit at `/AmazonWebServices/API Guide/search_upc.htm`.

Locating Services

Amazon provides access to a number of services such as the associates program and its own Amazon VISA card. You can make keyword requests for services that you need using the same techniques you use for finding books or other products. The list of Amazon service categories appears at `http://www.amazon.com/exec/obidos/subst/home/all-stores.html/`. Don't get the idea that services just include the mundane. You can also perform tasks such as looking up your favorite restaurant, reading reviews about it, and downloading the current menu. I find the restaurant service lets me find new places to try with minimal risk.

Acting as an Associate

One of the first uses of the Amazon Web Service, outside of searching for things, is to act as an associate. Today's economy actually makes being an associate a great idea because you can usually get a few dollars each month for very little work. An associate simply directs potential buyers to the appropriate Amazon Web site. When a potential buyer makes a purchase, the associate receives a commission. You can learn more about the associate program at `http://www.amazon.com/gp/browse.html/ref=sd_str_as_dir/?node=3435371`.

Most associates add product entries to their Web site. The Web site likely contains a description of the product and the potential buyer clicks on a link to go to the Amazon Web site to make the purchase. However, associates can use any number of application types to perform the same task. For example, you could create an intranet site for a group or even create a desktop application with an HTML interface. Amazon doesn't require you to provide the links in a specific way.

Depending on your application setup, you must refresh the content periodically to maintain your licensing agreement with Amazon. Normally, this means refreshing the content every 24 hours if you display just the content. You must refresh the content every hour if you display prices.

Providing Enterprise Services

Maintaining a corporate library, creating purchase lists, or researching product ideas all take considerable time if you rely on catalogs. Even searching for this kind of information online can take a long time. The process is also error prone because you normally have to read someone else's list and use the information to perform the search in some way.

A Web application that relies on Amazon Web Services could automate this process to an extent. Instead of having someone manually retrieve the product information and associated vendor information, the requestor could simply submit an electronic list that the Web application can process automatically. This technique greatly reduces the time requirements for finding products and reduces the number of errors made by the procurement staff.

Performing Research

Only your imagination limits the number of ways to research information using the Amazon Web Service. The "Using Overviews and Details" describes a number of search techniques you can use to find specific products. However, once you find these products, you can perform additional research to discover ways to save money, increase productivity, or reduce risk. For example, you can use a similarities search to locate products that do the same thing

Using Blended Searches to Your Benefit

A blended search lets you look across product boundaries. You perform a blended search by providing search parameters without any mode (product category such as books) or page (the page number of the result set) information. Generally, Amazon discourages blended searches because they return too much information—most of which is incorrect. However, blended searches are valuable in some situations.

One example of a good use for a blended search is a site that offers products in a specific category, rather than a specific type. For example, you might have a Pink Floyd site where you sell everything to do with the music group. A blended search is more likely to provide a complete list of items that you can sell from your site.

Another example of a practical blended search is when you need to perform research and don't know very much about the product. For example, you might be the proud recipient of an Aebelskiver pan. Aside from problems spelling the name if you don't speak Danish, you might have a hard time figuring out uses for the pan. A book search will prove disappointing, but a blended search will show results in both the Home & Garden and the Kitchen & Housewares categories.

as a current product, but for less money. In fact, you might find a used product that someone else doesn't need any longer. Performing a seller profile search lets you reduce risk by ensuring the seller is reputable. Finally, using a Web service to help in the purchasing process will result in a productivity gain.

Research can also include product comparisons. For example, you can create a hot word list and use it to perform comparisons against a list of products downloaded from Amazon. You might rate products based on the number of hot words contained in the list and add or remove points depending on how the vendor uses the hot word. Product research could include a look through the buyer comments too. The appearance of a hot word here could mean that the product provides superior support for that feature or might not include it at all.

Adding a Competitive Advantage

Sellers can also use research to their advantage. For example, you could build a Web service that automatically retrieves the sales rank information for your product and tracks that information over some time frame. The resulting statistics can help you understand how well your product is selling—at least on Amazon. (As Amazon gains popularity, the sales rank number begins to reflect the sales environment for the affected products as a whole.)

Amazon also encourages comment—all kinds of comments. Because the buyer is under no obligation to provide any particular input, you can receive and analyze all kinds of comments. In general, positive comments are what they seem—they tell you that your product satisfied some need better than a competitor's. Many negative comments also include some level of truth; although, you have to consider how much value the comment includes for your particular product.

As with buyers, you can perform keyword searches against your competitor's product to determine how their product compares with yours. The comparison can also reveal general buyer approval of the product and the strength of the competitor's marketing campaign.

Accommodating Personal Needs

Many people recognize the versatility of the Amazon Web site and realize that they can use the information it provides for more than just purchases. The problem is that the Web site often returns more information than they really need or the information isn't in the right format for their needs. For example, one person I recently read about uses the Amazon search site to create a shopping list of items needed at the store. (In this case, the person used the information at a department store when buying gifts.) Unfortunately, the search site doesn't provide information such as size directly, so creating a shopping list is error prone and not very efficient. This person eventually created a Web service that loads the shopping information into their cellular telephone. With telephone in hand, this person has a new way to go shopping where all of the details for each item are easily accessible.

Obviously, Amazon is hoping that each search of their Web site will bring a sale, but they're also realistic enough to understand that it takes multiple searches to garner the transaction. Consider the shopping list on the cellular telephone again. Suppose this person goes to the store and either can't find the item or learns that the store charges too much for it. Amazon is now in a position to get the sale even though the person originally had no intent of buying the item online. In short, supplying information can result in a sale.

Downloading and Installing the Kit

Before you begin working with the Amazon Web Service, you need to obtain the kit and a developer token. Once you have the kit, you need to install it and become familiar with its content. The following sections describe the kit-related tasks you need to perform.

Performing the Download

Downloading the kit is easy. You'll find the main Web services page at `http://www.amazon.com/webservices/`. Figure 1.4 shows that this page contains some information, along with two important links. Although the steps shown in the figure are numbered, you can perform the first two steps in any order. This chapter assumes that you want to download the Amazon Web Services Kit first.

Click the Download Our Free Developer's Kit link and you'll see a page that describes the kit. Click the Download Now link and you'll see a Save File dialog of some type (the precise presentation depends on the browser you use). It always pays to save this file to disk (in an easily located folder), rather than open it immediately, so that you have a permanent copy. In addition, you might want to name the kit something more descriptive than `Kit.ZIP`. I used `Amazon Web Services Kit.ZIP` for my kit and this name might appear in other areas of the book. The file is incredibly small for a developer product—a mere 511KB.

Getting a Developer Token

Once you complete the download process, click the Apply for Amazon Developer's Token link. You'll see a Web page that requests an email address and password. You'll see a complete copy of the licensing agreement below these fields. Make sure you read the licensing agreement because it contains important usage information in addition to the actual terms of use. Don't worry about copying the licensing agreement to disk—the kit includes a copy of the licensing agreement you can use for reference purposes later.

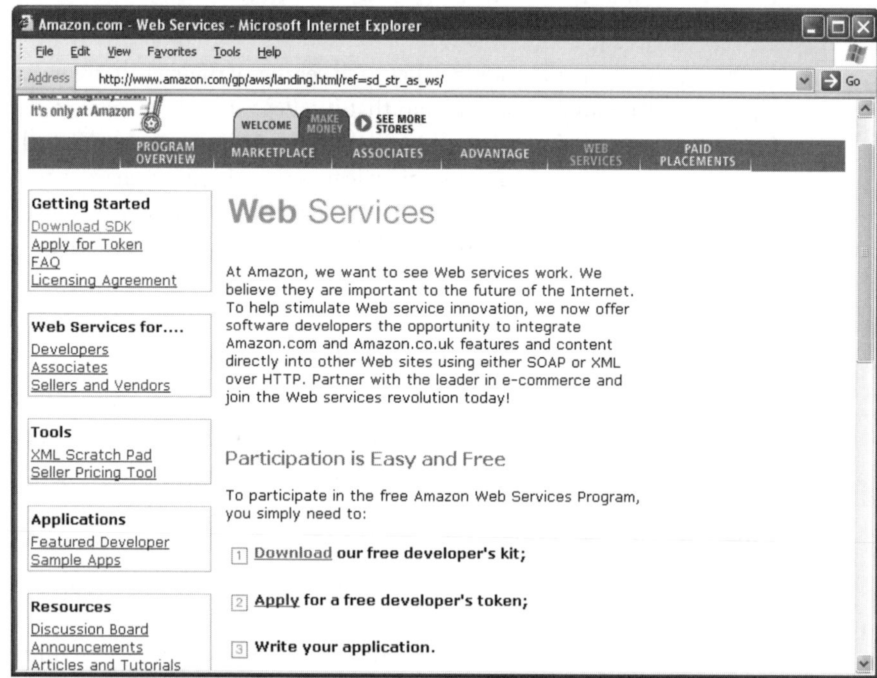

FIGURE 1.4: The Web Services site helps you obtain the kit and a developer token.

After you read the licensing agreement, check "I have read and accepted the Amazon Web Services terms and conditions." at the bottom of the page. Click Accept Terms and Conditions. (If you aren't an Amazon customer, you'll see additional Web pages requesting personal information. Fill out these Web pages so that Amazon knows who you are.) At this point, you'll see a message stating that Amazon will send your developer token to your email. I received mine in about an hour—you might need to wait more or less time depending on how busy Amazon is at the time. Make sure you save the email message containing the developer token because you'll need it for every transaction later.

Installing the Kit

The kit is actually a Zip file containing examples and documentation. If you're running Windows XP, the operating system provides a program to unpack the file for you. Otherwise, you'll need a special program that reads the compressed file and unpacks it for you such as WinZip (`http://www.winzip.com`).

You won't find any actual developer tools in the Zip file. The file does include complete path information, so you can unpack it in the root folder of your hard drive if you like. I used the D drive on my system, so the Amazon Web Services Kit appears in the `D:\AmazonWebServices` folder.

At this point, the kit is ready for use. However, before you go any further, you need to know about three files in the `\AmazonWebServices` folder. The `AMAZON.COM_LICENSE.TXT` file contains a copy of the license agreement that you saw online. Make sure you retain this file so that you can refer back to the usage terms as needed.

The `GNU_GENERAL_PUBLIC_LICENSE.TXT` file contains the distribution agreement for the Amazon Web Services Kit. These additional licensing terms don't affect how you use the kit. However, these terms do affect how to distribute any applications you create, so make sure you understand the licensing terms. You can learn more about the GNU General Public License at `http://www.gnu.org/copyleft/gpl.html` and `http://www.gnu.org/fsf/fsf.html`. This licensing policy is the same one used by other popular software such as Linux.

The `READMEFIRST.TXT` file contains useful information about the Amazon Web Services Kit and tells you where you can obtain additional information. This third file is very helpful because it contains URLs where you can obtain additional examples. It also has URLs for help sites and additional information. Finally, you'll want to read this file if you want to run the Java examples because it contains instructions for using them.

System Setup Considerations

Once you obtain the Amazon Web Services Kit and a developer token, it's easy to think that you're ready to write your first program. Theoretically, you can do just that. The problem with proceeding at this point though is that you don't know about the viability of your system configuration. For example, if you have a very fast processor and a lot of memory, it's easy to assume the page you've designed will work fine on all systems. However, once you load the resulting application on someone else's machine, it might not work very quickly (if at all).

Defining a usable development setup can save you considerable time and effort later. When you create a great development environment, you ensure that you'll see the application as the user does, which reduces the potential for deadly errors. Because the Amazon Web Services Kit is so accommodating, you'll need to spend a little extra time considering all of the possible usage scenarios. The following sections provide tips you can use to reduce the setup complexity.

Understanding Connectivity Requirements

You must consider three kinds of connectivity when you set up your development system. The first level of connectivity is your own machine. Make sure your machine has a connection to the Internet. Otherwise, any tests you run will fail. Remember that a Web service runs on the remote machine, not your local machine. You're borrowing the resources of that remote machine to perform useful work.

The second level of connectivity is the user's machine. If you create an associate Web site that simply contains links to Amazon's Web site, you can assume the user has a connection, but how fast is that connection? The best Web sites I've seen ask about the user's connection speed. This question allows the application to send the user the level of information that their connection can comfortably support. If you know that most users will rely on a dial-up connection for your Web site, make sure you also use a dial-up connection for testing. This additional step can greatly reduce the chances that you'll make the application too robust. Users who leave your site and don't use your application are users who are probably visiting someone else.

The third level of connectivity is the non-connected mode. You need to consider what happens when the user loses the connection or doesn't have one available. Applications can store static data locally to enable the user to continue using data they have already queried from the Web service. However, you need to observe any refresh requirements and ensure the data retains the same information the user would see online. For example, the local copy of the data must include any required copyright statements or trademarks.

Programming Setups for the Non-Developer

Many of the people reading this book have marginal experience with programming or do it as a hobby. It's true that Web services rely on the resources of the remote machine, but it's also true that the client must perform some work too. If you have a machine that's already marginal—that doesn't run applications well—trying to write a Web service application for it could make matters worse. The local machine must have some resources for using the Web service application.

Depending on the kind of application you create, you'll also need local resources for the programming environment. For example, VBA users have not only the Office application of choice running, but also the VBA development environment. The addition of the VBA development environment can reduce your system performance to a crawl and give you unrealistic performance for your application.

> **NOTE**
>
> Amazon places these requirements on your application. If the user doesn't connect often enough to refresh the data, Amazon doesn't hold you responsible.

It's also possible for you to speed things up too much. If the target platform is a 400MHz Pentium and you're using a 3GHz development machine, your application performance will look nothing like the user's performance in most cases. For a Web site, the machine performance differences might not be quite as significant as when you develop applications that run on the desktop.

Considering the User

Depending on how you use the Web application you build, user needs will take on significant importance. Many applications start out as projects that the developer is creating for personal use. Some of the best applications I've written fall into this category. However, you need to consider the user no matter who will use the application because you're a user too. At one time, I wrote rough applications that I understood but couldn't use efficiently because they were only for test purposes. After I ended up rewriting a number of the applications because I couldn't figure them out or other people asked me for copies, I began writing every program as if it were for someone else.

The applications you write with Amazon Web Services will likely see use from other people, even if you don't know it right now. Consequently, you need to consider what a hypothetical user will need. For example, you might need to include a few special search options. Sure, you could get the same results by typing a little extra text, but adding the functionality directly into your application makes it easier to use (faster in most cases as well).

It's also important to consider users with special needs. The "Addressing Users with Special Needs" section of Chapter 11 contains details on this topic, but you might need to perform setups before you even begin coding. For example, if you work on a Windows machine, you'll probably want to set up the Accessibility features (these features normally appear in the Control Panel and within the `Start\Programs\Accessories\Accessibility` folder).

Using Multiple Test Devices

If your application will appear on the Internet, you need to perform testing using multiple devices. It's no longer safe to assume that only desktop users will have any interest in your application. You might attract some Personal Digital Assistant (PDA) and cellular telephone users as well. This is especially true of a Web application that helps users find a particular kind of product quickly. People often rely on these applications when time is tight and they don't have time to look for a product themselves.

> **NOTE**
>
> This book doesn't teach you how to program, so make sure you spend at least a little time learning one of the programming languages discussed in this book before you begin working with the examples. I do provide good descriptions of the applications, but these descriptions won't be enough if you don't understand basic programming concepts.

It would be nice if everyone could afford to test every application on every device, but that's not realistic for the developer. Sometimes you need to use an emulator to perform the testing because you don't have the real device handy. Fortunately, you can find a vast array of useful emulators on the Internet—everything from the

Pocket PC to cellular telephones of all types. Emulators have limitations, but they do make good test devices in many cases. We'll discuss the advantages and concerns of using emulators in the "Working with Emulators" section of Chapter 9.

Sometimes it also helps to have multiple desktop machine setups. For example, you might need to consider how a Web page looks and acts in Netscape versus Internet Explorer. (Theoretically, you can run both browsers from the same machine, but doing so causes interference problems that some developers find distasteful.) Differences in how the browsers react to specific Web page designs could cause problems in your application. In some cases, you'll need multiple machines to perform this kind of testing. For example, you might need to consider how the application looks on a Macintosh versus a PC if your application has broad enough appeal. Obviously, you can still write Amazon Web Services applications if you don't have a multiple machine setup, but having more than one machine does make development tasks a lot easier and less error prone.

Emulating the Real World

Developers often live in a laboratory. In the laboratory, everyone has the proper equipment, fast machines, and an even faster connection. The user never disconnects unexpectedly and always knows how to get the most out of their computer. The problem with the lab is that it doesn't model the real world. In the real world, users get bored, try odd key combinations just to see what they do, don't understand their computer very well, but do know how to complain about the smallest application problems. If you want to avoid problems with the application you develop, you need to create a development environment that models the real world.

It's also easy to get lost in the development environment setup. Make sure you understand the person who uses your application. For example, it's quite possible that only desktop users will have any interest in your site on desktop machine maintenance, but you need to determine that fact in some way (online surveys work well). You also don't want to spend a lot of time testing the application to meet the needs of users who have no use for your product. Again, surveys and newsgroup polls are helpful in determining the real world environment that you must emulate with your system.

Your Call to Action

If you've read the entire chapter, you know what a Web service is, how Amazon Web Services fits within the general definition of a Web service, and what you can use Amazon Web Services to do. You can use this knowledge to create opportunities to use Amazon as a search engine for all kinds of tasks, not just as a means to extend the sales potential of your Web site. At this point, you also have a machine that's set up to create an Amazon Web Services application of some sort and you have the Amazon Web Services Kit installed.

The next step of the process is to evaluate where you're going based on the content of this chapter. You need to consider what you want to do with the information Amazon provides, how you plan to present it, your own capabilities, and the capabilities of the person using your application. This may sound like a lot of work, but it's important to create a firm foundation for your application. When you take these preliminary steps, you begin thinking about problems and solutions to those problems.

Chapter 2 builds on the knowledge you gained in this chapter. You learn what to expect from Web services and see examples of how Amazon Web Services could work for your application. Obviously, these examples are just starting points, but they do help you understand what takes place with a Web service and provide you with a little more information on how they work. Chapter 2 helps you understand why Web services are such a great idea and what Amazon Web Services can do for you in particular.

Chapter 2

Understanding How Web Services Output Data

Viewing Some Simple Examples

Changing the Data to Meet Specific Needs

Using Amazon Web Services to Your Advantage

Understanding that Web services provide data after you make a request is a good beginning but hardly adequate to work with a Web service. A Web service doesn't view information in the same way that a person views it. A computer has no concept of context and can't derive information from the placement of the data unless you use a special application (and even then, the interpretation is quite limited). Consequently, a Web service needs some type of structure to tell it what the data means and how to handle it. Your request doesn't mean much without this structure.

This chapter helps you understand the structure that a Web service requires. You'll begin seeing some XML in this chapter. Don't worry about the XML too much—Chapter 3 will introduce you to XML. The idea in this chapter is to understand how Web services fit within the grand scheme of things. In short, you'll discover a little more about Web services in general and the Amazon Web Service specifically.

Rather than spend a lot of time discovering how Web services work from a theoretical perspective, this chapter presents several examples. Each example shows how some aspect of Amazon Web Services works. Again, you don't really need to understand the code behind the examples; the chapter concerns itself more with the process involved in working with the Amazon Web Service. These examples provide hands-on time that you can use to develop an opinion of what makes Amazon Web Services useful to you and your organization.

Finally, this chapter begins a discussion on data manipulation. The data you receive from Amazon Web Services isn't ready for display. Your program must interpret the data, modify its appearance as needed, and then display it on screen for the user. This last section describes some of the handling and formatting issues you should consider as part of your application design process.

Knowing What to Expect As Output

Amazon expects many developers to access its Web site and build applications that use the Amazon Web Service. These developers will give or sell their applications to users who will increase the load on the servers. In short, hundreds of thousands of users could try to extract information from Amazon using custom applications, so Amazon had to devise a relatively generic way of formatting the data so everyone can use it. This format is XML. Using XML allows Amazon to send the data in pure text and still tell the recipient what the data means. The combination of pure text with explanation makes data transfers possible to a broad range of application types that reside on any number of platforms. However, the disadvantage is that the data requires interpretation.

The following sections describe what you can expect as output from Amazon Web Services to your application. Understanding the limitations of XML will help you create better applications. You don't have to understand XML to understand these sections. Remember that the goal in this chapter is to understand the process so that the programming examples later in the book make more sense.

Limitations of the Amazon Web Services Output

Many developers are used to working with a variety of data types when creating applications. Data types help define the kind of data you're using. For example, if a data element is a number, you might use an integer (a number without a decimal) or real (Single or Double for Visual Basic developers). A Web service has no concept of data type when it comes to the data itself. Every data transfer is text. The XML used to transfer the data does include type information, but of the sort that's normally associated with database fields, which means you have to know the field names to make an interpretation. For example, you might receive data in a message like the one shown here.

```
<SellerFeedback>
   <Feedback>
      <FeedbackRating>5</FeedbackRating>
      <FeedbackComments>Outstanding buyer!</FeedbackComments>
      <FeedbackDate>07/30/2003</FeedbackDate>
      <FeedbackRater>george_2003</FeedbackRater>
   </Feedback>
</SellerFeedback>
```

You don't have to understand the XML portion of this message segment, but look at the data. Amazon Web Services sends all data as characters (as do all other Web services) and defines the data using tags (the words between the angle brackets). For example, the line that contains `<FeedbackRating>5</FeedbackRating>` includes the `<FeedbackRating>` tag that tells you that this value is 5. The tag tells you what kind of information this is. By knowing the Amazon database layout, you also know the data type and other information about the entry. However, the information you receive from Amazon is still plain text. You can see other examples of XML responses in the \AmazonWebServices\XMLResponseSamples of the kit. Simply open them using Internet Explorer or another browser that supports XML. Figure 2.1 shows a typical view of one of the examples in the folder.

FIGURE 2.1: View some of the example files using Internet Explorer or other XML-compatible browser.

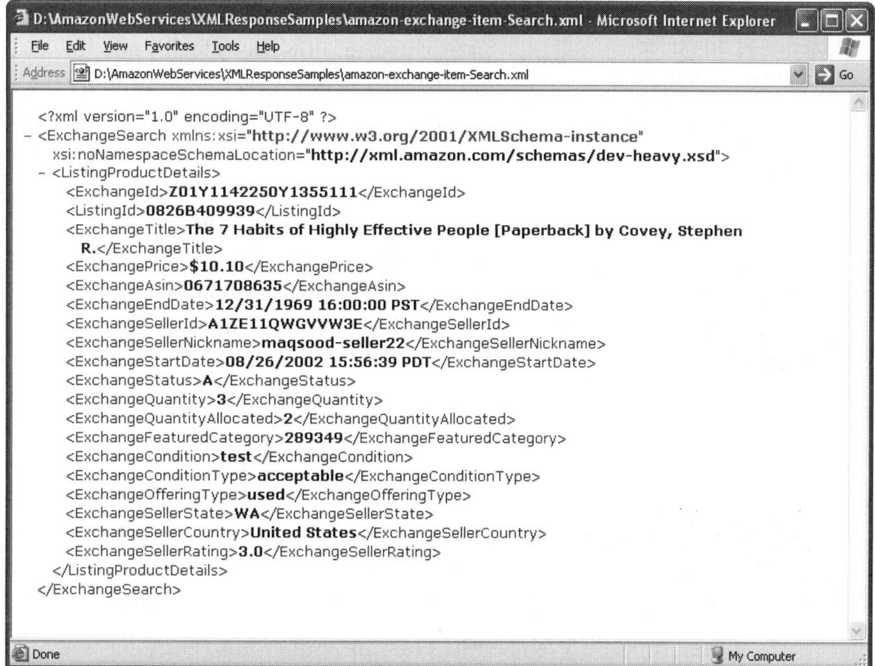

Your browser is actually very handy for viewing XML data, even if it might not make sense right now. The "Viewing XML Data in Your Browser" section of Chapter 3 discusses in detail how you can use your browser. For right now, all you need to know is that you can look at the various kinds of XML responses by opening the files in your browser.

Figure 2.1 points to another potential problem with Web service output. All of the tags and other information supplied in a request and response consume space. The file is larger than a text file with the same data because of all the tag information required. In addition, it's far more efficient to store many data types in their native format, rather than use characters. Consequently, Web service data suffers from bloat. The data uses more bandwidth than a

> **▶ NOTE**
>
> This section focuses on pure XML. Developers who use SOAP, instead of pure XML, will receive type information directly from Amazon. This information appears as an added attribute (an addition to the tag). The "Defining SOAP Messaging" section of Chapter 3 tells you more about the additions SOAP provides. You can find examples of SOAP responses in the `\Amazon-WebServices\SoapResponseSamples` of the kit.

binary message and, consequently, you could experience performance problems. Because of this issue, you need to create efficient queries for your application that maximize data throughput despite the limitations of the XML format. The "Making Sensible Queries" section of the chapter discusses this issue in detail.

Amazon Web Services output also has a limitation that might not be apparent at first. The kind of information you provide as input limits the output, but only as far as the Web service interprets the data. For example, it's possible to retrieve incorrect author information, even if you supply the author's full name. Figure 2.2 shows one case where I typed John Mueller and ended up with results for John Smiley when using the Web site search mechanism (the Web service also seems to provide this result, so this isn't a Web site–specific issue). Even though my name doesn't appear for the second book, I am one of the coauthors, so this result demonstrates a situation where the output is correct, but you wouldn't discover that fact until you probed deeper into the data. The reason output errors exist could range from a mention of the author as part of the other book's description to a glitch in the database entries for the Web service. In some cases, the search engine combines data in unexpected ways. The John Smiley book shows up because one of the other authors is Michael Mueller—the search engine combined the two authors' names to create a match to my name. Because you don't have direct control of either the Web service or its associated server, fixing these errors can become difficult. In general, you must provide code in your application to overcome this limitation.

A final Amazon Web Services output limitation to consider is accessibility. The fact that you can see a particular type of data on Amazon's Web site doesn't necessarily mean you'll also be able to access that data using Amazon Web Services. Amazon might hide certain types of data from view because the data represents sensitive information or simply because Amazon wants to keep it to itself for marketing purposes. To avoid data access problems, you must understand what the database can provide. The "Previewing the Amazon Database" section of Chapter 3 discusses this particular issue in more detail. I'll also provide resources in that section for keeping up-to-date with Amazon's current strategy online.

Making Sensible Queries

The Amazon Web Service can help you perform a number of tasks. The problem is that each request and response consumes resources. To get the most from this Web service, you need to optimize the requests and responses so that the value of the information you receive exceeds the cost of transmitting and manipulating the data.

Creating a request and then handling the response has several costs associated with it. Some of the costs are real world in that you must provide the infrastructure required to perform the task. Inefficient queries could mean adding additional bandwidth capacity or providing additional servers (if you make enough queries). Some costs are employee related—inefficient queries mean more waiting time as the computer crunches the data. Finally, inefficient queries can incur intangible costs. For example, people can become frustrated with poor query results, which affects their performance. Some of these costs are impossible to measure accurately, but they're real.

I often rely on the online search engine to help tune queries. Using the Search Books (`http://www.amazon.com/exec/obidos/ats-query-page/`) page (also called the power search page) shown in Figure 2.3 can help you define and tune searches to obtain maximum data with minimal resource use. For example, computer books don't typically have long shelf lives, so I normally provide a date range as part of my search. Using the online search to customize the date range for specific product types can greatly enhance performance.

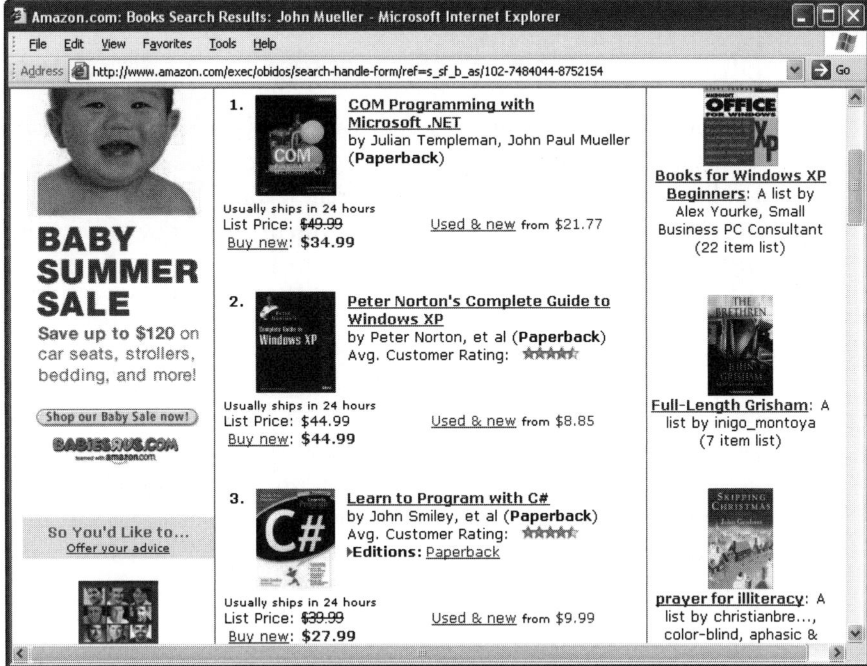

FIGURE 2.2: The Amazon Web Services output can glitch and produce unwanted results.

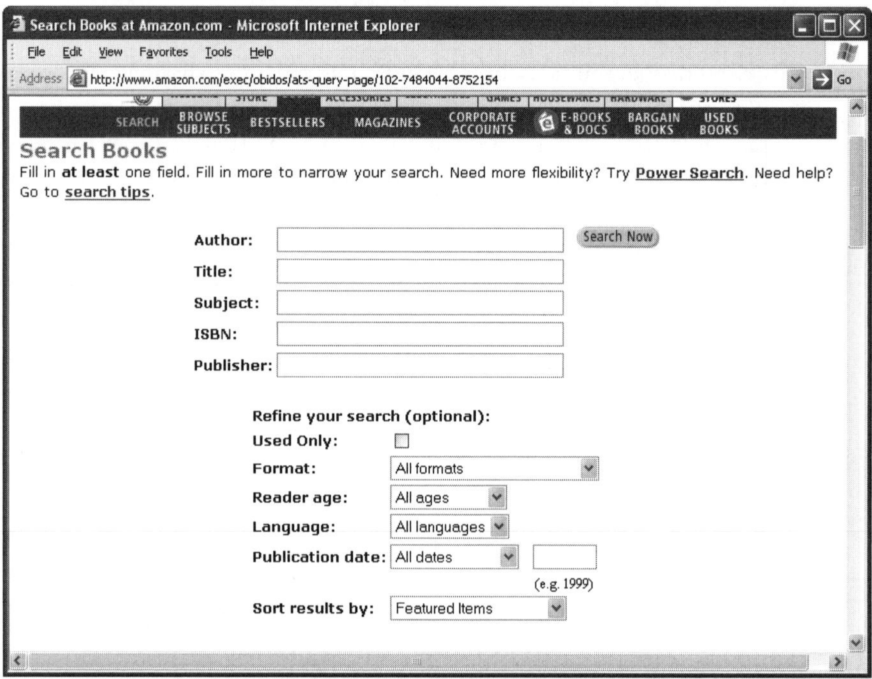

FIGURE 2.3: Use the Advanced Search to determine the type of queries to use in your application.

Notice that using the online search also allows you to define a sort order. Many people miss opportunities to optimize searches by not providing a sort order. Even when you retrieve a number of products for a particular search, sorting the results can make it easier to find the specific product you need. For example, you might sort by price to obtain the best product at the lowest cost or sort by the Bestselling category to obtain the product most people like best. The goal is to locate what you need quickly, whether it be products, services, or simply research.

Depending on your needs, some search features don't work quite as advertised (or perhaps not as you might think they work). For example, if you choose any of the age options, Amazon assumes that you want products for people ages 18 and under (the specific age depends on the search criteria), no matter how you word the query. The age options help ensure that younger users don't see products they can't buy—it's not a criteria that you would use to find products only for adults. Amazon assumes that anyone over 18 can also make use of the items for buyers under 18.

The language options also have problems now. You might think that you could request a book in French given that it is a popular language. The only two language selections that appear to work well are English and Spanish. (Obviously, this means that you can optimize your search for Spanish language books if desired.)

Defining Static and Dynamic Data

Web applications can include the concept of static and dynamic data. In fact, Amazon is concerned about this issue and addresses it in the licensing agreement (see Appendix B for details). Dynamic data is the best type to use for Web services because it reflects changes in the Amazon database. An application gains important benefits by using dynamic data. For example, you won't try to purchase a product that Amazon no longer carries because the dynamic nature of your application automatically tells you that product is no longer part of the Amazon catalog.

Unfortunately, dynamic data can also cause problems. For one thing, you need a connection to the Internet to work with dynamic data. When you use a desktop machine, maintaining a connection usually isn't a problem. However, many third party developers are working on applications where a connection might not be available, such as a shopping list application for a PDA. You download the information from the Amazon Web Service and then go shopping—the connection doesn't exist while you're at the store so the data is no longer dynamic.

Using the term dynamic to refer to application data is also somewhat of a misnomer. Nothing is truly a dynamic data application. The moment the response to your query leaves the Amazon server, it begins to age. The data doesn't change once it leaves the Amazon server, so in reality it isn't truly dynamic. The only way you can achieve a dynamic presentation of sorts is to make multiple queries. You must define how often is often enough for your needs, but Amazon defines minimum update requirements to achieve a sort of dynamic presentation.

> **▶ NOTE**
>
> The examples in this chapter all include the following string: `Your-Developer-Token`. To use the examples, you must replace this string with the developer token you receive from Amazon. Simply open the file and edit the string. When working with a text file (such as an HTML page or an eXtensible Stylesheet Language Transformations, XSLT, file), use a pure text editor such as Notepad. See the "Getting a Developer Token" section of Chapter 1 for details on getting a developer token if you don't have one. When working with a Visual Studio .NET application, you must replace the string and then recompile the application. Otherwise, the change will appear in the source code file, but not in the executable.

These facts lead into the discussion of static data. Truly static data never changes at all. Most Web sites still rely on static data presentation because the information they display doesn't change often enough to warrant a dynamic presentation. When you make a single query to the Amazon Web Service, the response you receive is static data. It's a snapshot of that particular part of the database at a specific time. The data won't change unless you make another query.

Understanding the static and dynamic nature of data is important when you design an application that relies on the Amazon Web Service. Errors creep into the presentation you create as the data from Amazon Web Services ages on your system. Part of the design process for your application is to determine how much error you can accept and to ensure you meet Amazon's minimum update requirements.

Working with Some Simple Examples

It's time to look at some Amazon Web Services examples. The following sections show how to work with many options that Amazon provides. The sections contain usage information, but no code unless it's necessary for the usage explanation. The book discusses source code in other areas—these examples acquaint you with Amazon Web Services through hands-on activities.

You can look at the source code if desired. You'll find these examples in the `\Chapter 02` folder of the source code located on the Sybex Web site.

Understanding the Example Types

I designed most of the examples in this section with Amazon Web Services process in mind. This means they aren't always the most realistic examples or that they'll provide results good enough to use for your next application. However, the examples demonstrate principles that make it easier for you to work with the Amazon Web Service as the book progresses. Most importantly, the examples serve as a basis for learning that Web services aren't difficult.

> **NOTE**
>
> You'll find the Sybex Web site at `http://www.sybex.com/`. Simply type the book title in the Search field, click Go, and you'll see a link for this book. The book page contains a link where you can download the code.

Many people won't actually build an application to work with Amazon. If they do build a simple application, it will be part of a Web page—not part of a Web server setup. The second set of examples demonstrates that this technique is possible, although it has limitations. The Web page approach is quite useful when you want to present someone with options or help them locate information associated with your Web site. It's not quite as helpful when you want to set up your system as an associate because the lack of application code means you can't track referrals.

The third set of examples demonstrates two kinds of application. The first type is for desktop users. Many people will build applications to make Amazon friendlier to their specific reference, referral, shopping, or other need. The book discusses a number of applications; this one simply demonstrates how the process works. The second example demonstrates that size is unimportant in many ways. Although you'll find that the Pocket PC does pose some limits on how you interact with Amazon, it's quite capable of performing many tasks.

> **NOTE**
>
> Originally, this chapter didn't include the browser example described in the "Using a Browser Example" section. I added this example after several people who read the manuscript complained that the examples still left the details hidden. You'd never want to query Amazon the way this example does, except for pure research—to see the results of a string you plan to use for another application. However, the technique in this example is still useful for experimentation.

Using a Browser Example

No one says that working with a Web service has to be hard or mysterious. Using a Web service is as easy as typing a URL in your browser in many cases. In fact, that's what this section demonstrates. You can literally type the following URL in your browser's Address field, press Enter, and get results back. Make sure you replace the string, "`Your-Developer-Token`" with your actual developer token. Note also that the URL is very long and wouldn't fit on a single line in the book. Simply type the entire URL without pressing Enter until you get to the end. Be sure you don't add any unnecessary spaces.

```
http://xml.amazon.com/onca/xml3?t=webservices-20&dev-t=Your-Developer-
Token&AuthorSearch=John%20Mueller&mode=books&type=lite&page=1&f=xml
```

This URL may look complicated, but it's relatively easy once you know what the individual entries mean. The `http://xml.amazon.com/onca/xml3` entry is the actual Web service URL for XML queries—SOAP queries use a different URL. All of the arguments—the description of the query—appear after the URL. You separate each argument with an ampersand (&). Here's a short description of each entry.

`t=webservices-20` This entry defines the associate tag you want to use to get credit for a sale. If you don't have an associate tag (perhaps because you're using Amazon for research), you can use the standard `webservices-20` tag instead.

`dev-t=Your-Developer-Token` This entry contains the developer token of the requestor. Every request must include a developer token or the Web service won't honor it.

`AuthorSearch=John%20Mueller` This entry contains the kind of search, an author, and the author's name. Notice the query replaces the space in my name with a %20. You can't use spaces in queries, so you use this special character combination instead. Read the "Sending Special Characters Using URL Encoding" section in Chapter 3 for additional details on using special characters.

`mode=books` This entry tells the Web service to look for books. You can also look for other product types.

`type=lite` This entry tells the Web service to provide only an overview of the information. You can also tell it to provide the details by specifying a heavy search.

`page=1` This entry tells the Web service to return the first page. If you want the second page, then you type `page=2` instead.

`f=xml` This entry defines the query format. In this case, we're using XML. Amazon Web Services can also work with SOAP requests.

Now that you understand that long URL a little better, try using it. Figure 2.4 shows typical results from this request. Note that I blanked my developer token out in the various places it appears in the figure.

FIGURE 2.4: Typical results from an Amazon Web Services request

Look at the top of the results and you'll see all of the arguments used to make the query. You'll also find the total number of results returned by the search (97) and the number of pages required to display those results (10). After the general information, you'll find a list of book entries. These entries include information like the title, authors, publisher, release date, and price.

You can easily make mistakes in formatting your query string. The most common mistake is not including enough arguments to perform the search. In this case, you receive an error message: "Your request has one or more parameters missing. Please check and retry." The most common missing argument is the developer token, but you should check all of the required arguments.

Another common error is not making the search specific enough. It may seem that you included enough information, but Amazon still returns the error message: "There are no exact matches for the search." When this happens, make sure you specify a `mode` argument. Figure 2.5 shows a typical error message. Notice the missing `mode` argument in this case. The list of arguments can help you locate problems with your request.

FIGURE 2.5: Use the argument information in an error message to find problems.

http://xml.amazon.com/onca/xml3?t=webservices-20&dev-t=D1A7ODOMNLFTZV&Aut...

File Edit View Favorites Tools Help

Address http://xml.amazon.com/onca/xml3?t=webservices-20&dev-t= &AuthorSearch=J Go


```
<?xml version="1.0" encoding="UTF-8" ?>
- <ProductInfo>
  - <Request>
    - <Args>
        <Arg name="locale" value="us" />
        <Arg name="AuthorSearch" value="John Mueller" />
        <Arg name="page" value="1" />
        <Arg name="dev-t" value="                    " />
        <Arg name="t" value="webservices-20" />
        <Arg name="f" value="xml" />
        <Arg name="type" value="lite" />
      </Args>
    </Request>
    <ErrorMsg>There are no exact matches for the search.</ErrorMsg>
  </ProductInfo>
```


Viewing the XML over HTTP Example

Once you know how to form a request string, you can begin adding it to a Web page. The Web page could also ask for the various bits of information you need to form a query. In short, you could make it into a simple tool for testing out queries. Figure 2.6 shows the simple example the chapter uses in this case.

FIGURE 2.6: This form automates the process of requesting pages from Amazon.

This example performs an author search, but you could probably extend it to perform other search types. Simply type the name of the author you want to find, the page of listings you want to locate, a return type (lite or heavy), and click Submit. The page returns results similar to those found in Figure 2.4.

The code for this page relies on simple HTML. You can use it on any Web site, even if you don't have access to the Web server. It doesn't require any special browser features, so just about any client can use it. In fact, you'll find this page works just fine with mobile devices such as a Palm. However, the screen may contain too many elements for cellular telephones. The most interesting feature of this example is that it loads extremely fast on any device, including mobile devices. You don't have to wait for Amazon's usual graphic display to load and there aren't any other hurdles to jump.

The point of this example is that you don't have to do anything too fancy to get information from Amazon Web Services if your only goal is to get some information quickly. One other consideration for this example is that the URL it produces is slightly different from the one in the previous examples. Here's the URL the page produces automatically (it will only span one line in your browser, even though it appears on two lines in the book).

```
http://xml.amazon.com/onca/xml3?t=webservices-20&dev-t=Your-Developer-
Token&AuthorSearch=John+Mueller&mode=books&type=lite&page=1&f=xml
```

Notice that the basic arrangement is the same, but that the author name has a plus sign (+) separating the first and last name. Amazon Web Services also recognizes the + as a separation character, so you don't necessarily have to use the %20 that appears in the "Using a Browser Example" section. The %20 is clearer, however, because it defines specifically which separator character to use.

Viewing the XSLT Example

The output from the previous examples is complete and usable if you want to read XML, but most people don't like to read XML directly. It's nicer to see a formatted presentation on screen. This example starts with the same form shown in Figure 2.6. You provide the same kinds of input as in the "Viewing the XML over HTTP Example" section, so there isn't anything too mysterious about the input data.

> **▶ NOTE**
>
> Most of the examples in this book assume that you're accessing Amazon using Internet Explorer 5.0 and above from a Windows system. Other browsers and platforms may require different scripting techniques than the ones demonstrated in this book.

Internally, the HTML for the page is about the same. The big difference is that clicking Submit doesn't use a standard HTML `<Submit>` tag to obtain the data. Instead, this button defines a handler for the `OnClick()` event. This event occurs whenever you click the button. The `OnClick()` event handler performs a number of tasks that the book discusses in "Using XSLT for Presentation" section of Chapter 3. For now, all you need to know is that the script stores the information it obtains from Amazon Web Services locally and processes it using an XSLT file. Figure 2.7 shows typical output from this example.

FIGURE 2.7: Using XSLT makes Amazon Web Services data much easier to read.

As you can see, the output from this example is far more readable than previous examples. I chose to include the calling arguments in this example so you could use the XSLT page for test purposes. However, a production page probably wouldn't use this information. The test page includes some overview information from the details section of the XML page. This information appears in any author search you perform, so it works for a number of test scenarios.

Viewing the SOAP Example

Many people need to access Amazon Web Services information from the desktop. The reasons for using a desktop application vary. It could simply be a matter of making the application more flexible than a Web application will allow or enabling the application to meet special requirements. For example, a user might have a special access need that you can't easily satisfy using a Web application. This section demonstrates a desktop application. It relies on a Visual C# .NET program, but you could easily use SOAP in a number of other forms too. In fact, I specifically chose this desktop example because the Amazon Web Services Kit doesn't contain any examples of this type.

> **▶ NOTE**
>
> Although this book uses XSLT relatively often to demonstrate how you can present Amazon information in a viewable manner, it doesn't discuss the details of using XSLT. The books, *Mastering XSLT* by Chuck White (Sybex, 2002) and *XML Schemas* by Chelsea Valentine, Lucinda Dykes, and Ed Tittel (Sybex, 2002) can help you learn more about this interesting technology. Make sure you also visit the W3C Schools at `http://www.w3schools.com/`. The XSL tutorial also contains XSLT specific information. In fact, you'll find tutorials on this site for many Web technologies.

This example uses a form similar to the ones for the Web applications. However, you can display the request and the results on the same page as shown in Figure 2.8. From a user perspective, the request process is about the same. However, from a developer perspective, requesting the information is actually easier because the methods and programming structures that Amazon Web Service provides (and the IDE builds on) make it harder to forget essentials and reduce the amount of information you have to provide.

The benefits of this approach are many. For example, without any additional programming, I can sort the results by any of the output columns. The application doesn't need to make additional requests of the Web service because the data is already available in memory. In fact, storing data could become a problem—you need to track just how long the data is in memory and require a refresh to meet licensing requirements. Although the data you receive using the SOAP technique is the same, it's easier to access using standard object-oriented programming techniques. In short, you gain a lot of flexibility and data access at a reduced cost in programming effort.

FIGURE 2.8:
Desktop applications can also make requests from the Amazon Web Service.

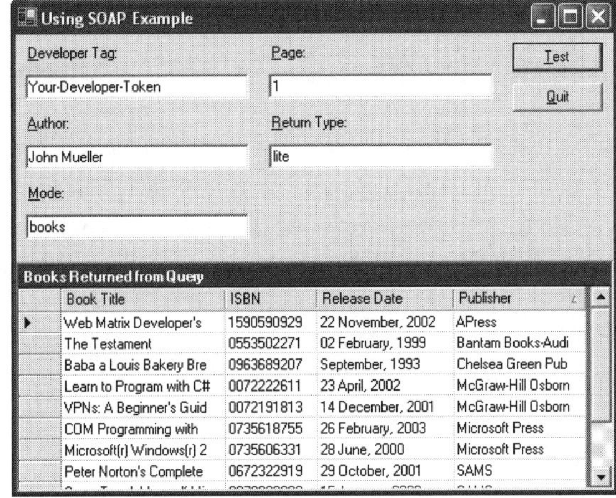

It might seem as if the SOAP approach is the best route to take. Unfortunately, every time you gain something in flexibility or programming speed, you end up paying for it in some way. The Web applications that appear in this chapter could possibly work on any machine. This example is very specific—it won't even work on every Windows machine. The user must have a copy of the .NET Framework installed to use this application. Don't assume that any other SOAP solution is better. If you use a SOAP-compatible IDE that has greater platform support, you usually lose something in programming speed or flexibility. There isn't any one best solution—only the solution that works best for you.

Viewing the Pocket PC Example

The Pocket PC example in this section relies on the .NET Compact Framework. As with the "Viewing the SOAP Example" section example, I chose this particular form for this chapter because you won't find an example of it in the Amazon Web Services Kit. The application works about the same as the desktop version. Of course, the form factor is different, so the application has to make some concessions. Figure 2.9 shows that the Pocket PC form of the application relies on a main entry form and a detail form to display the results. In all other ways, this example works like the desktop version. I was a little surprised that, except for form factor issues, the application works the same as the desktop version.

Manipulating Data to Meet Specific Needs

At some point, you'll have the data required to make your application functional. The problem is that raw data isn't that interesting, so you need to manipulate it to make it easier to read or provide conclusions based on the facts. The following sections discuss data manipulation needs you should consider for your application and how to use the Amazon examples to help you understand some of these data transformation needs.

Understanding Data Transformation Requirements

Getting data from Amazon often means transforming application data to text. Every input you provide to Amazon is text—it doesn't matter whether you use an XML or a SOAP request. This first form of data transition is relatively easy because you can perform most translations quickly. Most languages provide a method for changing a numeric page number to text. When you use a Web page, translation is actually unnecessary because the Web page stores all input data as text.

The difficult data transformations occur when you accept a response from Amazon and need to turn it into something your users will need. Not only is the data from Amazon somewhat bulky due to the XML storage requirements, you'll also find that little nuances in request strategy can make a big difference in what you receive and how your application reacts to it. For example, a lite request is going to return far fewer fields than a heavy request. If your application assumes the reader will always make a heavy request, it could fail when the user makes a lite request. Some of the fields are nonexistent or contain nothing (null data). Applications don't generally behave well under these circumstances unless you include extra functionality to handle the situation.

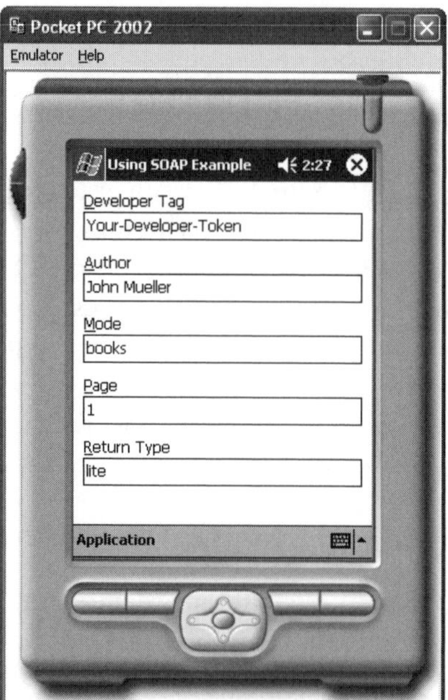

FIGURE 2.9: The Pocket PC form factor requires use of multiple forms.

Another problem is that some types of data defy easy analysis in code. For example, you'll find that Amazon uses attributes for some types of data and elements for other types. The book explains these design issues in better detail in Chapter 3. However, you'll want to consider the effect of data format on your use of the information Amazon provides.

Some data types require special handling. A book could have one or more authors, but you won't know how many authors until you receive the data. Likewise, a CD can have multiple artists and a video multiple actors. Again, if you decide that you only need to process one author, artist, or actor, the user could find that locating particular books, CDs, videos, or other products becomes difficult. To provide full functionality, your application needs to transform all of the authors into a readable form no matter how many (or few) authors worked on a particular book.

Viewing the Amazon Examples

Data manipulation takes a number of forms when you work with the Amazon Web Service. Some of these needs become obvious when you look at the examples provided with the kit. For example, the `\AmazonWebServices\XMLResponseSamples` contains a number of sample responses, just as you'd receive them from Amazon. When you view one of these examples (the chapter will use the `amazon-seller-search.xml` file), you'll see the XML shown in Figure 2.10. Likewise, the `amazon-seller-search-popup.xsl` file also displays what appears as a form of XML.

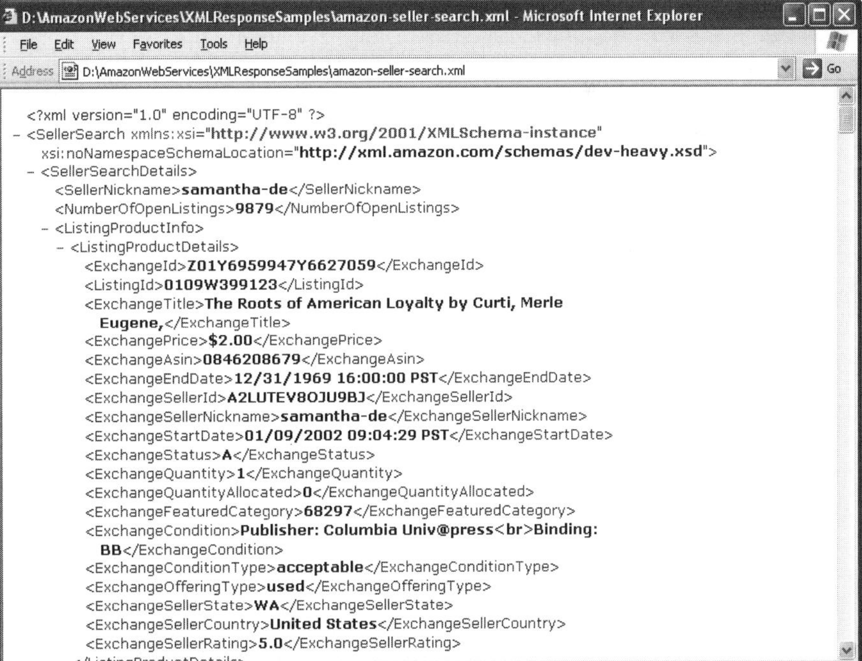
D:\AmazonWebServices\XMLResponseSamples\amazon-seller-search.xml - Microsoft Internet Explorer
File Edit View Favorites Tools Help
Address D:\AmazonWebServices\XMLResponseSamples\amazon-seller-search.xml
Go
<?xml version="1.0" encoding="UTF-8" ?>
- <SellerSearch xmlns:xsi="http://www.w3.org/2001/XMLSchema-instance" xsi:noNamespaceSchemaLocation="http://xml.amazon.com/schemas/dev-heavy.xsd">
- <SellerSearchDetails>
<SellerNickname>samantha-de</SellerNickname>
<NumberOfOpenListings>9879</NumberOfOpenListings>
- <ListingProductInfo>
- <ListingProductDetails>
<ExchangeId>Z01Y6959947Y6627059</ExchangeId>
<ListingId>0109W399123</ListingId>
<ExchangeTitle>The Roots of American Loyalty by Curti, Merle Eugene,</ExchangeTitle>
<ExchangePrice>$2.00</ExchangePrice>
<ExchangeAsin>0846208679</ExchangeAsin>
<ExchangeEndDate>12/31/1969 16:00:00 PST</ExchangeEndDate>
<ExchangeSellerId>A2LUTEV8OJU9BJ</ExchangeSellerId>
<ExchangeSellerNickname>samantha-de</ExchangeSellerNickname>
<ExchangeStartDate>01/09/2002 09:04:29 PST</ExchangeStartDate>
<ExchangeStatus>A</ExchangeStatus>
<ExchangeQuantity>1</ExchangeQuantity>
<ExchangeQuantityAllocated>0</ExchangeQuantityAllocated>
<ExchangeFeaturedCategory>68297</ExchangeFeaturedCategory>
<ExchangeCondition>Publisher: Columbia Univ@press
Binding: BB</ExchangeCondition>
<ExchangeConditionType>acceptable</ExchangeConditionType>
<ExchangeOfferingType>used</ExchangeOfferingType>
<ExchangeSellerState>WA</ExchangeSellerState>
<ExchangeSellerCountry>United States</ExchangeSellerCountry>
<ExchangeSellerRating>5.0</ExchangeSellerRating>

FIGURE 2.10: The XML pages provided with the kit display XML in your browser.

The XML file contains the data, while the XSL file contains the formatting information. Theoretically, placing these two files in the same folder should display formatted output in your browser, but it doesn't. You must connect the XML file to the XSL file. This is an example of a data transformation requirement. The default response doesn't include linkage information because Amazon has no way of knowing how you plan to format the information. Adding the following text to the XML file, immediately after the `<?xml version="1.0" encoding="UTF-8"?>` heading, creates the required connection.

```
<?xml-stylesheet type="text/xsl" href="amazon-seller-search-popup.xsl"?>
```

Now when you open the XML file, you'll see formatted output. Figure 2.11 shows the same `amazon-seller-search.xml` file as Figure 2.10, but with the required connection in place. When you build your application, you'll also need to add such linkage to the response so the user sees formatted output, rather than raw XML.

Your Call to Action

You now know how to work with Amazon Web Services from a user perspective. The examples in the chapter let you see how the Amazon Web Service can perform useful work for specific needs. In addition, you now know what to expect from the Web service in the way of output and understand the need to modify that information for display. In general, Amazon Web Services provides text data with formatting information to make conversion easy, but the data still requires some type of conversion for presentation purposes.

> **▶ NOTE**
>
> As with the examples supplied in this chapter, the Amazon examples all include a string that you replace with the developer token you request from Amazon. For example, in the `\AmazonWebServices\SoapRequestSamples` folder, many of the files contain this string: `<dev-tag>your-dev-tag</dev-tag>`. Unfortunately, the instructions for using the Amazon examples don't always indicate this requirement, so you need to remember to make the change.

Reading the material in the chapter will help you understand Amazon Web Services in theory. However, before you can really understand what's going on, it helps you get some hands-on time. If you haven't tried the examples yet, make sure you do. It's also a good idea to try the various examples that come with the Amazon Web Services Kit.

You've seen some XML examples in this chapter, but this chapter focuses mainly on the Web service process, so it doesn't discuss the actual XML implementation. Chapter 3 goes on to the next step of working with the Amazon Web Service—actually using XML to perform tasks. Chapter 3 discusses how XML works, shows examples of how various languages use XML, and describes some of the problems you'll encounter when using XML. For example, XML isn't secure and it causes privacy issues you'll need to consider. This next step helps you move from merely using the Web service to telling it what information you'd like to request.

FIGURE 2.11:

Creating a connection to the XSL file is important if you want to see formatted output.

Chapter 3

Previewing the Amazon Database
Understanding XML Basics
Using XSLT for Presentation

Working with Web Service Data

Defining SOAP Messaging
Understanding Privacy Issues
Understanding Security Issues

All Web services rely on some form of eXtensible Markup Language (XML) to receive requests and send information. Even the Simple Object Access Protocol (SOAP) is simply a way to package information within an XML envelope and the result looks similar to the XML that you see used in other places. This chapter isn't going to drown you in XML terminology, and it certainly won't make you an expert, but it does contain some helpful information on using XML with Amazon Web Services. The most important consideration is how Amazon uses XML to represent its database. Consequently, the first topic in the chapter isn't about XML—it's about the Amazon database.

You do need to understand some XML basics to get anything out of Amazon Web Services. The second section of the chapter helps you understand these basics. You'll receive enough information in this section to work with the examples in the book. However, once you start working with XML, you might find that you want to know more, so the section also includes a listing of resources (including tutorials) that you can use to increase your XML knowledge.

Many of the examples in Chapter 2 demonstrate that XML isn't necessarily easy for the average human to read. The eXtensible Stylesheet Language Transformations (XSLT) technology can transform XML into a readable Web page. Again, this section won't make you an expert, but you'll leave the section with enough information to create basic reports and informational layouts. Like the XML section, this section contains additional information on where you can learn more about XSLT.

The SOAP section of the chapter helps you understand how SOAP works, especially how it differs from straight XML. Most serious developers consider SOAP the best way to transfer data between systems today because you gain functionality. For example, SOAP supports the Web Services Description Language (WSDL), which many IDEs can turn directly into programming information for the developer. Instead of having to learn to write complex strings to request data, the developer concentrates on the data requirements and lets the IDE perform the complex part of the task.

Finally, this chapter discusses two essential issues. The first is the problem of maintaining privacy with Web service applications. Generally, you shouldn't run into too many privacy issues with Amazon Web Services unless you upload reviews or other input. The second is the problem of security. Fortunately, Amazon uses the HyperText Transport Protocol Secure (HTTPS) sockets protocol for third party vendor uploads.

Previewing the Amazon Database

Understanding the structure of data doesn't seem very important until you need a particular piece of data and can't find it. Most Web services hide the details of the database so that you don't become dependent on a particular data presentation. In addition, most Web services don't publish information about their databases because databases are reservoirs for proprietary information. Like most Web service providers, Amazon doesn't actually publish its database schema (a type of blueprint for the database layout). Even so, you do need to know what kinds of data you can expect to find and Amazon doesn't publish that information either except in the form of Web service calls. The request and response documentation provides a bare outline of some database elements, but doesn't really say much.

> **▶ WARNING**
>
> I based all of the information in this section on research I performed while creating applications. Amazon can change the Web service interface at any time. Consequently, you should view this information as a guideline, rather than fact. If Amazon does change the interface, the WSDL file you use to create applications will also change (letting you know about the new configuration) and Amazon will update its help files.

Fortunately, you can discover the public portions of the database by viewing the various files that Amazon does make available. Putting all documentation and examples together and then doing a little research on your own can yield interesting results. This section provides an overview of those results in tabular format. Table 3.1 shows the results you obtain for various kinds of searches. Each check in the table shows a data value you get for that search. The exception is the `TotalResults` field, which shows the number of results returned for a given search criteria (listed in the Search Value row, which isn't a field). This table doesn't tell about every kind of information, but it does provide enough information that you can see how the database works.

It's interesting to note that a lite search doesn't provide some of the kinds of feedback you might imagine. For example, it doesn't return an ISBN, even though it would be trivial to provide this output. Consequently, when you write an application, you need to use the ASIN field, not the ISBN field, as your source of data. Make sure you write your applications with the limitations of the database responses in mind.

All of these searches are nice, but what happens when you begin looking at other categories? Table 3.2 contains all heavy manufacturer searches, but for different search categories. Notice that the return information varies considerably by category. You can get a `RefurbishedPrice` for electronics, but not for any other category. On the other hand, books have a `CollectiblePrice` field. However, there are also some constants. For example, every

TABLE 3.1: Return Values from Typical Searches

Field Name	Lite Keyword	Heavy Keyword	Lite Author	Heavy Author	Lite ISBN	Heavy ISBN
Search Value	John Mueller	John Mueller	John Mueller	John Mueller	0735618755	0735618755
TotalResults	107	107	97	97	1	1
ASIN	X	X	X	X	X	X
Authors	X	X	X	X	X	X
Availability	X	X	X	X	X	X
BrowseList		X		X		X
Catalog	X	X	X	X	X	X
CollectiblePrice		X		X		X
ImageUrlLarge	X	X	X	X	X	X
ImageUrlMedium	X	X	X	X	X	X
ImageUrlSmall	X	X	X	X	X	X
ISBN		X		X		X
ListPrice	X	X	X	X	X	X
Manufacturer	X	X	X	X	X	X
Media		X		X		X
NumMedia		X		X		X
OurPrice	X	X	X	X	X	X
ProductName	X	X	X	X	X	X
ReleaseDate	X	X	X	X	X	X
Reviews		X		X		X
SalesRank		X		X		X
SimilarProducts		X		X		X
ThirdPartyNewPrice		X		X		X
UsedPrice	X	X	X	X	X	X

entry includes the three URL fields and a manufacturer. A few oddities also showed up—you won't find a UPC value for books no matter how hard you look, even though most books include a UPC.

TABLE 3.2: Comparison of Heavy Results for Amazon Queries

Field Name	Books	Kitchen	Music	Electronics
Search Value	Sybex	Braun	Columbia	Sony
Accessories		X		X
Artists			X	
ASIN	X	X	X	X
Authors	X			
Availability	X	X	X	X
BrowseList	X	X	X	X
Catalog	X	X	X	X
CollectiblePrice	X		X	
Features		X	X	X
ImageUrlLarge	X	X	X	X
ImageUrlMedium	X	X	X	X
ImageUrlSmall	X	X	X	X
ISBN	X			
ListPrice	X	X	X	X
Lists		X	X	X
Manufacturer	X	X	X	X
Media	X	X	X	X
NumMedia	X	X		X
OurPrice	X	X	X	X
ProductName	X	X	X	X
RefurbishedPrice				X
ReleaseDate	X		X	
Reviews	X	X	X	X
SalesRank	X	X	X	X
SimilarProducts	X	X	X	X
ThirdPartyNewPrice	X		X	X
Tracks			X	
UPC		X	X	X
UsedPrice	X		X	X

Understanding XML Basics

Almost everyone has heard about and used XML in some way. If nothing else, you've seen XML extensions on some Web pages because many magazines now use XML as a fast way to present highly formatted data online. However, XML sees more use than Web pages and Web services—it's becoming the glue that holds the Internet together. In many ways, knowing XML is a way to understand many of the things that are taking place on the Internet today. Although the following sections provide the information you need to work with Amazon Web Services, you'll eventually want to explore this topic further by using the resources in the "Learning More about XML" section.

> **▶ TIP**
>
> In some respects, you really don't learn much about Amazon Web Services database until you begin using SOAP with a product such as Visual Studio .NET. The process of creating a reference to the Web service also creates a file on disk that you can examine. Look in the `\Chapter 02\Simple-SOAP\Web References\com.amazon.soap` folder of the source code and you'll notice an innocuous file named `Reference.CS`. Viewing the file alone and with the Object Browser tells quite a bit about Amazon Web Services database. For example, most searches provide feedback in the form of a `ProductInfo` data structure. The data structure presents the public portions of that particular kind of data. The `ProductInfo` data structure represents a snapshot of that portion of the database for all searches, not just one or two.

Defining the Parts of an XML Message

All XML messages consist of three components: elements, attributes, and data. For all of the complexity of the examples in the previous chapters, XML doesn't contain very much in the way of complex information. In addition, XML messages consist entirely of text for the most part. Yes, you can attach encoded data, but the message itself is pure text, which makes XML quite readable. Here's a simple example that shows all three kinds of XML message components. You'll find this example in the `\Chapter 03\Sample XML` folder of the source code located on the Sybex Web site. (Note that some lines of code appear on more than one line in the book due to page width.)

```
<?xml version="1.0" encoding="UTF-8"?>
<Hello xmlns:xsi="http://www.w3.org/2001/
➥ XMLSchema-instance">
   <Element1>Some Text 1</Element1>
   <Element2 MyAttribute="SomeValue">Some Text
➥ 2</Element2>
</Hello>
```

The first line is an element. It's a special kind of element that every XML file has—the XML heading. The `<?xml?>` element (or tag as some books say) defines this file as an XML file of some kind. The `version` attribute further defines the XML file by telling the XML parser that this is a version 1.0 file. The `encoding` attribute states how the data preparer formed the characters within the file. The two most popular encoding techniques in use now are UTF-8 and UTF-7. You can learn more about the Unicode Transformation Format (UTF) standard at `http://czyborra.com/utf/` , `http://www.unicode.org/`, and `http://www.utf-8.com/`.

The second line also contains an element. However, notice this element has an opening and a closing tag. The opening `<Hello>` tag appears first, followed by two child elements, followed by the closing `</Hello>` tag. Standard elements all require an opening and closing tag unless they're self-contained. You can create a self-contained tag by adding the ending slash as part of the initial tag like this `<Hello />`. The `<Hello>` element includes a special namespace attribute. You can always detect namespace elements because they begin with `xmlns`, followed by a colon, followed by the name of the namespace (`xsi` in this case). The namespace normally has a URL attached to it. Whenever an XML parser sees a namespace attached to an element, it goes to the URL defined for that namespace to learn how to interpret the element, associated attributes, or data.

The `<Element1>` element is a child of the `<Hello>` element. Elements can have child/parent relationships. This element doesn't include any attributes, but it does have data in the form of `Some Text 1`. The value of `<Element1>` is `Some Text 1`. The XML Parser links the element to its data.

The `<Element2>` element is also a child of the `<Hello>` element and a sibling of `<Element1>`. This element also includes an attribute. In this case, the attribute is extra data that describes the element in some way. The value of MyAttribute appears in quotes after the attribute. To create an attribute, you must always provide a name, followed by the equals sign and a string value in quotes. An element can contain as many attributes as needed to provide a full description of its functionality.

Viewing XML Data in Your Browser

One of the problems of working with XML data is that it can become quite lengthy. The length of an Amazon search result can make it difficult to locate the very information you seek. Fortunately, you can see the formatted data in a browser such as Internet Explorer. The data contains indentations to show the relationships between parent and child. In addition, you can differentiate between elements, attributes, and data by looking at the colors. Finally, special elements such as processing instructions and the XML header appear in a different color.

Unless you know how a browser displays XML, you might conclude that the indentation and coloration are the only help you receive. However, browsers have a lot more to offer than that in most cases. At the very least, you can expand and collapse various levels of information.

Figure 3.1 shows an example of an Amazon response that relies on the ability of the browser to collapse information to present a clearer picture of the response. You'll find this example in the `\Chapter 03\Sample XML` folder of the source code located on the Sybex Web site.

FIGURE 3.1: Internet Explorer and other browsers can display XML files in a variety of ways.

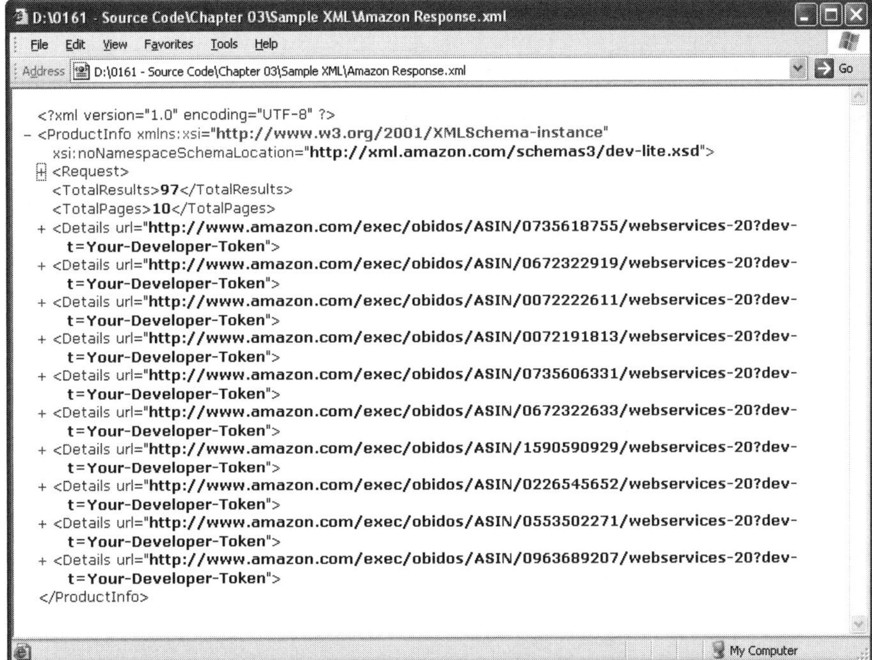

As you can see, the entire response now fits within one screen, making it easy to get an overview of the data. Notice the minus (–) sign next to the `<ProductInfo>` element. This symbol indicates that you can collapse this level. The plus (+) sign that appears next to the `<Request>` element shows that you can expand the level to show child entries. Clicking either a minus or plus sign performs that task within the browser, so you can display any level of detail desired.

Getting XML Data Tools

As noted in previous sections of the chapter, XML is almost, but not quite, readable by the average human. Reading simple files is almost trivial using a browser (see the "Viewing XML Data in Your Browser" section), but once you see the data nested a few layers deep, reading it can become tiresome. Consequently, many developers add an XML editor to their toolkit.

If you plan to perform detailed analysis of the information you receive from Amazon and don't necessarily want to do it using a browser, you need to get an XML editor. The only problem is that some of these tools cost quite a bit for the occasional user. Microsoft has remedied this problem a little with the introduction of XML Notepad. This utility is free for the price of a download and does a reasonable job of reading most XML files.

When you start XML Notepad, you'll see a blank project. Use the File ➢ Open command to display an Open dialog that helps you to open XML files from a local drive or from a Web site. All you need is a filename (and path) or a URL to get started.

Figure 3.2 shows the same Amazon response file used in other areas of the chapter. You'll find this example in the `\Chapter 03\Sample XML` folder of the source code located on the Sybex Web site. Notice that the elements match those found in Figure 3.1 (as well as Figure 2.4). Likewise, each of the child elements matches the name of one of the fields within the Amazon response. The right pane shows the data contained within each one of the child elements.

XML Notepad makes it easier to see various kinds of elements. For example, it represents attributes as purple diamonds. A leaf element (one that has no children) appears as a red slash. An element that does have children appears as a file folder. You can expand or collapse entries as needed, just as you can with a browser.

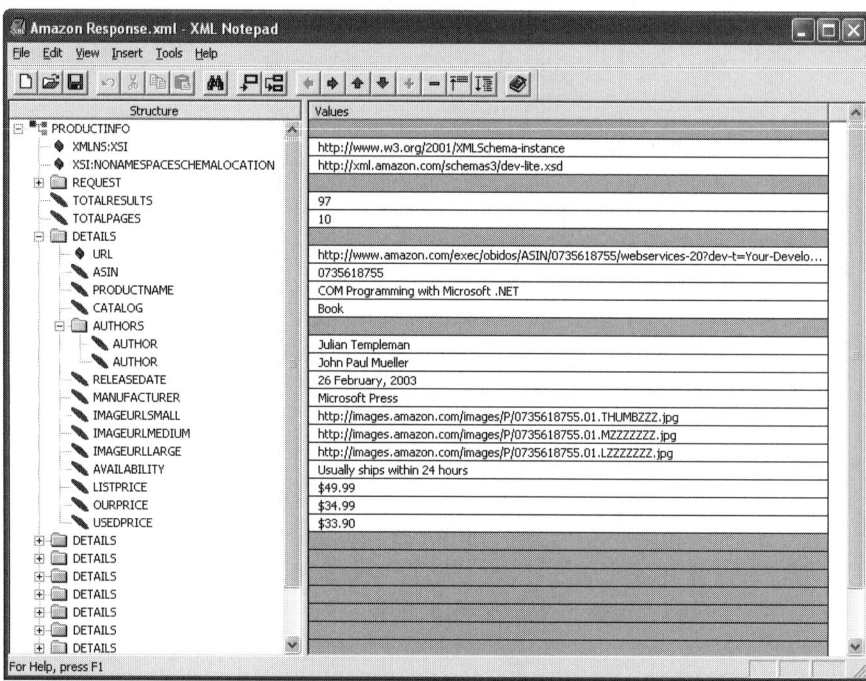

FIGURE 3.2: The names of the elements are important when working with exported data in XML format.

The benefit of having an XML editor is that you can also modify data when necessary. All you need to do is select an entry in the right and change the information. You can also right-click any of the existing icons and choose a new kind of entry to add. Creating new data for testing purposes is relatively painless once you see the exported data from an existing response. As a simple check of how easy XML Notepad is to use, try these steps.

1. Create a blank project using the File ➢ New command. XML Notepad creates a blank project that includes a Root Element and a Child Element.
2. Select the Root_Element entry and type **TheRoot**.
3. Select the Child_Element entry and type **Parent**. Highlight the entry to the right of the Parent entry and type **Parent Data**. You could stop at this point and have a perfectly acceptable XML file, but let's add a few other features.
4. Right-click Parent and choose Insert ➢ Comment from the context menu. You'll see a new comment entry added to the display. In the right pane, type **This is the parent comment**.
5. Right-click Parent and choose Insert ➢ Child Element from the context menu. The XML Notepad editor does something strange at this point—it actually creates two child elements. The first child element contains the Parent Data value created in Step 3, while the second child element is the one you wanted to create. A parent can't contain both data and children, so although this looks confusing, XML Notepad performed the task correctly. Name the first child element **`FirstChild`** and the second child element **`SecondChild`**, as shown in Figure 3.3. Notice that the figure also shows that I added data values to both children.
6. Right-click the SecondChild entry and choose Insert ➢ Attribute from the context menu. Notice that the SecondChild icon changes to a folder, but that it only adds one attribute icon. Name this attribute **FirstAttribute** and give it a value of **First Attribute Value**. Add a second attribute named **SecondAttribute** and give it a value of **Second Attribute Value**. Add a comment and give it a value of **Second Child Comment**. All three of these entries should nestle beneath

> **NOTE**
>
> Microsoft doesn't officially support XML Notepad. Consequently, you might have problems finding this download at the Microsoft site at `http://msdn.microsoft.com/library/default.asp?url=/library/en-us/dnxml/html/xmlpaddownload.asp`. Some alternate download sites include WebAttack at `http://www.webattack.com/get/xmlnotepad.shtml` and DevHood at `http://www.devhood.com/tools/tool_details.aspx?tool_id=261`. This section uses version 1.5 of the product (the installation program says it's the 1.0 version, but the About dialog box states that it's version 1.5). The Microsoft Knowledge Base article at `http://support.microsoft.com/support/kb/articles/Q296/5/60.ASP` is also a helpful source of information for this product.

the SecondChild entry. One final entry you need to consider is the text entry. Although Amazon Web Services doesn't use it very often, you might see this entry in other places.

7. Right-click the Parent entry and choose Insert ➢ Text from the context menu. Type **Here's some text.** as the text entry value. Your XML Notepad display should look similar to the one shown in Figure 3.4. Note that some of the entries could appear in a different order than the ones shown in Figure 3.4.

Save your new XML file as `SampleData.XML`. You might wonder how this file appears in a browser, so open it up with Internet Explorer. The first thing you should notice is that XML Notepad doesn't include the proper XML header, `<?xml version="1.0" encoding="UTF-8" ?>`, so that's something you have to add manually. In all other ways, XML Notepad creates well-formed XML with all of the required entries. The XML is even easy to read within Notepad because it contains carriage returns and the proper spacing to show the relationships between parents and children.

As you can see, XML Notepad doesn't have some of the bells and whistles of high-end products such as XML Spy (`http://www.xmlspy.com/`), but it's a good alternative if you only use an XML editor occasionally and don't want to spend a lot of money. The important consideration is that you have an XML editor that you can use to view the output from your applications.

FIGURE 3.3: XML Notepad correctly creates two children when necessary.

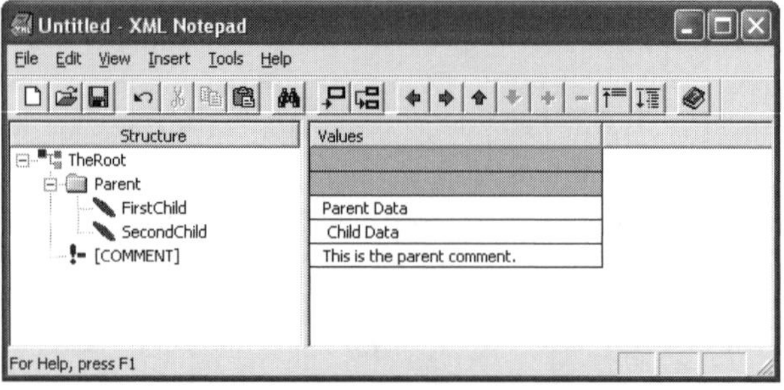

FIGURE 3.4: The final document created using XML Notepad.

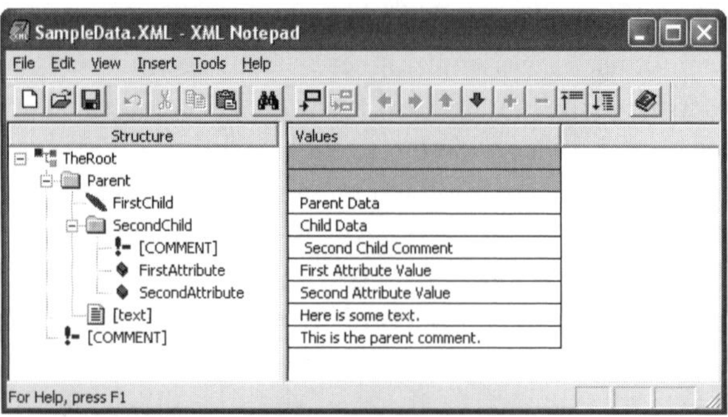

Sending Special Characters Using URL Encoding

For most people, working with Web sites is a unique experience because they encounter unexpected oddities that they haven't had to consider in the past. When you type a space into a word-processed document, nothing odd happens—the computer simply accepts the character. However, look at the word processor again. Notice how the word processor automatically looks at the space and uses it to determine where to split lines of text. The word processor does treat the space differently—it treats it as a delimiter (a fancy term that programmers use to mean a character that has a special meaning). Likewise, when you add a hyphen to a word, the computer could choose to split the sentence in the middle of the word. The hyphen acts as a delimiter.

The Internet also uses delimiters for a number of purposes, including URLs. When a Web server sees a space, it could assume that it has reached the end of the URL or the beginning of a new input parameter (or a number of other things). Consequently, you must replace spaces, question marks, and other characters with other characters that don't work as delimiters. The example in the "Using a Browser Example" section of Chapter 2 uses such a replacement for the author name. The example replaces a space between the author's first and last name with %20. The Web server interprets this special character sequence as a space.

At first, you might think that the character replacement is random, but there's some method to the madness. In fact, it's relatively easy to write a JavaScript function that performs the character replacement so you don't need to worry about it. Listing 3.1 shows this function. You'll find the complete source for this example in the `\Chapter 03\URL Encode` folder of the source code located on the Sybex Web site. Note that you can write similar functions in other languages; I'm just using this one because most people can run JavaScript using their browsers.

Listing 3.1 Replacing Characters in a String

```
function ReplaceCharacter(InputStr, Replace, UseInstead)
{
   // Define the length of the inputs.
   var InputLength = InputStr.length;
   var ReplaceLength = Replace.length;

   // Determine whether either input has a 0 length. If so,
   // the function can't succeed. However, because this is
   // a recursive function, the function does need to return
   // the original string.
   if ((InputLength == 0) || (ReplaceLength == 0))
      return InputStr;

   // Locate the first replacement value.
   var ReplaceIndex = InputStr.indexOf(Replace);

   // If the replacement value doesn't appear within the string,
```

```
    // then return. Again, keep the recursive nature of the
    // function in mind.
    if (ReplaceIndex == -1)
       return InputStr;

    // Create a string that includes the first part of the original
    // string and the replacement character, but not the rest of the
    // string.
    var Output = InputStr.substring(0, ReplaceIndex) + UseInstead;

    // Use recursion to process the string again if there is more data
    // to process.
    if (ReplaceIndex + ReplaceLength < InputLength)

       // Keep adding to the output string after each recursion.
       Output += ReplaceCharacter(
          InputStr.substring(ReplaceIndex + ReplaceLength, InputLength),
          Replace,
          UseInstead);

    // Return the output during each recursion.
    return Output;
}
```

This might look like a lot of very complicated code, but it's actually an easy program. It uses a special technique called recursion to perform its work. In recursion, the programmer writes a program that solves the simplest form of a problem, and then has that program keep calling itself until it achieves that simple form. No matter how complex the input is, the program can solve it (given enough memory and time) because eventually the input will reach this simple solution.

In this instance, the program keeps calling itself until one of several conditions occurs. First, the program could run out of text to process. Second, the program might have some text left, but it might not contain the special character you want to replace (such as a space). If that's the case, then the program has already performed all of the required work, so it can stop.

Once the program determines there's data to process, it uses the `substring()` function to look for that character in the string. The `substring()` function returns just the first part of the string—the part that doesn't contain the special character. To this string, the code adds the replacement characters, such as %20 for a space.

It's at this point that the recursion process occurs. The code still has the other part of the string to consider—the last half. The first half of the string is free of the special character, but not the second half. When the code detects that there's still string to process, it calls itself again with the last half of the string. This process continues until the code has processed all of the input string. Figure 3.5 shows typical output from this program.

Of course, the problem is figuring out which characters to replace and what numbers to use to replace them. Unfortunately, Amazon doesn't publish a list of offending characters, so you'll need to experiment a little with special characters that you want to use. A space never works and you have to exercise care with both double and single quotes. Determining what number to use is easy. Simply break out a copy of the Character Map utility that comes with Windows and you have everything needed. Figure 3.6 shows what this utility looks like.

Simply select the character you want and look at the number that appears at the bottom of the dialog box. This is the number you should use to replace the character in a string. You can also hover the mouse over the character and the program will display both the character name and the associated number, as shown in Figure 3.3. For example, you replace the quotation mark with %22 in a URL encoded string.

FIGURE 3.5:

The example program shows how you can perform URL encoding.

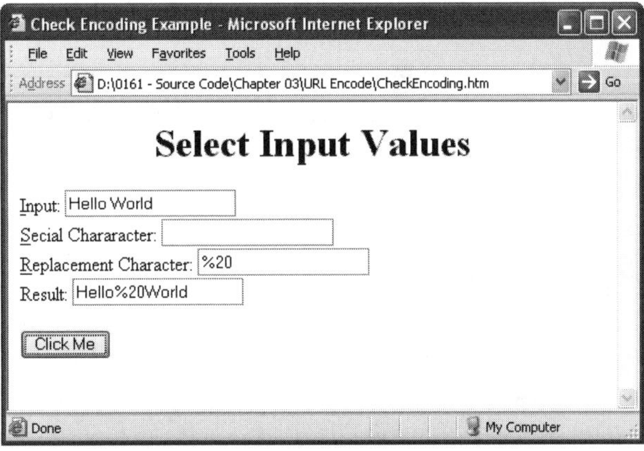

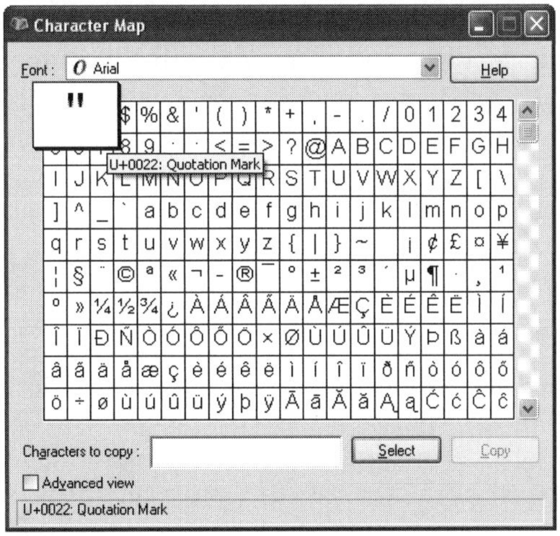

FIGURE 3.6:

Character Map makes it easy to learn the numbers associated with special characters.

Learning More about XML

Whether you know it or not, you'll run into XML many times during your computer use. The reason is simple—XML makes a great way to exchange data between disparate systems. Fortunately, XML is relatively easy to learn. Visit the W3C Schools site at `http://www.w3schools.com/xml/` to find a complete XML tutorial. You might also want to review the namespace tutorial at `http://www.zvon.org/index.php?nav_id=172&ns=34`.

Unlike many topics discussed in this book, there are multiple versions of XML so you can't rely on just one reference. The most important reference for Amazon Web Services appears at `http://www.zvon.org/xxl/xmlSchema2001Reference/Output/index.html`. However, make sure you also look at the references at `http://www.zvon.org/xxl/xmlSchemaReference/Output/index.html` for complete information. The annotated XML reference at `http://www.xml.com/axml/axml.html` is also handy for seeing the specification and expert commentary side-by-side.

You can also find a number of good general-purpose XML sites online. For example, the Microsoft XML Developer Center (`http://msdn.microsoft.com/nhp/default.asp?contentid=28000438`) is a great place to visit if you use Microsoft products.

Using XSLT for Presentation

For many people, reading XML borders on the impossible. Using XSLT can remedy the problem to a great extent, however, by telling a browser or application how to interpret the information the XML file contains. Presentation can mean everything once you get past the requirements of accurate data. Unfortunately, creating Web pages by hand to achieve a combination of great presentation and accurate data consumes a lot of time, so Webmasters have looked for an easier way to create a presentation online. The combination of XML (data) and XSLT (presentation) has become more than a convenience for many organizations. Using this technique helps companies create accurate presentations with little effort. Because Amazon Web Services relies on XML, XSLT also provides one of the best ways for you to create a great presentation. The following sections provide a good overview of XSLT. You'll also find a section with references to other XSLT information sources.

Using a Script to Call an XSLT Page

Amazon doesn't know how you want to present the data they provide, so the XML you receive doesn't include any form of XSLT declaration. This declaration appears as `<?xml-stylesheet type="text/xsl" href="amazon-seller-search-popup.xsl"?>` in the XML file. The `href` attribute tells where to find the XSLT file. Without this information, the browser will never display anything but XML on screen. It would seem that the situation is hopeless. However, you have other options, such as writing a script that performs the transformation process using another technique.

The example in Listing 3.2 shows how you can download a response from Amazon, store the information locally, and translate it using XSLT. The result is the same as modifying the XML file to include the required linkage information, but far more automatic. You'll find the complete source for this example in the `\Chapter 03\Viewing XSLT` folder of the source code located on the Sybex Web site.

Listing 3.2 Performing a Transformation in JavaScript

```
function GetData(XslFile)
{
   // Convert the author name to use %20 instead of spaces.
   var AuthName = SubmissionForm.AuthorSearch.value;
   AuthName = ReplaceCharacter(AuthName, ' ', '%20');

   // Build a string that will hold the complete URL.
   var XmlFile = "http://xml.amazon.com/onca/xml3?" +
                 "t=" + SubmissionForm.t.value + "&" +
                 "dev-t=" + SubmissionForm.devt.value + "&" +
                 "AuthorSearch=" + AuthName + "&" +
                 "mode=" + SubmissionForm.mode.value + "&" +
                 "type=" + SubmissionForm.type.value + "&" +
                 "page=" + SubmissionForm.page.value + "&" +
                 "f=" + SubmissionForm.f.value;

   // Create an XML document object and load the data from the
   // Amazon Web Service into it.
   var XMLData = new ActiveXObject("Msxml2.DOMDocument.5.0");
   XMLData.async=false;
   XMLData.load(XmlFile);

   // Create an XSLT document and load the transform into it.
   var XSLTData = new ActiveXObject("Msxml2.DOMDocument.5.0");
   XSLTData.async = false;
   XSLTData.load(XslFile);

   // Display the output on screen.
   document.write(XMLData.transformNode(XSLTData));
}
```

The script relies on named text boxes on the Web page for input. The first task the code performs is to URL encode the `AuthName` value (see the "Sending Special Characters Using URL Encoding" section for details). The code then combines the various values and the XML site URL into a request URL similar to the ones used throughout Chapter 2.

The next step is a little tricky and definitely Windows specific. The code creates an instance of the Microsoft XML component. The `ActiveXObject()` function performs this task. The `Msxml2.DOMDocument.5.0` string identifies the component. You might have to use `Msxml2.DOMDocument.4.0` on older machines—the last part of the string identifies the component version number. Setting the `async` property to false is important because you don't want the call to load the XML to return until the browser actually receives this file. Finally, the `XMLData.load()` function loads the response from Amazon Web Services.

The code now has a local copy of the data from Amazon. This local copy will disappear as soon as the function ends, so you don't have to worry about update requirements, but it's important to understand that the copy resides in memory on your machine somewhere.

At this point, the code has data to work with, but no XSLT file. The next step loads the XSLT file defined by the `XslFile` variable. The coupling between the XML response and the XSLT occurs in the `XMLData.transformNode()` function call. This call produces output that the `document.write()` function then sends to the current page. The result is that you see the transformed XML on screen, as shown in Figure 3.7. Notice that the URL doesn't change, even though the content differs, because you're still theoretically on the same Web page.

XSLT Transformation Example - Microsoft Internet Explorer
File Edit View Favorites Tools Help
Address D:\0161 - Source Code\Chapter 03\Viewing XSLT\SimpleHTML.htm
Go
Translated Amazon Web Server Results
Search Result Arugments
Name | Value
locale | us
AuthorSearch | John Mueller
page | 1
dev-t | Your-Developer-Token
t | webservices-20
f | xml
mode | books
type | lite
Books Returned from Query
Book Title | ISBN | Release Date | Publisher
COM Programming with Microsoft .NET | 0735618755 | 26 February, 2003 | Microsoft Press
VPNs: A Beginner's Guide | 0072191813 | 14 December, 2001 | McGraw-Hill Osborne Media
Peter Norton's Complete Guide to Windows XP | 0672322919 | 29 October, 2001 | SAMS

FIGURE 3.7: The results of using a script to transform XML data received from Amazon

Understanding How XSLT Works

Unlike an XML file, an XSLT file generates some type of presentation, using information from the XML file as input. Consequently, XSLT (or simply XSL) files often contain a combination of output text and XML. In fact, all XSLT files begin with the usual header and the special XSLT header shown here.

```
<?xml version="1.0" encoding="UTF-8"?>
<xsl:stylesheet version="1.0"
 xmlns:xsl="http://www.w3.org/1999/XSL/Transform"
 xmlns:fo="http://www.w3.org/1999/XSL/Format">
```

Remember that the `<?xml?>` element tells the XML parser that this is an XML file. The next element is an XSLT processing instruction. It tells the XML parser that this is an XSLT derivative of an XML file and it includes namespace pointers to Web sites that describe how to interpret XSLT. This instruction is important because otherwise the XML parser looks at this file as XML and won't have a clue what to do with all those XSLT instructions it contains.

An XSLT document describes how to transform an XML document into readable form. Therefore, the first thing it must do is tell the XML parser how much of the XML document to use for the transformation. You can choose anything from just one or two lines of the document to the entire document. Normally, XSLT documents are concerned with an entire XML document, so you'll see a line such as `<xsl:template match="/">` somewhere in the document.

It's important at this point to stress that XSLT doesn't have to output HTML. You can use XSLT to transform XML into anything you want. For example, I recently read an article in Visual Studio magazine where the author uses XSLT to transform XML data into program code. (See the article entitled "Generate .NET Code With XSLT" by Kathleen Dollard at `http://www.fawcette.com/vsm/2003_05/magazine/features/dollard/` for details.) That's right—she stores her coding requirements in XML and generates the required code automatically using XSLT.

Once you define a document as XSLT and define how much of the XML document input you want to process, you begin using a combination of text and XSLT processing instructions to transform the XML into some type of output. The "Writing a Simple XSLT Page" section shows a specific example of this transformation.

In general, XSLT is a programming language. One of the most common programming instructions retrieves a value from the XML file. For example, the instruction `<xsl:value-of select="ProductName"/>` retrieves the value of the `ProductName` element. However, XSLT doesn't limit you to simply retrieving data from the XML file. You can also use functions, such as the `count()` function that returns the number of nodes in a result set, to perform data manipulation on the XML input.

You'll also find that XSLT includes a limited number of loop and logic features. For example, you can tell XSLT that you want to perform the same task with every child of the current node using the `<xsl:for-each select="ProductInfo/Request/Args/Arg">` instruction. In this case, the `select` attribute tells which node to use for processing purposes.

A final consideration for this book is that XSLT also defines something called an axis. An axis defines a way of looking at the data. For example, the at (@) symbol tells XSLT to look at the attributes of a node, rather than the element. Another common axis is `parent`, which tells XSLT to look at the parent of the current element.

Writing a Simple XSLT Page

This section describes the XSLT page used with the transformation described in the "Using a Script to Call an XSLT Page" section (see Listing 3.2). Listing 3.3 shows how to create an XSLT page that outputs HTML code. You could use the same technique to create a report or any other form of output based on the XML input received from Amazon. You'll find the complete source for this example in the `\Chapter 03\Viewing XSLT` folder of the source code located on the Sybex Web site.

Listing 3.3 Designing an XSLT Page

```
<?xml version="1.0" encoding="UTF-8"?>
<xsl:stylesheet version="1.0"
 xmlns:xsl="http://www.w3.org/1999/XSL/Transform"
 xmlns:fo="http://www.w3.org/1999/XSL/Format">
<xsl:template match="/">
<html>
<head>
   <title>XSLT Transformation Example</title>
</head>
<body>
   <!-- Display a heading. -->
   <h1 align="center">Translated Amazon Web Server Results</h1>

   <!-- Displays the arguments used for the call. -->
   <table align="center" border="1" width="60%">
      <caption>Search Result Arguments</caption>
      <tbody>
         <tr>
            <th>Name</th>
            <th>Value</th>
         </tr>
         <xsl:for-each select="ProductInfo/Request/Args/Arg">
            <tr>
               <td><xsl:value-of select="@name"/></td>
               <td><xsl:value-of select="@value"/></td>
            </tr>
```

```
         </xsl:for-each>
      </tbody>
   </table>

   <!-- Display the search result values. -->
   <table align="center" border="1" width="100%">
      <caption>Books Returned from Query</caption>
      <tbody>
         <tr>
            <th>Book Title</th>
            <th>ISBN</th>
            <th>Release Date</th>
            <th>Publisher</th>
         </tr>
         <xsl:for-each select="ProductInfo/Details">
            <tr>
               <td><xsl:value-of select="ProductName"/></td>
               <td><xsl:value-of select="Asin"/></td>
               <td><xsl:value-of select="ReleaseDate"/></td>
               <td><xsl:value-of select="Manufacturer"/></td>
            </tr>
         </xsl:for-each>
      </tbody>
   </table>

</body>
</html>
</xsl:template>
</xsl:stylesheet>
```

The code begins with the usual declarations. It then outputs the heading. Notice that this is pure HTML and that the code isn't doing anything but outputting this text. The code moves on to the body where it outputs a heading.

The XSLT-specific code begins when the code starts creating a table. Notice the head of the table is standard HTML, but that the next selection is an `<xsl:for-each>` element. This statement tells the parser to look at all of the children of the `ProductInfo/Request/Args/` node. The system will process each `<Arg>` element in turn. The next step is to use the `<xsl:value-of>` element to retrieve the name and value attributes of each `<Arg>` element. Notice how the code uses the attribute axis to ensure the parser retrieves the attribute values and not the element values.

Once the code processes all of the arguments, it moves on to the `<Details>` element. The code uses the `<xsl:for-each>` element again to select each of the books in turn. It uses the `<xsl:value-of>` element to select each element value in turn. Notice that the code relies on an axis, in this case, because it uses the selected element directly. The code ends by completing the HTML page, and then completing both the template and the stylesheet.

Learning More about XSLT

This chapter only skims the surface of what you can do with XSLT. You can perform an incredible number of tasks using this technology. One of the better places to learn about XSLT is `http://www.w3schools.com/xsl/`. You should also view the examples in the XSLT reference at `http://www.zvon.org/xxl/XSLTreference/Output/index.html`. The XSL reference at `http://www.zvon.org/xxl/xslfoReference/Output/index.html` can also come in handy when you begin creating complex XSLT pages.

Make sure you check out some of the better third party XSLT reference sites. For example, the XSLT.com site at `http://xslt.com/` provides links and resources for XSLT from various vendors (not just Microsoft).

It also helps to have some great books on the topic. Make sure you read books such as *Mastering XSLT* by Chuck White (Sybex, 2002). It also helps to know something about XML schemas, so check out *XML Schemas* by Chelsea Valentine, Lucinda Dykes, and Ed Tittel (Sybex, 2002).

Defining SOAP Messaging

This chapter won't actually demonstrate SOAP messaging, but you do need to know how SOAP messaging works. You'll use this information in other parts of the book (especially in Chapters 6 and 9) to work with various platforms and programming languages. The following sections describe SOAP basics, tell you about some important SOAP issues, and provide a few pointers on where you can learn more about SOAP.

Determining Which SOAP Standard to Use

SOAP has gone through three major revisions. Each revision makes SOAP a better product to use for communication purposes. Almost no one uses the SOAP 1.0 standard anymore. Few vendors used this standard because it had some significant problems that the SOAP 1.1 standard quickly solved. The SOAP 1.1 standard is popular because it works well for most communication that doesn't require security. For example, you can safely use SOAP 1.1 products for most Amazon Web Services tasks because you aren't passing along anything that's secret.

The SOAP 1.2 standard originally appeared on the scene on July 9, 2001, (`http://www.w3.org/TR/2001/WD-soap12-20010709/`). However, the World Wide Web Consortium (W3C) didn't make it a recommendation until June 24, 2003 (`http://www.w3.org/TR/soap12-part1/`). Consequently, many of the products you see on the Internet today still rely on SOAP 1.1 and will probably continue to rely on this standard for some time. Even Microsoft's latest release of Visual Studio .NET still relies on SOAP 1.1.

SOAP 1.2 adds some very important features. The most important feature is added security. However, according an eWeek article (http://www.eweek.com/article2/0,3959,1137357,00.asp), the new standard includes over 400 fixes for previous problems. You can also find some interesting InfoWorld articles on the topic at http://www.infoworld.com/article/03/05/07/HNsoap_1.html, http://www.infoworld.com/article/02/12/19/021219hnsoapadvance_1.html?1220fram, and http://www.infoworld.com/article/02/11/01/021101hnsoap12_1.html?1104mnam. The last article is especially important because it points out another reason that vendors haven't embraced SOAP 1.2—potential patent issues were involved that the standards committee had to clear up.

> **▶ TIP**
>
> You can find many SOAP 1.1 resources now. The ZVON Web site at http://www.zvon.org/xxl/soapReference/Output/index.html provides a great reference you can use to learn more about SOAP. You'll find a SOAP tutorial at http://www.w3schools.com/soap/. The SOAP 1.1 specification appears at http://static.userland.com/xmlRpcCom/soap/SOAPv11.htm. Microsoft provides a SOAP testing tool that you can download at http://msdn.microsoft.com/library/en-us/dnsoap/html/soapvalidator.asp. Learn more about SOAP messages with attachments at http://www.w3.org/TR/SOAP-attachments. Finally, if you want to learn all the ins and outs of SOAP 1.1 with both Microsoft and third party products, get my book *Special Edition Using SOAP* (Que, 2001).

Given the current state of SOAP, you need to consider three things when you decide which standard to use. First, you need to know whether your product of choice even supports SOAP 1.2—most don't. Second, you need to consider whether the features SOAP 1.2 offers are essential to your organization. In many cases, using SOAP 1.1 still works fine. Third, you need to consider whether the remote sites you want to work with use SOAP 1.2. Using SOAP 1.1 until your partners catch up probably makes sense. You do want to use SOAP 1.2 sometime in the future, so planning for it today is a good idea.

Understanding the Parts of a SOAP Message

To understand SOAP, you need to consider the features that make up a SOAP message. A SOAP message includes the SOAP package, the XML envelope, and the HyperText Transfer Protocol (HTTP) or Simple Mail Transfer Protocol (SMTP) transport. Think about this system in the same way that you do a letter with SOAP acting as the letter, XML as the envelope to hold the letter, and HTTP or SMTP as the mail carrier to deliver the letter. The most common transport protocol in use today is HTTP, so that's what we'll look at in this section. Keep in mind, however, that SOAP can theoretically use any of a number of transport protocols and probably will in the future. Figure 3.8 shows a common

SOAP message configuration. Notice the SOAP message formatting. This isn't the only way to wrap a SOAP message in other protocols, but it's the most common method in use today.

The HTTP portion of a SOAP message looks much the same as any other HTTP header you may have seen in the past. In fact, if you don't look carefully, you might pass it by without paying any attention. As with any HTTP transmission, there are two types of headers—one for requests and another for responses. Figure 3.8 shows examples of both types.

As with any request header, the HTTP portion of a SOAP message will contain an action (`Post`, in most cases), the HTTP version, a `Host` name, and some `Content-Length` information. The `Post` action portion of the header will contain the path for the SOAP listener. Also located within a request header is a `Content-Type` entry of `text/xml` and a charset entry of `utf-8`. The `utf-8` entry is important right now because many SOAP toolkits don't support `utf-16` or other character sets.

FIGURE 3.8: An illustration of a typical SOAP message

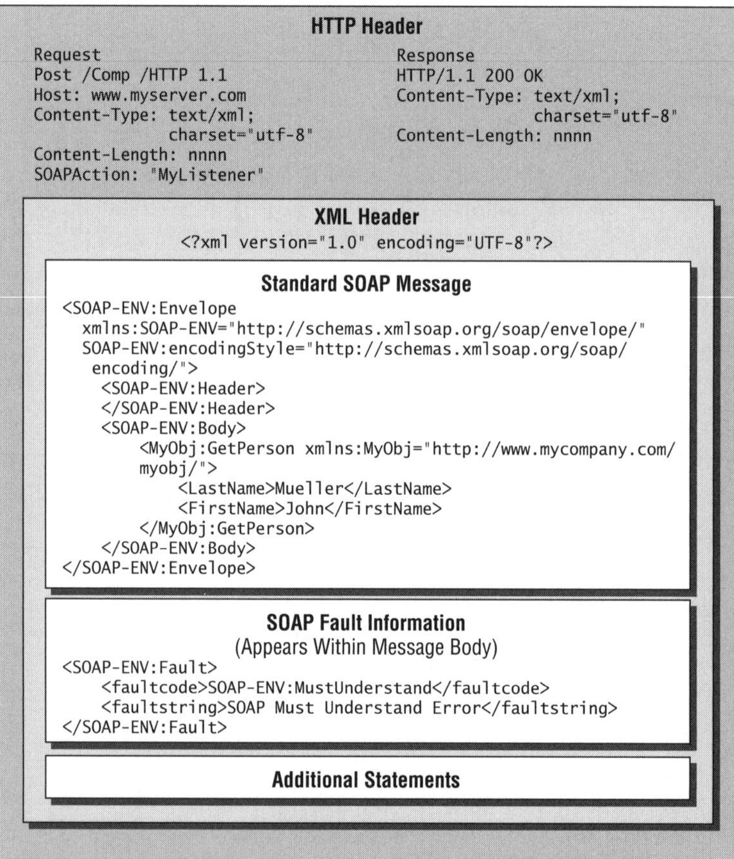

You'll also find the unique `SOAPAction` entry in the HTTP request header. It contains the Uniform Resource Identifier (URI) of the component used to parse the SOAP request. If the `SOAPAction` entry is "", then the server will use the HTTP `Request-URI` entry to locate a listener instead. This is the only SOAP-specific entry in the HTTP header—everything else we've discussed could appear in any HTTP formatted message.

The response header portion of the HTTP wrapper for a SOAP message contains all of the essentials as well. You'll find the HTTP version, status, and content length as usual. There are two common status indicators for a response header: 200 OK or 500 Internal Server Error. The SOAP specification allows use of any value in the 200 series for a positive response, but a server must return a status value of 500 for SOAP errors to indicate a server error.

Whenever a SOAP response header contains an error status, the SOAP message must include a SOAP fault section. We'll talk about SOAP faults in the "Defining Fault Tolerance in a SOAP Message" section of the chapter. All you need to know now is that the HTTP header provides the first indication of a SOAP fault that will require additional processing.

All SOAP messages use XML encoding. SOAP follows the XML specification and you can consider it a true superset of XML. In other words, it adds to the functionality already in place within XML. Anyone familiar with XML will feel comfortable with SOAP at the outset—all you really need to know is the SOAP nuances. Although the examples in the SOAP specification don't show an XML connection (other than the formatting of the SOAP message), SOAP messages always contain an XML header similar to the one shown in Figure 3.8.

A simple SOAP message consists of an envelope that contains both a header and a body (sort of the same arrangement used by an HTML page). The header can contain information that isn't associated with the data itself. For example, the header commonly contains a transaction ID when the application needs one to identify a particular SOAP message. The body contains the data in XML format. If an error occurs, the body will contain fault information, rather than data.

> **▶ TIP**
>
> Although SOAP 1.2 resources are still a little rare, you should look at the primer at `http://www.w3.org/TR/soap12-part0/`, the framework specification at `http://www.w3.org/TR/soap12-part1/`, and the adjuncts at `http://www.w3.org/TR/soap12-part2/`. You may also want to read about test collection methods at `http://www.w3.org/TR/soap12-testcollection/`. The W3C is also working on a number of additional specifications that aren't at the recommendation stage. These specifications include SOAP 1.2 attachments (`http://www.w3.org/TR/soap12-af/`), SOAP 1.2 email bindings (`http://www.w3.org/TR/soap12-email`), and SOAP 1.2 normalization (`http://www.w3.org/TR/soap12-n11n/`).

SOAP is essentially a one-way data transfer protocol. While SOAP messages often follow a request/response pattern, the messages themselves are individual entities. This means that a SOAP message is standalone—it doesn't rely on the immediate presence of a server, nor is a response expected when a request message contains all of the required information. For example, some types of data entry may not require a response since the user is inputting information and may not care about a response.

The envelope in which a SOAP message travels, however, may provide more than just a one-way transfer path. For example, when a developer encases a SOAP message within an HTTP envelope the request and response both use the same connection. HTTP creates and maintains the connection, not SOAP. Consequently, the connection follows the HTTP way of performing data transfer—using the same techniques as a browser uses to request Web pages for display.

> **▶ TIP**
>
> Working with the new capabilities provided by technologies like XML and SOAP means dealing with dynamically created Web pages. While it's nice that you can modify the content of a Web page as needed for an individual user, it can also be a problem if you need to troubleshoot the Web page. That's where a handy little script comes into play. Type **`javascript:'<xmp>'+document.all(0).outerHTML+'</xmp>'`** in the Address field of Internet Explorer for any dynamically created Web page and you'll see the actual HTML for that page. This includes the results of using scripts and other page construction techniques.

Defining Fault Tolerance in a SOAP Message

Sometimes a SOAP request will generate a fault message instead of the anticipated reply. The server may not have the means to answer your request, the request you generated may be incomplete, or bad communication may prevent your message from arriving in the same state as you sent it. There are many reasons that you may receive a SOAP fault message including messages that the client produces that the server can't process, errors on the server such as a missing application, and SOAP version mismatches.

When a server returns a fault message, it doesn't return any data. Look at Figure 3.8 and you'll see a typical client fault message. Notice the message contains only fault information. With this in mind, the client-side applications you create must be prepared to parse SOAP fault messages and return the information in such a way that the user will understand the meaning of the fault.

Figure 3.8 shows the standard presentation of a SOAP fault message. Notice that the fault envelope resides within the body of the SOAP message. A fault envelope will generally contain a `faultcode` and `faultstring` element that tells you which error occurred. All of the other SOAP fault message elements are optional. The following list tells you how they're used.

`faultcode` The `faultcode` contains the name of the error that occurred. It can use a dot syntax to define a more precise error code. The `faultcode` will always begin with a classification. For example, the `faultcode` in Figure 3.8 consists of a `SOAP-ENV` error code followed by a `MustUnderstand` subcode. This error tells you that the server couldn't understand the client request. Since it's possible to create a list of standard SOAP `faultcodes`, you can use them directly for processing purposes.

`faultstring` This is a human readable form of the error specified by the `faultcode` entry. This string should follow the same format as HTTP error strings. You can learn more about HTTP error strings by reading the HTTP specification at `http://www.normos.org/ietf/rfc/rfc2616.txt`. A good general rule to follow is to make the `faultstring` entry short and easy to understand.

`faultactor` This element points to the source of a fault in a SOAP transaction. It contains a Uniform Resource Identifier (URI) similar to the one used for determining the destination of the header entry. According to the specification, you must include this element if the application that generates the fault message isn't the ultimate destination for the SOAP message.

`detail` You'll use this element to hold detailed information about a fault when available. For example, this is the element used to hold server-side component return values. This element is SOAP message body specific, which means you can't use it to detail errors that occur in other areas like the SOAP message header. A detail entry acts as an envelope for storing detail subelements. Each subelement includes a tag containing namespace information and a string containing error message information.

> **▶ TIP**
>
> You can find a wealth of resources about WSDL on the Internet. One of the more interesting offerings includes the ZVON reference at http://www.zvon.org/xxl/WSDL1.1/Output/index.html. The W3C has a tutorial at `http://www.w3schools.com/wsdl/default.asp`. Originally, Microsoft and IBM promoted WSDL on their Web sites, but you can now find the specification on the W3C site at `http://www.w3.org/TR/wsdl`. You can find the IBM view of Web services at `http://www-106.ibm.com/developerworks/webservices/` and `http://www.alphaworks.ibm.com/tech/webservicestoolkit`. A WSDL search engine (where you can find services that rely on both SOAP and WSDL) appears at `http://www.salcentral.com/salnet/webserviceswsdl.asp`.

Understanding How WSDL Fits In

The documentation that comes with the Amazon Web Services Kit contains examples of how to format a message using SOAP. These examples include the XML header and all of the features discussed in the "Understanding the Parts of a SOAP Message" section of the chapter. Figure 3.9 shows a typical example from the kit. However, you won't need to use these examples in most cases.

WSDL provides a means for describing a Web service so that the Integrated Development Environment (IDE) you use can create the definitions needed. Some developers originally found WSDL less than helpful, and it doesn't work with every SOAP toolkit you can download. The SOAP samples help developers who must create messages manually get the format correct. However, if you use a product such as Visual Studio .NET, the IDE downloads the WSDL from the Amazon Web site and you'll find that you don't actually worry about the construction of the SOAP message.

Like many other topics discussed, WSDL relies on XML as a basis for communication. Figure 3.10 shows a typical example of the WSDL file for Amazon Web Services. Note that the Visual Studio .NET IDE automatically downloads this file as part of the process of creating a reference to the Web site—the "Creating a Web Reference" section of Chapter 6 describes how to perform this task.

Notice that the WSDL file contains a list of complex types, such as the `ProductInfo` data structure described in the "Previewing the Amazon Database" section of the chapter. It also contains a list of function names. You call a function such as `KeywordSearch()` in your code. The IDE automatically creates code to send a `KeywordSearchRequest` SOAP message and code that interprets the `KeywordSearchResponse` SOAP message the application receives from the server. The WSDL file is instrumental in performing all this work automatically.

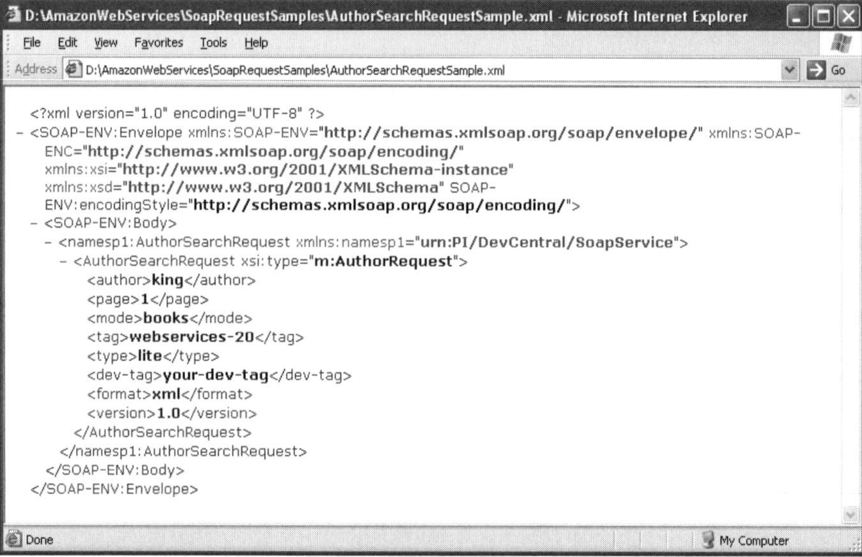

FIGURE 3.9: The kit contains a number of SOAP message examples.

FIGURE 3.10: Using WSDL makes SOAP messaging extremely easy for the developer.

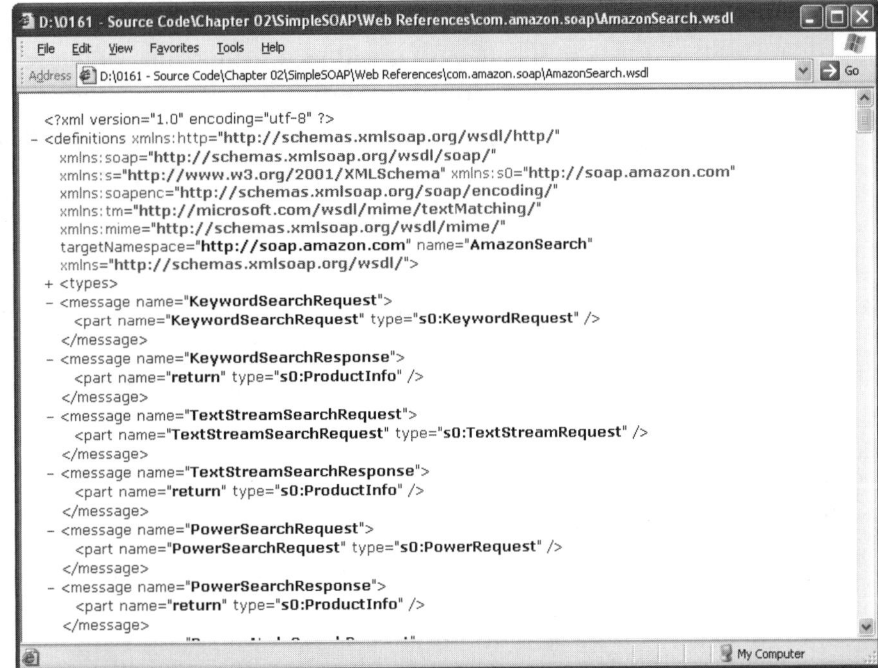

Understanding Privacy Issues

Generally, you won't run into privacy issues when you perform searches using Amazon Web Services because you don't send any personal information. If you only want to display information about products of interest on your Web site, you don't need to consider any privacy issues because they don't exist. The only privacy issue you might need to consider is the use of your developer token. You don't want to use this information in a way that could cause abuse of the system. Amazon can use the developer token to trace abuses back to you.

Most of the transactions that take place between your site and Amazon also keep privacy concerns to a minimum. You send your associate ID along with the ASIN of the product the user wants to Amazon using a special post message. Shopping carts, gift registries, and other forms of product information exchange rely on a generic object that doesn't include any user information. The only two items you need to consider are the object identifier and a security token used to identify the specific session. When a user is ready to make a purchase, you hand them off to Amazon and Amazon takes care of obtaining personal information. Even so, there's some risk of object number or security token contamination. For example, someone with an incredibly sick sense of humor could add a few items to the user's cart. To ensure you keep your risk to a minimum, never ask the user for any personal information.

Amazon also provides services such as a chat group now. You can connect to the various chat groups through your Web site. Again, Amazon takes care of getting most of the personal information for you. However, in this case, some personal information could end up on your Web site within a database. Although the chat is open to the public and there probably aren't any secrets passed using this method, you still need to exercise care in the handling of any data you acquire on your site. The safe bet is to purge any personal information as soon as possible and let Amazon address message handling and other concerns. (See the Amazon Chat details, including privacy and security concerns, at `http://www.amazon.com/exec/obidos/tg/browse/-/901886/`.)

Understanding Security Issues

It's not too hard to find disparaging news about security on the Internet—even Web services that shouldn't have security problems experience them. The security issues have kept many vendors from working with Web services. For example, the fact that you can't easily encrypt information for Web service use means that everyone can read it unless you take measures such as using Secure Sockets Layer (SSL). (Web sites that use `https` instead of `http` are using SSL.) Fortunately, most of the information you exchange with Amazon doesn't require security and Amazon takes care of most security concerns when you pass the user of your Web site along to them.

You still need to consider security for your site when it performs Web service tasks. One of the better whitepapers on how the standards groups are meeting security needs appears on the Microsoft site at `http://msdn.microsoft.com/library/en-us/dnwssecur/html/securitywhitepaper.asp`. This discussion also provides a road map of security services.

It's also important to consider other sources of security information. For example, the Worldwide Web Consortium (W3C) and Internet Engineering Task Form (IETF) released the XML Signature specification in 2002. An XML Signature can help a recipient validate the sender of XML data and the integrity of that data. You can read about this standard at `http://www.w3.org/TR/2002/REC-xmldsig-core-20020212/`. The W3C and IETF are still working on two other XML security standards: XML Encryption and XML Key Management.

Your Call to Action

You now know how to work with XML. This may not seem like much, but considering how important XML is to Web services, knowing how to work with XML is essential. Without knowing XML, you can't successfully build many Amazon Web Services applications. Viewing the XML you receive from Amazon helps you understand how various requests affect the information flow, which increases the chance that you'll develop efficient applications without a lot of extra effort.

This chapter is a beginning. You need to spend more time working with XML to become truly proficient with it. Make sure you visit at least some of the Web sites listed in this chapter to learn more about XML and related technologies such as SOAP and XSLT. It's also a good idea to spend time considering the Amazon database layout. You might want to use this information to formulate precise searches to obtain the most benefit for the lowest cost in terms of search time. Finally, if you don't have privacy and security policies in place, make sure you create the required documentation now, before something happens. Written policies are the best way to reduce risk. If you do have written policies, make sure you revisit them annually to ensure they still meet requirements of your organization, no matter how big or small.

Chapter 4 is the start of a new section. Rather than spending time looking at various techniques for developing applications and theoretical knowledge you need to implement an Amazon Web Services application, this section shows you how to perform the task. Chapter 4 presents concepts and techniques that everyone needs to work with Amazon Web Services. The chapters that follow begin looking at individual language requirements. In sum, Chapter 4 is the first chapter where you begin writing application code.

Part II

Writing Amazon Web Services Programs

Chapter 4

Selecting a Communication Method

Designing for One or More Platforms

Choosing a Development Language

Starting the Development Process

Designing with International Use in Mind

Writing application software is a discipline. You need to consider how you will implement the application before you begin coding it. Designing software includes a number of tasks this chapter doesn't consider, such as how to design the user interface. In addition, the chapter won't discuss creating schedules and other tasks that don't really relate to the topic at hand—connecting to Amazon Web Services and using the information it provides effectively. Consequently, this chapter discusses issues you probably didn't hear about in a computer science class, read in a book, learn about in a magazine, or discuss with a friend across the street.

Web services are all about communication. Your application uses some type of communication medium to transmit a request to a remote server and receive a response. The kind of communication you use makes a great deal of difference in the way you design and optimize your application. The communication method can also change the way your application operates and can affect performance.

You also need to consider the target platform for your application and choose the best language to meet your particular needs. As demonstrated in previous chapters, Amazon Web Services works well with a number of platforms and programming languages. Some developers attempt to take a one size fits all approach to selecting a language, but that's clearly not the best approach. This chapter helps you decide which platforms to target and which language to use for your specific needs.

Finally, most Web sites don't get visitors from just one country anymore. In fact, I've found that I use Google's translation service quite often now to translate sites in Japanese and German (among other languages). Often, these sites contain a bit of information I need to get a consulting job done or perform a writing task. Consequently, I understand the benefits that internationalization can provide. This final section discusses when internationalization can make your site more appealing and some of the steps you need to perform to do it.

Choosing a Communication Method

All of the examples to this point in the book have relied on some form of communication to achieve their goals. In fact, every Amazon Web Services application you create will include some type of communication with the remote server unless that application relies on static data. Even then, you need to consider significant licensing issues for updates because the updated data will have to come from some source. For example, a PDA could obtain updates from a local desktop, which avoids having the PDA connect to Amazon Web Services, but the desktop will still need some source of updated information (usually a direct connection).

Getting Additional Information about Application Design

This chapter doesn't discuss general application design. Make sure you augment the information in this chapter with some general design information from books such as *Designing Highly Usable Software* by Jeff Cogswell (Sybex, 2004). Another good book to consider is *Database Design for Mere Mortals: A Hands-On Guide to Relational Database Design*, Second Edition, by Michael J. Hernandez (Addison-Wesley, 2003). Finally, you might consider *Patterns of Enterprise Application Architecture* by Martin Fowler, David Rice, Matthew Foemmel, Edward Hieatt, Robert Mee, and Randy Stafford (Addison-Wesley, 2002).

Don't think that you're limited to reading books about design. You can also find a wealth of online sources for specific topics. For example, Microsoft provides a number of white papers online such as the article entitled "Modeling Your Application and Data" at `http://msdn.microsoft.com/library/en-us/vsent7/html/vxoriModelingYourApplicationData.asp`. You should also consider sources such as Rational's (now IBM) article entitled "Modeling Web Application Design with UML" at `http://www.rational.com/products/whitepapers/100462.jsp`. Sometimes online magazines provide great input. Check out the article entitled "Magic Quadrants: Business Modeling, Application Design" at `http://www4.gartner.com/pages/story.php.id.2648.s.8.jsp`—it provides some great resources you can use.

Make sure you also get any application design software you need. There are moderately priced solutions such as Microsoft Visio (`http://www.microsoft.com/office/visio/`). However, you should also consider shareware from sites such as Tucows (`http://idirect.tucows.com/`), ZDNet (`http://downloads-zdnet.com.com/2001-20-0.html`), and Nonags (`http://nonags.com/`). If your application is small enough, you can also use simple drawing programs such as Paint Shop Pro (`http://www.jasc.com`) or create the design by hand on paper. The point is to get the design down in print so that you can refer to it.

No matter what source of information you use and how you get your design in writing, you want to avoid one of the most common mistakes that developers make—starting an application without designing it. You wouldn't consider building a house without a blueprint—developing a blueprint for your application is the same. Although this chapter doesn't provide general design information, you'll find it essential in adding the Amazon Web Services twist to your application design.

The following sections discuss the design issues surrounding the various communication choices you have. You'll find that Amazon Web Services is quite flexible; which means you can exercise any of a number of options. However, the level of flexibility means you also have to consider those choices carefully. For example, you might consider speed more important than flexibility. In some cases, this means that you'll need to use Simple Object Access Protocol (SOAP), rather than an eXtensible Markup Language (XML) query to get the job done.

Using XML over HTTP

Of the communication choices, XML over HyperText Transport Protocol (HTTP) is the most flexible because you can use it from so many different products. The "Using a Browser Example" section of Chapter 2 demonstrates that you don't have to write a single line of code to use this method of communicating with Amazon. All you need is a properly formatted URL to receive an XML response that contains the information you requested.

As previously mentioned, this method does have certain problems. For example, you don't get formatted output. Of course, there are any number of ways around this issue—everything from using eXtensible Stylesheet Language Transformations (XSLT) to parsing the XML and providing it as part of a report. All of these issues have solutions of some sort, so you can work around them.

From a design perspective, you have other issues to consider when using the XML request method. The most critical problem is performance. You'll find that SOAP is far faster than using the XML request method because SOAP is formatted input that doesn't require as much interpretation on the part of the server or the client. The additional work required to use SOAP does boost performance. Just how much of a performance boost depends on a number of factors including communication speed, line conditions, and how busy Amazon is at any given time.

All types of communication are subject to damage. The probability of damage often reflects the complexity of the data or the formatting used to send it. The XML request method is especially subject to damage because the URL string must appear in precisely the correct format. A little thing, such as the use of a space instead of %20 (see the "Sending Special Characters Using URL Encoding" section of Chapter 3 for details) can damage the URL and make it unreadable. Consequently, you'll find that you have to repeat requests more often when using the XML request method. In addition, your application will require more error handling because the XML request method doesn't provide error handling in the same way that SOAP does (see the "Defining Fault Tolerance in a SOAP Message" section of Chapter 3 for details).

Using XSLT

All XSLT communication relies on the XML request method. You could possibly make the request using SOAP, but generally, you'll make an XML request. For example, when writing an application for the Pocket PC, you can use a product called PocketSOAP (`http://www.pocketsoap.com/`) that lets you make the call using JavaScript. The reason that I included XSLT as a separate communication method is that some people will use this technique to communicate with Amazon with scripts on a Web page, rather than write an application. For example, the "Viewing the XSLT Example" section of Chapter 2 demonstrates this technique.

Generally, you'll find that using JavaScript to create XSLT communication scenarios is the least complex method of providing full output to the user. You do have access to a number of underlying request methods, so this technique is also flexible when compared to other options, such as interpreting the XML from an XML request. Most browsers can also use both JavaScript and XSLT, so this is one of the few "universal" solutions at your disposal. Some developers might think otherwise, but this is also the easiest solution to debug because you don't need any special equipment.

The design considerations include performance. This is the slowest method you can use to work with Amazon. Every request requires interpretation using some type of script reader. Unlike an application, the script reader must interpret the script and convert it into something the user's machine can understand every time the user makes a request. Don't use this solution if speed is a concern.

Another potential problem is browser compatibility. Using JavaScript and a Web page might seem like the ideal solution, but you can run into numerous pitfalls when a user with a different browser than yours visits. Users can also decide to disable scripting, which prevents your page from working properly. In short, although using XSLT does cross boundaries that you'd normally have a hard time crossing, it isn't perfect.

Using SOAP

You'll find that SOAP is by far the most complex, yet fastest, method of communicating with Amazon. The problems with SOAP are many. For example, you need to consider whether the technology you use to access Amazon relies on document style or Remote Procedure Call (RPC) style SOAP. Microsoft products tend to use document style, while other products use RPC style SOAP. Unfortunately, Amazon uses the RPC approach. Generally, you'll find that newer products such as Visual Studio .NET make all of the required modifications for you, but at a slight performance cost (even with modifications, the SOAP solution is faster than the XML request method). Older products might require some special programming to adhere to Amazon's standard. Unfortunately, except for the examples Amazon provides, you don't find much documentation for this standard.

The lack of a description of Amazon's standard is important. Make sure you use the examples located in the `\AmazonWebServices\SoapRequestSamples` and `\AmazonWebServices\SoapResponseSamples` folders of the kit during the design process. Validate the output from your program using any of a number of interception programs if necessary. See the "Using a SOAP Interception Program" section of Chapter 6 for details. If nothing else, use the functionality provided by your programming language to build the required messages manually.

Selecting a Platform

You might think at the outset that only desktop users will need the Amazon Web Services application you create. In some cases, you might be right. Other kinds of users might not have a need to access your application in any way. However, it's surprising how many applications are seeing use on alternative platforms that many people would have considered impossible even a year or two ago. The problem for developers is seeing past preconceived ideas of how users will employ an application and decide which platforms the user could use. Once you make that determination, you have to go further and decide which platforms you want to support. The economic benefit of supporting a platform must outweigh the cost of implementing it.

The following sections discuss several platform design options. You'll find recommendations on ways to optimize your platform design decisions. These sections also contain a few surprises—things you might not have considered important. For example, the first section answers the question of whether you always need to implement a desktop application solution.

> ▶ **TIP**
>
> One of the most important additions you can make to your Web site is a survey form. The survey should ask users questions about the usability and information content of your site. In addition, you need to know what type of device the responder used to access your site, as well as the devices the responder would like to use to access your site. In some cases, you might find that you could double sales if you support an additional platform such as a cellular telephone.

Writing Desktop Applications

Desktop applications can serve a variety of needs. You can use a desktop application for everything from a corporate library reference that incorporates information from Amazon Web Services to a site for selling books on a particular topic as part of other services and information offered. This kind of application works well for family events, such as setting up a gift registry online for a wedding or making your favorite choices available for events such as birthdays. A small store could make an application available as a kiosk to sell goods that they might not normally carry or that the buyer needs to acquire from an online source. The application possibilities are endless.

The following sections describe three kinds of desktop applications. Obviously, you can write myriad application types for a desktop machine, but these three types work well with Amazon Web Services. Each application type has something special to offer in the way of flexibility, usability, performance, or compatibility. It's important to weigh your choices carefully, because even desktop machines aren't a one size fits all environment.

Using Standard Applications

Many users are unaware of the communication that goes on behind the scenes with many desktop applications today. The application could rely on standard desktop application controls—the same controls that developers have always used for this kind of application. In fact, you saw an example of this kind of application in the "Viewing the SOAP Example" section of Chapter 2. This application doesn't look like it has any type of connectivity to the outside world, but it does use an Internet connection to retrieve data from Amazon Web Services.

Use standard desktop applications for corporate needs. In many cases, it isn't important that the user know the source of the information used to perform a task; they simply need to know that the information exists. This kind of application could pull data in from a number of sources in a way that helps the user perform a task quickly and with less frustration than using a number of independent applications to perform the same task. Data source hiding is an important development principle to keep in mind. Hiding the source of the data means you don't have to retrain users every time the source of the data changes.

Using Web-enabled Applications

Some developers use the term Web-enabled to mean any browser application that sits on the desktop. However, this description doesn't really fit today's application development products. You can easily create an application that looks like a standard desktop application, but uses a browser interface by adding one of many HTML controls to the application. It doesn't matter whether you use a high-end product such as Visual Studio or an Office product such as Word—the interface still looks like a standard application, but the presentation is all HTML. Microsoft actually uses this technique for most help setups in their applications today.

This kind of application can work well when you need to combine local and remote sources. For example, employees at a nursery work with thousands of plants. A nursery often has detailed books on each plant, but new plants come out each year, making it necessary to buy books on those plants. A Web-enabled application would allow the employee to search local books for the plant first, and then bookstores online if the plant doesn't appear in any of the local resources.

A side benefit of this approach is that you can combine sources into one page. A nursery employee might see a single page that has a picture of the plant at top and a list of books that support that plant beneath the picture. The picture could come from an online source when none of the local sources can provide one. Web-enabled applications help you present text and graphics without a lot of difficult programming.

Using Browser Applications

A browser application can reside on a desktop or anywhere else for that matter. The user clicks on a link that opens Internet Explorer and takes them to the location of the application. The application could reside on a local intranet or on the Internet. A desktop browser application is usually simple compared to other kinds of browser applications. At most, the application needs to determine what type of browser the user has so that it can account for any compatibility issues.

It's important to consider browser compatibility because you don't know which of the many browsers available a user will choose. However, getting the vendors to tell you the facts is nearly impossible. You can find various charts that show browser compatibility issues online. One of the better charts is the Webmonkey Browser Chart at `http://hotwired.lycos.com/webmonkey/reference/browser_chart/index.html`. The advantage of using this chart is that the owner updates it regularly to reflect new browsers. Figure 4.1 shows a typical example of this chart.

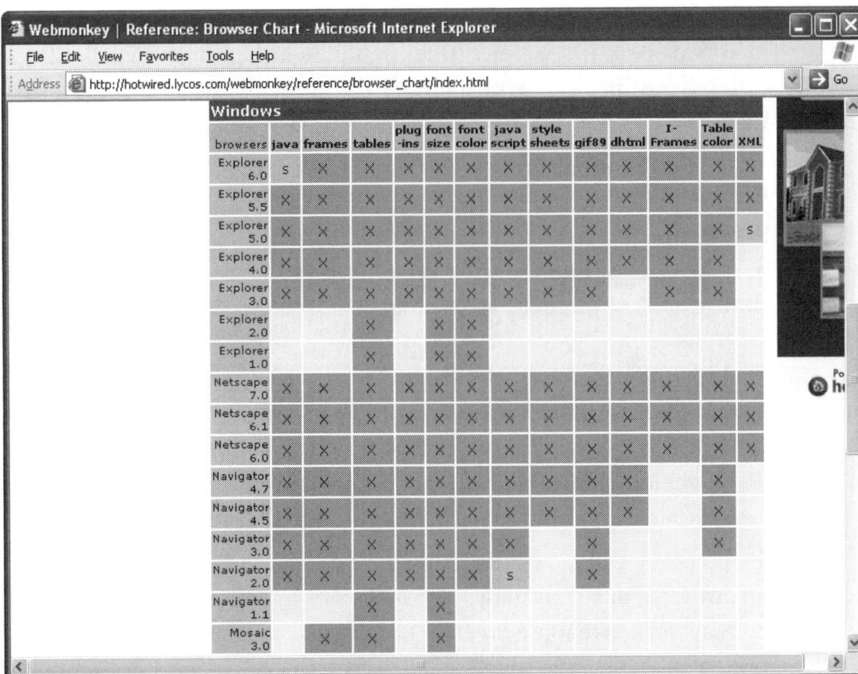

browsers	java	frames	tables	plug -ins	font size	font color	java script	style sheets	gif89	dhtml	I-Frames	Table color	XML
Explorer 6.0	S	X	X	X	X	X	X	X	X	X	X	X	X
Explorer 5.5	X	X	X	X	X	X	X	X	X	X	X	X	X
Explorer 5.0	X	X	X	X	X	X	X	X	X	X	X	X	S
Explorer 4.0	X	X	X	X	X	X	X	X	X	X	X	X	
Explorer 3.0	X	X	X	X	X	X	X	X	X		X	X	
Explorer 2.0			X		X	X							
Explorer 1.0			X		X	X							
Netscape 7.0	X	X	X	X	X	X	X	X	X	X	X	X	X
Netscape 6.1	X	X	X	X	X	X	X	X	X	X	X	X	X
Netscape 6.0	X	X	X	X	X	X	X	X	X	X	X	X	X
Navigator 4.7	X	X	X	X	X	X	X	X	X	X		X	
Navigator 4.5	X	X	X	X	X	X	X	X	X	X		X	
Navigator 3.0	X	X	X	X	X	X	X		X			X	
Navigator 2.0	X	X	X	X	X	X	S		X				
Navigator 1.1			X		X								
Mosaic 3.0		X	X		X								

FIGURE 4.1: Always check the assumptions you make about browser compatibility against a reliable chart.

As you can see, the Webmonkey Browser Chart presents a wealth of information about the features that each browser supports. Note that this chart only supports Windows browsers—Webmonkey also provides charts for the Macintosh (`http://hotwired.lycos.com/webmonkey/reference/browser_chart/index_mac.html`), Unix/Linux (`http://hotwired.lycos.com/webmonkey/reference/browser_chart/index_nix.html`), and other platforms (`http://hotwired.lycos.com/webmonkey/reference/browser_chart/index_other.html`). Make sure you consider Webmonkey's other offerings, such as a chart that shows how to create special characters and a JavaScript reference library.

Use browser applications when you think you might need to connect to other platforms. For example, using a browser application makes it much easier to move the application to the Pocket PC or even a cellular telephone. Browser applications do tend to face a variety of compatibility problems, and they're not very fast when compared to other application types, but they're the flexibility option of choice.

Writing Small Form Factor Applications

Many users now carry about some type of small form factor device such as a Personal Digital Assistant (PDA). The PDA is the most popular form, but you could consider some types of notebook computers in this category too. The small form factor device is very portable, generally sees use on the road, and has limits in processing power, memory, and local storage. Notebooks and PDAs don't suffer quite the limitations of a cellular telephone, but you may still find it difficult to write a program that fits on most of these devices and delivers everything needed.

The following sections discuss two kinds of small form factor application: desktop and browser. The Pocket PC is one of the easiest and most powerful PDAs to program, so the first section discusses how you can create desktop applications for this platform. Most people use a Web application of some type for less capable devices, such as the Palm, because local storage and the difficulty of writing an application for these platforms becomes a factor.

Using Pocket PC Applications

The Pocket PC provides a number of great programming options. For example, you can write directly to Windows CE or use the .NET Compact Framework. Developing a Pocket PC–specific application has many of the same advantages of creating standard desktop application. (See the "Using Standard Applications" section for details.) One of the biggest benefits of the Pocket PC application is that you don't need a Web server to host it in most cases.

Currently, many businesses favor the programmability the Pocket PC provides for applications such as warehouse inventory. The user has a need for a mobile device, a laptop or notebook won't work, and the user can carry a Pocket PC in a holster.

Like many other uses of Amazon Web Services, this one is nontraditional. A company can act as a third party provider on Amazon. Given the brisk pace of sales, your warehouse manager might have to keep track of inventory listed on Amazon to ensure the amount of stock your entries say exists actually appears in the warehouse.

Obviously, you can also perform searches and buy products using a Pocket PC. The advantage of the Pocket PC application, however, is that you can also do the unexpected. Many users will see the advanced applications and say that they didn't know you could do that.

Using Generic PDA Applications

All PDAs can use a Web interface, including the Palm and Pocket PC. When you create a generic PDA application, you normally need to host it on a Web server because you can't assume anything about the processing power of the client. A host can detect the type of mobile device and provide output for that device in the form of a Web page.

From a design perspective, you need to consider the devices you want to support at the outset of the project. Everything from screen design to coding technique must consider the devices you expect to use the application. In fact, you normally need to provide settings within the application that instruct the server how to react to specific devices. A Palm might require three pages to display a Web site, while a Pocket PC can display the same information in two pages. The information is the same, but the form factor of the device is different.

One of the biggest advantages of using this approach is that you can support any device. Many users find the advanced features of the Pocket PC less than useful and the larger size of the device annoying. An office manager doesn't want to carry a Pocket PC around in a holster all day. A Palm that fits in a pocket is much better because it stays out of the way until needed.

> **▶ TIP**
>
> It's possible to write a local application with a Web basis for the Pocket PC. For example, you can use products such as PocketSOAP (`http://www.pocketsoap.com/`) to write an application that relies on JavaScript to make a SOAP request locally. The PDA uses a Web interface, but it doesn't rely on contact with a server to make the request—everything occurs locally. One of the benefits of using PocketSOAP is that the vendor also makes a compatible product for desktop machine so you can use the same code base for both platforms.

Writing Cellular Telephone Applications

At one point, I wondered how someone would use a cellular telephone with Amazon Web Services. Then, someone sent me an article about a developer who uses a cellular telephone to hold a shopping list of products. The product list comes from Amazon Web Services. By storing the information in a cellular telephone, the developer can go to the local store, compare prices, and buy from the source that costs least. The best part of this application is that it stores specific information about the product such as color, size, and features.

Cellular telephones are here to stay. Some people try to use them for every communication need. As cellular telephones increase in capability, it becomes easier to write Web-based applications that really do make a difference. Imagine that you're in a meeting and the boss tells you to order a product as the result of a conversation. With the proper Amazon Web Services application, you could place the order immediately right from the meeting.

Although cellular telephones are extremely convenient, they also have severe limitations. You don't want to try to build an industrial strength application with one because they simply don't have the processing speed, memory capacity, or communication speed to support such an application. In short, for development purposes, consider the cellular telephone as an option for shopping list, search, or other light applications.

Writing Mixed Environment Applications

It's important to consider the fact that you might not be able to support just one device and make your Amazon Web Services application work. Sometimes you need to support two or even three platforms to ensure that everyone who wants to contact you can do so. You might think that this means writing separate applications for each device, but that's not necessary anymore as long as you consider the requirements of each device before you begin writing code.

Mixed environment applications commonly work on more than one device or environment (and sometimes both). In the past, you wrote mixed environment applications using Web programming techniques because the various platforms didn't offer much in the way of commonality. For example, you can write an ASP application that detects the device type (desktop browser version, PDA model, or cellular telephone model) and outputs a page specifically tailored for that device. The essential code doesn't change and you use a single code base for every device. Only the interface changes to meet the needs of a particular device.

Today, it isn't necessary to write your application as a Web application. For example, you can use Visual Studio .NET to write an application that works on a PDA or a desktop machine. Your code base remains the same, but you do need to compile the application for each kind of device. In addition, you must work within the confines of the .NET Compact Framework, rather than assume the full resources of the .NET Framework are available.

The ability to write applications that work on more than one platform or in more than one environment is so compelling that other vendors will follow suit. Eventually, you might be able to write an application that works equally well on any device without much thought.

Unfortunately, although the development environment is better today, it's still not perfect—the goal of writing mixed environment applications that truly work everywhere with little effort on the developer's part is a long way off.

Selecting a Development Language

Some developers have a mind-set that their particular language is the only perfect language in the world and they never plan to use anything else. I've love to say these developers are really on to something because it would greatly reduce the efforts I go to in order to maintain proficiency with multiple languages. The sad truth is the world has yet to discover the perfect language and probably never will. Some development languages work best for one situation, and others work best in another situation. Good developers either realize the limitations of the one language they do know or have multiple languages available in their programming toolkit.

Of course, the question is how language choice affects your use of Amazon Web Services. Look again at the examples in Chapters 2 and 3. You'll notice that all of the examples return a result from a simply constructed request. The problem is using the data you receive in some useful way. Displaying a search result with XSLT isn't a problem and you can add scripting to the resulting page to make it more flexible, but trying to build a high-end application using this technique is difficult. The sections that follow won't tell you specifically which language to use to meet your development needs, but it will help you match a language to a specific kind of project.

Choosing a Language that Meets Specific Needs

Some developers look at me rather strangely when I tell them that I develop applications in VBA about as often as I do in other languages such as C++ or C#. I find that using VBA provides me with a way to quickly prototype Office-specific applications and reduce the user's learning curve by using an environment they already know. In addition, VBA is enough like other languages I know that I don't have a big learning curve to contend with every time I start a new project. That's also the reason you'll find a VBA chapter in this book.

In fact, the language-specific chapters (Chapters 5 through 9) each demonstrate the functionality provided by a specific language. For example, the VBA examples deal with tasks you can perform more easily in Office than you can any other environment, such as creating reports or generating a list of gift ideas. You'll also see how to perform statistical analysis and generate graphs. Perhaps you sell products on Amazon (through the third-party program) and want to track the sales rank of your various offerings to see how each product performs.

However, VBA and Office don't provide the level of accessibility needed for some tasks and you definitely wouldn't want to set up a Web site that relies on VBA. The other chapters in the book cover other kinds of applications such as a Web site that offers items for sale, along with the information you have always provided. The idea is to select a language that meets the needs of the application so that you don't become frustrated trying to use a hammer where a screwdriver would work better.

Considering Your Skills and Abilities

It would be easy to assume that you want and can devote hours to your Amazon project simply because you're reading this book. However, the fact is that many of you have time constraints and probably don't have much of an inclination to become a developer (unless you're already a professional developer). It may be that you won't want to create a Web site that instantly produces sales or tracks sales records—maybe you just want to do a little research. Along with considering the needs of the application, you also have to consider your skills and abilities. Trying to take on a full-fledged shopping cart program when all you really know how to do is write a little HTML is going to become frustrating—you might never finish the project.

The development language you choose has to match the project, but it also has to match your skills and abilities. Often, the choice of language determines just how much you should attempt to do with Amazon Web Services. In other cases, you might know that you want to perform certain tasks, but that the programming language skills you possess don't quite fit in with your plans. The planning process can point out the need to call in a consultant to help with the programming part of the job. In addition, by knowing your skills and understanding the needs of the job, you can find a developer with the qualifications you need from a point of knowledge.

Honestly assessing your skills and abilities can have another effect. One person I know went back to school to learn the skills required to develop their Web application. The person didn't have nearly as many time constraints as he did cash flow problems (a consultant was out of the question). Although he didn't graduate with a degree in computer science, this person now knows how to maintain a Web site that has built his business. In short, this book might help you choose a programming language that you want to learn to use Amazon Web Services to meet a specific need effectively.

Defining Language Limitations

Part of the design process is to understand the limitations of the language you choose. You must consider both the current application requirements and those that you need to address in the future. Moving an application from one language to another is definitely not a fun task.

Consequently, you need to consider what you plan to do today and how you plan to expand the application in the future. In some cases, accomplishing this task means defining the limitations of the language.

If you choose JavaScript to create an application for your Web site, it's going to be quite flexible and most browsers won't have a problem accessing the information. In addition, you can perform most Amazon Web Services tasks without buying an expensive server or incurring many startup costs. JavaScript is the low-price solution for many developers. However, JavaScript is hardly the most robust programming language, and you'll find your expansion opportunities limited. For example, this probably isn't the right choice for creating complex reports, but it is a good solution if you want to offer a means to make purchases on Amazon or perform quick searches for products.

You might think that Java or Visual Basic .NET will solve all of your development problems. They're certainly robust enough to help you perform any task you might want to do. However, I probably wouldn't use either language if my main goal were tracking product statistics. In addition, both Java and Visual Basic .NET require the skills of a good programmer to create successful applications. Good programmers don't come cheap—plan to spend quite a bit to create the Web application of your dreams.

Understanding Internationalization Issues

Many developers don't consider internationalization issues when they develop a Web application today, but it's an important issue. Unless you know that no one who speaks another language will ever have any reason to access your site, you have to consider the possibility that internationalization could benefit your site. Not every site requires internationalization, but many do. You also have to consider how to handle the internationalization of your site. In many cases, you can simply ensure that the site handles more than one type of currency; but in others, you need to provide pages in more than one language. The following sections discuss these issues as they apply to Amazon Web Services.

Determining When to Internationalize a Site

It's important to consider not only how to internationalize your site, but also when. Sometimes the question is even "if" you should internationalize your site. Adding a second language or a second country to your site isn't a small undertaking. Even if you choose to use the least expensive approach possible, supporting two languages still means providing two sets of identical Web pages. Experience shows that even with the best of intentions, one language is bound to remain behind the other in updates. Adding more languages only compounds the problem. The point is that you need to consider the monetary problems of maintaining more than one language. You need to be sure that the cost of supporting more than one language is going to result in a quantifiable gain.

The gain doesn't always have to include a monetary value. For example, you might be the librarian for your company and some employees might need to use Amazon Web Services in a different language. Although you can't point to a specific gain for your department, the improved performance of the employees in their department does qualify as a quantifiable gain.

However, most Amazon Web Services developers will need to consider the money end of things at some point. You need to perform research to discover whether the addition of another language makes sense. For example, you could include a survey on your Web site. Check search sites such as Google for other sites that provide services similar to your own. In many cases, you'll see the languages these other sites support and may find that you need to support them as well to remain competitive. In most cases, you need to know that the language addition will at least pay for itself to ensure you can maintain it.

Considering the User's Location

The user's location affects the way you handle internationalization from more than one perspective. Of course, the first problem to avoid is confusing the user's language with the user's location—the two aren't always the same. Someone in the United States could prefer speaking Spanish, even though the language spoken by most Americans is English. Likewise, someone in the United Kingdom could prefer to speak Hindi. However, even when you offer your page in Hindi or Spanish, you still need to consider the user's location because the location affects the currency used (see the "Overcoming Currency and Other Internationalization Issues" section for details on currency issues), postal regulations, and even Amazon requirements to a degree.

> **▶ TIP**
>
> It's important to consider language issues when you develop a Web site. For example, many people have never even heard of Hindi, yet 180 million people use it as their first language and another 300 million use it as their second language (see `http://www.cs.colostate.edu/~malaiya/hindiint.html` for details).

As an author, I send copies of my books all over the world. Every time I go to the post office to send a book, the postmaster has to spend some time looking up the regulations for that country. He then has to figure out whether I can even send my book to that country and how much to charge for postage. I have the luxury of learning about the regulations for mailing my books as I need to mail them, but you might not have that luxury. Even though Amazon takes care of many of the details for you, your Web site will likely have some information about sending products to other countries. Make sure you know the regulations before you accept orders for that country.

You also need to consider Amazon requirements for service in other countries. They currently have Web service sites in these countries.

- United States (`http://www.amazon.com/`)
- United Kingdom (`http://www.amazon.co.uk/`)
- Germany (`http://www.amazon.de/`)
- Japan (`http://www.amazon.co.jp/`)

Notice that Amazon doesn't have an office in every country. If you live in a country where Amazon doesn't have an office, you need to determine which country with an office will meet your needs best. For example, someone living in Mexico might choose the United States office. To do this, you would need to provide your page in Spanish and use the Amazon resources to convert the dollar amounts to pesos.

When you decide to branch out and work with users in other countries, you also need to have an associate tag for each country. The use of multiple associate accounts means that you need to agree to the terms for each country (the terms will differ based on that country's requirements) and set up separate pages for each country. Let's look at the URL shown in Chapter 2 again.

```
http://xml.amazon.com/onca/xml3?t=webservices-20&dev-t=Your-Developer-
Token&AuthorSearch=John%20Mueller&mode=books&type=lite&page=1&f=xml
```

This URL works for an American site that doesn't require an associate tag (you're just performing research or something of that nature). When you want to set this URL up for use with an associate tag, you change the `t` argument of `webservices-20` to match your associate tag for the country in which you conduct business. You use the same URLs as you normally do for all searches. Referral URLs may change as Amazon develops its Web services, so you need to exercise care in using the correct associate identifier and URL for all sales in other countries.

> **▶ TIP**
>
> You might find it impossible to offer online payment in some situations. In this case, you can set up an Amazon Honor System. Check the Honor System help topic in the kit at `\AmazonWebServices\API Guide\honor_system_payments.htm` for details.

The Web services provided to other countries are also somewhat limited when compared to the U.S. offering. (Amazon plans to address these issues soon.) For example, although the remote shopping cart is available to developers in the United Kingdom, the help file recommends that users not use the feature if they want to ensure they receive credit for the referral. The problem is that the Web service doesn't properly record the associate tag. You might also find that services such as the Wish List, Wedding Registry, and Baby Registry service don't work at all or product unexpected results. (See the "Understanding Amazon Web Services Limitations" section for details.)

Performing Language Encoding

When you internationalize a site, it often means using other languages. Unless you know the target language well enough to perform the translation, you need to find someone who can translate the pages. Sometimes you can get the translation free. For example, the Free-Translation.com site at `http://www.freetranslation.com/` will accept your input and output translation in a number of languages. Figure 4.2 shows an example of such a translation from English to Spanish. The free translations on this site focus on translating English to another language, although you can find some translations that go the other direction (from Spanish to English, for example). Unfortunately, the quality of the translation on these sites varies from acceptable to poor. In many cases, you'll want to use a professional translator to ensure the quality of a translation remains high. (It's interesting to note that many of the sites providing free translation services also offer paid human translations as well.)

Most developers have more than just a few words to translate, and they still might not want to pay the price of using a professional translation service. You do have another option. The Google translation service works relatively well on simple Web pages. The more complicated your Web page becomes, the harder it is to get an acceptable translation. You call the Google translation service using an URL such as this:

```
http://translate.google.com/translate?hl=fr&sl=en&u=http://www.mwt.net/~jmueller
```

This URL translates my home page from English to French. All you need supply are three items. First, you must supply the host language (the `hl` argument), which is a two-letter abbreviation such as *en* for English, *fr* for French, and *de* for German. You can find a list of standard two-letter abbreviations at `http://www.loc.gov/standards/iso639-2/englangn.html`. Make sure you use the two-letter and not the three-letter abbreviations. Second, you must provide a source language (the `sl` argument), which relies on the same two-letter code system as the host language. Finally, you must supply the URL you want to translate (the `u` argument).

> **NOTE**
>
> If you choose to work with Amazon in more than one country, you need more than one version of Amazon Web Services Kit. You can find the version that works with the United Kingdom, Germany, and Japan at `http://www.amazon.com/gp/browse.html/104-6680872-1199104?node=3435361`. Make sure you keep this version of the kit completely separate from any other kit you use. This particular kit uses English as its language.

Understanding Amazon Web Services Limitations

One of the critical limitations you'll face when you try to internationalize your application is that Amazon Web Services works mainly in English. The Amazon offerings are mainly English offerings, with a very few Spanish offerings added. The lack of language capability in Amazon Web Services means that you'll have to do a lot more work in presenting the information using another language. In some cases, you might need to hire an interpreter to assist in the

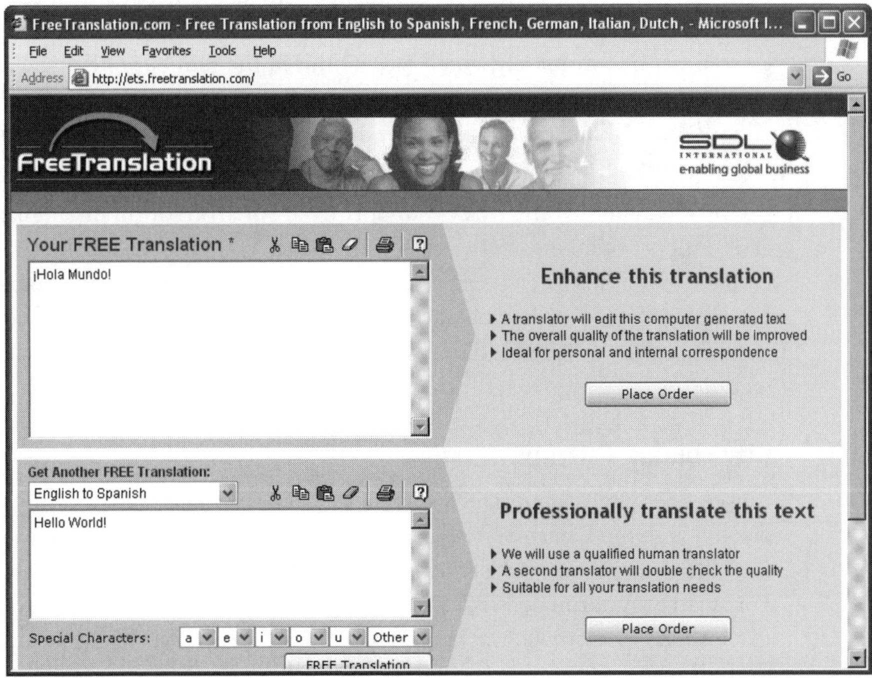

FIGURE 4.2: Sometimes you can translate a limited amount of text free.

language translation—in other cases, you might need to use the automated translation services offered on some Web sites. In short, you won't resolve this issue easily, but you can do it.

This problem might become less noticeable in the future. Eventually, Amazon Web Services will allow queries in other languages and you should be able to receive responses in those languages too. The first two languages that will probably arrive are Japanese and German—the only two languages that I can confirm at the time of this writing. It's likely that Amazon will move on to other languages such as Spanish and Hindi at some point.

NOTE

Google does support most common languages, but they don't support every language. If you see the translated page in the original language, it normally means that Google doesn't provide support for the host language. In most cases, serious translations require serious translation services.

Another problem is that you don't have full control over the entire process in some situations. For example, when a user makes a purchase, you turn them over to the Amazon site. Amazon gets the user's personal information, makes payment arrangements, and ensures the user receives their product. An internationalized site could fail at any of these points if you don't exercise caution in addressing limitations of Amazon Web Services in handling international customers. Unfortunately, you'll face a limit in the number of languages and currencies you can support at this time because Amazon only provides services for the United States, United Kingdom, Germany, and Japan. (See `http://www.mitsukatta.com/` for examples of multi-language support.)

Don't assume that the lack of support from Amazon for other languages means that you can't support them indirectly—it simply means you have to do a lot more work to accomplish the task. For example, you can run a search service in just about any language so long as you're willing to provide some type of translation. In many cases, you can find free translation services that work well enough to perform a search (see the "Performing Language Encoding" section for details).

Overcoming Currency Issues

Amazon definitely supports the currencies from the four countries with Web services, so anyone living in the Unites States, United Kingdom, Germany, or Japan has their monetary needs met. However, the world is much larger than four countries, so it's hard to know what to do. Fortunately, Amazon doesn't leave you without options for converting currency from one form to another. For example, the United Kingdom site lets you choose a currency conversion using this URL `http://www.amazon.co.uk/exec/obidos/select-preferred-currency/`. To use this service, the user must have an account and set up the preference in advance. The best you can do is direct them to the site in question and tell them how to fill out the required form.

Your Call to Action

This is the first chapter that really discussed programming techniques to the extent that you're planning for a Web site or application that relies on Amazon Web Services. Previous chapters have demonstrated the useful features of Amazon Web Services and even shown how these features work by exposing the Web service process. Completing this chapter means that you're ready to look at language-specific issues and get your application running.

Now that you've spent some time discovering the Web service process and deciding what Amazon Web Services can do for you, it's time to consider the design of your application. This chapter presented useful information that you need to develop a good design. However, it concentrated on Amazon Web Services, rather than general development principles. Now is the time to learn about these other principles, if you haven't worked with them already. In addition, you need to consider the design of your application. A written specification is nice (and required for larger companies), but just the act of thinking about what you want to do is essential.

Chapter 5 is the first language-specific chapter in the book. This chapter helps VBA users get started using Amazon Web Services. You'll discover how to perform specific kinds of analysis, store data for later use, and create reports based on the information you find. I chose VBA as the first language to present because many people rely on this language to work with Office and other applications. In general, Chapter 5 demonstrates not only that VBA is quite capable of doing amazing things with Amazon Web Services, but that you won't find many limits of the other languages.

Chapter 5

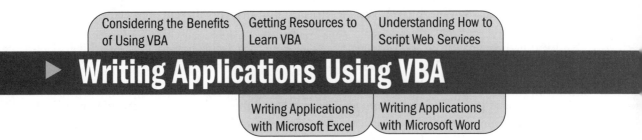

Considering the Benefits of Using VBA

Getting Resources to Learn VBA

Understanding How to Script Web Services

Writing Applications Using VBA

Writing Applications with Microsoft Excel

Writing Applications with Microsoft Word

Many people associate Visual Basic for Applications (VBA) with Microsoft Office. While it's true that Microsoft Office does rely on VBA as a development language, you'll find VBA used with other applications too. Microsoft provides a list of companies that have licensed VBA at `http://msdn.microsoft.com/vba/companies/company.asp`. (Make sure you read the "Other Companies That Use VBA" sidebar for additional ideas too.) Therefore, even though the examples in this chapter do rely on Microsoft products, you can use the information it contains with any product that supports VBA.

This chapter explores methods of coupling Amazon Web Services to an application with VBA capability. You can use Amazon Web Services to meet a number of needs. For example, you can write an application that draws current sales ranking information for a product you sell from Amazon Web Services and then uses Excel to chart the progress of that product. Likewise, you can obtain information from Amazon Web Services to create a report in Word. You might use such a report to help management understand the current resources available on a particular subject—perhaps a new area the company plans to target for business.

Unfortunately, one chapter can't do everything that you normally find in a whole book. You won't learn how to use VBA in this chapter, and I'm assuming you also know how to use the application in question. The chapter doesn't leave you completely in the dark, however. The "Resources for Learning VBA" section contains information on where you can learn more about VBA. Knowing how to use VBA is a prerequisite for this chapter.

Understanding the Benefits of Using VBA

Most of the examples you'll see for Amazon Web Services outside this book probably focus on Web technologies. Developers use Amazon Web Services to create connections to their Web site (to make sales) or their cellular telephone (to generate shopping lists). However, VBA lets you view Amazon Web Services from an entirely different perspective. Instead of looking for the next sale or generating some type of search result, using VBA with your application lets you concentrate on data—it helps you decide how to use the data that Amazon provides for your own needs.

It's possible to create the kind of links described in the previous paragraph using full-fledged programming environments such as Visual Studio. You can also create a great Web environment that mimics some of these features using languages such as PHP Hypertext Processor (PHP). However, the point is that VBA works in concert with the host application. You don't have to write a lot of the code that you normally need to write because the host

Other Companies That Use VBA

Companies other than Microsoft use VBA, but you might not know about them right now. Corel makes software such as WordPerfect and Draw. WordPerfect is a word processing program, and you'll find that many legal offices still use it. One of my first professional writing jobs required use of WordPerfect. Draw is a drawing program that many professionals enjoy using. It supports a wealth of features. I drew the original versions of all of the line art in this book using Corel Draw. All of my drawing setups are performed automatically using VBA programs.

You'll also want to check out Micrografx's iGrafx Series. This product helps you create flowcharts or organizational charts and this product can help you. Unlike a lot of drawing tasks, both flowcharts and organizational charts are extremely repetitive—making them a perfect place to use VBA.

Another good product to check for VBA is IMSI's TurboCad. TurboCad is the drawing program I prefer to use. It's relatively inexpensive and the VBA programs I've created for it automate many of the drawing tasks.

So, how do these products benefit from Amazon Web Services? Corel WordPerfect and Corel Draw are the easiest matches. You can use them to create reports, charts, and graphs based on information you retrieve from Amazon Web Services. Likewise, the Micrografx iGrafx product can use input from Amazon Web Services to create charts of various types. The question remains: how do you use a CAD application with Amazon Web Services? Actually, I've tried it out as a resource for finding third party vendors. Sometimes I need a specific product for a project. All I do is highlight the name of the product I need and ask Amazon Web Services if someone sells it. The underlying technology is a VBA application that makes a search query from Amazon.

application provides the required functionality for you. In fact, if you choose the right host application, writing an Amazon Web Services interface can become mind numbingly simple. Just a few lines of code will help you perform tasks in seconds, rather than hours.

So, why not write every application in VBA? To say that VBA is a cure-all for every problem is incorrect. VBA answers a specific range of needs, but doesn't handle every need. In fact, the needs that VBA answers are somewhat specialized. This chapter helps you understand some of the applications where VBA can save you considerable time and expense. It also demonstrates that you can achieve truly amazing results with just a modicum of programming. The important point is to match VBA and the host application to a particular Amazon Web Services application need.

Resources for Learning VBA

This chapter won't teach you how to use VBA. I'm assuming that you already know enough about VBA to create your own simple applications. If you don't already have this knowledge, you can get it from a number of sources. The first place to look is my book, *VBA for Dummies*, Fourth Edition (Wiley, 2003). This book introduces you to VBA and takes you through examples using all of the major Microsoft Office applications.

You'll also want to look at some of the resources that Microsoft provides. For example, you'll find a Microsoft Office 2000 Resource Kit at `http://www.microsoft.com/office/ork/xp/default.htm`. This site includes some interesting tools at `http://www.microsoft.com/office/ork/2000/appndx/toolbox.htm`. Office 2003 users can find similar information on their product. At the time of this writing, Office 2003 is still in beta, but you can find the beta version at `http://www.microsoft.com/office/ork/xp/beta/default.htm` and `http://www.microsoft.com/office/ork/xp/journ/orkbeta.htm`.

> **NOTE**
>
> The VBA language has basic concepts that are the same across all products. A loop in Word is the same loop that you find in Excel or Corel Draw for that matter. However, every product has special objects that it includes for working with VBA. These objects vary by product, so it's usually best if you can locate a VBA tutorial for your specific product.

It's amazing to see how many third party sources you can find online for VBA. Many sites have free code, specialized examples, chat forums, tutorials, or other offerings that make your VBA experience better. For example, you can download a VBA tutorial at `http://freedownloadswindows.com/windows/Visual-Basic/656996/L-Basic.html`. Online Excel VBA tutorials appear at `http://lacher.com/toc/tutvba1.htm` and `http://lacher.com/toc/tutvba2.htm`.

Don't forget to visit newsgroups with your VBA questions. Microsoft sponsors VBA newsgroups at:

- `microsoft.public.office.developer.vba`
- `microsoft.public.excel.programming`
- `microsoft.public.frontpage.programming.vba`
- `microsoft.public.office.developer.outlook.vba`
- `microsoft.public.outlook.program_vba`
- `microsoft.public.project.vba`
- `microsoft.public.visio.developer.vba`
- `microsoft.public.word.vba.addins`
- `microsoft.public.word.vba.beginners`
- `microsoft.public.word.vba.customization`
- `microsoft.public.word.vba.general`
- `microsoft.public.word.vba.userforms`
- `microsoft.public.word.word97vba`

If you noticed the overwhelming number of Word VBA newsgroups, it's because many people develop for this particular product. The `microsoft.public.word.vba.beginners` newsgroup is an exceptionally good place to start your VBA programming journey. PowerPoint doesn't have a specific VBA newsgroup, so you'll need to use the general `microsoft.public.powerpoint` newsgroup instead. If you want to work with Access, be sure to look at task-specific newsgroups such as `microsoft.public.access.formscoding`.

You can also find third party newsgroups (often with better peer information, but no Microsoft help) at newsgroups such as `alt.comp.lang.vba`. Some third party products also sport their own VBA newsgroups such as AutoCAD (`autodesk.autocad.customization.vba`). In some cases, the name of the newsgroup won't be obvious, as with Corel Draw (`corel.developer.draw`).

Understanding Scripting of Web Services

In many respects, VBA is a scripting or macro language, rather than a full development language such as Visual Basic or C#. The host application interprets the VBA code when you run the macro based on an event such as selecting a menu entry, clicking a button, or opening a file. Consequently, the host application performs every task in real time—you can't decide much in advance. Although VBA is far more powerful than Web scripting languages such as JavaScript, it still has some of the benefits and problems of any scripting language. The following sections discuss how VBA scripting can affect your application and one technique for circumventing scripting issues.

Advantages and Disadvantages of VBA

VBA is a good scripting language and far more capable than VBScript (but less capable than Visual Basic). One of the biggest advantages of using VBA is that you get instant feedback. You don't have to compile the application nor do you have to do anything fancy to see the result of your code—all you need to do is run it. This means the development cycle is much shorter and you can get your application going faster.

Unlike JavaScript and browser applications in general, most VBA environments provide good debugging. You run the program in a special environment that lets you see variables and the short-term results of operations. This is especially helpful when working with Amazon Web Services because you can see how your code interacts with the Web service without resorting to using on-screen data presentation or similar tricks required for browser applications in many cases.

A new developer can also learn VBA relatively quickly compared to a full-fledged programming language such as Visual Basic or C#. VBA is a subset of Visual Basic, which means it has fewer commands to learn. However, even with fewer features, VBA developers can create robust Amazon Web Services applications. Many of the advanced features that VBA lacks don't affect applications of this type.

The biggest disadvantage of using VBA is performance. Most interpreted languages are slower than compiled languages because an interpreter (a special program that reads the code) must convert the human readable information into machine code during runtime. VBA developers use a variety of techniques to improve performance, but

> **▶ TIP**
>
> If you ever have a problem finding a Microsoft newsgroup, open your browser and type the name of the Microsoft news server and the name of the newsgroup. For example, if you want to access the `microsoft.public.word.vba.addins` newsgroup, type `news://news.microsoft.com/microsoft.public.word.vba.addins` in the browser's Address field and press Enter. The browser will locate the newsgroup, open your newsreader, and display that newsgroup from the Microsoft server. You can also use online resources such as Google Groups (`http://groups.google.com/`) to locate VBA newsgroups. Simply type the name of the newsgroup in the Search field, click Google Search, and you'll see a list of messages in that newsgroup.

even great programming techniques can only improve performance so much. At some point, the application runs as fast as possible and you have to live with the performance implications.

From an Amazon Web Services perspective, VBA also presents display problems. You can only display data in the way that the host application allows. It's possible to force the application to display data in nonstandard ways, but only at the cost of long development time and poor performance. Choosing the correct application for your needs is essential when using VBA.

An Alternative to VBA

One issue to consider before you invest a lot of time in VBA is whether you need VBA at all. Most Office applications and many third party applications let you place a hyperlink within a document. As you saw in the "Using a Browser Example" section of Chapter 2, all you really need is a simple URL to contact Amazon and obtain the needed data. The problem is that this approach returns XML data, which isn't easy to read. The example in the "Viewing the XSLT Example" section of Chapter 2 shows that you can avoid the display issue by using a script to translate the data using an XSLT file. However, this approach isn't as convenient as using a hyperlink.

The example in this section demonstrates a technique that works especially well with applications that support hyperlinks. The code actually asks XSLT to download and load the Amazon file for processing. Using this technique means that the XML file from Amazon doesn't need the linking instruction used for other examples in the book—the link appears as part of a third file. Listing 5.1 shows an example of the special XSLT file you need to create. You'll find this example in the `\Chapter 05\HyperLink Technique` folder of the source code located on the Sybex Web site.

Listing 5.1 Using XSLT to Call Amazon Web Services

```
<?xml version="1.0" encoding="UTF-8"?>
<xsl:stylesheet version="1.0"
 xmlns:xsl="http://www.w3.org/1999/XSL/Transform"
 xmlns:fo="http://www.w3.org/1999/XSL/Format">
<xsl:template match="ResultData">
<ResultData>
   <xsl:apply-templates
select="document('http://xml.amazon.com/onca/xml3?t=webservices-20%26dev-t=Your-
Developer-
Token%26AuthorSearch=John%20Mueller%26mode=books%26type=lite%26page=1%26f=xml')"
/>
```

```
</ResultData>
</xsl:template>

<xsl:template match="ProductInfo">
<html>
<head>
   <title>XSLT Transformation Example</title>
</head>
<body>
   <!-- Display a heading. -->
   <h1 align="center">Translated Amazon Web Server Results</h1>

   <!-- Displays the arguments used for the call. -->
    ... Display Code ...

   <!-- Display the search result values. -->
   ... Display Code ...

</body>
</html>
</xsl:template>
</xsl:stylesheet>
```

This XSLT file uses the same display code used in Listing 3.3, so this section doesn't describe that part of the process again. However, this XSLT file includes several important differences. First, notice the `<xsl:template match="ResultData">` element. A standard entry matches everything—this entry matches just the node that begins as `<ResultData>`. This entry makes a connection between the input file and the loaded file. If you match everything, the template won't work.

The next line applies a template to a file loaded using the `document()` function. The `<xsl:apply-templates>` element tells XSLT to apply a template; the `select` attribute tells what data to use. In this case, the same URL used for many other examples in the book retrieves the XML from Amazon Web Services. You should see something odd about this string. All of the ampersands in previous examples now appear as `%26`, the URL encoded version of the ampersand. If you don't make this replacement, the XSLT parser will complain about errors. At this point, the template ends, rather than process the data. This step cuts off the input file because the input file won't match the second template in the XSLT file.

The second template begins with the `<xsl:template match="ProductInfo">` element. Only the incoming Amazon input includes this element, so the XSLT parser only translates the incoming file. The resulting display looks the same as the example in Chapter 3 (see Figure 3.7).

You still need to call the XSLT file in some way. Just because Listing 5.1 shows a way to load the XML you actually want to process doesn't mean you avoid providing an input file. Listing 5.2 shows the input file in this case.

Listing 5.2 XML Referral Example

```
<?xml version="1.0" encoding="UTF-8"?>
<?xml-stylesheet type="text/xsl" href="default.xsl"?>
<ResultData xmlns:xsi="http://www.w3.org/2001/XMLSchema-instance">
   <FirstChild>This is the Child.</FirstChild>
</ResultData>
```

Notice that this file doesn't contain much. However, it does contain two essential entries that work with the XSLT file. First, notice that this file contains the XSLT reference the XML from Amazon Web Services doesn't contain. You still must include this glue between the input file and the XSLT file. Second, notice that the root node is `<ResultData>`. The XSLT file looks for this same element.

You have everything needed to get formatted data from Amazon using a simple hyperlink in a document. To create the hyperlink in an application such as Word, right-click the location in the document that you want to contain the hyperlink and choose Hyperlink from the context menu. When you see the Insert Hyperlink dialog box shown in Figure 5.1, choose the XML file that contains the code shown in Listing 5.2. Click OK. Now, whenever you Ctrl+click the hyperlink, Word will request the information from Amazon Web Services.

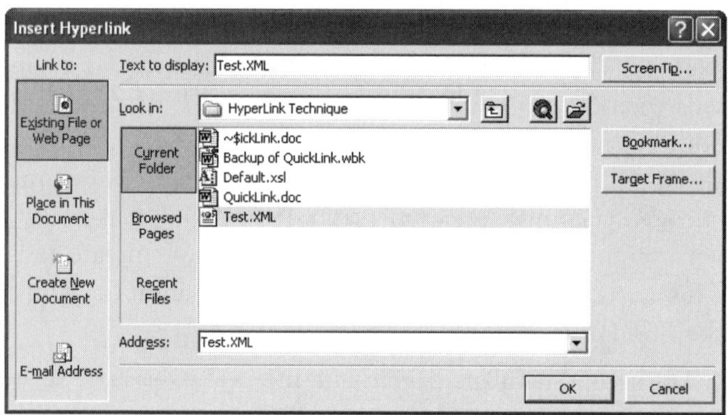

FIGURE 5.1: Use the Insert Hyperlink dialog box to add a hyperlink to your application.

Word 2003 users have another alternative. You can also open the `Test.XML` file directly, rather than place a hyperlink to it in your code. When you open the file, you may see a Convert File dialog box. Make sure you select the XML Document option (Word should highlight it automatically) and click OK. When the document opens, you'll see the `Test.XML` file, which might be a little disappointing. However, look at the XML Document pane shown on the right side of Figure 5.2 and you'll notice that you can select `Default.XSL`. Once you select this option, you'll notice the Word view changes to the same structured presentation used for XML and HTML documents. When you combine this display with the proper stylesheet, you can create reports directly from Word without relying on any VBA code.

As with many alternatives, this one has problems. First, you might have noticed that I hard coded the Web service query into the XSLT file, making each XSLT file good for only one request. Unfortunately, you probably won't find a way around this problem, which means that you have to use this technique carefully. Second, this solution means that the data often appears in your browser, rather than as part of the application display. Even when it does appear as part of the application display, the data is still HTML, not your document's native format. Consequently, while this technique does work well, it has limitations that make it unsuitable for some needs.

FIGURE 5.2: Word 2003 can also interpret XML files for you.

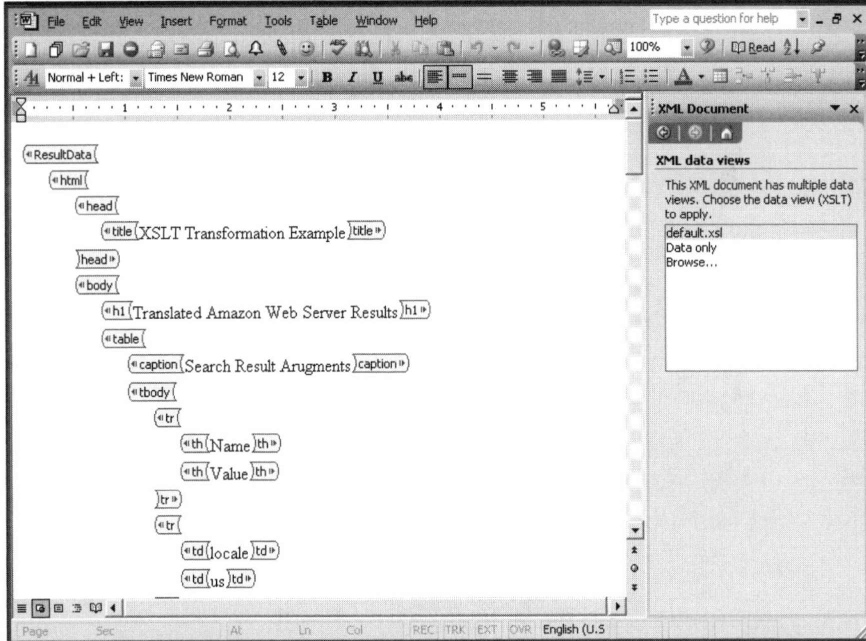

Developing with Microsoft Excel

Microsoft Excel provides a number of interesting features that can help you manipulate the data you receive from Amazon Web Services. Sometimes you have to gather this data over time. For example, you might collect the sales rank for a product each day at 10:00. After some time, you can chart the sales rank information to see the general direction of sales for your product—at least on Amazon.

> **TIP**
>
> Some types of statistical analysis for Amazon Web Services are very time sensitive. Consequently, you'll want to use something like Task Scheduler to ensure the system gathers the data at the same time each day. You can perform this task in a number of ways, including relying on the automatic document execution feature of Excel. Simply opening the document ensures the macro to gather the data runs.

The following sections demonstrate some ways to use Microsoft Excel with Amazon Web Services. It's important to remember that these sections are just examples—you can probably use Amazon Web Services in other ways. All you really need is an idea of how the data you can obtain from Amazon works into your company's use of the Web site. For an in-depth treatment of the topic, see *Mastering Excel 2003 Programming with VBA* by Steven M. Hansen (Sybex, 2004).

Creating a Data View Using XML over HTTP

The first task you have to perform is getting the data into Excel. The example in this section won't perform a lot of fancy formatting or provide input screens. However, it does show you how to use XML parsing techniques to place data you receive from Amazon into an Excel spreadsheet.

Before you can begin working with this example, you need to add a reference to your project using the Tools ➢ References command. Figure 5.3 shows the References dialog box. As you can see, you need to choose the Microsoft XML, v5.0 component and then click OK. This reference lets you use the XML parsing capabilities provided with Microsoft Office. If you don't see the 5.0 version of this component, you can use older versions—they might not have all of the features of the 5.0 version.

Listing 5.3 shows the code you need to parse the data. You'll find this example in the `\Chapter 05\Excel` folder of the source code located on the Sybex Web site.

Listing 5.3 Parsing XML Data Retrieved from Amazon

```
Public Sub FetchAmazonData()
   Dim XMLFile As String
   Dim XMLData As DOMDocument
   Dim CurrentNode As IXMLDOMNode
```

FIGURE 5.3:

Add a reference to the Microsoft XML component to parse the Amazon data.

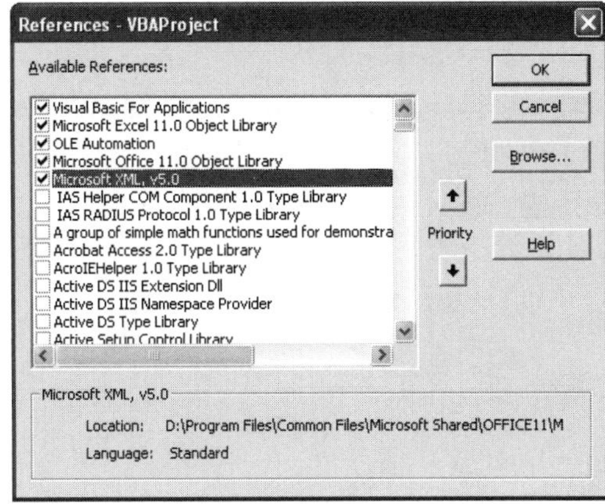


```
Dim NodeCount As Integer
Dim CellOffset As Integer

' Create the string.
XMLFile = "http://xml.amazon.com/onca/xml3?t=webservices-20" + _
          "&dev-t=Your-Developer-Token&AuthorSearch=John%20" + _
          "Mueller&mode=books&type=lite&page=1&f=xml"

' Load the data.
Set XMLData = New DOMDocument
XMLData.async = False
XMLData.Load XMLFile

' Display a heading.
Sheet1.Cells(1, 1) = "Arguments"
Sheet1.Cells(3, 1) = "Name"
Sheet1.Cells(3, 2) = "Value"

' Get the ProductInfo/Request/Args node
Set CurrentNode = XMLData.childNodes(1).childNodes(0).childNodes(0)
For NodeCount = 0 To CurrentNode.childNodes.Length - 1
   Sheet1.Cells(NodeCount + 4, 1) = _
      CurrentNode.childNodes(NodeCount).Attributes(1).Text
   Sheet1.Cells(NodeCount + 4, 2) = _
      CurrentNode.childNodes(NodeCount).Attributes(0).Text
Next

' Display the next heading.
CellOffset = NodeCount + 5
Sheet1.Cells(CellOffset, 1) = "Book Information"
CellOffset = CellOffset + 2
Sheet1.Cells(CellOffset, 1) = "ISBN"
```

```
    Sheet1.Cells(CellOffset, 2) = "Name"
    Sheet1.Cells(CellOffset, 3) = "Publisher"
    Sheet1.Cells(CellOffset, 4) = "Release Date"

    ' Get the ProductInfo/Details.
    For NodeCount = 3 To XMLData.childNodes(1).childNodes.Length - 1
       Set CurrentNode = XMLData.childNodes(1).childNodes(NodeCount)
       Sheet1.Cells(CellOffset + NodeCount - 2, 1) = _
          "'" + CurrentNode.childNodes(0).Text
       Sheet1.Cells(CellOffset + NodeCount - 2, 2) = _
          CurrentNode.childNodes(1).Text
       Sheet1.Cells(CellOffset + NodeCount - 2, 3) = _
          CurrentNode.childNodes(5).Text
       Sheet1.Cells(CellOffset + NodeCount - 2, 4) = _
          CurrentNode.childNodes(4).Text
    Next
End Sub
```

This short example relies on the same query string used for so many other examples. However, the technique works with any query string so long as you consider the format of the XML data that Amazon returns. The code begins by creating the `XMLData` object (which is a `DOMDocument` type). Using the `Load()` method of this object loads the data from Amazon Web Services into the local variable. Unlike JavaScript, you can view the data directly within the VBA debugger.

Now that the application has access to the data, it's time to do something with it. This means parsing the data—a process of separating the piece of data you need from the rest of the data. The code performs this task by creating the `CurrentNode` variable (object type of `IXMLDOMNode`). This variable contains a single node of the data. A node is an element, its attributes, and children. Consequently, when the code retrieves the `ProductInfo/Request/Args` node, it also places the individual `Arg` elements within `CurrentNode` as well. A `for` loop retrieves each `Arg` element in turn and uses the `Attributes` property to obtain access to each attribute within the element. Notice how the code performs this task using numbers—you really don't know where you're at in the hierarchy unless you carefully check the schema of the incoming XML.

After the code retrieves the arguments and displays them on screen, it performs the same process with the `ProductInfo/Details` nodes. In this case, the data resides in an element, not an attribute, so the retrieval process is somewhat different. You must determine the number of the element you want to retrieve and use the `childNodes` property to locate it. Figure 5.4 shows the output from this example.

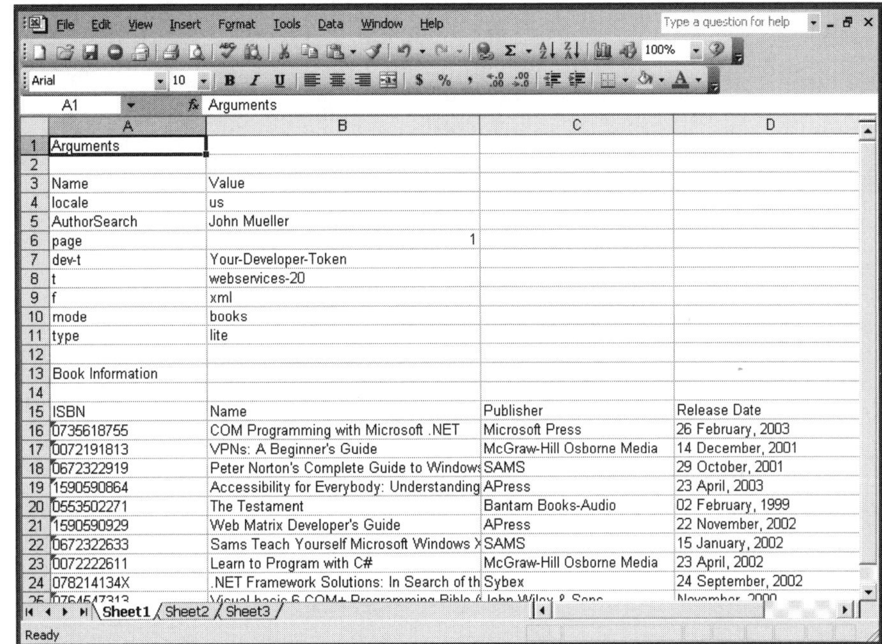

FIGURE 5.4: You can use the output from this example for a number of purposes.

Defining Graphs and Charts

Sometimes nothing illustrates data better than a chart or graph. Visual data presentation lets you see the differences in the data in a way that numbers don't. Many companies rely on visual data to make decisions, so it's more than likely that someone in your company will need a visual presentation of data from Amazon Web Services. For example, you might want to compare the prices of various products to a base price or an average price. You might use this information to change the price of your product to match the competition better or to reflect the price of materials you use. Listing 5.4 shows a typical example of code used to request data from Amazon and then present that information as a graph. You'll find this example in the `\Chapter 05\Excel` folder of the source code located on the Sybex Web site.

Listing 5.4 Charting Amazon Web Services Statistics

```
Public Sub ChartData()
   Dim XMLFile As String                 ' Contains the search criteria.
   Dim XMLData As DOMDocument            ' The information returned.
   Dim Details As IXMLDOMNodeList        ' Details within the document.
   Dim CurrentDetail As IXMLDOMNode      ' A single detail.
```

```
Dim ProductData As IXMLDOMNodeList   ' All of the product data.
Dim CurrentData As IXMLDOMNode       ' A single product data element.
Dim Pages As Integer                 ' The total number of pages.
Dim CurrentPage As Integer           ' The current page.
Dim ProcessMore As Boolean           ' Keep processing data?
Dim RowNumber As Integer             ' Current spreadsheet row.
Dim ChartSeries As Series            ' The chart reference.

' Set the current page.
CurrentPage = 1

' Set the row number.
RowNumber = 1

' Keep processing data until complete.
ProcessMore = True
While ProcessMore

   ' Create the string.
   XMLFile = CreateKeyString("webservices-20", _
                             "Your-Developer-Token", _
                             "Microsoft%20Office%202003", _
                             "books", _
                             "lite", _
                             CStr(CurrentPage))

   ' Load the data.
   Set XMLData = New DOMDocument
   XMLData.async = False
   XMLData.Load XMLFile

   ' Store the total pages.
   Pages = CInt(XMLData.childNodes(1).childNodes(2).Text)

   ' Get the details.
   Set Details = XMLData.childNodes(1).childNodes

   ' Add the data to the worksheet.
   For Each CurrentDetail In Details

      ' Verify this is a product node.
      If CurrentDetail.baseName = "Details" Then

         ' Store the product information.
         Set ProductData = CurrentDetail.childNodes

         ' Look for specific data.
         For Each CurrentData In ProductData

            ' Add the ISBN.
```

```
            If CurrentData.baseName = "Asin" Then
               Sheet1.Cells(RowNumber, 1) = "'" + CurrentData.Text
            End If

            ' Add the product name.
            If CurrentData.baseName = "ProductName" Then
               Sheet1.Cells(RowNumber, 2) = CurrentData.Text
            End If

            ' Add the list price.
            If CurrentData.baseName = "ListPrice" Then
               Sheet1.Cells(RowNumber, 3) = CurrentData.Text
            End If
         Next

         ' Update the row number.
         RowNumber = RowNumber + 1
      End If
   Next

   ' Update the current page.
   CurrentPage = CurrentPage + 1

   ' Compare the current page with the total pages.
   If CurrentPage > Pages Then
      ProcessMore = False
   End If
Wend

' Calculate the average.
Sheet1.Cells(RowNumber + 1, 3) = _
   "=Sum($C$1:$C$" + CStr(RowNumber - 1) + ")/" + CStr(RowNumber - 1)

' Copy the average to the D column.
Sheet1.Cells.Range("C" + CStr(RowNumber + 1)).Copy
Sheet1.Cells.Range("D1", "D" + CStr(RowNumber - 1)).PasteSpecial

' Add and configure the Individual Value series.
Chart1.SeriesCollection.Add _
   Source:=Worksheets("Sheet1").Range("C$1:C$" + CStr(RowNumber - 1))
Set ChartSeries = Chart1.SeriesCollection(1)
ChartSeries.Name = "Individual Values"
ChartSeries.XValues = _
   Worksheets("Sheet1").Range("A$1:A$" + CStr(RowNumber - 1))

' Add an configure the Average Value series.
Chart1.SeriesCollection.Add _
   Source:=Worksheets("Sheet1").Range("D$1:D$" + CStr(RowNumber - 1))
Set ChartSeries = Chart1.SeriesCollection(2)
ChartSeries.Name = "Average Value"
End Sub
```

This is the first example where the code processes multiple pages. In fact, it processes every page for the specified keyword search. The code begins by creating a number of variables to track the current position on the worksheet and the number of pages processed. It then uses a function to put the search string together. Nothing is very different from the previous example to this point. The example even uses the same technique to load the XML file from the Web site. However, the added flexibility helps the application process multiple pages quickly.

Previous examples assumed that Amazon would provide the data in a specific format using an exact data ordering. This isn't a good assumption to make because Amazon could change the ordering of the data at any time. This example shows techniques you can use to isolate your code from potential data ordering changes. Notice it doesn't use specific child element numbers. Instead, the code uses two `For Each...Next` loops to process the data based on the `baseName` element value. This element determines the kind of data found within the nodes. Consequently, the loops process all of the data, but they don't fail if the required data doesn't appear within the loops.

When the code finds the `Asin` (ISBN), `ProductName`, and `ListPrice` elements, it records their values in the worksheet. At the time of writing, there were 52 entries matching Microsoft Office 2003. Notice how the code uses the number of pages contained within the responses to determine when it doesn't have any more pages to process. At this point, the main processing loop ends and the code begins creating the chart.

The first task the code performs is determining the average book price. It copies this information to the same number of rows in which the individual prices appear to make the chart work properly.

The second task the code performs is to create two series. The first series contains the individual book prices. This series receives a name and `XValues` to provide names for each entry along the X-axis. The second series contains the average value and appears as a straight line on the chart. Figure 5.5 shows typical output from this example. It's not too hard to see how this data bears little resemblance to the information you can garner online, yet it's a helpful depiction of sales information for this particular book type.

Developing with Microsoft Word

I normally use Word for reports of various kinds with Amazon Web Services. You could potentially use it for other purposes, such as the price list discussed in this section. The problem with printed formats is that they often cause problems with the Amazon licensing terms. For example, you need to refresh prices often enough to meet the requirements of the Web service, so printed formats aren't necessarily useful unless you're planning on using the information immediately (such as in a meeting to discuss potential purchases).

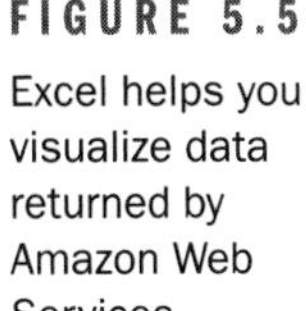

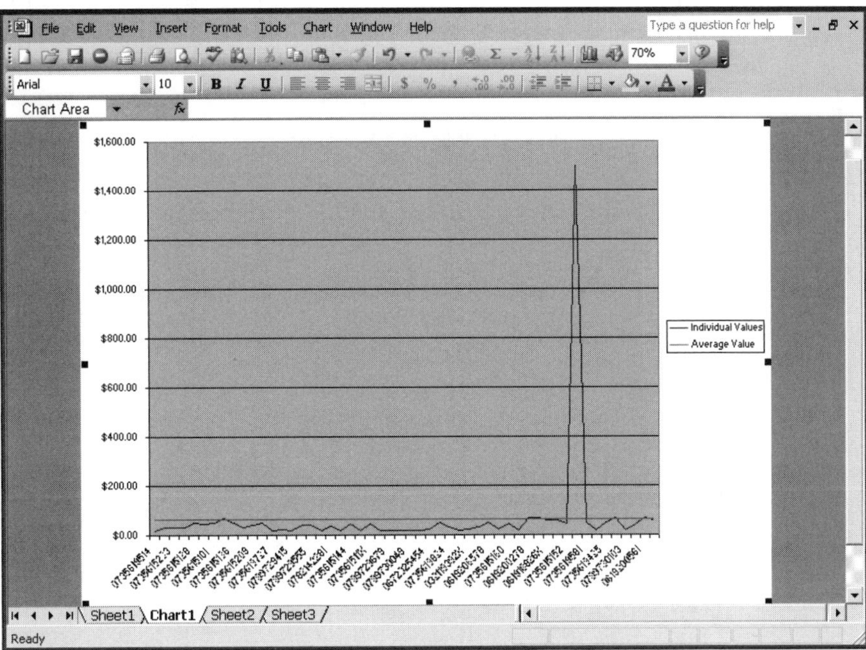

FIGURE 5.5: Excel helps you visualize data returned by Amazon Web Services.

Automating Reports Using SOAP

So far, all of the examples in this chapter have relied on the XML over HTTP technique to obtain data. You don't have to use this technique if you don't want to with VBA. It's relatively easy to use SOAP instead. The example in this section creates a report using the SOAP technique. The biggest advantage of using the SOAP method is performance—using SOAP is up to three times faster than the XML over HTTP method. The example in this section also demonstrates a major problem in using SOAP with VBA—development time. You'll spend considerably more time writing and debugging a SOAP application than you will an XML over HTTP application.

Before you can proceed with the example, you'll need to add a reference to the module. You still use the Tools ➢ References command to display the References dialog box. In this case, locate the Microsoft SOAP Type Library entry, check it, and click OK to add the reference. This example also requires use of the Microsoft XML, v.5.0 component used for the Excel examples in the chapter. (An older version of the Microsoft XML library probably won't work in this case.) However, this example uses that

> **▶ NOTE**
>
> The data in Figure 5.5 is unreadable. I just want you to get an idea of what the chart looks like because the data in your chart will differ from mine.

component in a different way. Listing 5.5 shows the code you need for this example. You'll find this example in the `\Chapter 05\Word` folder of the source code located on the Sybex Web site.

Listing 5.5 **Using Low-Level SOAP Access**

```
Public Sub CreateReport()
   Dim Connector As SoapConnector      ' Connection to Web Service
   Dim DataSend As SoapSerializer      ' Sends data to Amazon.
   Dim DataReceive As SoapReader       ' Receives data from Amazon.
   Dim Details As IXMLDOMNodeList      ' Contains all of the detail nodes.
   Dim CurrentBook As IXMLDOMNode      ' Contains just one book.
   Dim Counter As Integer              ' Loop counter.

   ' Create a connection to Amazon.
   Set Connector = New HttpConnector
   Connector.Property("EndPointURL") = _
      "http://soap.amazon.com/onca/soap3"
   Connector.Property("SoapAction") = _
      "http://soap.amazon.com"

   ' Tell Amazon that the application is sending a request.
   Connector.BeginMessage

   ' Associate the data serializer with the connection.
   Set DataSend = New SoapSerializer
   DataSend.Init Connector.InputStream

   ' Start creating a request, including the SOAP envelope.
   With DataSend

      ' Create the envelope and associated namespaces. Don't
      ' include namespaces that VBA already includes.
      .startEnvelope
      '.SoapAttribute "xmlns:SOAP-ENV", , _
      '               "http://schemas.xmlsoap.org/soap/envelope/"
      '.SoapAttribute "xmlns:SOAP-ENC", , _
      '               "http://schemas.xmlsoap.org/soap/encoding/"
      .SoapAttribute "xmlns:xsi", , _
                     "http://www.w3.org/2001/XMLSchema-instance"
      .SoapAttribute "xmlns:xsd", , _
                     "http://www.w3.org/2001/XMLSchema"
      .SoapAttribute "SOAP-ENV:encodingStyle", , _
                     "http://schemas.xmlsoap.org/soap/encoding/"

      ' Create the SOAP body.
      .startBody

      ' Start creating the request.
      .startElement "namesp1:AuthorSearchRequest"
      .SoapAttribute "xmlns:namesp1", , "urn:PI/DevCentral/SoapService"
```

```
      .startElement "AuthorSearchRequest"
      '.SoapAttribute "xsi:type", , "m:AuthorRequest"

      ' Add the author information.
      .startElement "author"
      ThisDocument.Bookmarks("Author").Select
      .writeString ThisDocument.ActiveWindow.Selection.Text
      .endElement

      ... Other information elements ...

      ' Add the developer token information.
      .startElement "devtag"
      ThisDocument.Bookmarks("DevTag").Select
      .writeString ThisDocument.ActiveWindow.Selection.Text
      .endElement

      ' Close all of the open tags.
      .endElement
      .endElement
      .endBody
      .endEnvelope
   End With

   ' Tell Amazon the request is complete.
   Connector.EndMessage

   ' Receive the response from Amazon.
   Set DataReceive = New SoapReader
   DataReceive.Load Connector.OutputStream

   ' Place the Details node into a local variable.
   Set Details = DataReceive.RPCResult.ChildNodes(2).ChildNodes

   ' Set the counter value.
   Counter = 2

   ' Delete unneeded rows from the table.
   While ThisDocument.Tables(1).Rows.Count > 2
      ThisDocument.Tables(1).Rows(3).Delete
   Wend

   ' Process each book in the Details node one at a time.
   For Each CurrentBook In Details

      ' Place the ISBN, name, publisher, and release data in the
      ' table provided.
      ThisDocument.Tables(1).Cell(Counter, 1).Range.Text = _
         CurrentBook.ChildNodes(1).Text
      ThisDocument.Tables(1).Cell(Counter, 2).Range.Text = _
         CurrentBook.ChildNodes(2).Text
      ThisDocument.Tables(1).Cell(Counter, 3).Range.Text = _
         CurrentBook.ChildNodes(6).Text
```

```
        ThisDocument.Tables(1).Cell(Counter, 4).Range.Text = _
           CurrentBook.ChildNodes(5).Text

        ' Increment the counter.
        Counter = Counter + 1

        ' Add a row to the table if necessary.
        If Details.Length > Counter - 2 Then
           ThisDocument.Tables(1).Rows.Add
        End If
     Next
  End Sub
```

This may look like a lot of code, but it really isn't once you understand what's going on. Most developers refer to this as the low-level SOAP technique. Essentially, you build the message and send it manually, rather than allow classes to perform the work for you. Using this technique provides the flexibility needed to work with the complex data that Amazon provides. The high-level SOAP object (`SoapClient`) is found in the Microsoft SOAP Type Library. One of the benefits of using this technique is that you learn exactly how SOAP messaging works, which makes it easier for you to diagnose and fix problems later.

The code begins by creating a connection between VBA and Amazon Web Services. You have access to a number of connector types but will probably use the `HttpConnector` most often. This connector requires that you define two properties: an endpoint (the other end of the conversation) and an action (a URL that defines what the connection should do). Both properties rely on values located in the WSDL file you can download from `http://soap.amazon.com/schemas3/AmazonWebServices.wsdl`. The endpoint appears as part of the service description shown here.

```
<service name="AmazonSearchService">
   <!-- Endpoint for Amazon Web APIs -->
   <port name="AmazonSearchPort" binding="typens:AmazonSearchBinding">
      <soap:address location="http://soap.amazon.com/onca/soap3"/>
   </port>
</service>
```

The `location` attribute of the `<soap:address>` element describes the endpoint for this service (and any other service you might want to use). The SOAP action appears as part of an operation description. The Web service describes operations, or tasks, that you can perform. Here's the operation description for the author request.

```
<operation name="AuthorSearchRequest">
   <soap:operation soapAction="http://soap.amazon.com"/>
   <input>
      <soap:body use="encoded" encodingStyle=...URL  namespace=...URL>
   </input>
   <output>
```

```
      <soap:body use="encoded" encodingStyle=...URL namespace=...URL/>
    </output>
  </operation>
```

Notice the soapAction attribute of the <soap:operation> element. This attribute tells you where that action will take place. At this time, all Amazon Web Services operations use the same soapAction value, but it's something you need to track as you develop applications.

Once the code establishes a connection to Amazon Web Services, it begins a message. This call tells Amazon Web Services to listen for the application's request. To send data, the code associates the input stream of Connector with DataSend. At this point, the code begins constructing an author request using the AuthorSearchRequestSample.XML file from the \Amazon-WebServices\SoapRequestSamples folder of the kit as a template. It's important to note that you don't have to provide every entry in that file. The example code shows the attributes you can leave out.

It's essential that you provide the correct number and type of ending tags or Amazon Web Services won't understand the request. Notice that the code places these ending tags in a separate location to make them easier to track. Once the code completes the message, it issues an EndMessage() call with the Connector. Amazon Web Services obtains the response and feeds it to the application using DataReceive.

At this point, the application has a response that it must parse using the XML functionality that VBA provides. Notice how the code places the complex data into local variables and then builds the output data. This data appears within a table on the application. Figure 5.6 shows typical output from this application.

Using the Web Service References Tool

The "Automating Reports Using SOAP" section demonstrates that it's possible to create a reference to the SOAP portion of Amazon Web Services manually. However, there's an easier way to perform this task. You can use the Web Service References Tool for simple queries. A simple query is one that doesn't rely on complex data types for either the request or the response. For example, you could use this technique if your company already runs a Web service for mobile users that delivers a simple response given a simple request. In some cases, you can also use it with Amazon Web Services, which is the method this section considers. (See the MSDN article entitled "Handling Complex SOAP Data Types in XML Web Services" at http://msdn.microsoft.com/library/default.asp?url=/library/en-us/dnxpwst/html/odc_wsrtct.asp for details on the complex data issues with the Web Service References Tool.)

> **▶ WARNING**
>
> Due to the limitations in earlier versions of the Web Service References Tool, I don't recommend this approach for earlier versions of Office. It works marginally with Office XP and Microsoft has promised better support for Office 2003.

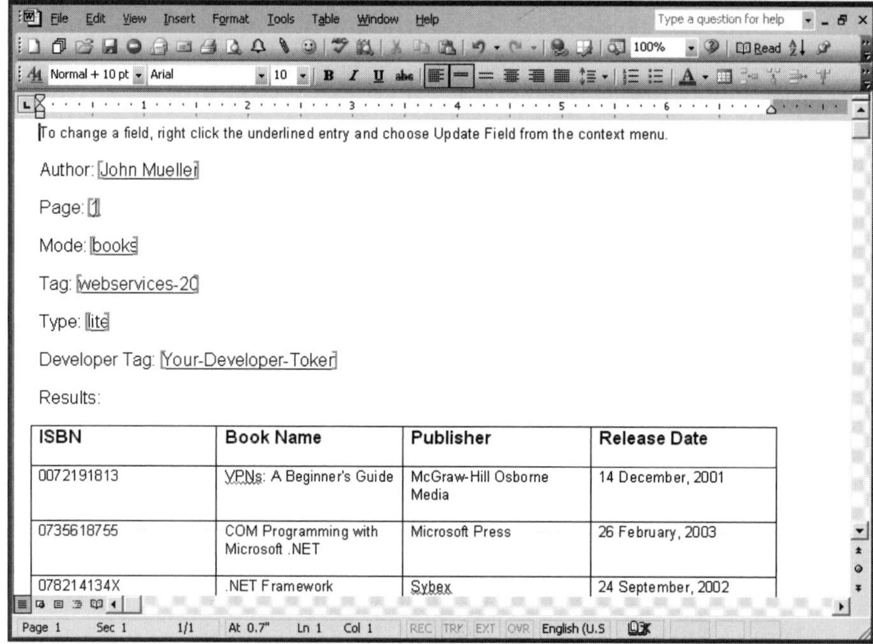

To change a field, right click the underlined entry and choose Update Field from the context menu.

Author: John Mueller

Page: 1

Mode: books

Tag: webservices-20

Type: lite

Developer Tag: Your-Developer-Token

Results:

ISBN	Book Name	Publisher	Release Date
0072191813	VPNs: A Beginner's Guide	McGraw-Hill Osborne Media	14 December, 2001
0735618755	COM Programming with Microsoft .NET	Microsoft Press	26 February, 2003
078214134X	.NET Framework	Sybex	24 September, 2002

FIGURE 5.6: This form and associated table contain the information for the report.

To use this technique, you must have the Web Service References Tool loaded on your machine. Use the Add-Ins ➢ Add-Ins Manager command to display the Add-In Manager dialog box shown in Figure 5.7. Ensure the Web Service References add-in is both loaded and started, as shown in the figure.

FIGURE 5.7: Use the Web Service References add-in to make using SOAP easier.

The Web Services Reference Tool adds new menu entries to the VBA IDE. Once you know that the Web Service References add-in is running, you can use the following steps to create a reference to Amazon Web Services.

1. Use the Tools ➢ Web Service References command to display the Web Service References Tool 2.0 dialog box.
2. Select the Web Service URL option and type **`http://soap.amazon.com/schemas3/AmazonWebServices.wsdl`** in the URL field.
3. Click Search. After a few seconds (up to a minute), the Web Service References Tool 2.0 dialog box displays information for Amazon Web Services, as shown in Figure 5.8. (Figure 5.8 shows the hierarchical list extended.)
4. Check the AmazonSearchService option and click OK. At this point, the VBA IDE will go a little crazy as VBA automatically creates the code required to access Amazon Web Services. You'd have to write this code yourself normally.

You still have to make one change to the automatically generated code. Amazon made an unfortunate choice in variable names for their Web service that doesn't seem to affect some development environments, but does affect VBA. In this case, the problem is the use of the word *type* as a variable name. VBA reserves this word, so you'll have to find all occurrences of it and replace it with something else. I used *atype* as a replacement.

> **NOTE**
>
> If you get an error message that VBA can't find the Web Service References Tool add-in on your machine, download the Microsoft Office XP Web Services Toolkit 2.0 at `http://www.microsoft.com/downloads/details.aspx?FamilyId=4922060F-002A-4F5B-AF74-978F2CD6C798&displaylang=en`. (You should also check for the 2003 version if you're using Office 2003, but the Office XP version seems to work.) Install the toolkit, open the Office XP Web Services Toolkit Overview, and then click the Web Services Reference Tool link on the Welcome page to install the tool.

Once you make the required changes, you can use the Web Service References Tool approach to make simple queries. Listing 5.6 shows the code you need for this example. You'll find this example in the `\Chapter 05\Web Service References Tool` folder of the source code located on the Sybex Web site.

Listing 5.6 Creating a Shopping Cart

```
Public Sub CreateShoppingCart()
   ' Define a list of items.
   Dim ItemList(0) As struct_Item
   Set ItemList(0) = New struct_Item
   ItemList(0).Asin = "0735618755"
```

```
    ' Create the request.
    Dim TheReq As struct_AddShoppingCartItems
    Set TheReq = New struct_AddShoppingCartItems
    TheReq.devtag = "Your-Developer-Token"
    TheReq.Items = ItemList
    TheReq.tag = "webservices-20"

    ' Create the response object.
    Dim Response As struct_ShoppingCart

    ' Make the request.
    Dim AmazonReq As clsws_AmazonSearchService
    Set AmazonReq = New clsws_AmazonSearchService
    Set Response = AmazonReq.wsm_AddShoppingCartItemsRequest(TheReq)
End Sub
```

This example only creates a shopping cart. If you want to add items to the shopping cart, you need to include other information such as the security code contained in the Keyed-Hashing for Message Authentication Code (HMAC) variable contained in the `struct_ShoppingCart` object, `Response`, on return from this call.

The code begins by creating a list of items to add to the new shopping cart. Include as much information as possible to ensure the application actually adds the correct item. Once the code creates an array of items, it adds them to a request object based on `struct_AddShoppingCartItems`. This request object includes your developer token, associate token, and the item array.

FIGURE 5.8: The Web Service References Tool 2.0 dialog box displays the AmazonSearchService and its functions.

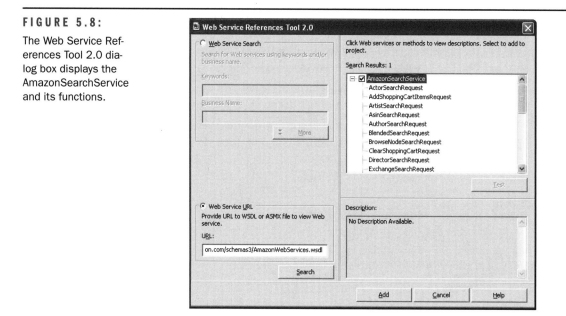

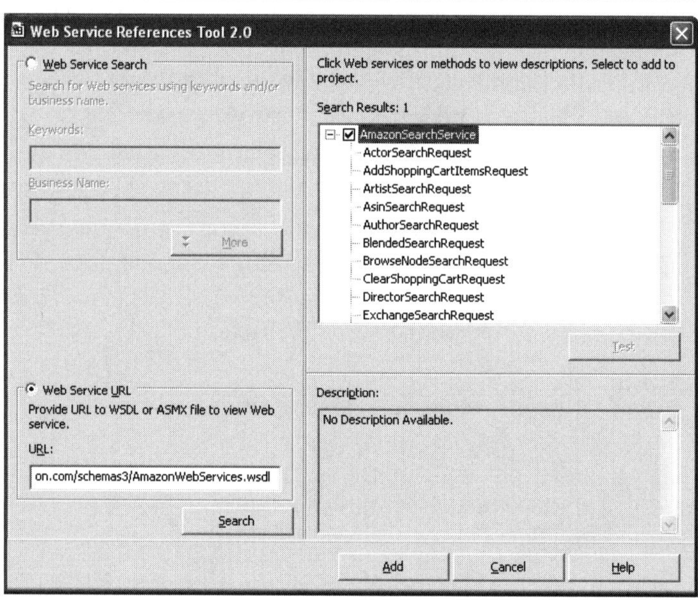

All requests require the `clsws_AmazonSearchService` class. This class contains all of the code required to make the request, so your development efforts focus on getting the right data put together. The code ends by making the request and storing the results in the `Response` object. Make sure you keep track of this `Response` object because it contains essential information such as the `HMAC` for keeping the cart updated.

Your Call to Action

This chapter has demonstrated how you can use VBA to write programs that use Amazon Web Services. It's essential to remember that the techniques in this chapter work with any application that supports VBA, not just Microsoft Office. The capabilities of the application also affect how you interact with Amazon Web Services. Yes, you can force a spreadsheet to act as a word processor, but the results usually aren't easy to use, flexible, or robust. Finally, this chapter demonstrates that you can do a lot more than just buy books using Amazon Web Services—this product definitely provides room for all kinds of application types.

> **▶ TIP**
>
> The error reporting provided with the default Web Services Reference Tool code is less than helpful. Amazon Web Services provides more information—the code just doesn't present it to you. You can easily improve the amount of information you receive from Amazon Web Services by modifying a single line of code in the `AmazonSearchService-ErrorHandler()` method of the `clsws_Amazon-SearchService` class. Make the SOAP error line read as `Err.Raise vbObjectError, str_Function, sc_Amazon-SearchService.Fault-String + vbCrLf + vbCrLf + sc_Amazon-SearchService.Detail` and you'll receive a lot more information during failed calls.

It's your turn to begin creating macro add-ons that rely on Amazon Web Services for your favorite application. VBA is a very flexible programming language. When you couple this language with the unique functionality provided by a specific application, you can create robust add-ons using a minimum of code and time. Of course, you can't confuse theses add-ons with full-fledged applications—the macro couples the add-on to the host application.

You might decide that you really do need a full-fledged application—that working with a specific host application just won't work for your need. Chapter 6 discusses techniques you can use to write full-fledged applications using Visual Studio. This chapter doesn't target a specific version of Visual Studio because many people don't have the latest product. Instead, the chapter discusses several languages included with both Visual Studio 6 and Visual Studio .NET so that you can choose the language that works best for your specific need.

Chapter 6

Finding Resources to Learn Visual Studio
Creating Visual Basic 6 Applications
Creating Visual C++ Applications
Creating Visual Basic .NET Applications

Writing Applications Using Visual Studio

Creating Web Applications
Developing Microsoft Access Applications
Developing SQL Server Applications

One of the best ways to work with Amazon Web Services when you want to create a free-form desktop application is to use Visual Studio. With Visual Studio, you have access to a full user interface, Web service, and database tools. Given time and resources, you can create seamless access to Amazon Web Services for any need, including many forms of Web application access. If you use Visual Studio .NET, mobile applications become relatively easy to create as well. In sum, this is the approach to use when you require maximum flexibility, have the required development skills, and have the time and resources to create a complete application.

The two most popular versions of Visual Studio now are Visual Studio 6.0 and Visual Studio .NET. This chapter explores both versions of Visual Studio. Visual Studio 6.0 developers will find examples for Visual C++ and Visual Basic. Visual Studio .NET developers will find examples for Visual C# and Visual Basic .NET. Most developers will find a Visual Studio flavor they like in these sections.

Visual Studio developers can create desktop or Web applications with equal ease. This chapter explores some of the differences between the two kinds of application development. You need to consider the unique issues of each environment as you create your application. For example, Web applications don't always lend themselves to extensive formatting with the same ease as desktop applications.

This chapter also considers the use of a database for various kinds of data storage, both short and long term. You might find that you need to use local storage that provides automatic data entry updates to achieve a given level of performance for your application. In some cases, you might also need to store customer or company specific short-term information as part of your application. This chapter presents two database sections. Information about applications that rely on SQL Server appears in the "Using SQL Server as a Database" section. You can find information about applications that rely on Access in the "Using Microsoft Access as a Database" section.

Using Web Services from Any Visual Studio Version

Chapter 5 demonstrates that you have a number of options for working with Amazon Web Services when using Microsoft Office. You can use the alternative eXtensible Stylesheet Language Transformations (XSLT), the eXtensible Markup Language (XML) over HyperText Transport Protocol (HTTP), or the Simple Object Access Protocol (SOAP) methods. In fact, you have a number of sub-options within these major access categories. Visual Studio also lets you access Amazon Web Services using any of these techniques. The difference is that this environment is more robust. Visual Studio provides a number of additional tools that Office developers can only dream about.

However, just because Visual Studio provides a robust development environment, doesn't mean that all versions of Visual Studio are equal. You have a number of choices to consider when working with Visual Studio. The .NET version has a definite ease-of-use advantage not provided by previous editions. Instead of manually figuring out how to access the Web service, you simply add a reference to it using the technique discussed in the "Creating a Web Reference" section of the chapter.

I'd love to say that Visual Studio .NET is a positive advance in every way, but it isn't the right choice for some needs. This version of Visual Studio relies on the .NET Framework to perform tasks. The .NET Framework is a library of programming routines similar in purpose to the Windows API. The difference is that it also relies on a runtime engine in the form of the Common Language Runtime (CLR). Unless the person who needs your application has both CLR and the .NET Framework installed on their system, they can't run your application.

Visual Studio 6.0 has a distinct advantage in that it's familiar and you can produce native or Windows 32-bit Application Programming Interface (Win32 API) code using it. Every version of Windows can use applications created by this version of Visual Studio. Consequently, you have decisions to make when selecting which version of Visual Studio to use. Although all of the languages in this chapter can access Amazon Web Services, each language has features that make it better suited to specific needs.

Resources for Learning Visual Studio

This book assumes that you already know how to use Visual Studio and at least one supported language. Except as needed, I won't discuss the IDE or basic programming techniques. Of course, the chapter will discuss how to use Amazon Web Services in detail, but you still need to know the essentials of the IDE and language you want to use. The following sections provide some resources you can use to learn Visual Studio (although these lists are by no means complete).

Using Visual Studio 6

Visual Studio is the last version of Microsoft's language product to provide full support for native applications—those that run directly from the Win32 API. Developers who don't want to adopt Microsoft's .NET strategy have continued to use this version of Visual Studio and it will probably remain viable for a long time. This book discusses the two most popular languages included with Visual Studio 6: Visual Basic 6 and Visual C++ 6. I'm assuming that you have installed the latest service pack from Microsoft (SP5 at the time of this writing).

It helps if you have a good book when learning any computer language, but especially when working with the intricacies of Visual Studio. A good starting Visual C++ book is *Beginning Visual C++ 6* by Ivor Horton (Wrox, 2003). Visual C++ developers will probably want to look at my books, *Visual C++ 6 from the Ground Up*, Second Edition (Osborne, 1998) or *Windows 2000 Programming Bible* (IDG, 1999) as their second book. Make sure you check out *Mastering C++ 6* by Michael J. Young (Sybex, 1998) as well.

For Visual Basic 6 developers, one of the best books on the market is *Visual Basic 6 for Dummies* by Wallace Wang (IDG, 1998). Another good book once you understand a few of the basics is *Mastering Visual Basic 6* by Evangelos Petroutsos (Sybex, 1998).

Make sure you also spend some time looking at source code examples. For example, you can find great source code examples at Planet Source Code (`http://www.pscode.com/`). This site includes both Visual Basic and Visual C++ examples, along with helpful tutorials. Note that this site also caters to .NET users. Another good place to look for Visual Basic code is A1VBCode at `http://www.a1vbcode.com/`. The TutorGig site at `http://www.tutorgig.com/` provides tutorials for both Visual Basic and Visual C++.

Normally, I recommend spending time on Microsoft's newsgroups such as `microsoft.public.vb.bugs` or `microsoft.public.vc.database`. However, if you're a Visual Basic developer, many online forums present great information without the usual Microsoft bias. For example, the Extreme Visual Basic Forum at `http://visualbasicforum.com/` provides a number of message lists you can use to discuss issues such as adding a Windows XP interface to your application.

Using Visual Studio .NET

Visual Studio .NET promises to deliver a lot in the way of language functionality, so it's almost a shame that I only cover C# and Visual Basic in this chapter. You still have an option to use Visual C++ for development purposes. See my book *Visual C++ .NET Developer's Guide* (Osborne, 2002) for details on using this language. In fact, the inclusion of new designer tools for Visual C++ developers in Visual Studio .NET 2003 makes this language a viable choice (the first version of Visual Studio .NET didn't provide Visual C++ developers with designer support). However, I'm currently working with PERL in .NET (see `http://www.activestate.com/Products/Visual_Perl/` for details) and there are other choices too. You can see a list of languages at `http://msdn.microsoft.com/netframework/technologyinfo/Overview/default.aspx`. It's also interesting to look at the language list at `http://www.gotdotnet.com/team/lang/`.

One of the best places to learn about C# is *A Programmer's Introduction to C#*, Second Edition, by Eric Gunnerson (Apress, 2001). Once you get a basic start, check out my book *Visual C# .NET Developer's Handbook* (Sybex, 2002). If you want a great .NET book that includes both Visual Basic and C#, check out *.NET Programming 10-Minute Solutions* by Russell Jones and Mike Gunderloy (Sybex, 2003).

Visual Basic .NET developers also have a wealth of information sources at their disposal. One book to try is *Beginning VB.NET* by Richard Blair, Jonathan Crossland, Matthew Reynolds, and Thearon Willis (Wrox, 2003). Many people also find *Microsoft Visual Basic .NET Step by Step* by Michael Halvorson (Microsoft Press, 2002) quite helpful.

As with any other language, seeing coding examples and trying them out on your machine is a good way to learn. One of the best places to obtain coding examples for Visual Basic .NET or Visual C++ .NET is GotDotNet (`http://www.gotdotnet.com/`). Some of the Microsoft developers frequent this site, as well as expert programmers who don't have any Microsoft affiliation. You can also learn a lot from my free .NET Tips, Trends & Technology eXTRA newsletter (sign up at `http://www.free-newsletters.com/`). Send me your .NET questions and I'll answer them in the newsletter. I've also written a number of articles for InformIT (`http://www.informit.com/isapi/authorid~{67CBE1B0-99DC-4A19-8BFB-5D224A0F34A7}/authors/author.asp`). Finally, Matthew Reynolds' .NET 247 site at `http://www.dotnet247.com/` is packed with helpful examples and other information.

> **TIP**
>
> Many of the books that you'll see online say they're for the novice, but the author has targeted them to a specific need. For example, you might see a book for database programming or using Crystal Reports. These books are helpful, but first try to find a .NET book that focuses on the language, rather than tasks you can perform with the language.

Microsoft supports a number of .NET newsgroups. The important thing to remember is that most of these newsgroups have "dotnet" in the name. For example, if you want to learn about .NET Framework interoperability problems, you should visit the `microsoft.public.dotnet.framework.interop` newsgroup. When you need help with Visual Basic .NET, check the `microsoft.public.dotnet.languages.vb` newsgroup. Likewise, you can visit the `microsoft.public.dotnet.languages.vc` newsgroup for help with Visual C++ .NET questions.

Developing with Visual Basic 6

Visual Basic 6 is still a favorite with developers today because it makes building applications easy when they compare it to a language such as C and still produces a native executable. Many organizations have documented the developer productivity benefits of using Visual Basic 6. You can produce both desktop and Web applications with equal ease. The design interface makes working with databases simple. In fact, if there's a problem with Visual Basic, it's that the product does too much and ends up hiding low-level functionality that developers need. Consequently, this is the language to use if you need a native code application to access Amazon Web Services and developer productivity is high on your list of priorities. The following sections describe how you can use Visual Basic 6 to build an Amazon Web Services application.

Getting the Microsoft SOAP Toolkit

Visual Studio 6 arrived on the scene well before the SOAP arrived on the scene. Consequently, none of the languages in Visual Studio 6 includes native support for SOAP. To add SOAP support, download the Microsoft SOAP Toolkit 3.0 from `http://www.microsoft.com/downloads/details.aspx?FamilyId=C943C0DD-CEEC-4088-9753-86F052EC8450`. Once you download the toolkit, install it on your system. Make sure you have Visual Studio 6 installed before you install the toolkit so the installation routine can make any required changes to your Visual Studio 6 setup. Note that accessing Amazon Web Services doesn't require all of the features provided in the Microsoft SOAP Toolkit, but it's a good idea to install everything in case you want to perform other types of SOAP development later.

> **NOTE**
>
> Microsoft still offers the Microsoft SOAP Toolkit 2.0 SP2 for download. This version of the toolkit works fine with the examples in this book. In fact, you can download this version of the toolkit from `http://www.microsoft.com/downloads/details.aspx?FamilyId=147ED727-0BE8-48A1-B1DA-D50B1EA582CB&displaylang=en`. However, it's better to use the newer version of the Microsoft SOAP Toolkit if possible and the version-specific information in this section reflects that toolkit's contents.

The Microsoft SOAP Toolkit contains a number of files that you need to know about before you can create an application with it. Table 6.1 provides a list of the files (including DLLs) provided in the Microsoft SOAP Toolkit. This table tells how you'll use the DLLs within an application and the utilities to create application resources or perform testing. Note that some filenames include version information that might vary from the version you have installed. In addition, you might find the files in a slightly different location and some toolkit versions could include files not listed in Table 6.1.

TABLE 6.1: Files provided with the Microsoft SOAP Toolkit

DLL Name	Location	Description
MSSOAP1.DLL and MSSOAP30.DLL	\Program Files\CommonFiles\MSSoap\Binaries	This is the first SOAP DLL that you'll use on a high-level API access client or server. Use the MSSOAP30.DLL file for version 3.0 access. The Microsoft SOAP Library contains a number of classes, but you'll always begin by creating either a SoapClient or SoapServer object. These objects support a single method call, Init(), that tells SOAP which WSDL file to use. Other classes perform tasks such as serializing data for output and reading input. This is the DLL that you'll use for simple requests with Amazon Web Services.
MSSOAPR.DLL and MSSOAPR3.DLL	\Program Files\Common Files\MSSoap\Binaries\Resources\1033	This file contains resources for SOAP use in general and normally you won't need to reference it directly. The MSSOAPR3.DLL file contains resources specifically used by the 3.0 version of the toolkit.
MsSoapT3.EXE	\Program Files\MSSOAP\Binaries	Use this file to start the Microsoft SOAP Trace utility. In most cases, you won't need this diagnostic tool when working with Amazon Web Services. However, it's helpful to know how to use it so that you can troubleshoot problems when they occur.
SOAPIS30.DLL	\Program Files\Common Files\MSSoap\Binaries	Use this DLL to add WSDL support to your Internet Information Server (IIS). The "Specifying an ISAPI Listener" topic of the SOAP Toolkit 3.0 help file tells how to add this file to the server. It's unlikely that you'll use this file with Amazon Web Services, unless you create a referral type application where a user uses a Web service application on your Web server to access Amazon Web Services.

Continued on next page

TABLE 6.1 CONTINUED: Files provided with the Microsoft SOAP Toolkit

DLL Name	Location	Description
`WHSC30.DLL`	`\Program Files\Common Files\MSSoap\Binaries`	This DLL contains the Windows HTTP SOAP Connector Library. This library provides SOAP connector service to a remote location. You'll also use this DLL to receive and send low-level SOAP messages. Use this library for complex requests, especially when working with searches, to avoid receiving unwanted data from the server. Avoid using this library with Windows 9x systems—use the Windows Internet Connector Library instead.
`WISC10.DLL` and `WISC30.DLL`	`\Program Files\Common Files\MSSoap\Binaries`	These DLLs contain the Windows Internet Connector Library. The version 3.0 toolkit includes the `WISC30.DLL` file. Both DLLs provide essentially the same services as the Windows HTTP Library Connector described earlier. This lower performance library works with Windows 98, Windows ME, Windows NT, and Windows 2000. As with the Windows HTTP SOAP Connector Library, use this DLL for complex requests.
`WSDLGen3.DLL` and `WSDLGen3.EXE`	`\Program Files\MSSOAP\Binaries`	The WSDL generation tools create the WSDL files used to describe Web services that you create. You never need to use this tool with Amazon Web Services because Amazon provides the required WSDL file for you. This file resides at `http://soap.amazon.com/schemas3/AmazonWebServices.wsdl` for users in the United States and Japan, and `http://soap-eu.amazon.com/schemas3/AmazonWebServices.wsdl` for United Kingdom and German users.

As you can see from Table 6.1, the library that you're going to use most often is the Microsoft SOAP Library. It contains everything you need to begin a conversation between client and server using the high-level API. What the table doesn't show is that you'll also need the latest version of the Microsoft XML Library. This library doesn't appear in the same directory as the rest of the SOAP files. The Microsoft SOAP Toolkit installation program automatically adds the latest version of the Microsoft XML Library to your System or System32 directory.

On those few occasions where you do need low-level API access, make sure you include one of the low-level API access libraries in Table 6.1. All of the sample programs provided with the Microsoft SOAP Toolkit rely on the Windows Internet Connector Library. This doesn't make the other selections any better or worse, it simply means you'll spend a little additional time figuring out how to use them. It helps that all the low-level libraries work about the same way, contain about the same classes with the same methods, and that you could theoretically use any of the three with the same boilerplate code.

> **▶ TIP**
>
> You might find that you have additional questions about the Microsoft SOAP Toolkit for your own needs. The `microsoft.public.xml.soapsdk` newsgroup is a good place to start asking questions about this product.

Adding a SOAP Toolkit Reference to Visual Basic 6

Before you can develop an application using the SOAP toolkit, you need to add a reference to it in your application. The following steps tell how to perform this task.

1. Select the Project ➢ References command. You'll see a References dialog box such as the one shown in Figure 6.1.
2. Locate the Microsoft SOAP Type Library 3.0 entry in the list and check it.
3. Locate the Microsoft XML, v4.0 entry in the list and check it.
4. Click OK.

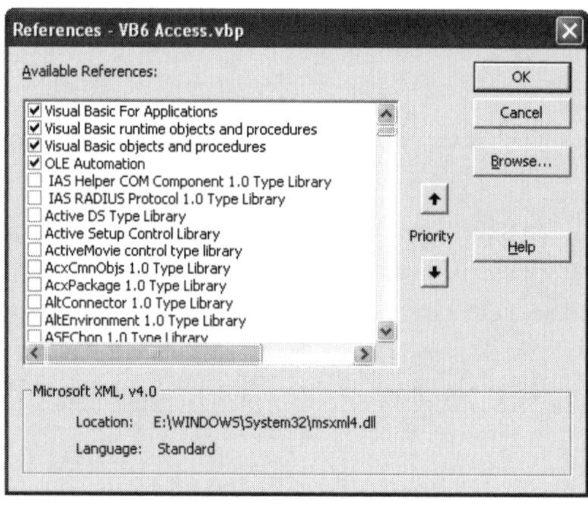

FIGURE 6.1: Add a reference to the appropriate type libraries using this dialog box.

You also need to add the FlexGrid control to your application to make this example work properly. To add this control, right-click the Toolbox and select Components from the context menu. Check the Microsoft FlexGrid Control 6.0 option in the Components dialog box. Click OK and you'll see the component added to your Toolbox.

▶ **TIP**

One of the first places you should look when experiencing client-side errors in your SOAP application is the Microsoft XML Library. My workstation has four versions of this library installed. Although the library versions are clearly marked, you could find that you selected the wrong one by mistake. The current version of the Microsoft SOAP Toolkit relies on version 4 of the Microsoft XML Library found in `MSXML4.DLL`.

Performing an Author Search with Visual Basic 6

Some of the searches you perform on Amazon won't produce the results you anticipated. For example, when searching for some author names, you'll find that some books not produced by that author also show up. However, on closer examination, you'll find that two coauthors with the requisite names did write the book. For example, when searching for Stephen King, you might get a book produced by Stephen Miller and Audrey King. The search engine doesn't filter any of these mismatches for you. Listing 6.1 shows how you can filter the Amazon output using a custom application. You'll find this example in the `\Chapter 06\VB6 Access` folder of the source code located on the Sybex Web site.

Listing 6.1 Accessing Amazon Web Services in Visual Basic 6

```
Private Sub btnTest_Click()
   Dim Details As IXMLDOMNodeList        ' Contains the detail nodes.
   Dim CurrentBook As IXMLDOMNode        ' Contains just one book.
   Dim BookDetails As IXMLDOMNodeList    ' Details for one book.
   Dim BookItem As IXMLDOMNode           ' An individual book detail.
   Dim AuthDetails As IXMLDOMNodeList    ' All the authors.
   Dim Author As IXMLDOMNode             ' A single author.
   Dim AuthList As String                ' The list of authors
   Dim IsAuthor As Boolean               ' Is this the correct author?
   Dim Counter As Integer                ' Loop counter.

   ' Get the requested information.
   Set Details = GetData

   ' Fill in the data grid.
   For Each CurrentBook In Details

      ' Get the book details.
      Set BookDetails = CurrentBook.childNodes
```

```
' Look for specific book items.
For Each BookItem In BookDetails

   ' Determine which action to take.
   Select Case BookItem.baseName
      Case "Asin"
         fgOutput.Col = 0
         fgOutput.Text = BookItem.Text
      ... Other Standard Actions ...
      Case "Authors"
         ' Make sure the author list is blank.
         AuthList = ""
         Counter = 1

         ' Get the author list.
         Set AuthDetails = BookItem.childNodes

         ' Verify the author check is false.
         IsAuthor = False

         ' Process each author.
         For Each Author In AuthDetails
            ' Add the author name.
            AuthList = AuthList + Author.Text

            ' Add the appropriate author name
            ' separator.
            If AuthDetails.length > 1 And _
               Counter < AuthDetails.length Then
               If Counter = AuthDetails.length - 1 Then
                  AuthList = AuthList + ", and "
               Else
                  AuthList = AuthList + ", "
               End If
            End If

            ' Update the counter.
            Counter = Counter + 1

            ' Check for the author.
            If UCase(Author.Text) = UCase(txtAuthor.Text) Then
               IsAuthor = True
            End If
         Next

         ' Set the column text.
         fgOutput.Col = 3
         fgOutput.Text = AuthList
   End Select
Next
```

```
         ' Blank this row if the author wasn't found.
         If Not IsAuthor Then
            fgOutput.Col = 0
            fgOutput.Text = ""
            ... Other Blanked Columns ...
         Else
            ' Add a new row.
            fgOutput.AddItem " "
            fgOutput.Row = fgOutput.Row + 1
         End If
      Next
   End Sub
```

A filtering application is as much about on-screen presentation and data manipulation as it is about requesting data from Amazon. This part of the list requests the information from Amazon using the `GetData()` method described as part of Listing 6.2. However, assume for the moment that you've retrieved the details for the request. The `Details` object contains a list of 10 books, but only some of those books actually match the author name you requested. In fact, Figure 6.2 shows that many of the entries aren't from the requested author (John Mueller). For example, look at the first entry. The authors John Mairs and Michael Mueller satisfied the author search because Amazon combined the first name of one author and the second of another. However, these aren't the authors the example is looking for, so this book shouldn't appear in the list. In fact, if you look through the list, you'll find that only two books precisely match the criteria, but eight match the criteria if you don't consider middle names.

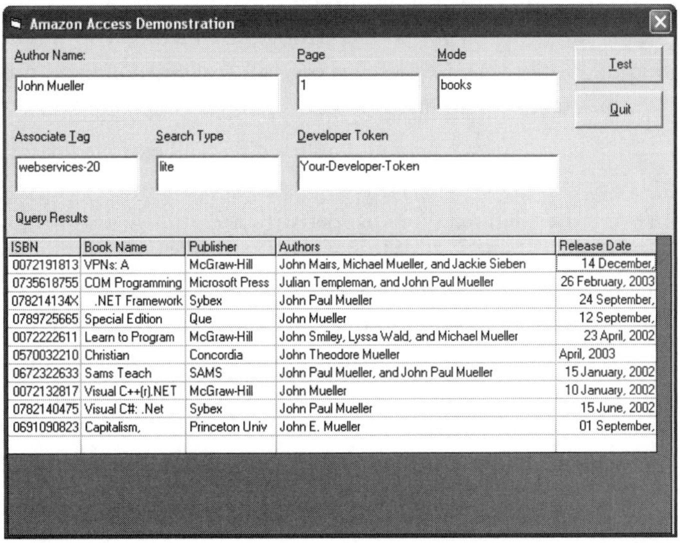

FIGURE 6.2: Unfiltered output from Amazon Web Services can contain undesirable data elements.

The code uses a combination of the IXMLDOMNodeList object, IXMLDOMNode object, and For Each...Next loop to process the data. Every time the code needs to go down another level of detail, it creates an IXMLDOMNodeList object with all the details, and then uses a For Each...Next loop to process the individual items in the list. Using this technique tends to insulate your code from some of the effects of getting data lists of indeterminate length.

The Select Case structure chooses an action based on the kind of data that a particular book data element contains. The code bases the decision on the BookItem.baseName value, which is a string that tells what kind of data the element contains. In most cases, the only thing the code needs to do is place the BookItem.Text value into the data grid because the information consists of a single element.

Processing an author requires more work. A book can have more than one author (or a CD more than one artist), so Amazon sends this data back as another node list. As you can see, the code uses the same node list technique as usual to read the author names from the BookItem object. Because the list can contain multiple authors and you don't know which author might be the one you need, it's important to use some type of flag to indicate that the record has the appropriate author name in it. The code has two tasks to perform. First, it creates a formatted string containing all of the author names. Second, notice that the code checks for the specific author name the user has requested. If this author name is present, the code sets the IsAuthor flag to True.

When the code finishes processing a BookItem, it uses the IsAuthor flag to determine whether to keep or delete the record. Deleting the record means blanking the individual columns in that row and using the same row for the next BookItem. Keeping the record means adding a new row and updating the FlexGrid row pointer. Figure 6.3 shows the filtered output. Notice that the match is precise. You'd need to add code to perform wildcard matches, but the example demonstrates that such filtering is possible.

To perform most searches, you need to send complex data to Amazon. You can perform this task using a number of techniques. For example, you could create a custom SOAP mapper or a user defined type mapper with the high-level API. (See the "Handling Complex Types" help topic in the Microsoft SOAP Toolkit help file for details.) It might at first appear that using the high-level API would require less coding because the examples in the help file don't rely on very complex data. Working with Amazon Web Services is another story—the data is extremely complex. You'd spend many hours creating and perfecting the type information for mapping the data with the high-level API, which is why I suggest using the low-level API technique shown in Listing 6.2 with Visual Basic 6 and Visual C++ 6. Using this technique, you can create functions that appear in a separate file and encapsulate the details for you.

Listing 6.2 Getting the Data Using Low-Level Calls in Visual Basic

```
Private Function GetData() As IXMLDOMNodeList
   Dim Connector As SoapConnector30     ' Connection to Web Service
   Dim DataSend As SoapSerializer30     ' Sends data to Amazon.
   Dim DataReceive As SoapReader30      ' Receives data from Amazon.

   ' Create a connection to Amazon.
   Set Connector = New HttpConnector30
   Connector.Property("EndPointURL") = _
      "http://soap.amazon.com/onca/soap3"
   Connector.Property("SoapAction") = _
      "http://soap.amazon.com"

   ' Tell Amazon that the application is sending a request.
   Connector.BeginMessage

   ' Associate the data serializer with the connection.
   Set DataSend = New SoapSerializer30
   DataSend.Init Connector.InputStream

   ' Start creating a request, including the SOAP envelope.
   With DataSend

      ' Create the envelope and associated namespaces. Don't
      ' include namespaces that Visual Basic already includes.
      .StartEnvelope
      '.SoapAttribute "xmlns:SOAP-ENV", , _
      '               "http://schemas.xmlsoap.org/soap/envelope/"
      '.SoapAttribute "xmlns:SOAP-ENC", , _
      '               "http://schemas.xmlsoap.org/soap/encoding/"
      .SoapAttribute "xmlns:xsi", , _
                     "http://www.w3.org/2001/XMLSchema-instance"
      .SoapAttribute "xmlns:xsd", , _
                     "http://www.w3.org/2001/XMLSchema"
      .SoapAttribute "SOAP-ENV:encodingStyle", , _
                     "http://schemas.xmlsoap.org/soap/encoding/"

      ' Create the SOAP body.
      .StartBody

      ' Start creating the request.
      .StartElement "namesp1:AuthorSearchRequest"
      .SoapAttribute "xmlns:namesp1", , "urn:PI/DevCentral/SoapService"
      .StartElement "AuthorSearchRequest"
      '.SoapAttribute "xsi:type", , "m:AuthorRequest"

      ' Add the author information.
      .StartElement "author"
```

```
            .WriteString txtAuthor.Text
            .EndElement

            ... Other Required Elements ...

            ' Add the developer token information.
            .StartElement "devtag"
            .WriteString txtDevTag.Text
            .EndElement

            ' Close all of the open tags.
            .EndElement
            .EndElement
            .EndBody
            .EndEnvelope
        End With

        ' Tell Amazon the request is complete.
        Connector.EndMessage

        ' Receive the response from Amazon.
        Set DataReceive = New SoapReader30
        DataReceive.Load Connector.OutputStream

        ' Return the data.
        Set GetData = DataReceive.RpcResult.childNodes(2).childNodes
    End Function
```

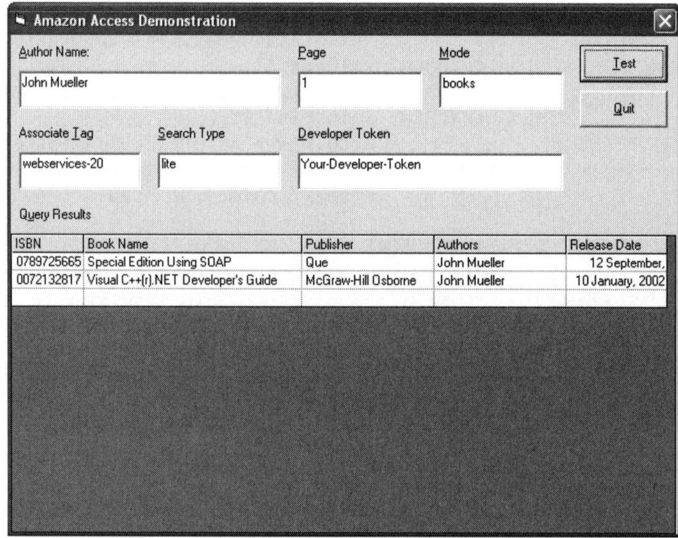

FIGURE 6.3: Filtering application output makes it easier to find what you need.

The code begins by creating a connection to Amazon Web Services (`Connector`), an object to send data to the service (`DataSend`), and an object to receive data from the service (`DataReceive`). Notice that all of these objects are Microsoft SOAP Toolkit 3.0 specific. You can also use the older version objects, but they don't provide the reliability, features, and speed of the newer objects.

The first task the code performs is creating a connection to Amazon Web Services. To do this, the code must specify the endpoint, which is essentially the place on the Internet to send the data. The connector must also include a SOAP action so the Web service knows what to do with the information. The connection doesn't actually take place until the `Connector.BeginMessage()` method call. If the connection parameters aren't correct, the code will usually fail at this point.

The second task the code performs is sending a request to the server. You must create a request message that simulates the format shown in the files found in the `\AmazonWebServices\SoapRequestSamples` folder. Note that all of these examples contain a mysterious `xsi:type="m:AuthorRequest"` attribute in the second `<AuthorSearchRequest>` element that will cause your request to fail. Don't include this attribute in the request. Notice how the code starts the envelope, creates the required namespace entries, defines the body, and then closes everything up so that the message includes the closing tags. Each request tag also includes a starting and closing element, along with the data you want to send. The code sends the message when it sees the `Connector.EndMessage()` method call.

The third task is to receive the response from Amazon Web Services. In most cases, all you need is the detail nodes, so the code shown in the listing is precisely the code you'll use for all of your applications as well. You can return the additional information, but generally, you won't need it. Notice that the code uses the `RpcResult` node because Amazon Web Services uses the Remote Procedure Call (RPC) technique, rather than the document technique normally used by Microsoft products.

Developing with Visual C++ 6

Most developers who use Visual C++ 6 are looking for low-level flexibility and application execution speed. Given the flexibility this environment provides, some types of data manipulations are much simpler than with a product such as Visual Basic. The problem with Visual C++ 6 is that you pay a price in developer productivity when using it. An Amazon Web Services application can take two or three times longer to build than with Visual

> **▶ NOTE**
>
> RPC refers to a data exchange (formatting) technique in this case, not the actual technology. Consequently, worms such as Blaster that normally attack RPC technologies such as DCOM using port 135 don't have an effect on SOAP.

Basic, given applications of the same capability. In addition, building database support into a Visual C++ 6 application is more difficult and time consuming than when you use Visual Basic. Visual C++ 6 is the language of choice when you value flexibility and performance over ease of use and productivity.

Adding a SOAP Toolkit Reference to Visual C++ 6

You really need to know the location and names of the SOAP Toolkit files when working with Visual C++ because the IDE doesn't perform any hand-holding. This lack of support is one reason that Table 6.1 is so important. The following steps will help you install the SOAP Toolkit, XML, and FlexGrid support required for this example.

1. Use the Project ➢ Add to Project ➢ Components and Controls command to display the Components and Controls dialog box shown in Figure 6.4.
2. Double-click the Registered ActiveX Controls folder. Locate the Microsoft FlexGrid Control, and then click Insert. Visual C++ will ask if you want to insert this component.
3. Click OK. You'll see a Confirm Classes dialog box similar to the one shown in Figure 6.5. Normally, you don't have to change any of the entries on this dialog box. However, you may need to change the names if there's a conflict with another class.
4. Click OK. Visual C++ adds the new classes to your application and you'll see the new control in the Toolbox.
5. Click Close to close the Components and Controls dialog box.

FIGURE 6.4: Use the Components and Controls dialog box to add SOAP, XML, and FlexGrid support.

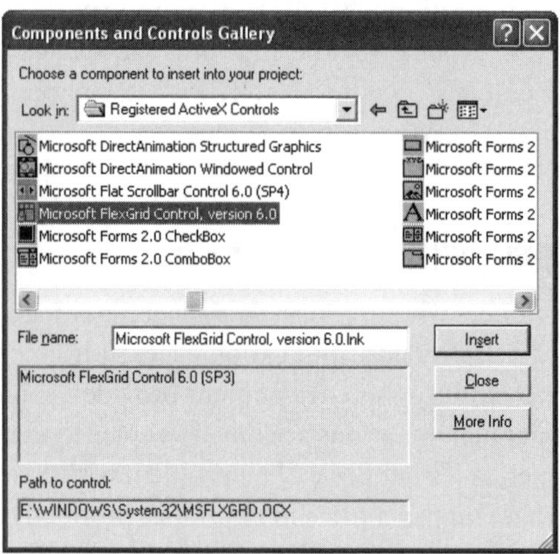

FIGURE 6.5:
The Confirm Classes dialog box shows which classes the IDE adds to support the FlexGrid.

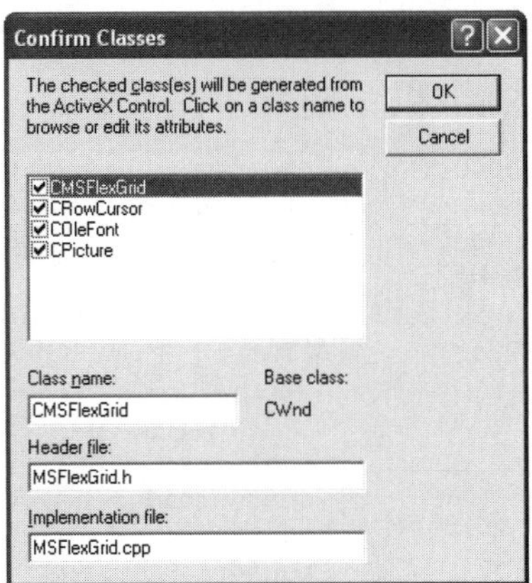

You add the XML and SOAP reference to the application by adding code to the file. In general, you'll use the following code to add the SOAP toolkit and XML references.

```
// You must change these locations to match your setup!
#import "MSXML4.DLL"
using namespace MSXML2;
#import "E:\Program Files\Common Files\MSSoap\Binaries\MSSOAP30.DLL" \
   exclude("IStream", "IErrorInfo", "ISequentialStream", \
   "_LARGE_INTEGER", "_ULARGE_INTEGER", "tagSTATSTG", "_FILETIME")
using namespace MSSOAPLib30;
```

Notice that the `MSSOAP30.DLL` file has a specific directory attached because it doesn't appear in the `\Windows\System32` folder. You must change this folder to match your system or the code won't compile. Also, notice that the `#import` reference excludes a number of elements from the `MSSOAP30.DLL` file. If you don't include these exclusions, the code probably won't compile because it will detect errors with existing files. The IDE automatically adds the support required by the `#import` statements when you build the application the first time.

> **▶ NOTE**
>
> You must have the Microsoft SOAP Toolkit installed on your system to work with the examples in this section. Learn more about this toolkit in the "Getting the Microsoft SOAP Toolkit" section of the chapter.

Performing an Author Search with Visual C++ 6

The example in this section is very similar to the one shown in the "Performing an Author Search with Visual Basic 6" section of the chapter. I included similar examples so that you could use them for comparison between Visual Basic 6 and Visual C++ 6. Listing 6.3 shows how you can filter the Amazon output using a custom application. You'll find this example in the `\Chapter 06\VC6Access` folder of the source code located on the Sybex Web site.

Listing 6.3 Accessing Amazon Web Services in Visual C++ 6

```
void CVC6AccessDlg::OnTest()
{
   IXMLDOMNodeList*  Details;        // Contains all the detail nodes.
   IXMLDOMNode*      CurrentBook;    // Contains just one book.
   IXMLDOMNodeList*  BookDetails;    // Details for one book.
   IXMLDOMNode*      BookItem;       // An individual book detail.
   IXMLDOMNodeList*  AuthDetails;    // All the authors.
   IXMLDOMNode*      Author;         // A single author.
   CString           AuthList;       // The list of authors
   bool              IsAuthor;       // Is this the correct author?
   long              CountBook;      // Loop counter.
   long              CountDetail;    // Loop counter.
   long              CountAuthor;    // Loop counter.
   int               Counter;        // Loop counter.
   long              BookCount;      // Number of books returned.
   long              DetailCount;    // Number of details per book.
   CString           BaseNameTxt;    // BaseName field value.
   int               CurrDGRow;      // Current data grid row.
   CString           DGRowTxt;       // Text data grid row.
   CString           AuthChk1;       // First part of Author check.
   CString           AuthChk2;       // Second part of Author check.

   // Initialize the COM environment.
   CoInitialize(NULL);

   // Get the requested information.
   Details = GetData();

   // Set the data grid row.
   CurrDGRow = 1;

   // Determine the number of books and process each book in turn.
   // Fill in the data grid.
   Details->get_length(&BookCount);
   for (CountBook = 0; CountBook < BookCount; CountBook++)
   {

      // Get the book details.
      Details->get_item(CountBook, &CurrentBook);
      CurrentBook->get_childNodes(&BookDetails);

      // Look for specific book items.
      BookDetails->get_length(&DetailCount);
      for (CountDetail = 0; CountDetail < DetailCount; CountDetail++)
      {
         // Get the book item.
         BookDetails->get_item(CountDetail, &BookItem);

         // Determine which action to take.
         BaseNameTxt = (const char*)BookItem->baseName;
```

```
      if (BaseNameTxt == "Asin")
      {
         m_Output.SetCol(0);
         m_Output.SetText((const char*)BookItem->text);
      }
         ... Other Standard Actions ...
      if (BaseNameTxt == "Authors")
      {
         // Make sure the author list is blank.
         AuthList = "";

         // Get the author list.
         BookItem->get_childNodes(&AuthDetails);

         // Verify the author check is false.
         IsAuthor = false;

         // Process each author.
         AuthDetails->get_length(&CountAuthor);
         for (Counter = 0; Counter < CountAuthor; Counter++)
         {
            // Get the individual author.
            AuthDetails->get_item(Counter, &Author);

            // Add the author name.
            AuthList += (const char*)Author->text;

            // Add the appropriate author name separator.
            if ((CountAuthor > 1) && (Counter + 1 < CountAuthor))
            {
               if (Counter == CountAuthor - 2)
                  AuthList += ", and ";
               else
                  AuthList += ", ";
            }

            // Check for the author.
            m_NameWnd.GetWindowText(AuthChk1);
            AuthChk2 = (const char*)Author->text;
            AuthChk1.MakeUpper();
            AuthChk2.MakeUpper();
            if (AuthChk1 == AuthChk2)
               IsAuthor = true;
         }

         //  Set the column text.
         m_Output.SetCol(3);
         m_Output.SetText(AuthList);
      }
   }

   // Blank this row if the author wasn't found.
   if (! IsAuthor)
```

```
         {
            m_Output.SetCol(0);
            m_Output.SetText("");
            ... Other Blanked Columns ...
         }
         else
         {
            // Add a new row.
            CurrDGRow++;
            itoa(CurrDGRow, DGRowTxt.GetBuffer(6), 10);
            DGRowTxt.ReleaseBuffer(-1);
            m_Output.AddItem("", _variant_t(DGRowTxt));
            m_Output.SetRow(CurrDGRow);
         }

      }

      // Uninitialize the COM environment.
      CoUninitialize();
   }
```

This code performs essentially the same task as the Visual Basic code explained in Listing 6.1. The two applications output the same data so you can perform a comparison of the two languages. However, you also need to note some differences in the handling of data for this example. Some differences are due to the language itself—Visual C++ doesn't have a `For Each...Next` statement, so you must use loops. The `switch` statement is hostile toward the data types used for XML, so it's more efficient to use the `if` statement.

Notice that the example code makes as much use of Visual C++ native types as possible. For example, the data you receive from Amazon appears as a `BSTR`, rather than the `String` type used for Visual Basic. Consequently, you'll want to convert these values to a `CString` so that you can manipulate the data easily. Use the `(const char*)` override to ensure a good conversion. You also have to perform data conversions when you send data to Amazon or use one of the XML data objects. The easiest way to accomplish this task in many cases is to use the `_variant_t()` method.

The `GetData()` method shown in Listing 6.4 follows the same strategy as the Visual Basic example in Listing 6.2. However, like this example, it also includes a few surprises.

Listing 6.4 Getting the Data Using Low-Level Calls in Visual C++ 6

```
IXMLDOMNodeList* CVC6AccessDlg::GetData(void)
{
   ISoapConnectorPtr    Connector;     // Connection to Web Service
   ISoapSerializerPtr   DataSend;      // Sends data to Amazon.
   ISoapReaderPtr       DataReceive;   // Receives data from Amazon.
   CString              TempStr;       // Transitions the input text.
```

```
IXMLDOMElement*      RpcElement;     // Holds entire RPC result.
IXMLDOMNodeList*     List;           // Contains the 3 RPC nodes.
IXMLDOMNode*         DataElement;    // Holds the data node of List.
IXMLDOMNodeList*     Details;        // Holds up to 10 detail nodes.


// Create a connection to Amazon.
Connector.CreateInstance(__uuidof(HttpConnector30));
Connector->Property["EndPointURL"] =
   "http://soap.amazon.com/onca/soap3";
Connector->Property["SoapAction"] =
   "http://soap.amazon.com";

// Tell Amazon that the application is sending a request.
Connector->BeginMessage();

// Associate the data serializer with the connection.
DataSend.CreateInstance(__uuidof(SoapSerializer30));
DataSend->Init(_variant_t((IUnknown*)Connector->InputStream));

// Create the envelope and associated namespaces. Don't
// include namespaces that Visual C++ already includes.
DataSend->StartEnvelope("", "", "");
//DataSend->SoapAttribute "xmlns:SOAP-ENV", , _
//                  "http://schemas.xmlsoap.org/soap/envelope/"
//DataSend->SoapAttribute "xmlns:SOAP-ENC", , _
//                  "http://schemas.xmlsoap.org/soap/encoding/"
DataSend->SoapAttribute("xmlns:xsi", "",
                 "http://www.w3.org/2001/XMLSchema-instance", "");
DataSend->SoapAttribute("xmlns:xsd", "",
                 "http://www.w3.org/2001/XMLSchema", "");
//DataSend->SoapAttribute("SOAP-ENV:encodingStyle", "",
//                  "http://schemas.xmlsoap.org/soap/encoding/", "");

// Create the SOAP body.
DataSend->StartBody("");

// Start creating the request.
DataSend->StartElement("namesp1:AuthorSearchRequest", "", "", "");
DataSend->SoapAttribute("xmlns:namesp1",
                        "",
                        "urn:PI/DevCentral/SoapService", "");
DataSend->StartElement("AuthorSearchRequest", "", "", "");
//.SoapAttribute "xsi:type", , "m:AuthorRequest"

// Add the author information.
DataSend->StartElement("author", "", "", "");
m_NameWnd.GetWindowText(TempStr);
DataSend->WriteString(TempStr.AllocSysString());
DataSend->EndElement();
```

```
        ... Other Required Elements ...

    // Add the developer token information.
    DataSend->StartElement("devtag", "", "", "");
    m_DevTagWnd.GetWindowText(TempStr);
    DataSend->WriteString(TempStr.AllocSysString());
    DataSend->EndElement();

    // Close all of the open tags.
    DataSend->EndElement();
    DataSend->EndElement();
    DataSend->EndBody();
    DataSend->EndEnvelope();

    // Tell Amazon the request is complete.
    Connector->EndMessage();

    // Receive the response from Amazon.
    DataReceive.CreateInstance(__uuidof(SoapReader30));
    DataReceive->Load(_variant_t((IUnknown*)Connector->OutputStream),
                      "");

    // Build the output value.
    DataReceive->get_RpcResult(&RpcElement);
    RpcElement->get_childNodes(&List);
    List->get_item(2, &DataElement);
    DataElement->get_childNodes(&Details);

    // Release the COM objects.
    Connector.Release();
    DataSend.Release();
    DataReceive.Release();

    // Return the data.
    return Details;
}
```

From an Amazon Web Services perspective, notice that the Visual C++ code eliminates the `SOAP-ENV:encodingStyle` attribute. Visual C++ applications send this attribute automatically; Visual Basic applications don't. If you don't remove this extra attribute, Amazon Web Services will report a duplicate attribute error.

Notice the code for creating and instantiating the `Connector`, `DataSend`, and `DataReceive` objects. You must create and track these objects as you use them at a much greater level of detail than you would for a Visual Basic application. Also, notice that you must include specific code to release these three objects because you created them in your code. The `Release()` method sets the objects to a 0 reference (you can see it easily in the debugger). The application will create a substantial memory leak if the code fails to release the objects.

Unlike Visual Basic, you can't simply ignore any of the arguments for the various methods. However, you can pass null strings to placate the compiler without passing any data. If you run into data errors when working with Amazon Web Services, it's a good idea to verify that you placed the null strings in the correct places and don't need to pass additional data, such as URLs, to ensure the Web service knows where to find information.

Notice how much code Visual C++ uses to obtain the `<Details>` node of the return value. Unlike Visual Basic, where you can combine all of the required data manipulation in a single statement like this:

```
Set GetData = DataReceive.RpcResult.childNodes(2).childNodes
```

you must perform each step individually in Visual C++. For example, to get to the `RpcResult`, you need to use the `DataReceive->get_RpcResult(&RpcElement)` method call and then move further down the node list. Don't attempt to combine calls. Even though the code compiles, Visual C++ won't transfer the data from level to level, which means you'll end up with a null data set.

> **WARNING**
>
> Visual C++ and Visual Basic map data types and work with the Amazon data nodes differently. Don't assume a data type in Visual Basic will simply map to the same data type in Visual C++. See the "Data Type Mappings" and "Data Types Generated by the WSDL/WSML Generator" help topics in the Microsoft SOAP Toolkit help file for details. In addition, because Visual C++ works directly with pointers and Visual Basic hides this issue, you need to perform additional work with the nodes. For example, the `IXMLDOMNodeList` and `IXMLDOMNode` class methods that return a value directly tend not to work in Visual C++; you must use the lowercase methods shown in Listings 6.3 and 6.4 to work with the nodes so that you can pass a pointer to the object.

The final consideration for this example is the data conversion techniques used to work with Amazon Web Services. Notice the use of the `AllocSysString()` method to create the `BSTR` values Amazon Web Services requires. Also notice how the code uses the `_variant_t((IUnknown*)Connector->OutputStream)` call to marshal the data from Amazon Web Services to Visual C++.

Developing with Visual Basic .NET

Visual Basic .NET isn't the same language as Visual Basic 6—the two are so different that many developers gave up trying to move code from one to the other. Many of the changes in Visual Basic .NET are actually advantageous, especially for Amazon Web Services application designers. For example, you have better access to the low-level details of your application now. In addition, Visual Basic .NET comes with many Web service support items built in. The following sections discuss how to use Visual Basic .NET to work with Amazon Web Services.

Creating a Web Reference

Visual Studio .NET introduces a number of automation features. One of these features is the ability to create a reference to a DLL, EXE, service, or other form of executable code both locally and remotely. One type of remote reference relies on Web services. You'll see this feature listed as a Web Reference in Solution Explorer. Use the following steps to create a reference to Amazon Web Services.

1. Right-click the project entry in Solution Explorer and choose Add Web Reference from the context menu. You'll see an Add Web Reference dialog box similar to the one shown in Figure 6.6. Notice that this dialog box already has the URL for Amazon Web Services WSDL file entered.
2. Type **`http://soap.amazon.com/schemas3/AmazonWebServices.wsdl`** in the URL field as shown in Figure 6.6. Click Go. After a few minutes, the Add Web Reference dialog box will display a list of methods available on Amazon Web Services as shown in Figure 6.7.

FIGURE 6.6: The Add Web Reference dialog box helps you create a connection to Amazon Web Services.

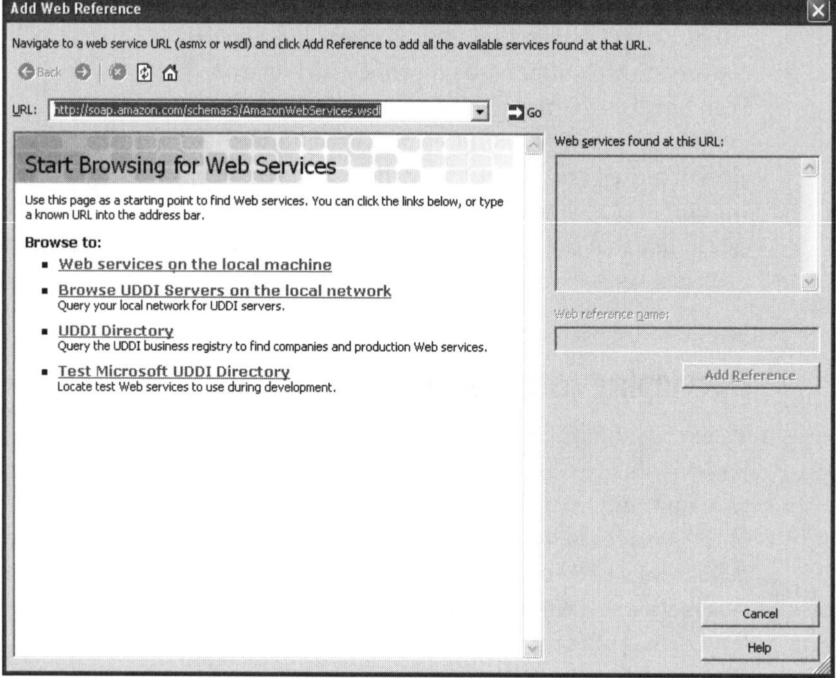

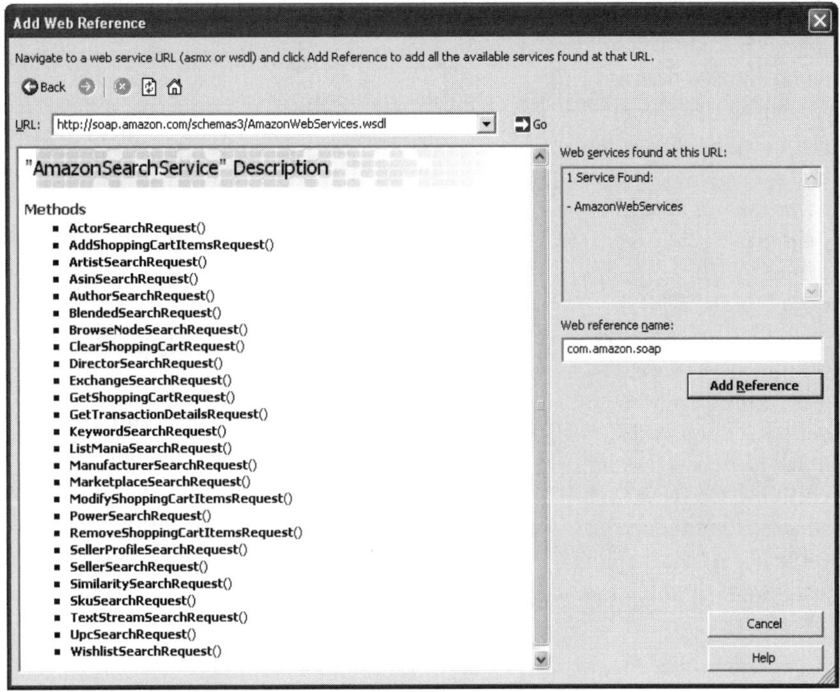

FIGURE 6.7: Scroll through the list of Amazon Web Services methods to learn more about it.

3. Type a new name for the reference in the Web Reference Name field if desired. The only time you need to perform this task is when you think your application could experience a naming conflict or you want to change the name to match your application better. The examples in this chapter will use the default name of `com.amazon.soap`.
4. Click Add Reference. After a few moments, you'll see a new reference added to Solution Explorer like the one shown in Figure 6.8.

FIGURE 6.8: Check Solution Explorer for the new Web reference once the IDE finishes its work.

> **▶ TIP**
>
> If you don't own Visual Studio .NET, but would like to try it out, you can find a 60-day demonstration version at `http://msdn.microsoft.com/vstudio/productinfo/trial/default.aspx`. All you need to do is order the CD and install it. You can also find an online trial of Visual Studio .NET at `http://msdn.microsoft.com/vstudio/tryit/`. In general, the 60-day trial version is a better option when working with Amazon Web Services.

Adding the Web reference also adds a new file to the project. You'll find this file in the `\Chapter 06\AmazonQuery\Web References\com.amazon.soap` folder for the example in this section. The `References.VB` file contains all the information your application needs to interact with Amazon Web Services. Other languages will create similar folders and reference files. It's interesting to look through this file to see how the Web service reference works. However, make sure you don't change any of the code in the file if you do open it. Changes can cause the Web service interface to stop working.

Defining the Request in Terms of a Function

Once you create a reference for Visual Basic .NET, accessing Amazon Web Services is very similar to any other type of function access you might require. An application uses functions to access the Web service, generates exceptions when you pass an invalid request, and returns the resulting data in a structure. The example shown in Listing 6.5 demonstrates all three basic tasks. Pay special attention to the technique used to catch errors—most examples in the book won't include this extra code for the sake of clarity. You'll find this example in the `\Chapter 06\AmazonQuery` folder of the source code located on the Sybex Web site.

Listing 6.5 Creating a Request from Visual Basic

```
Private Sub btnTest_Click(ByVal sender As System.Object, _
                          ByVal e As System.EventArgs) _
                          Handles btnTest.Click
   Dim AR As AuthorRequest                ' The author request.
   Dim PI As ProductInfo                  ' Data returned from request.
   Dim Service As AmazonSearchService     ' Connection to the service.
   Dim Counter As Int32                   ' Loop counter
   Dim Output As StringBuilder            ' Output data

   ' Instantiate the objects.
   AR = New AuthorRequest
   PI = New ProductInfo
   Service = New AmazonSearchService

   ' Create the author request.
   AR.author = txtAuthor.Text
   AR.devtag = txtTag.Text
   AR.mode = txtMode.Text
   AR.page = txtPage.Text
   AR.type = cbType.Text
```

```
AR.tag = "webservices-20"  ' Use the default associate tag.

' Add optional request items as needed.
If txtKeywords.Text.Length > 0 Then
   AR.keywords = txtKeywords.Text
End If
If txtLocale.Text.Length > 0 Then
   If Int32.Parse(txtLocale.Text) > 0 Then
      AR.locale = txtLocale.Text
   End If
End If
If txtPrice.Text.Length > 0 Then
   AR.price = txtPrice.Text
End If
If Not (cbSort.Text = "None") Then
   Select Case (cbSort.Text)
      Case "Featured Items"
         AR.sort = "+pmrank"
      Case "Bestselling"
         AR.sort = "+salesrank"
      Case "Average Customer Review"
         AR.sort = "+reviewrank"
      Case "Price (Low to High)"
         AR.sort = "+pricerank"
      Case "Price (High to Low)"
         AR.sort = "+inverse-pricerank"
      Case "Publication Date"
         AR.sort = "+daterank"
      Case "Alphabetical(A - Z)"
         AR.sort = "+titlerank"
      Case "Alphabetical(Z - A)"
         AR.sort = "-titlerank"
   End Select
End If

' Make the request.
Try
   PI = Service.AuthorSearchRequest(AR)
Catch SOAPErr As System.Web.Services.Protocols.SoapException

   ' Handle any SOAP errors.
   MessageBox.Show(SOAPErr.Code.ToString() + vbCrLf + _
                   SOAPErr.Message + vbCrLf + _
                   SOAPErr.Detail.InnerText, _
                   "Amazon Request Error", _
                   MessageBoxButtons.OK, _
                   MessageBoxIcon.Error)

   ' Exit the routine.
   Exit Sub
End Try
```

```
    ' Display a result.
    Output = New StringBuilder
    For Counter = 0 To PI.Details.Length - 1
       Output.Append(PI.Details(Counter).ProductName)
       Output.Append(vbCrLf)
    Next
    MessageBox.Show(Output.ToString, _
                    "Book List", _
                    MessageBoxButtons.OK, _
                    MessageBoxIcon.Information)

End Sub
```

When you create a reference to Amazon Web Services, the Visual Studio IDE creates a file with all the structures and function call declarations you need. You use the data structure that matches the request. In this case, the application creates an `AuthorRequest` object, `AR`. The code begins by getting all of the required data from the input form and placing it in `AR`.

One of the things you'll notice immediately is that the `AuthorRequest` class has more fields than the SOAP documentation provided by Amazon would seem to allow. The example code shows how these optional fields come into play. It places any additional information into `AR` as you define it on screen, which means that you'll normally leave these entries blank.

Notice the special handling of the `AR.sort` field. The text you need to pass to Amazon as part of the request is difficult to read and isn't very consistent. For example, a price sort uses `+pricerank` for low to high and `+inverse-pricerank` for high to low. Yet, an alphabetical search uses `+titlerank` and `-titlerank` for essentially the same kinds of search. The example uses understandable phrases for the search order, as you should for any application you create.

Once the code creates the `AuthorRequest` object, it makes the request. Notice the code creates an `AmazonSearchService` object, `Service`, for this task. This object contains a complete list of Amazon Web Services methods. If the call fails, then CLR raises a `System.Web.Services.Protocols.SoapException` exception that includes the fault code, fault message, fault actor, and fault detail elements from the SOAP response. This code shows how you can use this information to display an error message on screen.

The example ends by parsing the information returned from the search. In this case, the code simply presents a dialog box containing the names of the books returned by the search.

Understanding the .NET Difference

Once you build a few Amazon Web Services applications with Visual Studio 6 and Visual Studio .NET, you begin to notice the .NET difference. Most developers find that Visual Studio .NET languages as a whole reduce the labor required to work with Amazon Web Services and present the data in a pleasing way. Microsoft went through a lot of effort to increase developer productivity and reduce labor-intensive actions. It would seem that an upgrade to Visual Studio .NET would instantly reap large rewards for any developer making the change.

The problem is that the decision isn't nearly as easy as Microsoft would have you believe. Other sections of the chapter have already discussed obvious benefits of using Visual Studio 6, such as the ability to output native code whenever you need it. Not every Windows machine has the .NET Framework installed and many won't ever have the .NET Framework, which means a .NET application is useless on these machines. However, you must think about several subtle issues when considering the .NET difference.

> **WARNING**
>
> The one additional field that doesn't seem to work is `AR.price`. In many cases, using this field will generate a Bad Request error. Using the `AR.locale` field can also prove tricky—make sure you verify the input is a number and optionally that it matches one of the recognized locale identifiers (LCIDs). You can find a list of LCIDs at `http://www.microsoft.com/globaldev/reference/lcid-all.mspx`. Make sure you pass the decimal value as a string. For example, the LCID for United States English is 1033.

One of the most important issues is the matter of debugging. You'll notice that the Microsoft SOAP Toolkit contains a Transmission Control Protocol (TCP) tracing tool so that you can see the interaction of your system with Amazon Web Services. The low-level debugging offered by this tool lets you check the precise format of the message and ensure compatibility problems aren't the cause of a miscommunication. The .NET package offers no such solution and you'll find that it's very hard to implement such a solution because you don't have full knowledge of the code.

This brings up the second problem with the .NET solution. The IDE generates a lot of the code you need in the background. This feature is good because it decreases development time. It can also reduce programming errors by reducing the amount of custom code a developer creates. However, the negative side is that you don't really know much about that code. When an error occurs, the debugger could take you to an area of that code and you might not have any idea of how to fix the problem. Even if you could fix the problem, the fact that the IDE generates this code automatically means you might revisit the problem more than once because the IDE could break whatever you fixed by regenerating the code.

Whether the .NET solution is the one you need depends on what you want out of your Amazon Web Services programming experience. The .NET solution is definitely better in more ways that this book will discuss. For example, you can't easily generate the applications found in Chapter 9 using Visual Studio 6—it just doesn't include the required projects and support. However, it's important to weigh the cost. This chapter shows both kinds of development side by side so that you can make a good decision on which programming language product to use for your Amazon Web Services application.

Developing with Visual C# .NET

Visual C# .NET is a new language that made its appearance as part of Visual Studio .NET. The language combines the flexibility of C++ with some of the programmer productivity benefits of using Visual Basic. In addition, it bears a striking resemblance to Java in many ways. In fact, many developers say that C# is Microsoft's attempt to create something as useful as Java.

No matter how you feel about C#, it's a capable language that lets you perform some tasks that Visual Basic .NET doesn't. For example, Visual Basic doesn't let you create unsafe code—that is, code that contains unmanaged pointers. C# lets you create such code so that you can perform some low-level tasks that Visual Basic isn't designed to perform. From an Amazon Web Services perspective, the two languages are probably equivalent and the choice of language comes down to coding style. However, it's important to keep the differences between Visual Basic and C# in mind if you plan to create a complex application. The following sections show how to create a basic C# Amazon Web Services application.

> **NOTE**
>
> Use the information contained in the "Creating a Web Reference" section of the chapter to create a reference to Amazon Web Services. You won't be able to create the code as shown in this section without the reference. Creating a Web reference is the same for all versions of Visual Studio, so you could use this information with any .NET language, including languages like PERL.NET.

Defining a Simple Request

Many developers have moved to C# because it provides a superb combination of flexibility, low-level access, and developer productivity aids. In general, you won't need the extra power of C# to access Amazon Web Services—that part is actually simple compared to data manipulation. What you do with the data is important because it determines the user's perception of that data. The example in this section focuses on the access portion of the picture. However, unlike the Visual Basic example in the "Defining the Request in Terms of a Function" section, this example will focus a little on data presentation techniques.

Listing 6.6 demonstrates the basic techniques for accessing Amazon Web Services from C#. In this case, the example concentrates on essential inputs and doesn't provide error handling. The output is a `DataSet` used to fill a `DataGrid`. You'll find this example in the `\Chapter 06\SimpleSOAP` folder of the source code located on the Sybex Web site.

Listing 6.6 Defining a Request with C#

```
private void btnTest_Click(object sender, System.EventArgs e)
{
   AuthorRequest        AR;      // The author request.
   ProductInfo          PI;      // Data returned from request.
   AmazonSearchService  Service; // Connection to the service.
   DataRow              DR;      // Output data.
   Int32                Counter; // Loop counting variable.

   // Instantiate the objects.
   AR = new AuthorRequest();
   PI = new ProductInfo();
   Service = new AmazonSearchService();

   // Create the author request.
   AR.author = txtAuthor.Text;
   AR.devtag = txtTag.Text;
   AR.mode = txtMode.Text;
   AR.page = txtPage.Text;
   AR.type = txtType.Text;

   // Make the request.
   PI = Service.AuthorSearchRequest(AR);

   // Display the results on screen.
   for (Counter = 0; Counter < PI.Details.Length; Counter++)
   {
      // Create a new row to hold the data.
      DR = dsAmazon.Tables["AuthorOut"].NewRow();

      // Add the data to the row.
      DR["Book Title"] = PI.Details[Counter].ProductName;
      DR["ISBN"] = PI.Details[Counter].Asin;
      DR["Release Date"] = PI.Details[Counter].ReleaseDate;
      DR["Publisher"] = PI.Details[Counter].Manufacturer;

      // Display the row on screen.
      dsAmazon.Tables["AuthorOut"].Rows.Add(DR);
   }
}
```

The example begins by creating an `AuthorRequest` object, `AR`. As with Visual Basic .NET, C# builds a number of classes to hold various kinds of data. This example shows the minimum number of inputs you can provide for a SOAP request. Interestingly enough, an XML over HTTP request would probably fail if you didn't include the associate tag value, but a SOAP request works fine. (Amazon is addressing this problem.) You must include the author name, developer tag, search mode, return page, and the search type as shown.

The code makes the information request from Amazon Web Services and returns the data in the `ProductInfo` object, `PI`. This example shows how you can place the data into a `DataSet`. Notice the use of the `NewRow()` method to create an individual row, which the code fills with data, and then adds to the `DataSet` using the `Add()` method. The `DataGrid` automatically reflects any changes to the `DataSet`. Figure 6.9 shows the output from this application.

FIGURE 6.9:

Check Solution Explorer for the new Web reference once the IDE finishes its work.

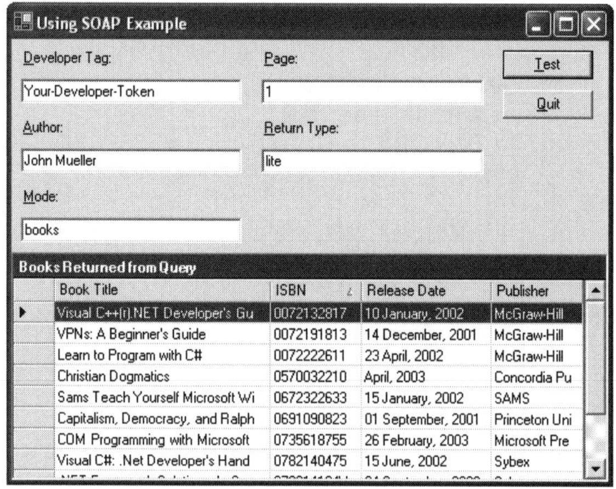

Working with Web Servers

You can easily create desktop applications that access Amazon Web Services. In many cases, a desktop application is the right solution. However, you might find that a Web application can do the job more efficiently or with fewer problems in some cases. For example, your company might decide that it needs to support more than one platform. In this case, a Web application is a good answer because you can write a single application to support multiple platforms. This chapter can't provide a full discussion of the merits of using Web applications versus desktop applications, but both have their place. The following sections provide details on using both Active Server Pages (ASP) and ASP.NET to create an Amazon Web Services application for your IIS server.

Creating an ASP Application

Most ASP applications can use the low-level SOAP method to good advantage. This technique is friendly to resource management and faster than the XML over HTTP technique. However, it does require more code to implement, so you have to weigh the advantages of each technique. If you decide to use the XML over HTTP technique, Listing 3.2 will provide you with everything you need.

You implement a SOAP design for an ASP page in three phases. The first phase is to create the object references. Make sure you have the Microsoft SOAP Toolkit installed on the server or ASP won't find the component. Here is the code required to create the reference (make sure you change the locations to match your machine configuration).

```
<!--METADATA TYPE="TypeLib"
FILE="D:\WINDOWS\System32\msxml4.dll"
-->
<!--METADATA TYPE="TypeLib"
FILE="D:\Program Files\Common Files\MSSoap\Binaries\MSSOAP30.dll"
-->
```

The second phase of this example is to retrieve the data from Amazon Web Services. The example shown in Listing 6.7 shows the second phase. You'll find this example in the `\Chapter 06\ASPExample` folder of the source code located on the Sybex Web site.

Listing 6.7 Accessing Amazon Using ASP

```
Dim Connector       ' Connection to Web Service
Dim DataSend        ' Sends data to Amazon.
Dim DataReceive     ' Receives data from Amazon.
Dim Details         ' Contains all of the detail nodes.
Dim CurrentBook     ' Contains just one book.
Dim BookDetails     ' Details for one book.
Dim BookItem        ' An individual book detail.

' Create a connection to Amazon.
Set Connector = CreateObject("MSSOAP.HttpConnector30")
Connector.Property("EndPointURL") = "http://soap.amazon.com/onca/soap3"
Connector.Property("SoapAction") = "http://soap.amazon.com"

' Tell Amazon that the application is sending a request.
Connector.BeginMessage

' Associate the data serializer with the connection.
Set DataSend = CreateObject("MSSOAP.SoapSerializer30")
DataSend.Init Connector.InputStream

' Start creating a request, including the SOAP envelope.
With DataSend

   ' Create the envelope and associated namespaces.
   .StartEnvelope
   .SoapAttribute "xmlns:xsi", , _
                  "http://www.w3.org/2001/XMLSchema-instance"
   .SoapAttribute "xmlns:xsd", , _
                  "http://www.w3.org/2001/XMLSchema"
   .SoapAttribute "SOAP-ENV:encodingStyle", , _
                  "http://schemas.xmlsoap.org/soap/encoding/"
```

```
      ' Create the SOAP body.
      .StartBody

      ' Start creating the request.
      .StartElement "namesp1:AuthorSearchRequest"
      .SoapAttribute "xmlns:namesp1", , "urn:PI/DevCentral/SoapService"
      .StartElement "AuthorSearchRequest"

      ' Add the author information.
      .StartElement "author"
      if Request.QueryString("AuthorSearch") = "" then
         .WriteString "John Mueller"
      else
         .WriteString Request.QueryString("AuthorSearch")
      end if
      .EndElement

      ... Other Elements ...

      ' Close all of the open tags.
      .EndElement
      .EndElement
      .EndBody
      .EndEnvelope
   End With

   ' Tell Amazon the request is complete.
   Connector.EndMessage

   ' Receive the response from Amazon.
   Set DataReceive = CreateObject("MSSOAP.SoapReader30")
   DataReceive.Load Connector.OutputStream

   ' Return the data.
   Set Details = DataReceive.RpcResult.childNodes(2).childNodes
```

This example works similarly to the Visual Basic example described in the "Developing with Visual Basic 6" section, but there are definite differences. For one thing, you don't define variable types—you just define the variables. The code also can't make assumptions that a Visual Basic developer could make. It's impossible to know whether the user will supply any inputs, so you need to provide default values. Consequently, the code checks for user input using the `Request.QueryString` property. Supply an index to this property to retrieve a specific value as shown in the code.

The one other item to note is that you can't use the `New` operator. You must use the `CreateObject()` method to create the various objects. Notice that the code uses both the component and class name as you would normally. Even the latest SOAP functionality appears as part of the `MSSOAP` component as shown in the code.

The third phase of this example is to display the code on screen. This part is definitely different from anything else in the chapter because you have to create HTML output, rather than text. Listing 6.8 shows typical code for this type of output in tabular form.

Listing 6.8 Creating ASP Output Based on Amazon Data

```
<%
' Process the data retrieved from the Web site.
For Each CurrentBook In Details

   ' Output a row tag.
   Response.Write("<tr>")

   ' Get the book details.
   Set BookDetails = CurrentBook.childNodes

   ' Look for specific book items.
   For Each BookItem In BookDetails

      ' Determine which action to take.
      Select Case BookItem.baseName
         Case "Asin"
            Response.Write("<td>")
            Response.Write(BookItem.Text)
            Response.Write("</td>")
            Response.Write(vbCrLf)
         ... Other Cases ...
      End Select
   Next

   ' Output the closing row tag.
   Response.Write("</tr>")
   Response.Write(vbCrLf)
Next
%>
```

Fortunately, ASP supports the `For Each...Next` statement, which makes processing the data a lot easier. You need to output each item individually. Trying to concatenate the strings usually results in errors. I include the carriage returns in the output to make the result easier to read for debugging purposes, but you don't have to add this information. Figure 6.10 shows the output from this application.

Creating an ASP.NET Application

The example in this section lets you perform a manufacturer search. Some manufacturers, such as Microsoft, can appear in more than one product category or mode. This means that the mode entry that has remained somewhat useless for other examples in the book now has a new meaning. It also means you have to become familiar with the modes that Amazon supports. You can find a list of modes in the "Common Modes and Browse IDs" help topic of the Amazon Web Services Toolkit at `/AmazonWebServices/API Guide/common_modes.htm`.

> **NOTE**
>
> Use the information contained in the "Creating a Web Reference" section of the chapter to create a reference to Amazon Web Services. You won't be able to create the code as shown in this section without the reference.

One issue you must be careful about is the international implication of modes. Not every country supports all modes and every country uses a different mode for the same product category. For example, only the United States site supports a universal mode. The United Kingdom site supports the toys-uk mode that is the same as the toys mode in the United States site and that no other country supports this mode as of this writing.

Now that you have some idea of how this example will work, look at Listing 6.9. You'll find this example in the `\Chapter 06\ASP_NET_Example` folder of the source code located on the Sybex Web site.

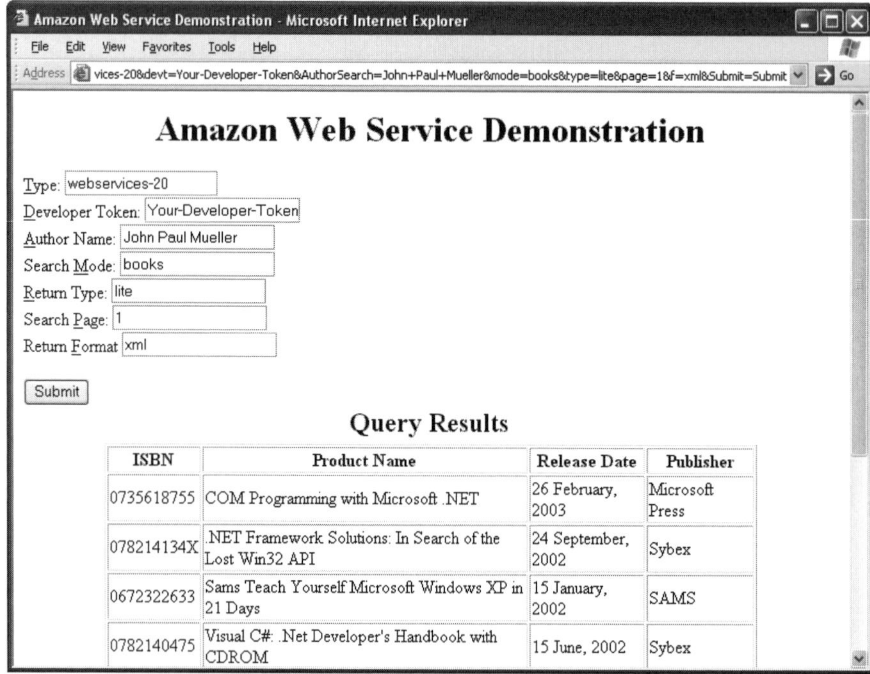

ISBN	Product Name	Release Date	Publisher
0735618755	COM Programming with Microsoft .NET	26 February, 2003	Microsoft Press
078214134X	.NET Framework Solutions: In Search of the Lost Win32 API	24 September, 2002	Sybex
0672322633	Sams Teach Yourself Microsoft Windows XP in 21 Days	15 January, 2002	SAMS
0782140475	Visual C#: .Net Developer's Handbook with CDROM	15 June, 2002	Sybex

FIGURE 6.10: An ASP page can provide an effective way to work with Amazon from your Web server.

Listing 6.9 Using ASP.NET to Perform a Manufacturer Search

```
private void btnSubmit_Click(object sender, System.EventArgs e)
{
   ManufacturerRequest  MR;      // The manufacturer request.
   ProductInfo          PI;      // Data returned from request.
   AmazonSearchService  Service; // Connection to the service.
   TableRow             TR;      // A table row.
   TableCell            TC;      // Individual table item.
   Int32                Counter; // Loop counting variable.

   // Instantiate the objects.
   MR = new ManufacturerRequest();
   PI = new ProductInfo();
   Service = new AmazonSearchService();

   // Create the author request.
   MR.manufacturer = txtManufacturer.Text;
   MR.devtag = txtDevTag.Text;
   MR.mode = txtMode.Text;
   MR.page = txtPage.Text;
   MR.type = txtType.Text;
   MR.tag = txtTag.Text;

   // Make the request.
   PI = Service.ManufacturerSearchRequest(MR);

   // Display the results on screen.
   for (Counter = 0; Counter < PI.Details.Length; Counter++)
   {
      // Add a new row.
      TR = new TableRow();

      // Create the ASIN cell.
      TC = new TableCell();
      TC.Controls.Add(new LiteralControl(PI.Details[Counter].Asin));
      TR.Cells.Add(TC);

      // Create the Product Name cell.
      TC = new TableCell();
      TC.Controls.Add(
         new LiteralControl(PI.Details[Counter].ProductName));
      TR.Cells.Add(TC);

      // Create the List Price cell.
      TC = new TableCell();
      TC.Controls.Add(
         new LiteralControl(PI.Details[Counter].ListPrice));
      TR.Cells.Add(TC);
```

```
            // Add the row to the table.
            tblOutput.Rows.Add(TR);
        }
    }
```

This example works essentially the same as a desktop C# application. The code creates the required request structure, instantiates the Amazon Search Service, and then makes the request. The `ProductInfo` data structure holds the information on return from the call, unless the application experiences an error. However, the similarities end at this point.

To make this example work, you must use ASP controls on your form. Otherwise, the code behind application has a very hard time reading the data values (you can still access them, but it's more work than you really need to perform). However, notice that you can access these controls just as you would the controls on a desktop application form. The only difference is that you need the connection between the Web form and your application.

The code creates HTML output, which means you need some type of ASP control that emulates a grid for the Web application. The example uses the `Table` control. You can theoretically create a `DataSet` and use a `DataGrid` control, but using a `DataGrid` is overkill for this application. Notice how the application uses the `LiteralControl` instead of another control such as a `Label`. You can use other controls, but the `LiteralControl` works best in most situations because it represents HTML data that doesn't require processing on the server. Figure 6.11 shows typical output from this application. It's interesting to make changes to the mode, while leaving the rest of the request the same. For example, you'll see a big difference with Microsoft when you select video games and books.

Using the ASP.NET Applications in this Book

All of the ASP.NET applications in this book follow the same pattern as the example in the "Creating an ASP.NET Application" section of the chapter. You'll find two folders associated with every example on the Sybex Web site. The first folder, such as `\Chapter 06\ASP_NET_Example`, contains the files that you should place on your development machine. The second folder, such as `\Chapter 06\ASP_NET_Example (Server)`, contains the files that you should place on your Web server in the appropriate `\Inetpub\wwwroot` folder.

Once you place the files on your system, open the SLN (Solution) file for the project using a plain text editor such as Notepad. The top of this file will contain several lines of information similar to the ones shown here:

```
Microsoft Visual Studio Solution File, Format Version 8.00
Project("{FAE04EC0-301F-11D3-BF4B-00C04F79EFBC}") = "ASP_NET_Example",
"http://winserver/0161/Chapter6/ASP_NET_Example/ASP_NET_Example.csproj"
```

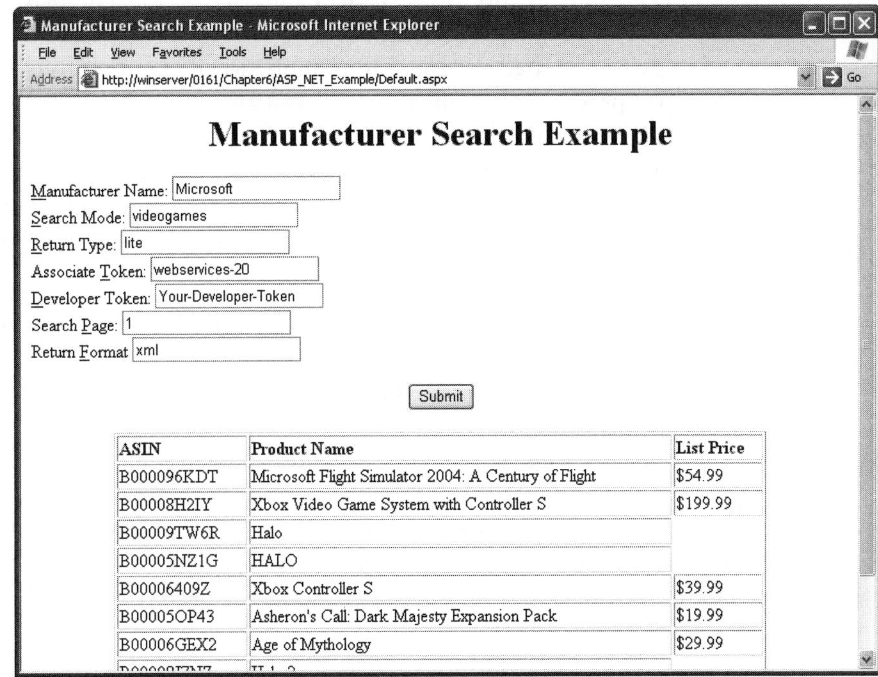

FIGURE 6.11: The results of a manufacturer search vary by product mode.

Change the URL on the third line to match the location of the files on your Web server. Once you make this change, save and close the file. When you open the SLN file, the Visual Studio .NET IDE will automatically open the correct project files on your Web server. This technique lets you use a single machine by changing the Web server to localhost if desired. Make sure you recompile the application using the Rebuild Solution option to ensure that all of the compiled references also match your server setup.

Using Microsoft Access as a Database

In many cases, it's just not efficient or convenient to query Amazon Web Services for every need. For example, when you plan to perform lengthy analysis of some product online, you don't want to query Amazon again for every calculation—it's just inefficient. Likewise, when you want to take some product information on the road, you'll need a database to store it because it's just not convenient (or even possible) to query Amazon from a remote location. In other cases, you need to store the data to build a data store of information over time, such as when you want to perform analysis of sales data.

The storage requirements for an Amazon query aren't that complex or demanding, unless you want to save every bit of information. In general, you only need to save the information needed to perform a specific task. For example, when you want to track the sales ranking for a group of products, you only need to maintain a list of the ASIN and the sales ranking elements. You might also want to keep track of the product name and manufacturer, but you wouldn't need all of the sales data unless this information is also part of the statistics you need. Because you can reduce the storage elements to a simple subset of the data that Amazon returns, it's possible to use products such as Microsoft Access for temporary or even long-term storage.

The example in this section assumes that you want to track statistical information, but don't want to store it in an Excel spreadsheet as in the example in the "Defining Graphs and Charts" section of Chapter 5. The Access database stores the date, ASIN, and sales rank information over a number of days. A second table relates the ASIN to a book title. The C# application manipulates the data directly. Although you could create this example as a Notification Area application so that the program could detect the time and download the information directly, the example forgoes the complexity and simply lets you get the data as needed. Listing 6.10 contains the important code for this example. You'll find the complete source code for this example in the `\Chapter 06\Access Storage` folder of the source code located on the Sybex Web site.

Listing 6.10 Using Access for Short-Term Data Storage

```
private void btnAddISBN_Click(object sender, System.EventArgs e)
{
   FrmISBN               GetISBN; // Used to get the ISBN.
   AmazonSearchService   Service; // The search service.
   AsinRequest           AR;      // The request data.
   ProductInfo           PI;      // Data returned from search.

   // Create and display the dialog box.
   GetISBN = new FrmISBN("Enter a New ISBN");
   if (GetISBN.ShowDialog() == DialogResult.OK)
   {
      // Create the service.
      Service = new AmazonSearchService();

      // Get the ASIN from Amazon to determine the book title.
      AR = new AsinRequest();
      AR.asin = GetISBN.NewISBN;
      AR.devtag = "Your-Developer-Token";
      AR.mode = "books";
      AR.tag = "webservices-20";
      AR.type = "heavy";
      PI = Service.AsinSearchRequest(AR);
```

```
        // Verify the search worked.
        if (PI.Details[0].ProductName == null)
        {
           // If not, display an error and exit.
           MessageBox.Show("Nonexistent ISBN",
                           "Search Error",
                           MessageBoxButtons.OK,
                           MessageBoxIcon.Error);
           return;
        }

        // Use the new ISBN to create a BookTitle table entry.
        dsAmazon.BookTitle.AddBookTitleRow(GetISBN.NewISBN,
                                           PI.Details[0].ProductName);
        daBookTitle.Update(dsAmazon.BookTitle);

        // Also add the first scanned information to the DataStore table.
        dsAmazon.DataStore.AddDataStoreRow(GetISBN.NewISBN,
                                           PI.Details[0].SalesRank,
                                           DateTime.Now);
        daDataStore.Update(dsAmazon.DataStore);

        // Refresh the data grid.
        dsAmazon.DataView.Clear();
        daDataView.Fill(dsAmazon.DataView);
     }
     else
        // Tell the user the action was cancelled.
        MessageBox.Show("Action Cancelled by User",
                        "ISBN Result",
                        MessageBoxButtons.OK,
                        MessageBoxIcon.Exclamation);
  }

  private void btnGetData_Click(object sender, System.EventArgs e)
  {
     AmazonSearchService  Service; // The search service.
     AsinRequest          AR;      // The request data.
     ProductInfo          PI;      // Data returned from search.

     // Create the search service and request structure.
     Service = new AmazonSearchService();
     AR = new AsinRequest();

     // Verify there are ASINs to scan.
     if (dsAmazon.BookTitle.Rows.Count == 0)
     {
        // If not, display an error and exit.
        MessageBox.Show("Enter some ISBN (ASIN) numbers to scan!",
                        "Database Error",
                        MessageBoxButtons.OK,
```

```
                         MessageBoxIcon.Error);
         return;
      }

      // Process each ASIN in turn.
      foreach (DataRow DR in dsAmazon.BookTitle.Rows)
      {
         // Get the ASIN from Amazon to determine the book title.
         AR.asin = DR.ItemArray[0].ToString();
         AR.devtag = "Your-Developer-Token";
         AR.mode = "books";
         AR.tag = "webservices-20";
         AR.type = "heavy";
         PI = Service.AsinSearchRequest(AR);

         // Add the scanned information to the DataStore table.
         dsAmazon.DataStore.AddDataStoreRow(DR.ItemArray[0].ToString(),
                                            PI.Details[0].SalesRank,
                                            DateTime.Now);
         daDataStore.Update(dsAmazon.DataStore);
      }

      // Refresh the data grid.
      dsAmazon.DataView.Clear();
      daDataView.Fill(dsAmazon.DataView);
   }
```

The example includes two important functions. The first, `btnAddISBN_Click()`, adds new ISBNs to the list of ISBNs to process (not shown is a function for removing old ISBNs). The second, `btnGetData_Click()`, scans all of the ISBNs you've selected and obtains their current sales rank. Both examples rely on the `AsinSearchRequest()` method to obtain information for individual books. However, you can use the same function to retrieve information for any ASIN, not just books. If you want to track Braun shaver sales, you can do that using the same technique shown here—all you need is the ASIN from the Amazon Web site.

The `btnAddISBN_Click()` method begins by displaying a form that requests an ISBN from the user. You can easily ask for an ASIN or other identifying information. The code determines whether the user entered a value and clicked OK. It then fills out the `AsinRequest` fields with data. Notice that the only input the user need provide is the ASIN in the form of an ISBN. To obtain sales rank information, you must use a heavy search as shown in the code.

Once the function returns, the code determines whether the `ProductInfo` object contains a `ProductName` field entry. You might think that you could use the `TotalResults` field for this check, but the `AsinSearchRequest()` method doesn't fill this field out—it's always `null`. The code adds the data returned in `PI` to the `BookTitle` and `DataStore` tables, which act as input to the `DataView` query used for display purposes. The reason the code doesn't interact directly with the query is that this approach can cause problems—the data adapter for an Access query usually doesn't provide complete functionality.

The code ends by refreshing the `DataGrid` object content indirectly through the `DataView` query data adapter. You must use the `Clear()` method to get rid of the current results before you update the information using the `Fill()` method. Figure 6.12 shows typical results of using this application. Notice that you can sort the information as needed to track the sales rank. You could also use the Access database as input to Excel to chart the sales information.

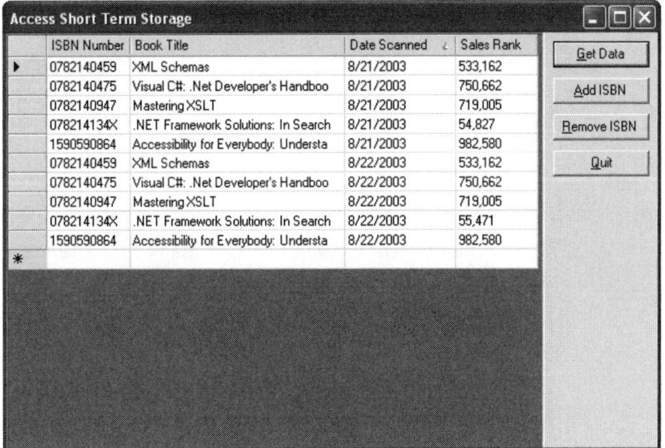

Access Short Term Storage
ISBN Number
Book Title
Date Scanned
Sales Rank
0782140459 XML Schemas 8/21/2003 533,162
0782140475 Visual C#: .Net Developer's Handboo 8/21/2003 750,662
0782140947 Mastering XSLT 8/21/2003 719,005
078214134X .NET Framework Solutions: In Search 8/21/2003 54,827
1590590864 Accessibility for Everybody: Understa 8/21/2003 982,580
0782140459 XML Schemas 8/22/2003 533,162
0782140475 Visual C#: .Net Developer's Handboo 8/22/2003 750,662
0782140947 Mastering XSLT 8/22/2003 719,005
078214134X .NET Framework Solutions: In Search 8/22/2003 55,471
1590590864 Accessibility for Everybody: Understa 8/22/2003 982,580
Get Data
Add ISBN
Remove ISBN
Quit

FIGURE 6.12: The application stores the sales rank information for selected books over time.

Using SQL Server as a Database

You can use SQL Server for long- or short-term storage of Amazon data. The enterprise nature of this database makes it easier for multiple users to share the same data, which can make statistical analysis and other types of data use easier and more efficient. However, SQL Server isn't exactly portable, so you wouldn't use it as the data storage solution for your laptop. The differences in functionality between Access and SQL Server make one more appropriate than the other in some circumstances. Use SQL Server for large quantities of data shared by a number of people and Access for more personalized storage that requires some level of mobility.

The example in this section demonstrates the storage capability of SQL Server using C#. The application first checks for required data in the SQL Server database. If the data isn't present or it's outdated, the application requests the information from Amazon Web Services. In this case, the application stores the data within SQL Server for future use. As with the

Access example in the "Using Microsoft Access as a Database" section, this example doesn't store all of the data returned by the query—it only returns the subset of data the company actually needs. However, the application stores more data because more than one user and application needs the information. Therefore, even if the current application can't use a particular piece of data, it still stores the data so everyone can use the same data store. Listing 6.11 contains the code for this example. You'll find this example in the `\Chapter 06\SQL Server Storage` folder of the source code located on the Sybex Web site.

Listing 6.11 Using SQL Server for Long-Term Data Storage

```
private void btnTest_Click(object sender, System.EventArgs e)
{
   dsAmazon.DataStoreRow   DSR;         // DataRow containing request.
   MemoryStream            PictStrm;    // Memory stream for image.
   Bitmap                  Pict;        // Bitmap form of image.

   // Get the data.
   DSR = dsAmazon.DataStore.FindByUPC(txtUPC.Text);

   // If the data isn't available locally, generate a request.
   if (DSR == null)
   {
      GenerateRequest();
      return;
   }

   // If the data is too old, erase the old data and
   // generate a request.
   if (DSR.Scanned.AddHours(24) < DateTime.Now)
   {
      DSR.Delete();
      GenerateRequest();
      return;
   }

   // The data is available and isn't too old, so use it.
   txtASIN.Text = DSR.ASIN;
   ... Other Display Code ...
   lblURL.Text = DSR.Product_URL;

   // Generate the picture.
   PictStrm = new MemoryStream(DSR.Picture);
   Pict = new Bitmap(PictStrm);
   pbAlbumCover.Image = Pict;

   // Close the memory stream.
   PictStrm.Close();
}
```

```
private void GenerateRequest()
{
   UpcRequest                Request;     // The UPC of the CD.
   AmazonSearchService       Service;     // Amazon Search Service
   ProductInfo               PI;          // Returned information.
   String                    PictStr;     // Product image.
   DiscoveryClientProtocol DCP;           // Download service for image.
   MemoryStream              PictStrm;    // Memory stream for image.
   Bitmap                    Pict;        // Bitmap form of image.

   // Create the service.
   Service = new AmazonSearchService();

   // Create and define the request.
   Request = new UpcRequest();
   Request.devtag = txtTag.Text;
   Request.mode = txtMode.Text;
   Request.tag = "webservices-20";
   Request.type = txtType.Text;
   Request.upc = txtUPC.Text;

   // Get the data.
   PI = Service.UpcSearchRequest(Request);

   // Add data to the appropriate places on screen.
   txtASIN.Text = PI.Details[0].Asin;
   ... Other Display Code ...
   lblURL.Text = PI.Details[0].Url;

   // Download the image from Amazon and place it in local memory.
   DCP = new DiscoveryClientProtocol();
   PictStrm = (MemoryStream)DCP.Download(ref PictStr);

   // Convert the MemoryStream into a Bitmap.
   Pict = new Bitmap(PictStrm);

   // Load the Bitmap into the PictureBox control.
   pbAlbumCover.Image = Pict;

   // Create a new row to hold the data in the database.
   dsAmazon.DataStore.AddDataStoreRow(
      txtASIN.Text,
      txtUPC.Text,
      txtName.Text,
      txtManufacturer.Text,
      txtAvailability.Text,
      lblURL.Text,
      Decimal.Parse(txtPrice.Text.Substring(1)),
      DateTime.Parse(txtReleaseDate.Text),
      PictStrm.GetBuffer(),
      DateTime.Now);
```

```
        // Update the row in the database.
        daDataStore.Update(dsAmazon.DataStore);

        // Close the MemoryStream.
        PictStrm.Close();
    }
```

The code begins with the `btnTest_Click()` method. The first task is to locate the UPC entered by the user in the `DataSet` retrieved from the database using a special `DataStoreRow` object created by the IDE for you. If this object is null after calling the `FindByUPC()` method, then the UPC doesn't exist in the `DataSet`. It's important to note that the `DataSet` can contain outdated information unless you clear and refill it as needed. Someone else might visit the same site, which makes the second trip unnecessary. When the code detects that the UPC is unavailable, it calls the `GenerateRequest()` method described later in this section.

The second check determines the data of the information in `DSR`. This check represents one way to abide by the licensing agreement for Amazon Web Services and still maintain high data availability. If the data in DSR is too old, the code deletes that row from the `DataSet` and calls `GenerateRequest()`.

At this point, the code displays the data on screen. For the most part, all the code needs to do is move data from DSR to the appropriate entry on screen. In some cases, this means performing some data translation because the database stores some information in a form that's convenient for analysis. Notice the technique used to transfer the CD cover image from the SQL Server database to the screen. You can use other, more direct, methods, but this technique ensures the image remains available in a multiuser environment, reduces the probability of error with individual images, and makes it easier to manipulate the image when necessary.

> **NOTE**
>
> Entering a UPC can be tricky if you don't understand how they work. Look at a UPC for a music CD and you'll see a 10-digit number immediately below the symbol. However, look to the left and right of this number and you'll see two, barely visible, numbers, for a total of 12-digits. You must include these two numbers as well. Otherwise, Amazon will fail to recognize the UPC as valid.

The `GenerateRequest()` method begins by creating a `UpcRequest` object. It uses this object to perform a `UpcSearchRequest()` call using the `AmazonSearchService` object. You'll notice that the `Request.mode` value can vary by music type. For example, you'd use a value of `classical` for classical music, and `music` for popular tunes. Using the incorrect value can result in a failed search, even when Amazon stocks the particular CD.

Once the request is complete, the code transfers data from `PI` to the display. This example also displays the product picture. However, `PI` only contains the URLs for the three sizes of product picture that Amazon supports—not the actual image. It's not difficult to display the product picture when working with a Web application, but a .NET desktop application requires a little more work. The example code shows one technique for obtaining the picture using a `DiscoveryClientProtocol` object. The `Download()` method obtains the image from the Amazon Web site and places it in a `MemoryStream` object, which is then displayed on screen.

At this point, the data appears on screen, but you also need to add it to the database so that other users can access the information. The example uses the `dsAmazon.DataStore.AddDataStoreRow()` method to perform this task. Notice that the record contains all of the data displayed on screen, plus the time the application scanned the information as a final entry. Figure 6.13 shows typical output from this application.

To test this application, you need to make the same request twice. Depending on the speed of your Internet connection, you may notice a significant difference in response times for this application between the first and second request. The second request is significantly faster because the application is using the local data store.

One other interesting feature to note in Figure 6.13 is the Product URL field. Notice that this field is an URL. If you click the field, the application will open a copy of your browser and load the page from the Amazon site. This particular feature can be very useful in a number of situations because the URL includes both your developer token and associate tag. Amazon creates this URL for you automatically as part of the request, so you don't have to create the URL manually.

FIGURE 6.13:

This application uses a database storage technique to make repeated searches faster.

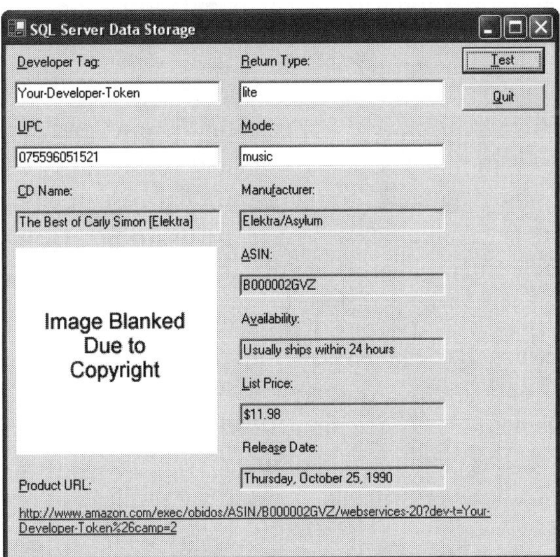

Writing a Program with Database Support

The two database applications in this chapter don't demonstrate everything you can do with Amazon Web Services, but they do demonstrate some important principles you need to consider as part of your development effort. The following list describes these issues.

Store Only What You Need The immediate temptation is to store every bit of information the `ProductInfo` structure can provide. However, most applications won't ever use all that information. Storing everything increases the size of the database and reduces application performance. More importantly, storing excess information increases the risk of application error because Amazon doesn't return every piece of data for every product or product type.

Perform Record Aging You must keep the database in synch with Amazon Web Services. This means performing some type of automatic aging as needed. Something as simple as storing a scanning (or download) date can help you keep the information updated. The easiest way to perform this task is to check the scan date before you use the record. However, you could also create a service for the server that performs scanning of the entire database for old records. This second technique is more complex, but ensures that the application doesn't fill the database with records that no one will ever use.

Trap Errant Results There's no guarantee that every request to Amazon Web Services will result in useful information. A user can detect problems immediately when an application doesn't include database support and make the request again. However, a database application could become corrupted during the request process and add errant data to the database. Consequently, database applications require an additional measure of error trapping.

Perform Automated Processing Whenever Possible It's often easier to automate the request process than ask the user to make the requests repeatedly. For example, you can store the requested information in a database when the user needs to make the request more than once. Using a database to store the request ensures the user can make the requests quickly and using precisely the same criteria every time. This technique ensures that you base any statistical analysis you perform on accurate information.

Convert Data to Convenient Types Amazon Web Services returns everything as a string. This data format works well for Web services because it's easier to transfer across firewalls. However, once the data arrives at your application, you need to convert it to a convenient type. Using the correct type reduces data storage requirements and can increase application performance because the application only has to perform the required conversion once.

Your Call to Action

This chapter demonstrates various techniques you can use to access Amazon Web Services using Visual Studio products such as Visual C++, Visual Basic, Visual Basic .NET, and Visual C#. Most developers will select one of these languages to create most applications, but all of them work well. The choice of language depends on personal taste and existing application infrastructure as much as the techniques for accessing Amazon Web Services. You also learned how to mix Visual Studio applications with SQL Server. In most cases, you'll use SQL Server for short-term storage of intermediate results or customer data. However, you can use SQL Server with Amazon as you would any other database application. The use of a database simply makes it easier to manipulate and analyze the data.

It's time to consider how you'll use Visual Studio to create applications to access Amazon Web Services. The choice of language is important because each language does excel in specific areas. Visual C++ is a great choice when application performance and flexibility are prime considerations, but Visual Basic provides the best database access for many purposes. Visual C# and Visual Basic both provide superior database access and developer productivity. However, the cost of using these products is that every machine that uses the resulting application must have the .NET Framework loaded. Because .NET is a relatively new programming technology, you can't make assumptions about the user's machine unless you have control over the machine configuration.

Chapter 7 is the first Web-specific chapter in the book. It demonstrates techniques for accessing Amazon Web Services using PHP. You'll find that working with PHP is relatively easy and that support for PHP is very good. Many developers create all of their Web applications in PHP because the language is so popular and short-term costs so low. Whether PHP is the right solution for your Amazon Web Services application or not depends on how you plan to work with Amazon Web Services in the long term. Chapter 7 can help you make a good decision about the viability of using PHP for your Amazon Web Services project.

Chapter 7

Defining the Benefits of Using PHP
Locating Resources to Learn PHP
Working with the Amazon PHP Example

Writing Applications Using PHP

Creating an XML over HTTP PHP Application
Working with MySQL as a Database
Creating a PHP Application with Database Support

Many developers have learned to use PHP over the years because it's a good solution for creating Web pages and the price is right. The PHP acronym is like many other new acronyms for the Internet—the acronym is recursive (refers back to itself). PHP stands for *PHP Hypertext Processor*. This general-purpose HTML scripting language works much like ASP (see Chapter 6) or other page description languages you might have used. Essentially, you mix HTML with scripting information. When the PHP process sees HTML, it sends the text directly to the user. It processes any scripting information, and passes the resulting HTML to the user as well.

This chapter helps you discover how PHP works with Amazon Web Services. I'm assuming that you already know something about PHP, but the first two sections provide some suggestions on how to learn more about PHP. Because PHP runs on so many platforms, you'll also find some suggested resources for getting and installing PHP for your particular server. These instructions might require a little technical knowledge on your part, so make sure you understand what the instructions require before you perform them.

The examples in this chapter show how to use PHP to create an Amazon Web Services application. The first example provides simple instructions for accessing the Web service without any fancy application features. You'll also find an application that shows how to use PHP with MySQL, an open source database. In fact, you can download every piece of software in this chapter free and try out all of the examples without spending a penny—that's one of the benefits of using open source.

I've also provided a number of tips to help you with your PHP applications. You'll find that the open source support system is adequate, but you won't get the same level of hand-holding that you do with paid products such as Visual Studio. Open source solutions tend to require a motivated developer, so it might not be the right solution if you need a packaged approach that doesn't require a lot of fiddling on your part. With this in mind, the chapter also provides some ideas on where you can get help when you need it.

Understanding the Benefits of Using PHP

PHP has a number of interesting benefits, especially for a company on a budget. One of the biggest benefits is that PHP is essentially free because it's open source, as is the main Web server it runs on—Apache. All you need to do is download the required products and install them on your system. In fact, you'll find an amazing array of products you can use with Apache and PHP on the Apache Software Foundation site at `http://www.apache.org/index2.html`. Note that this site also keeps you informed about many of the conferences associated with the open source movement and many of the political issues as well.

Another important benefit of using PHP is that it runs just about anywhere. The Apache server comes in versions for Windows, NetWare, Linux, Macintosh OS/X, and most Unix systems. You can also find Apache support for larger systems such as the AS/400. In fact, there are few places that Apache doesn't run. Anywhere you can run Apache, you can likely run PHP. In the few cases you can't find a version of Apache to use for your copy of PHP, it's quite possible you can find a version of PHP that runs on another Web server for that platform.

Understanding the Usage of *Free* with Software

Free can be a subjective term. Free doesn't necessarily mean without cost. In many cases, you see the word *free*, but it doesn't mean that everything about a product is free. The problem is that I haven't come up with better terminology. The use of the term free has caused so much worry for users that some of them have sued vendors over the use of the term free because it really doesn't mean inclusively free for the entire product. This article sums up the situation: `http://www.infoworld.com/article/03/08/29/34FElinux_1.html`.

As you can see from this (and other) articles, the experts haven't yet placed a price tag on the supposedly free Linux. Yes, you can download a generic copy of Linux free, but most people choose a customized version, so that costs money, but it costs less than a copy of Windows. Unfortunately, the cost of the operating system is a relatively small percentage of the whole cost of installing a system. Even if a company chooses the free generic version of Linux, no one can say that it's truly free, but few experts agree on the actual cost.The political part of the equation comes from the uncertainty of cost. If you're Microsoft and you want to dissuade someone from buying Linux, then you make those costs as high as you can without losing support from the "independent" experts who will back up your claim. On the other hand, if you're a member of the open source community, you want to make those costs as low as possible without calling your sanity into question.

This chapter won't discuss the political issues that surround the concept of *free*. For the purposes of this book, free means the product won't cost anything to download. You still have to consider support, installation, and management costs as part of any solution you use.

PHP is relatively easy to transport from one system to another. Because PHP applications run as scripts (essentially text), any application you create for PHP on one platform is likely to work with a few tweaks on another platform. Amazon Web Services developers should find that PHP works especially well for multiple platforms. Problems can occur when you begin adding platform-specific features to an application to make it look nicer or perform better.

The creators of PHP have improved it a great deal since its initial release. For example, you no longer need Apache to run PHP (many Web sites and articles still say this is a requirement). See the "Downloading and Installing PHP" section for additional information on this topic. The open source community also provides regular patches for PHP, including the all important security patches. You can find these patches on the PHP download site. Because these patches receive an open review, many developers consider them better coded and more stable than the proprietary solutions available on the market.

> **NOTE**
>
> I'm using the Apache 2.0.47 Windows and PHP 4.3.3 versions for this chapter. You might notice some differences between these product versions and other versions available on the download sites. Because of the way PHP works, the example code should work fine on any newer version of Apache and PHP you choose to use. Older versions of both Apache and PHP could encounter problems when they don't support the features found in the current products.

Resources for Learning PHP

This chapter assumes that you already know how to use PHP and simply want to learn how to use it with Amazon Web Services. Consequently, the chapter doesn't include essential language instruction that you might need if you're a PHP novice. If you think you might want to learn to use PHP for your next Web application, the resources in this section will help. One of the first places you should look for PHP information is the PHP site at `http://us2.php.net/manual/en/introduction.php`. Once you spend some time with the PHP tutorial, you'll also want to look at the PHP manual at `http://us2.php.net/manual/en/index.php`. The manual tells you how to use various PHP commands.

The Webmonkey Web site has an excellent PHP tutorial (`http://hotwired.lycos.com/webmonkey/01/48/index2a.html?tw=programming`). Another tutorial will help you understand PHP and MySQL Usage (`http://hotwired.lycos.com/webmonkey/programming/php/tutorials/tutorial4.html`). However, you'll also want to view the other PHP topics on this Web site (`http://hotwired.lycos.com/webmonkey/programming/php/index.html`) to learn more about PHP and see how you can use it with other products such as Oracle.

A number of other sites also provide PHP tutorials. For example, the Free Webmaster Help.com site at `http://www.freewebmasterhelp.com/tutorials/php` provides a seven-part tutorial that includes information on using forms. The tutorials on Dev Shed (`http://www.devshed.com/Server_Side/PHP/`) are a little more advanced. The tutorials on this site help you discover how to work with the local hard drive and even create PDFs as output from your application. You'll also find a number of articles about error handling and other developer topics. However, you'll want to save this site as your last stop because many of the articles get quite detailed and you could find yourself lost quickly.

It's also helpful to have a good book on the topic. Take a look at *Creating Interactive Web Sites with PHP and Web Services* by Eric Rosebrock (Sybex, 2004). This book shows how to install and configure development and production platforms of Apache, PHP, and MySQL on both Windows and Linux systems, and teaches Web development with PHP from a problem-solving viewpoint. Also visit Eric's wildly popular Web site PHP Freaks (`http://www.phpfreaks.com`).

Downloading and Installing PHP

One of the first places you'll want to visit is the Webmonkey site at `http://hotwired.lycos.com/webmonkey/00/44/index4a.html?tw=programming`. Use this tutorial to get PHP setup on your system and learn a little about this product. This PHP tutorial will also introduce you to the language. Unfortunately, the tutorial is also a little outdated and many of the links no longer work. Here's a list of links you can use instead of the links provided with the Webmonkey article (the article information is still very good, so don't be concerned about the outdated links).

- Apache Server Download (`http://httpd.apache.org/download.cgi`)
- Apache Documentation (`http://httpd.apache.org/docs-2.0/`)
- PHP Download (`http://us2.php.net/downloads.php`)
- PHP Manual (`http://us2.php.net/manual/en/index.php`)

Because the Webmonkey article is a little outdated, you'll also want to spend time with the official PHP installation documentation found at `http://us2.php.net/manual/en/installation.php`. Although this text isn't quite as readable as the Webmonkey version, it's definitely current. Make sure you base any installation decisions, such as whether to use CGI or ISAPI, on the content of the official documentation.

One thing you won't need to do to work with Amazon Web Services is add any extensions. All of the examples in this chapter work fine with the default extensions. You might need to add extensions to process the data, but it's a good idea to work with Amazon Web Services for a while using the default PHP configuration. Using the default configuration ensures you won't run into any extension-specific errors.

Don't get the idea that PHP only comes in versions for Apache users. It's true that many people use PHP with Apache, but you can also use it with Internet Information Server (IIS), Personal Web Server (PWS), and Xitami (among other servers). Many of the other servers require that you use the CGI version of PHP, but you can also get an ISAPI version for IIS. The ISAPI version will provide superior performance and a little more flexibility, as well as improved reliability and recoverability. If you want the ISAPI support, you must download the Zip version of the PHP file, not the installer version, which includes only the CGI files.

You can run into a number of issues with Apache that none of the documentation mentions. For example, you might run into a situation where Apache installs and even starts, but you can't access it. Make sure you don't have another Web server installed on the same system. The second Web server could make it difficult or impossible to access the Apache server. This problem is especially prominent on Windows systems because Microsoft simply assumes that every server should have IIS installed.

Amazon Web Services can accept either XML over HTTP or SOAP requests from PHP. The choice of interface depends on what you plan to achieve with the Web service. In many cases, you can achieve acceptable results using the XML over HTTP approach with less coding and effort than using the SOAP approach. If you decide to use the SOAP approach, you'll need to download a SOAP library to use with PHP. You can find this

▶ TIP

Like most programming languages, you'll find a variety of third party support sites for PHP. One of the better sites, ByKeyword.com (`http://www.bykeyword.com/pages/php.html`) includes a list of utilities to edit, manage, and even convert your PHP code. Make sure you also visit sites like Tucows (`http://tdconline.tucows.com/`). A simple search can net a list of useful shareware and freeware products you can use.

▶ NOTE

At the time of this writing, Webmasters have closed some PHP sites temporarily as a protest against the legal wrangling occurring in the open source community. For example, the php4win site (`http://www.php4win.de/`) won't allow any access at all. Consequently, if you see that one of the sites mentioned in this chapter is closed, try it again after a month or so.

library at `http://cvs.sourceforge.net/cgi-bin/viewcvs.cgi/nusoap/lib/nusoap.php`. This file must appear in a central location or in the same folder as your other application files.

Using the Amazon Supplied File Example

The Amazon Web Services Kit includes a PHP example you can use for experimentation. This example is useful in several ways. Obviously, it shows how to develop a PHP application. However, the example includes a second file, `AmazonSearch.PHP`, which greatly simplifies your SOAP programming needs if the functions it includes meets your requirements. This section discusses both uses of the example.

First, you need to make a change to the source code for the `Amazon.PHP` file. The example won't work properly as a Web page as written now. Open the file in any plain text editor. You can use Notepad, but an editor designed for the task works better. I wrote all of the examples in this chapter using PHP Expert Editor (`http://www.phpexperteditor.com/`). You can find a list of additional editors at `http://phpeditors.linuxbackup.co.uk/editorlist.php`. At line 58 of the `Amazon.PHP` file, you'll find a line that reads

```
if (count($argv) == 1)
```

Change this line so it reads

```
if (count($argv) <= 1)
```

Now that you have the code fixed, copy the entire `\PHPSample` folder to the `\Program Files\Apache Group\Apache2\htdocs` folder of your server. In addition, copy the `NuSOAP.PHP` file to this folder. You should find four files in the `\Program Files\Apache Group\Apache2\htdocs\PHPSample` folder at this point. Make sure the server has a connection to the Internet and access to the example. Figure 7.1 shows typical output from the example. Note that you can obtain a better view of the data by right-clicking the browser window and selecting View Source from the context menu.

While the example is interesting, it's not the complete picture. The `AmazonSearch.PHP` file is the one that contains the code that makes everything happen. Amazon wisely placed this code in a separate file so you could easily use the functions it contains in your own applications. Using this file makes the SOAP technique almost too simple because all you need to know is which function to use and how to parse the incoming data.

> **NOTE**
>
> The Amazon developer originally intended this application to run at a command prompt as a script, not as a Web page. The code change allows you to run the code as either a script or a Web page. However, the arguments mentioned at the top of the file only work when you use the example at the command line. To use the code this way, you would type **`PHP Amazon.PHP -a`** at the command prompt and press Enter to obtain the author query results. Make sure you include any required path information to locate the `PHP.EXE` file.

Most applications you create using the Amazon supplied files require three steps. The first step is to create a request and retrieve results from that request. Listing 7.1 shows an example of how you can use the `AmazonSearch.PHP` file to perform this first step. You'll find this example in the `\Chapter 07\AmazonSearch` folder of the source code located on the Sybex Web site.

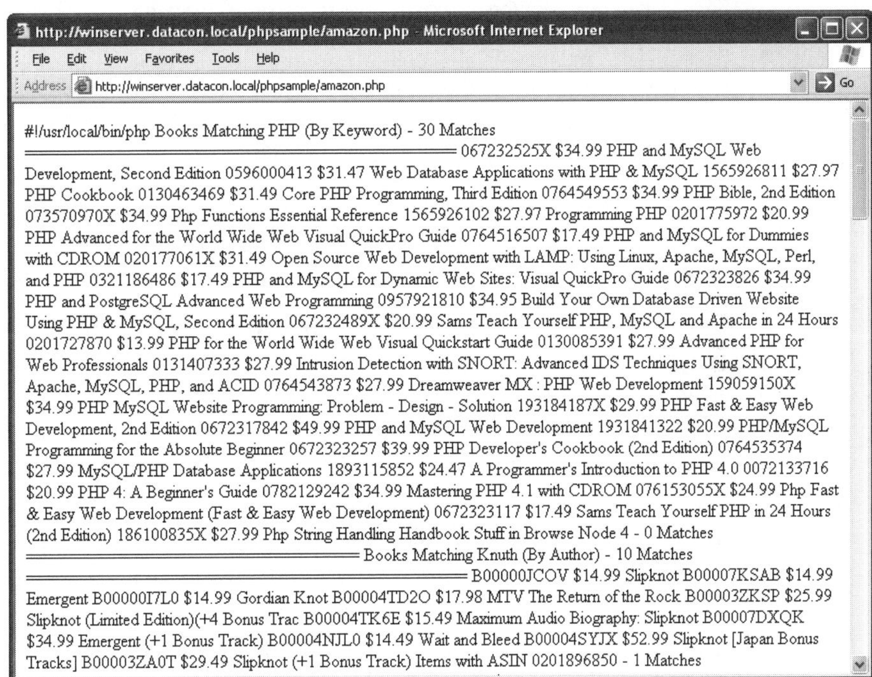

FIGURE 7.1: The Amazon PHP example shows some of the results you can achieve.

Listing 7.1 Building an Application Using the Amazon Supplied Files

```
<?php
// Set up the variables used to make the request.
$Debug   = false;   // Use debug mode?

// Associate token.
if ($_REQUEST["txtTag"] == null)
   $Tag    = "webservices-20";
else
   $Tag    = $_REQUEST["txtTag"];

... Other Inputs ...

// Number of return results.
if ($_REQUEST["txtNumber"] == null)
   $Return = 10;
```

```
else
   $Return = $_REQUEST["txtNumber"];

// Load Amazon Search object
require("./AmazonSearch.php");

//  Initialize the search service.
$Service = new AmazonSearch($DevTag, $Tag, $Debug);

//  Perform an Author search.
$Results = $Service->DoAuthorSearch($Author, $Type, $Mode, $Return);

?>
```

The code checks each input for a request value and uses a default if it doesn't find one. As in many cases, a user could open the page directly or as the result of clicking Submit on the form. You could simply display the form without making a request if the user hasn't pressed Submit.

Once the code has input values to use, it creates an instance of Amazon Web Services. This object is actually the class that Amazon supplies as part of the kit. You need to create all of the data that the class creates by hand if you decide that the predefined class won't do what you need. Notice that the constructor requires both the developer and associate tokens. You can also place the class in a debug mode by setting `$Debug` to true.

At this point, the code can make a query. The example uses the `DoAuthorSearch()` method, which requires the four inputs shown. One of the advantages of this method is that you can define the number of results you want returned from the query. Theoretically, you could make just two calls to Amazon Web Services to obtain all of the results for a particular request. The first call simply retrieves the number of results available, while the second call requests the full number of results. The only problem with this method is that you can't select a page. The method always begins with the first page of available results, which means every request returns the same starting information. It's possible to change the Amazon supplied code to add functionality such as the starting page and sort order, so you may still want to use this file as a starting point.

The second step of the process displays the HTML portion of the Web page. Listing 7.2 shows a typical example of this portion of the code.

Listing 7.2 Creating the User Display Using the Amazon Supplied Files

```
<html>

<head>
<title>Author Amazon Search Demonstration</title>
</head>
```

```
<body>

  <form action="http://YourWebsiteURL/AmazonSearchDemo.PHP"
        id="SubmissionForm"
        method=get
        name="SubmissionForm">
     <h1 align=center>
        <label id="Heading">Query Entry Form</label>
     </h1><p />
     <label id="Type">Associate
        <span style="TEXT-DECORATION: underline">T</span>ag:
     </label>
     <input id="t" accesskey="T" type="text"
        <?php
           if ($_REQUEST["txtTag"] == null)
              print('value="webservices-20"');
           else
           {
              print('value="');
              print($_REQUEST["txtTag"]);
              print('"');
           }
        ?>
        name="txtTag"><br/>

     ... Other Labels and Inputs ...

     <div align="center">
        <input id="Submit" type=submit value="Submit" NAME="Submit">
     </div>
  </form>

  <table align=center width=80% border=1>
     <caption>
        <span style="FONT-WEIGHT: bold; FONT-SIZE: large">
           Query Results
        </span>
     </caption>
     <tr>
        <th>ISBN</th>
        <th>Product Name</th>
        <th>Release Date</th>
        <th>Publisher</th>
     </tr>
```

For the most part, this code looks like a standard PHP page. It does include special code to display the results of any changes the user makes to the page and submits to the server. Because Amazon Web Services code relies on these changes, you must include code of this type to ensure the user changes remain in place. I also chose to place the output table outside the form to avoid problems with data submissions.

The third step of the process is to display the data retrieved with the Amazon request. Listing 7.3 shows one way to work with this data.

Listing 7.3 Processing the Results Using the Amazon Supplied Files

```
<?php
  foreach($Results as $Detail)
  {
     // Start a row.
     print("<tr>");
     print("\r\n");

     // Get the ISBN.
     print("<td>");
     print($Detail["Asin"]);
     print("</td>");
     print("\r\n");

     ... Other Results ...

     print("</tr>");
     print("\r\n");
  }
?>
```

As you can see, PHP provides a `foreach` statement that works well with the data because of the way it's organized. The `AmazonSearch` class treats the return value as an array—each array element contains one book detail record. This record is arranged the same as any Amazon `ProductInfo` data structure. Consequently, you can retrieve some values such as the ASIN directly, but other values, such as Authors, require further processing. Figure 7.2 shows typical output from this application.

Developing an XML over HTTP PHP Application

You might run into a situation where you want to use the XML over HTTP technique with PHP. Certainly, putting the message together is much easier than working with SOAP and you don't need to download anything extra—the standard PHP setup includes everything you need. Some people also find this solution a tad more flexible because you can perform tasks at the start of the element, during the reading of the character data, and again at the end of the element. The example in this section performs a simple query of Amazon. Processing the data requires two steps. The first step is to open the remote connection, get the data, and start the processing loop. This step appears in Listing 7.4. You'll find this example in the `\Chapter 07\XMLDemo` folder of the source code located on the Sybex Web site.

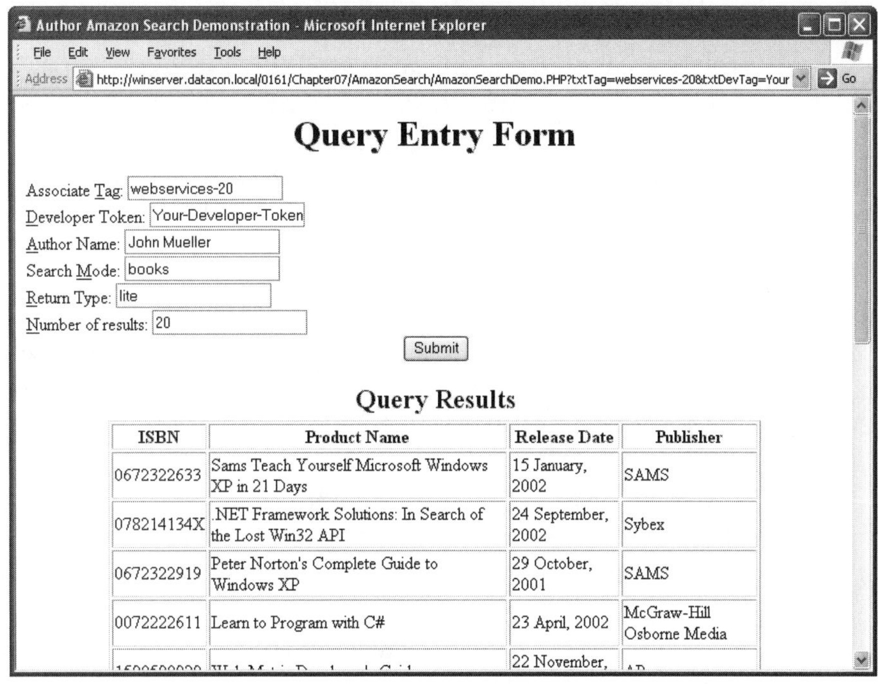

FIGURE 7.2: Typical output from the sample application includes as many entries as needed.

Listing 7.4 Initiating the XML Processing Loop

```
// Define the XML parser and set the parsing functions.
$Output = xml_parser_create();

// Define the element parser.
xml_set_element_handler($Output, "StartElement", "EndElement");
xml_set_character_data_handler($Output, "CharacterData");

// Open a connection to Amazon using the XML over HTTP method.
$FilePointer = fopen("http://xml.amazon.com/onca/xml3?" .
                     "t=webservices-20&dev-t=Your-Developer-Token&" .
                     "AuthorSearch=John%20Mueller&mode=books" .
                     "&type=lite&page=1&f=xml", "r");
if ($FilePointer == null)
   // Display an error message an exit.
   die(print("Couldn't open the Amazon site."));
else
{

   // Keep reading the data until there isn't any more to read.
   while ($DataStream = fread($FilePointer, 4096))
```

```
      {
         // If the program can't parse the data, raise an
         // error.
         if (!xml_parse($Output, $DataStream, feof($FilePointer)))
         {
            // Display an error message and exit.
            die(sprintf("XML error: %s at line %d",
               xml_error_string(xml_get_error_code($Output)),
               xml_get_current_line_number($Output)));
         }
      }
   }
```

The code begins by creating the XML parser, `Output`, using the `xml_parser_create()` function. It then assigns an element handler and a character data handler to the XML parser using the `xml_set_element_handler()` and `xml_set_character_data_handler()` functions. These three functions actually process the incoming data.

Now that the code has an XML parser to use, it opens a pointer to the XML data using the `fopen()` function with the same string as the example in the "Using a Browser Example" section of Chapter 2. If the `fopen()` function is successful, the code begins the processing loop.

Processing involves reading data from the data stream into `$DataStream` using the `fread()` function. The code parses the resulting data using the `xml_parse()` function. What actually happens in this loop is that the code calls the three functions found in Listing 7.5 in turn.

Listing 7.5 Outputting the Processed Data as HTML

```
$CurrentElement = "";

function StartElement($Parser, $Name, $Attributes)
{
   // Store the current element name.
   global $CurrentElement;
   $CurrentElement = $Name;

   // Start a table containing the arguments.
   if ($Name == "ARGS")
   {
      print('<table align=center width=50% border=1>');
      print('<caption>');
      print('<span style="FONT-WEIGHT: bold; FONT-SIZE: large">');
      print('Arguments</span>');
      print('</caption>');
      print('<tr>');
      print('<th>Name</th>');
```

```
      print('<th>Value</th>');
      print('</tr>');
   }

   // List each argument in turn.
   if ($Name == "ARG")
   {
      print('<tr><td>');
      print($Attributes["NAME"]);
      print('</td><td>');
      print($Attributes["VALUE"]);
      print('</td></tr>');
   }

   // End the arguments table and print the total results.
   if ($Name == "TOTALRESULTS")
   {
      print("</table>");
      print("<LABEL>Total Results: ");
   }

   // Print the total number of pages.
   if ($Name == "TOTALPAGES")
      print("<LABEL>Total Pages: ");

   // Print the ASIN.
   if ($Name == "ASIN")
      print("<tr><td>");

   ... Other Data Values ...

}

function EndElement($Parser, $Name)
{
   // End the Total Result value.
   if ($Name == "TOTALRESULTS")
      print("</LABEL><br/>");

   // End the Total Pages value. Also set the
   // page up to print the details table.
   if ($Name == "TOTALPAGES")
   {
      print("</LABEL>");
      print('<table align="center" border="1" width="90%">');
      print('<caption>');
      print('<span style="FONT-WEIGHT: bold; FONT-SIZE: large">');
      print('Books Returned from Query</span>');
      print('</caption>');
```

```
         print('<tbody>');
         print('<tr>');
         print('<th>ISBN</th>');
         print('<th>Book Title</th>');
         print('<th>Release Date</th>');
         print('<th>Publisher</th>');
         print('</tr>');
      }

      if ($Name == "ASIN")
         print("</td>");

      ... Other Data Values ...

   }

   function CharacterData($Parser, $Data)
   {
      // Get the current element name.
      global $CurrentElement;

      // Print the Total Results value.
      if ($CurrentElement == "TOTALRESULTS")
         print($Data);

      // Print the Total Pages value.
      if ($CurrentElement == "TOTALPAGES")
         print($Data);

      if ($CurrentElement == "ASIN")
         print($Data);

      ... Other Data Values ...

   }
```

You must think about the three functions in terms of how you want data to appear on screen. The easiest method is to process the data as it comes from Amazon, which is what this example does. The processing look also calls these three functions in turn, which means that it passes an <Args> element to the `StartElement()` function first, but then it processes all of the <Arg> child elements by calling both the `StartElement()` and `EndElement()` functions before it calls `EndElement()` for the <Args> element. It's handy to keep a browser display of the raw data similar to the one shown back in Figure 2.4 to help create your code.

In this case, the code begins by creating a table in the `StartElement()` function to display the arguments on screen. It then processes the <Arg> elements as a table. Notice how the code uses strings to access the $Attributes array for the <Arg> elements. The StartElement() function continues by beginning to process the <TotalResults> and <TotalPages> elements. Element character data isn't accessible in this function, so the code only creates the beginning label. Likewise, since elements such as <Asin> use character data instead of attributes, the code only creates the required supporting tags.

Look now at the CharacterData() function. As you can see, it keeps track of the current element using the global variable, $CurrentElement. Whenever the code comes to an element that contains data that it should present on screen, it simply prints the $Data variable.

Now that the code has printed an opening tag and the required data, the Web page requires a closing tag. The EndElement() function takes care of this task. The tags that you need to output depends on what you want to do with that element, what you did in the StartElement() function, and what the next element will need to work right. In this case, most of the entries are obvious—they simply output the closing tag. However, the <TotalPages> element also marks the beginning of the details processing. Because the details aren't contained within a parent element, adding the table tags here makes sense. Figure 7.3 shows the output from this example.

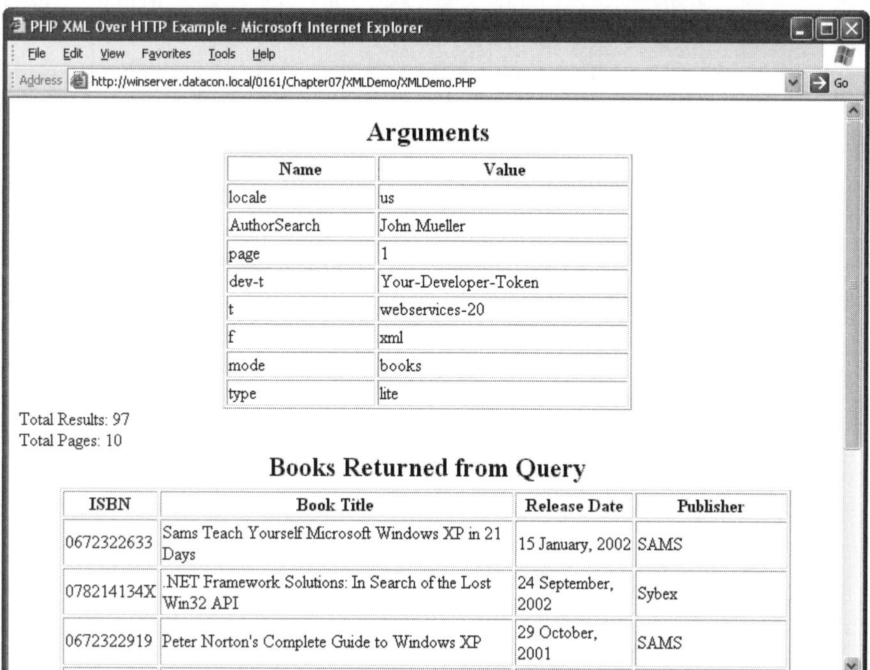

FIGURE 7.3: This example relies on XML over HTTP to provide detailed results.

Using MySQL as a Database

You'll probably want to improve the efficiency of your PHP application, at some point, by storing some data locally. It's likely that you'll use a database to perform this task. One of the more popular databases on the market is MySQL. It provides robust capability and the price is right. In addition, MySQL seems to enjoy better than average support from a cadre of developers who use it.

Like everything else in this chapter, MySQL is open source. Normally, you don't have to buy this product—just download it. However, there are some situations where you do need to buy a license, such as when you create an application for commercial (shrink-wrap) distribution where you'll realize a profit from the sale of the application. Make sure you understand the distribution requirements for MySQL by reading them at `http://www.mysql.com/downloads/index.html`.

The example in this chapter relies on MySQL 4.0, the latest production version at the time of writing, which you can download at `http://www.mysql.com/downloads/mysql-4.0.html`. You'll notice that MySQL comes in quite a few versions for various platforms including Linux, Windows, Solaris, FreeBSD, Mac OS X, HP-UX, IBM AIX, Novell NetWare, SCO OpenUnix, SGI Irix, and DEC OSF. You can also download the source code and create your own flavor of MySQL if necessary. The test system for this chapter uses the compiled Windows version with default settings applied by the installer. If you use some other form of MySQL, your screenshots will vary from mine.

Once you download the version of the product you need, install it according to the vendor directions. In most cases, this means starting the installer or unpacking the product and performing a manual install. The Windows Installer version is very easy to use—just double-click the executable that you download and follow the prompts.

Learning to use MySQL is relatively straightforward. You can find the complete product documentation at `http://www.mysql.com/documentation/index.html`. The documentation comes in two formats: PDF, for a printed version, or HLP, for a desktop electronic version. Part of the documentation is a tutorial that you'll find at `http://www.mysql.com/doc/en/Tutorial.html`. The vendor provides training and certification courses that you can learn about at `http://www.mysql.com/training-and-certification.html`. The Webmonkey site at `http://hotwired.lycos.com/webmonkey/programming/php/tutorials/tutorial4.html` provides an excellent online MySQL tutorial. Another good tutorial appears on the TAASC site at `http://www.analysisandsolutions.com/code/mybasic.htm`. In fact, you can find a number of tutorials on this product.

Writing a PHP Application with Database Support

The example in this chapter replicates most of the functionality of the example in the "Using SQL Server as a Database" section of Chapter 6. Of course, that application runs on a desktop machine and this one works as a browser application, so there are some differences. For one thing, the application stores the URL of the local copy of the image, rather than the image itself in the database.

Setting Up the Database

Before you can begin using PHP with MySQL, you need a database. The `\Chapter 07\Data` folder of the source code located on the Sybex Web site contains a SQL script called `AmazonData.SQL`. Copy this file into the `\MySQL\bin` folder of your server (assuming you used a default setup). At the command line, type **`MySQL MySQL < AmazonData.SQL`** and press Enter. Your system will pause for a moment and return to the command prompt. That's all you need to do to create the database for this example.

You can use the MySQL utility to verify the presence of the database, table, and data at the command line. Simply type **`USE AmazonData;`** and press Enter. If the `AmazonData` database is present, the utility will use that database. Type **`SELECT * FROM DataStore`** and press Enter. You'll see a lot of data stream by if the script successfully created the table and filled it with data. An easier way to achieve the same results on a Windows system is to use the `WinMySQLadmin` utility shown in Figure 7.4. Simply select the Databases tab and you'll see the database, table, and associated fields.

> **TIP**
>
> Even though the example in this chapter stores the URL of the local copy of the image, you can replicate the functionality of the example in Chapter 6 almost exactly by adding a third party library to your PHP setup. This technique requires a platform-specific library and can cause browser compatibility issues in some cases. Because of these issues, I chose to discuss techniques that will work on most platforms with most browsers. The Dev Shed article at `http://www.devshed.com/Server_Side/PHP/ImageGeneration/page1.html` discusses the PHP image generation technique in detail.

Writing the Sample Application

This example application requires five processing phases. First, you must create the local variables and determine whether the user has passed any information as part of the query. This part of the process works precisely the same as the processing described in Listing 7.1.

FIGURE 7.4:

The WinMySQLadmin utility validates the success of the script on a Windows machine.

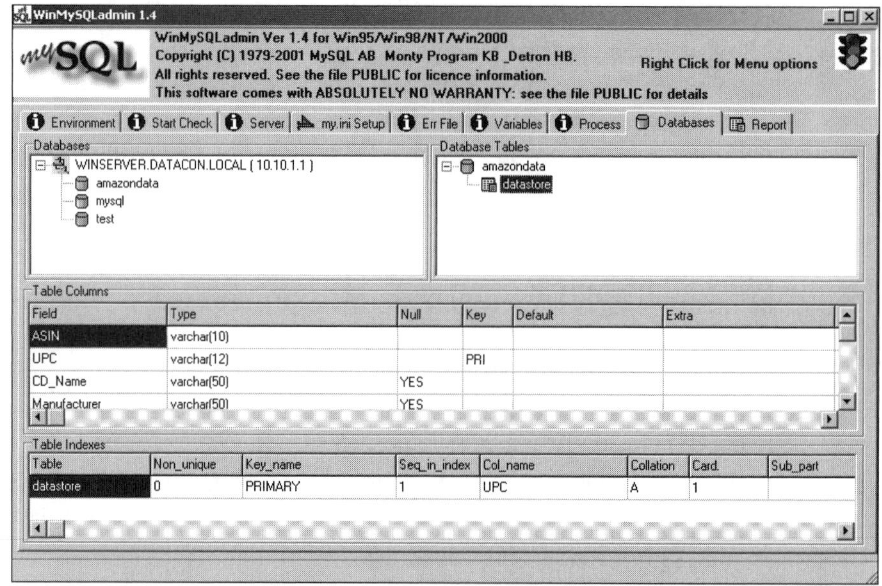

The second phase is to display the HTML on screen. The request process works just the same as the code in Listing 7.2. The difference is that the request screen is the only thing that the user sees during the initial request. Only after the user clicks Submit does the return data appear. The reason for this change is that you don't know where to get the data from until the user makes the request.

The third phase detects the type of processing the request requires. In this case, the code determines whether the data appears in the local database or it needs to request the data from Amazon. Listing 7.6 shows this phase. You'll find this example in the `\Chapter 07\MySQLDemo` folder of the source code located on the Sybex Web site.

Listing 7.6 Determining How to Process a Request

```
// Create a database connection.
mysql_connect("localhost")
or die ("Cannot connect to the database.");

// Select the database.
mysql_select_db("AmazonData")
or die ("The database doesn't exist or is inaccessible.");

// Obtain the data.
$Output = mysql_query("SELECT * FROM DataStore WHERE UPC = '$UPC'");

// Verify the data is in the database.
```

```
if (mysql_num_rows ($Output) == 0)
   $Row = GetData();

else
{
   // Get the display data.
   $Row = mysql_fetch_row($Output)
   or die ("No Data in Query Row.");
}

// Get the current date and convert it to a timestamp.
$ConvDate = strtotime($Row[9]);

// Add 24 hours.
$ConvDate = $ConvDate + 86400;

// Verify the data isn't too old.
if ($ConvDate < time())
   $Row = GetData();
```

The code begins by using the `mysql_connect()` function to create a connection to the MySQL server. Depending on how you configure your database, you might also need to provide a username and password (or request this information from the user). The `mysql_select_db()` function to connect to the `AmazonData` database—this is the database that contains the information for the example. Finally, the code uses the `mysql_query()` function to obtain the data from the database if it exists.

The first check of the data determines whether the query returned any rows using the `mysql_num_rows()` function. If `$Output` is blank, then the UPC doesn't reside in the database and the code requests it using the `GetData()` function described later in this section. Even if `$Output` contains the requested data, there's no guarantee that this data is current. The next code check verifies the date the application last downloaded the data from Amazon. If the data is too old, then the code calls `GetData()` to retrieve the data.

The act of verification often leads into an optional fourth processing phase. The code might have to retrieve the data from Amazon. Listing 7.7 shows a straightforward SOAP technique you can use to perform this task without relying on the `AmazonSearch.PDF` file used for the example in the "Using the Amazon Supplied File Example" section.

Listing 7.7 Querying Amazon for Data Using SOAP

```
function GetData()
{
   // Access the global variables.
   global $UPC;
   global $Mode;
   global $Type;
```

```
global $DevTag;

// Create a new SOAP client.
$Client = new
soapclient("http://soap.amazon.com/schemas3/AmazonWebServices.wsdl",
true);

// This proxy helps you access the Amazon WSDL methods directly.
$Proxy = $Client->getProxy();

// Create an array to hold the request values.
$Parameters = array
(
   'upc'    => $UPC,
   'mode'   => $Mode,
   'tag'    => 'webservices-20',
   'type'   => $Type,
   'devtag' => $DevTag
);

// Invoke the Amazon method.
$AllData = $Proxy->UpcSearchRequest($Parameters);

// Retrieve the Details.
$DetailsNode = $AllData["Details"];
$Details = $DetailsNode[0];

// Get the image from online.
$ImageData = file($Details["ImageUrlMedium"]);

// Create a filename based on the existing filename.
$PathArray = parse_url($Details["ImageUrlMedium"]);
$Path = $PathArray["path"];
$FileArray = pathinfo($Path);
$File = $FileArray["basename"];

// Save the file on disk.
$FilePointer = fopen($File, "w");
for ($Counter = 0; $Counter < count($ImageData); $Counter++)
   fwrite($FilePointer, $ImageData[$Counter]);

// Remove the existing record (if any).
mysql_query('DELETE FROM DataStore WHERE UPC = "' . $UPC . '"');

// Get the scanning time.
$ScanTime = strftime("%y/%m/%d %H:%M:%S");

// Convert the release date.
$ReleaseTime = strftime("%y/%m/%d %H:%M:%S",
```

```
      strtotime(ereg_replace(",", " ", $Details["ReleaseDate"])));

   // Create the query string.
   $UpdateQuery =
      'INSERT INTO DataStore (ASIN, UPC, CD_Name, Manufacturer,
         Availability, Product_URL, List_Price, Release_Date, Picture,
         Scanned)
      VALUES ("' . $Details["Asin"] . '" , "' . $UPC . '" , "' .
         $Details["ProductName"] . '" , "' . $Details["Manufacturer"]
         . '" , "' . $Details["Availability"] . '" , "' .
         $Details["Url"] . '" , "' . substr($Details["ListPrice"], 1)
         . '" , "' . $ReleaseTime . '" , "' . $File . '" , "' .
         $ScanTime . '")';

   // Update the database.
   mysql_query($UpdateQuery)
   or die ("Error Updating Database");

   $Result = array($Details["Asin"], $UPC, $Details["ProductName"],
                   $Details["Manufacturer"], $Details["Availability"],
                   $Details["Url"], $Details["ListPrice"],
                   $Details["ReleaseDate"], $File, $ScanTime);
   return $Result;
}
```

The code begins by creating a SOAP client using the `soapclient()` constructor. This URL points to the same WSDL page that other example in this book uses. Once the code accesses the WSDL page, it creates a proxy for it so that the application can access Amazon Web Services. At this point, you can begin making requests of the service.

The code creates a specially formatted array to hold the request data. The capitalization of the array elements follows the capitalization in the Amazon Web Services Kit help file. It appears that these entries are case sensitive. Once the code creates a request array, it uses it to make the request using the `$Proxy->UpcSearchRequest()` method.

The request returns the same `ProductInfo` XML data as usual, so you need to parse through the various levels to find the `Details` node. Note that PHP treats the XML nodes as arrays, so you can use the same techniques that you use with any other array to access data members.

It's important to download the image for the product so the user can see it. To perform this task, the code opens the required image using the `file()` function. It then creates a local file with the same name with the `fopen()` function and uses the `fwrite()` function to store the image to that file. Make sure you use binary safe function calls to perform this task. The technique shown might not work with older versions of PHP. The documentation tells which versions support binary files.

At this point, the code has everything it needs to store the data in the table, so it uses the `mysql_query()` function to delete the existing record, if necessary. The call doesn't fail if the table doesn't contain the record, so you don't lose anything by making it. You'll find that MySQL is a little fussy about time formats and unfortunately, those formats aren't necessarily the same formats that PHP accepts. Consequently, the code performs some conversion of the two dates that the table must store—the released date and the date that the application last requested the data from Amazon. The final step is to insert the new record into the table using the `mysql_query()` function. Make sure you pay special attention to how the code creates `$UpdateQuery`. If you don't format the string correctly, the table stores incorrect data. For example, notice how the code removes the dollar sign from the incoming list price. The database stores a 0 for the list price if you don't perform this task.

The final step creates a `$Result` array from the data retrieved from Amazon and returns it to the caller for display. Notice that the code calls on the `$Details` array several times for the same data. In general, it's easier to use the technique shown to create the array, but you could possibly increase performance by storing the data in local single variables rather than read them from arrays every time you need them.

The fifth processing phase displays the data on screen. Like the other examples in the chapter, this phase uses the `print()` function to output a combination of HTML and data from the variables. The only surprises here are those that deal with differences in the way Amazon returns the data and the method used to store the data in the database. You need to detect the display issues and handle them in code as shown here.

```
// Display the list price.
print("<label>List Price: ");
if (substr($Row[6], 0, 1) <> "$")
   print("$");
print($Row[6]);
print("</label></br>");

// Display the release date.
print("<label>Release Date: ");
if (strstr($Row[7], "-"))
   print strftime("%d %B, %Y", strtotime($Row[7]));
else
   print($Row[7]);
print("</label></br>");
```

As you can see, the code detects the problem areas by looking for key strings within the variable. The database stores financial values without the dollar sign (or other monetary symbol), so the code adds it back in for a local response. Likewise, the database stores the date in a different format from Amazon, so the code needs to translate the database format to make it match the Amazon output. Figure 7.5 shows the output from this example.

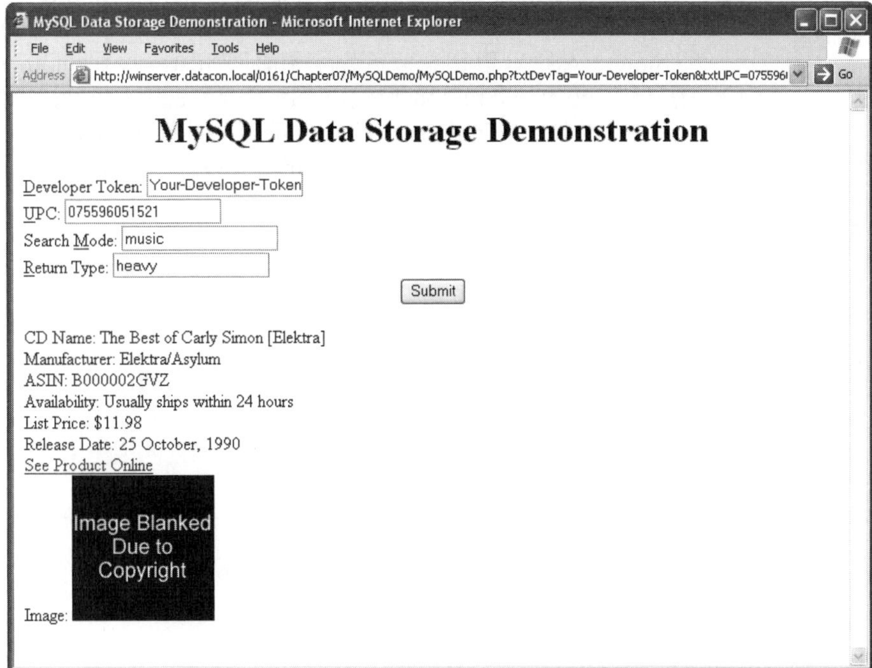

FIGURE 7.5: This application demonstrates the use of MySQL storage for Amazon data.

Your Call to Action

This chapter has helped you understand some of the essentials for using PHP with Amazon Web Services. PHP is a good solution for developers who want to create a capable Web site without relying on heavy amounts of scripting. In addition, PHP is the most portable solution you can use to build Amazon Web Services applications. Of course, this solution only works for Web applications—not for desktop applications such as those found in Chapter 6. In general, you can use other alternatives to get the same results with less coding or effort. Finally, PHP is a good solution for developers with a tight budget because you can get the required software free.

At this point, you have to decide whether you want to use a product like PHP to develop your next Web application. Most developers find PHP easy to work with and the price is right. Once you do decide to use PHP, make sure you get a good start by checking out the tutorials and other user help information in this chapter. Expert PHP developers can start writing their Amazon Web Services application immediately. The chapter shows several examples that demonstrate applications of varying complexity.

Chapter 8 moves from PHP to Java. You'll find that Java is another extremely popular choice and that the Amazon Web Services Kit provides good support for this language. Although Java isn't quite as easy as PHP to transfer from one platform to another, it's a more popular choice. In addition, you'll find that Java applications run faster because Java performs some of the interpretation required to run the application during a compile cycle. Java still doesn't run as fast as a native code application, but it's a very good choice.

Chapter 8

Discovering the Benefits of Using Java

Discovering Places to Learn Java

Uncovering Java Browser Issues

Writing Applications Using Java

Working with the Amazon Supplied Code

Creating a Simple Java Application

Creating a Java Application with Database Support

Most people have heard about Java and many people have worked with it. Java appears on Web sites with some regularity because it lets Web designers create solutions that work with a number of browsers. Developers create Java applets for many Web-enabled applications as well as desktop applications. In short, Java appears in numerous places, so it's no wonder that you can use Java with Amazon Web Services too.

This chapter discusses techniques for using Java with Amazon Web Services. The examples show various strategies you can use to improve the user experience, while keeping the cost of development low. In general, you'll find many resources for using Java online. In addition, because Sun essentially owns Java, you'll find that it enjoys a level of support that most solutions can only dream about and openness not normally found with fully proprietary solutions.

However, using Java can become problematic in some cases. Java isn't fully proprietary, nor is it fully open. Consequently, there's some contention surrounding Java and you need to consider the issues that using Java can cause. (Read about these issues at `http://www.infoworld.com/article/03/05/12/HNfowler_1.html`.) This chapter doesn't examine these issues in detail, but it does provide enough information that you can learn more about the issues yourself and make a decision about the suitability of Java for your next application. As part of the Java overview, you'll also learn where you can find out more information about the language. As with all other languages in the book, I assume you've already learned Java and performed the required software installation before you begin this chapter.

Understanding the Benefits of Using Java

Java is popular because it can do so many things well. You can use Java on either the client or the server, or even both at the same time. This feature makes Java different from other solutions such as PHP because it provides flexibility in determining where an application runs. Unlike many other solutions, Java enjoys wide platform support, so a solution you create for one platform has a good chance of working on other platforms, too. In fact, you'll find numerous Java applications available for download that run on multiple platforms. For example, a single byte-code file (compiled code) can run on Macintosh OS X, OS/2, UNIX, VMS, and Windows.

Many developers use Java for both desktop and Web-based applications, although most people equate Java with Web development where it's a much stronger presence. The fact that you can use it for multiple application types makes Java a good solution for many multi-environment scenarios. Even though you'd need to make changes to an application (desktop) to run it as an applet (Web), the changes are minimal compared to other languages. However, make sure you understand the limits of Java compared to platform-specific solutions such as Visual Basic before you decide to use it in more than one place.

> **▶ NOTE**
>
> The examples in this chapter rely on the Java 2 Platform, Standard Edition (J2SE) version 1.4.2 available at `http://java.sun.com/j2se/1.4.2/download.html`. Older versions of the product might work, but you may need to modify the example code to exclude new features or functionality. In addition, I used the Windows platform for writing many of the applications and associated explanations. While the source code will work on any platform that supports the latest version of Java, you might need to modify some of the usage instructions slightly for other platforms.

Using Java for Web applications has many significant benefits. The most important benefit is that so many platforms support Java natively. You can develop Web-based applications using products such as Shockwave or Flash, but this solution often forces the Web site visitor to download a browser plug-in. Given Microsoft's recent loss of a lawsuit allowing plug-ins, using Macromedia Shockwave or Macromedia Flash might not even be an option in the future (see the eWeek article at `http://eletters.eweek.com/zd/cts?d=79-181-2-3-67152-23278-1` for details). Java applications generally work without any additional effort at all on the part of the user. In addition, Java is more capable than most other languages used for Web application presentation because it allows full interactivity between the client and server.

One feature that could be a benefit or a problem, depending on how you view it, is the fact that Java applications rely on a runtime engine that keeps them in a secure environment known as a sandbox. A Java application can only use the resources allotted to it by the runtime engine or Java Virtual Machine (JVM). This feature is beneficial because it improves security and makes it less likely that an errant Java application will cause other applications to fail (crash). The feature can cause problems by making it difficult to access resources the application needs to perform essential tasks such as writing data to the hard drive.

Another feature that you can view as a benefit or problem is the fact that Java tends to take a one-size-fits-all approach to platform support. Yes, every platform requires a special JVM, but that JVM tends to have the same functionality as every other JVM. This means you face fewer problems porting Java applications from one platform to the next. In fact, except for text-based products such as PHP, Java is one of the easiest languages to port. However, the one-size-fits-all approach also means that you'll experience problems using advanced features a specific platform has to offer. Microsoft tried to address the lack of platform-specific support in Java (among other things) by creating its own version of the JVM (see the "Understanding Java Browser Issues" section for details).

Resources for Learning Java

Learning any high-end language is difficult. However, some developers have complained that Java is one of the harder languages to learn because it lacks tools that other high-end languages provide. Sun is apparently aware of the complaints because it's promised to provide better tools (see the article at `http://www.infoworld.com/article/03/06/09/23NNjavaone_1.html` for details). Ease of use issues aside, Java is still a very powerful and flexible language, so you should honestly consider this solution for your next Amazon Web Services application. A single chapter can't show you everything about Java, so this section provides some resources where you can learn more.

> **▶ TIP**
>
> The court of public opinion on whether .NET or Java is the best solution to use for Web services is about split. According to a survey late in 2002 (see `http://www.infoworld.com/article/02/10/09/021009hndevsurvey_1.html?1010thap` for details), developers are spending equal time on both technologies. In short, both technologies are popular—you need to decide which one meets your needs best.

One of the best places to learn about Java is the Sun Web site at `http://java.sun.com/docs/books/tutorial/`. This site provides a good overview of Java and some great introductory material you can use to learn the language. For example, this tutorial explains the difference between a stand-alone application and an applet. Note that this Web site does provide separate instructions for Windows, Linux/UNIX, and Macintosh developers. You might find it helpful to read the instructions for your platform of interest, and then quickly glance through the other two sections to pick up platform-specific issues.

If you need another basic tutorial, then look at Brewing Java: A Tutorial at `http://www.ibiblio.org/javafaq/javatutorial.html`. The author of this tutorial actually expanded it into a book that he also mentions on the site. If you find the whole concept of object-oriented programming with Java difficult to understand, you'll want to view the Don't Fear the OOP tutorial at `http://sepwww.stanford.edu/sep/josman/oop/oop1.htm`.

An excellent beginner tutorial is Phil Heller's *Ground-Up Java* (Sybex, 2004). *Ground-Up Java* assumes no programming experience, but gets the reader up and running as a Java programmer quickly. The unique aspect of this book is the collection of powerful animated illustrations on the accompanying CD-ROM. They provide a crash-free environment to experiment with Java programming. The animated illustrations combined with the graded exercises that conclude every chapter and Phil's clear explanations of concepts and techniques make *Ground-Up Java* a programming course and computer lab rolled into one.

Choosing a Java Editor

The Sun tutorial suggests using Windows Notepad or a similar text editor for creating your Java applet code. However, you should consider using a good Java editor to make the development experience a lot better. The Sun ONE Studio 4, Community Edition IDE mentioned in the tutorial isn't available for download any longer—Sun has replaced it with a 60-day demonstration version of Sun ONE Studio 5, Standard Edition. You can get the Sun ONE Studio 5, Standard Edition IDE at `http://wwws.sun.com/software/sundev/`. The advantage of using the official IDE is that Sun designed it for Java and the IDE provides Java-specific help.

In some cases, a third party product such as SlickEdit (`http://www.slickedit.com/`) is actually a better deal. The SlickEdit solution provides support for multiple languages, which means you only have to learn one editor. Although this is a shrink-wrapped application, you can obtain a limited use trial version from the company Web site.

You might also consider using a product such as jEdit (`http://www.jedit.org/`) because the same executable runs on Macintosh OS X, OS/2, UNIX, VMS, and Windows. The author wrote this editor in Java and it points out the platform independence this language provides in a real world application. You'll find that jEdit has great community support, so you can download any of a number of add-on products for it. I used the jEdit editor to write the AmazonSearch and SimpleApplication examples in this chapter and found the color coding it provides extremely helpful. You can download this open source product free.

Another great IDE is JCreator (`http://www.jcreator.com/`). You can get the freeware version of the product and use it as long as you like. The professional version of the product is shareware, so you can download and use it free for 30 days. I also tried this editor while working on the DatabaseStore and SimpleApplication examples for this chapter. (The JCreator version of the SimpleApplication example appears on the Sybex Web site.) It's a great choice for developers who have worked with VBA or Visual Studio and are familiar with the IDE for those products. This is also one of the better editors for large projects because it helps you organize your project better and includes features such as a debugger.

Once you learn a little about Java, try some of the more advanced developer tutorials offered by Sun at `http://developer.java.sun.com/developer/onlineTraining/`. The tutorials on this site are diverse and some are complex, so make sure you understand the requirements for using the tutorial before you get too involved (the requirements normally appear as part of the tutorial's introduction). The feature I like most about this site is that all of the tutorials have dates, so you know how old the information is before you get started.

A number of third parties also provide advanced tutorials and this section doesn't even begin to list them all. One of the more interesting offerings is The Advanced Java/J2EE Tutorial at `http://my.execpc.com/~gopalan/java/java_tutorial.html`. This tutorial begins with a comparison of the various communication technologies (including Java/RMI, DCOM, and CORBA). You might also want to look at Java Coffee Break at `http://www.javacoffeebreak.com/` because it includes a wide range of tutorials (some advanced) as well as other resources.

Newsgroups can also provide essential information to the Java developer. One of the best newsgroups to try is `comp.lang.java`. Note that this newsgroup has numerous subfolders you'll also want to visit. For example, you can keep track of Java bugs on the `comp.lang.java.bugs` newsgroup. The `comp.lang.java` newsgroup enjoys broad support and some people even support it on their Web sites. For example, check out The comp.lang.java FAQ List at `http://www.ibiblio.org/javafaq/javafaq.html`. You can also try newsgroups such as `alt.comp.lang.java`. Make sure you check any vendor specific Java newsgroups groups such as `borland.public.jbuilder.java` when you use a particular product.

Understanding Java Browser Issues

As previously mentioned, you can use Java in a client, server, or mixed solution. The problem with developing either a client or mixed solution is that you have to consider the user's browser. The media has documented the combat between Sun and Microsoft over the JVM. (See the story at `http://archive.infoworld.com/articles/hn/xml/02/12/05/021205hnmsblames.xml?1205tham` as just one example.) Microsoft, as usual, decided to produce its own version of the JVM, which is incompatible with Sun's version. Some users might have this incompatible version installed, even though Sun won a lawsuit over the issue and Microsoft no longer produces it.

The latest twist in the battle is that some versions of Windows no longer come with the JVM installed, which means that the client can't run your Java application at all. Microsoft originally shipped Windows XP without a JVM—the operating system downloaded the JVM on demand, rather than supply it as a default (see the story at `http://archive.infoworld.com/articles/hn/xml/02/06/18/020618hnjavasupport.xml?0620thap` for details). Sun is trying to get around the Windows JVM problem by signing individual companies to distribute it (see the InfoWorld article at `http://www.infoworld.com/article/03/06/11/HNjavadell_1.html` for details). The two companies are still in court over this issue (see the story at `http://www.infoworld.com/article/03/04/03/HNmsorder_1.html`). Because of this contention, you can't be sure which version of the JVM a client has or even if the client has the JVM installed.

Even if the client has the JVM installed, crackers have made Java one of their tools of choice. Consequently, many people turn off support for the JVM in their browsers. This task is amazingly easy with products such as Internet Explorer. Because you don't know whether the client has the JVM installed, telling them to turn the JVM on in an error message is unlikely to produce the desired results in many cases.

Finally, it might seem like everyone would have a JVM installed and all the proper browser support, but that's not true. Many browsers simply don't have the required support. You can view the Webmonkey charts at the following locations for specific platform support of Java.

- Windows

  `http://hotwired.lycos.com/webmonkey/reference/browser_chart/index.html`
- Macintosh

  `http://hotwired.lycos.com/webmonkey/reference/browser_chart/index_mac.html`
- Linux

  `http://hotwired.lycos.com/webmonkey/reference/browser_chart/index_nix.html`
- Other

  `http://hotwired.lycos.com/webmonkey/reference/browser_chart/index_other.html`

The bottom line is that you have to know the client capabilities of the users of your application or develop a server-side solution. Java is a great solution because it's so flexible, but it also carries a number of problems that you might not run into with less flexible or less capable solutions. You need to decide whether the potential browser problems with Java are going to interfere with your Amazon Web Services application.

Using the Amazon Supplied Code

The Amazon Web Services Kit provides a lot of Java support—you'll find example code in both the `\AmazonWebServices\JavaCodeSample` and `\AmazonWebServices\PriceTracker` folders. Make sure you read the instructions found in the "Instructions on how to use the Java Sample" and "Instructions on how to use the Java Price Tracking Program" sections of the `READMEFIRST.TXT` file found in the `\AmazonWebServices` folder as a first step for using these examples. However, you'll find that the instructions leave out a few steps and contain a little outdated information. The topic in this section provides some updates you should know about before using the examples.

You'll find that the Amazon supplied code is a lot more than a simple example—you can use this code as the basis for your own applications. Consequently, the second topic in this section tells you how to make use of the Amazon code for your own applications. Using this technique is a good first step because it greatly reduces the work you need to do to get an initial application running.

> **NOTE**
>
> Do not follow the Apache Axis installation instructions unless you plan to create your own Web service. You only need the library files to create the Java files required for the client portion of Amazon Web Services.

Performing the Required Setup

This section describes some of the tasks you should perform to ensure your Java applications work well with Amazon Web Services. The instructions for creating the Amazon examples are clear enough, but they leave out a few important steps that can make your experience a bit better. Make sure you get the latest versions of the Java Development Kit (JDK) and the Axis Simple Object Access Protocol (SOAP) provider. At the time of this writing, you can obtain the Java 2 Platform, Standard Edition (J2SE) version 1.4.2 at `http://java.sun.com/j2se/1.4.2/download.html`. All of the Apache Axis versions appear at `http://ws.apache.org/axis/`. Do not use the Beta 3 version mentioned in the Amazon documentation—at least not on Windows, where it caused a number of errors including a non-reproducible system reboot. I used the Final 1.1 version for the book with good success.

Java must have access to the files required to build the SOAP stubs. This means that you must place the Axis files in the same folder as the WSDL file or you must create a class path for the library. You can use this second technique by adding the `-classpath` switch to the command line (edit the `Client.Axis.BAT` file to include it for Windows developers). The class path must include all of the `JAR` files located in the `\Axis-1_1\Lib` folder. If you receive a `java.lang.NoClassDefFoundError` message, it means that Java can't find the Axis libraries. You'll find a modified version of the `Client.Axis.BAT` file, with the WSDL file I used for the examples and the resulting `.JAVA` files in the `\Chapter 08\WSDL2Java` folder of the source code on the Sybex Web site.

> **NOTE**
>
> Move the `\com\amazon\soap\axis` folder to the `\AmazonWebServices\PriceTracker` example folder before you attempt to compile the PriceTracker example. The Amazon documentation doesn't make it clear that you have to perform this step. Make certain that you use the modified versions of the batch files for both examples.

Java takes a piecemeal approach to SOAP support. In addition to Axis, you also need XML parser support. The Axis documentation recommends using the Xerces-J parser found at `http://xml.apache.org/dist/xerces-j/`. You don't need the XML parser to create the SOAP stubs, but you do need it to create the example executable using the `javac` command listed as Step 5 in the Amazon instructions. Again, make sure you provide a class path for the XML parser. You can find a sample batch file `XercesCompile.BAT` file located in the `\Chapter 08\WSDL2Java` folder of the source code on the Sybex Web site that performs this step.

At this point, you might see a listing of errors. These errors occur because the capitalization of functions in the Axis-generated stubs differs from the capitalization of function calls in the Amazon example files. Generally, you must fix an entry in the Amazon SOAP files. For example, if you see an error for `class com.amazon.soap.axis.SellerRequest`, you'll need to change the `SellerProfileSoap.JAVA` file. All you need to do is compare the Axis capitalization to the Amazon capitalization to fix the error.

Once the program compiles, you can run it. Make sure you include the class path, as you did for the other steps. The `RunExample.BAT` file located in the `\Chapter 08\WSDL2Java` folder of the source code on the Sybex Web site shows how to perform this step. Figure 8.1 shows typical output from the example in the `\AmazonWebServices\JavaCodeSample` folder. The drop-down list selects a query type. Simply fill in the fields and click Send to see the results.

FIGURE 8.1:

The Amazon Java Code Sample helps you understand the techniques for making a request in Java.

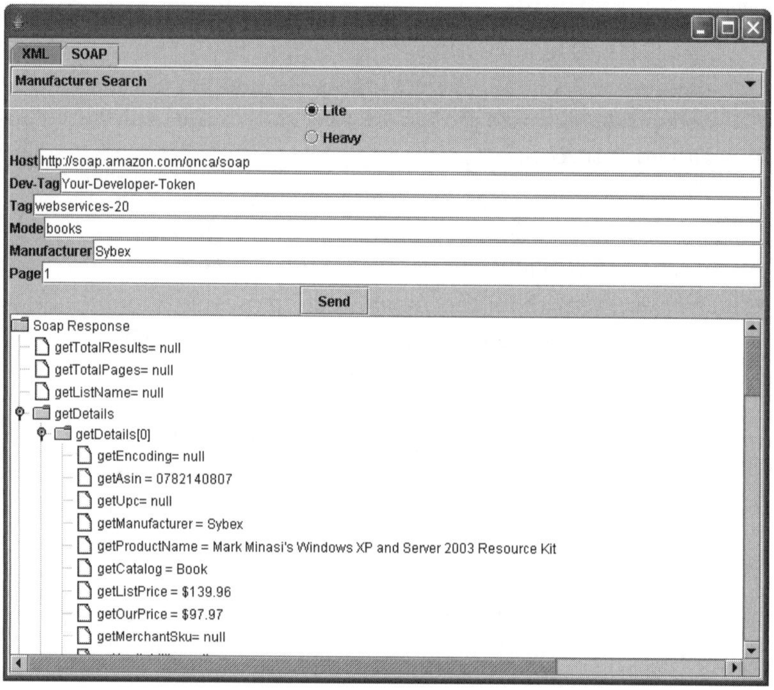

Note that you don't really get to see the benefit of the PriceTracker example until after you generate a few searches. Open the `asinRecord.CSV` file in an application such as Excel and you'll see columns indicating the data you requested for a particular ASIN as shown in Figure 8.2. For example, if you request a list of used products for a particular ASIN, you'll see the Asin, Exchange Id, Offer Type, Last Price, Current Price, Tracking Start Date, and Condition Type columns in the file. Track this information over time and you can start defining trends for the ASIN.

Using the Examples for Your Own Code

Now that you've performed all the work required to get the Amazon examples working, you might wonder what good they do you except to look neat on screen. It turns out that the example code in the `\AmazonWebServices\JavaCodeSample` folder is quite helpful in creating applications of your own. In fact, this code can reduce the problem of working with Amazon Web Services to the few lines needed to grab the data and then whatever code you need to present the information on screen. In addition, you don't have to worry about using all of the code—three files might be all you need to accomplish a given task. For example, if you want to make an author request, then all you need are these files.

- `AbstractSoapQuery.JAVA`
- `AuthorSoap.JAVA`
- `SoapQuery.JAVA`

FIGURE 8.2: Use a product such as Excel to view the output of the PriceTracker example.

	A	B	C	D	E	F	G
1	Asin	Exchange Id	Offer Type	Last Price	Current Price	Tracking Start Date	Condition Type
2	078214134X	Y02Y5895743Y8055809	new	0	29.98	9/5/2003 11:24	new
3	078214134X	Y04Y6948888Y6328620	new	0	29.99	9/5/2003 11:24	new
4	078214134X	Y01Y1315359Y0006583	new	0	37.74	9/5/2003 11:24	new
5	078214134X	Y01Y0732475Y5851066	used	31	31	9/5/2003 11:25	mint
6	078214134X	Y02Y5607286Y2694307	new	0	36.9	9/5/2003 11:24	new
7	078214134X	Y01Y2125909Y9235367	new	0	29.99	9/5/2003 11:24	new
8	078214134X	Y02Y4055568Y3216526	new	0	29.99	9/5/2003 11:24	new
9	078214134X	Y01Y1248142Y7191228	used	41	41	9/5/2003 11:25	verygood
10	078214134X	Y02Y6647666Y3686201	new	0	30.55	9/5/2003 11:24	new
11	078214134X	Y01Y2384005Y4263087	used	29.38	29.38	9/5/2003 11:25	verygood
12	078214134X	Y03Y3181312Y9347742	used	36.9	36.9	9/5/2003 11:25	mint
13	078214134X	Y04Y2047372Y0695929	used	41.15	41.15	9/5/2003 11:25	mint
14	078214134X	Y02Y0662307Y0007945	used	29.38	29.38	9/5/2003 11:25	verygood
15	078214134X	Y03Y5588767Y7996907	new	0	36.75	9/5/2003 11:24	new
16	078214134X	Y03Y2953173Y4339740	used	41	41	9/5/2003 11:25	verygood
17	078214134X	Y04Y2089348Y9914249	new	0	30.55	9/5/2003 11:24	new

You also need the contents of the `\com\amazon\soap\axis` folder when you want to create a SOAP application. However, you only need to generate this folder once until Amazon changes the interface. In short, you need to check your WSDL file to ensure it isn't outdated. The Amazon Web Services Kit help topic at `/AmazonWebServices/API Guide/dtd_xsd_soap_wsdl.htm` contains all the information you need to update your WSDL file. Placing the Amazon SOAP stubs in a central location so you can access them from all applications saves time. The example code uses a local copy for each example to reduce the risk of compilation problems on your system.

> **▶ WARNING**
>
> Don't attempt to change the automatically generated Axis files. These files appear in the `\com\amazon\soap\axis` folder and reflect the current state of the Amazon WSDL files. When you generate these files again, all the errors you fixed earlier will reappear. Always change the Amazon example files.

The example in this section eschews the usual interface elements to make the Amazon Web Services access process clearer. Once you add display elements, it's easier to lose track of the request process. Consequently, you'll see some simple output at the command prompt for this example and won't be able to change the input values without recompiling the application. Listing 8.1 contains the code you need for this example. You'll find this example in the `\Chapter 08\AmazonSearch` folder of the source code located on the Sybex Web site.

Listing 8.1 Building a Java Application Using the Amazon Supplied Files

```
import com.amazon.soap.axis.*;

public class MainApp
{
   AuthorSoap  Request;    // Contains the request information.
   ProductInfo Result;     // Holds all of the results.
   Details     BookData;   // Holds an individual book.

   public MainApp()
   {
      // Create the request.
      System.out.println("Setting up SOAP request...");
      this.Request = new AuthorSoap();
      this.Request.parameters.put("Author","John Mueller");
      this.Request.parameters.put("Page","1");
      this.Request.parameters.put("Mode","books");
      this.Request.parameters.put("Tag","webservices-20");
      this.Request.parameters.put("Type","lite");
      this.Request.parameters.put("Dev-Tag","Your-Developer-Token");

      // Place the actual request transfer in a try block. Check for
      // each of the common exceptions. When the call is successful,
      // place the return value in a ProductInfo object.
      try
```

```
            {
               this.Request.issueRequest();
               this.Result = (ProductInfo)this.Request.getResult();
            }
            catch(java.net.MalformedURLException e)
            {
               System.out.println("A MalformedURLException error occurred.");
               System.out.println(e);
            }
            catch(javax.xml.rpc.ServiceException e)
            {
               System.out.println("A ServiceException error occurred.");
               System.out.println(e);
            }
            catch(java.rmi.RemoteException e)
            {
               System.out.println("A RemoteException error occurred.");
               System.out.println(e);
            }

            // Process the Details array.
            for (int Count = 0;
                 Count < this.Result.getDetails().length;
                 Count++)
            {
               // Retrieve the data for an individual book.
               this.BookData = (Details)this.Result.getDetails()[Count];

               // Print out the information.
               System.out.println(this.BookData.getProductName());
               System.out.println(this.BookData.getAsin());
               System.out.println(this.BookData.getManufacturer());
               System.out.println(this.BookData.getReleaseDate());

               // Add an extra line between books.
               System.out.println("");
            }
         }
      }
```

The example assumes that you've placed the three Amazon files in the same folder as the example application. It relies on the `XercesCompile.BAT` and `RunExample.BAT` batch files to start the applications. You must import the Axis-generated classes as shown in the code.

The code begins by creating a request. The `Request` object includes parameters specific to each request type, so you need to view the content of the associated `JAVA` file. In this case, you'd need to view the `AuthorSoap.JAVA` file. Depending on the editor you use, you might see this information without actually opening the file. The code uses the `parameters.put()` method with the name of a request argument and the request value as the two input values.

To make the request, the code uses the `issueRequest()` method. You must place this method within a `try...catch` block to ensure the application can retrieve any required fault information. The code retrieves the entire result set using the `getResult()` method. Again, this call should appear within a `try...catch` block—you can use the same block as the request submission.

The final step is to process the data. As with all return structures returned by Amazon, this one is a set of XML nodes that Java treats as arrays or individual data values as needed. Notice that you treat each detail as an array element and use the `getDetails()` method to obtain the entire detail array. Note that this is the only method for obtaining an individual result.

Developing a Simple Java Application

The application in this section moves beyond simple Amazon Web Services access into something you could start using as an application. In this case, the example performs a manufacturer search using a dialog-based application. The example doesn't rely on any of the Amazon example files, so the application has to perform all of the SOAP operations based on the Axis files. The first section that follows shows how to configure the JCreator editor to make using the Axis-specific files a lot easier. The subsequent sections discuss the example.

Configuring the JCreator Editor

The professional version of the JCreator editor can make working with Amazon Web Services a lot easier because it provides more help with the various packages and libraries. You don't have to spend time working with batch files because the application compiles within the IDE. In addition, the debugger makes it easier to see how requests to and responses from Amazon Web Services work. To obtain all these benefits, you need to perform the following configuration steps.

1. Create a new workspace using the File ➢ New command. The new workspace automatically contains a single project file. The first configuration step is to add the Amazon SOAP support.
2. Choose the Project ➢ Add Directory Contents command. You'll see an Insert Files from Directory dialog box similar to the one shown in Figure 8.3.
3. Type the root directory of the Amazon SOAP files created by Axis. You can also use the browse button to locate the files. Check the Include Subdirectories option. Select Create Project Folders by Package Name. Click Insert. JCreator will add the Amazon SOAP files to the project. You'll see the Amazon SOAP files as `com.amazon.soap.axis` in the Package View window.

4. Choose the Project ➢ Project Settings command. You'll see the Project Settings dialog box.
5. Select Required Libraries. This is where you enter the information for the Axis and Xerces libraries.
6. Click New. You'll see a Set Library dialog box similar to the one shown in Figure 8.4 (this one has the Axis library settings in place).
7. Type a name for the library in the Name field.
8. Choose the Add ➢ Add Archive button (the button displays several options when you click it). You'll see an Open dialog box.
9. Locate the target library files on your hard drive. Select all of the required `.JAR` files. Click OK.
10. Click OK to close the Set Library dialog box.
11. Check the new library entry in the Project Settings dialog box. JCreator adds the library files to the `ClassPath` field at the bottom of the dialog box.
12. Perform Steps 6 through 11 for both the Axis and the Xerces libraries.

FIGURE 8.3:

Use the Add Directory Context dialog box to add the Amazon SOAP files to your project.

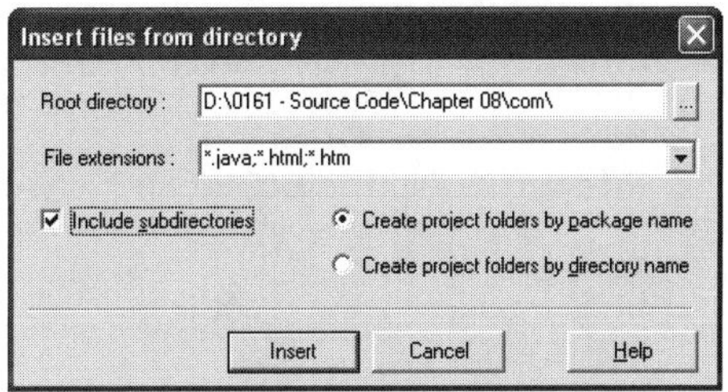

FIGURE 8.4:

Use the Set Library dialog box to add libraries to the class path.

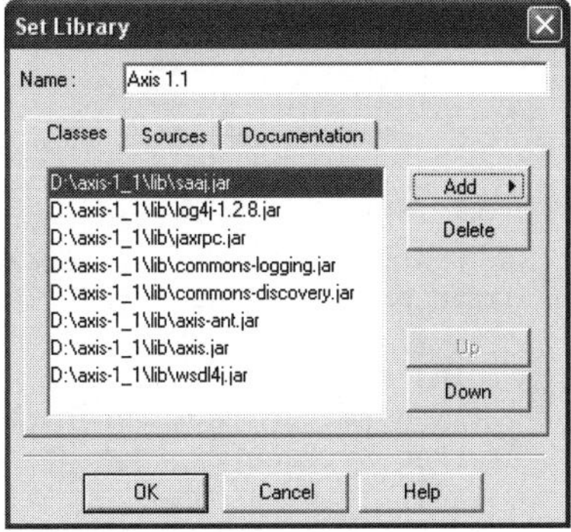

You've configured JCreator for use with Amazon Web Services at this point. These steps probably seem like a lot more work than simply typing what you need into a batch file, but it's also less error prone and somewhat easier to configure. Generally, you'll find modification and updates are much easier to perform using this editor.

Writing the Application

In this section, you learn how to perform a manufacturer search using Java and Amazon Web Services. Manufacturer searches are helpful when you want a product made by that particular vendor, rather than the broad range of vendors that Amazon supports. Listing 8.2 shows the essential code for this example—the listing isn't complete. You'll find the complete code for this example in the `\Chapter 08\SimpleApplication` folder of the source code located on the Sybex Web site.

Listing 8.2 Developing a Manufacturer Search

```
// This class handles button click events.
private class ButtonHandler implements ActionListener
{
   AmazonSearchService  Service;    // Amazon Search Service Object.
   AmazonSearchPort     Port;       // Port used to access Amazon.
   ManufacturerRequest  DataReq;    // Request data object.
   ProductInfo          DataResult; // Response to request.
   Details              ProdData;   // An individual product.

   public void actionPerformed(ActionEvent AE)
   {
      // End the program.
      if (AE.getSource() == btnQuit)
         System.exit(0);

      // Issue a request and receive a response.
      if (AE.getSource() == btnTest)
      {
         try
         {
            // Create the required SOAP objects.
            Service = new AmazonSearchServiceLocator();
            Port = Service.getAmazonSearchPort(
               new URL("http://soap.amazon.com/onca/soap"));
            DataReq = new ManufacturerRequest();

            // Insert the request data.
            DataReq.setManufacturer(txtMfg.getText());
            DataReq.setPage(txtPage.getText());
            DataReq.setMode(txtMode.getText());
```

```
            DataReq.setType(txtType.getText());
            DataReq.setTag(txtTag.getText());
            DataReq.setDevtag(txtDevTag.getText());

            // Get the result.
            DataResult =
               (ProductInfo)Port.manufacturerSearchRequest(DataReq);
         }
         catch(java.net.MalformedURLException e)
         {
            System.out.println("A MalformedURLException error.");
            System.out.println(e);
         }
         catch(javax.xml.rpc.ServiceException e)
         {
            System.out.println("A ServiceException error occurred.");
            System.out.println(e);
         }
         catch(java.rmi.RemoteException e)
         {
            System.out.println("A RemoteException error occurred.");
            System.out.println(e);
         }

         // Clear the response table.
         for (int RCount = 0;
              RCount < 10;
              RCount++)
            for (int CCount = 0;
                 CCount < 4;
                 CCount++)
                tblResp.setValueAt("", RCount, CCount);

         // Output the result.
         for (int Count = 0;
              Count < DataResult.getDetails().length;
              Count++)
         {
            // Retrieve the data for an individual product.
            ProdData = (Details)DataResult.getDetails()[Count];

            // Print out the information.
            tblResp.setValueAt(ProdData.getAsin(), Count, 0);
            tblResp.setValueAt(ProdData.getProductName(), Count, 1);
            tblResp.setValueAt(ProdData.getReleaseDate(), Count, 2);
            tblResp.setValueAt(ProdData.getListPrice(), Count, 3);
         }
      }
   }
}
```

> **NOTE**
>
> JCreator includes a package `myprojects.databasestore` or similar statement in the templates, which prevents you from running the application from the command prompt. The examples in this chapter don't include the statement so you'll find the compiled code and `RunExample.BAT` file in the `classes` subfolder, rather than in the `classes\myprojects` subfolder as usual. Make sure you add this statement if you want to run the application from within the JCreator IDE.

Listing 8.2 shows the SOAP-specific code for this example. It begins by creating the objects needed to access Amazon Web Services. Because this example doesn't rely on the Amazon example files, it needs to perform a few tasks by hand, such as defining the access port. You must perform all of these tasks within a `try...catch` block as shown in the example. Fortunately, you still only need to check for three exception types as the code progresses (see the example in Listing 8.1 for details).

Once the code instantiates the Amazon Web Services connection, creates a search port, and obtains a `ManufacturerRequest` object, it begins filling `DataReq` with the information required for the request. The example provides `JTextField` objects as an interface with the user. You must provide the six values shown in Listing 8.2 as a minimum. Amazon Web Services will also accept values that order the information for presentation on screen.

At this point, the code makes the request. Notice that communication occurs through the `Port` object created earlier. Axis sets up the various search request methods when it reads the WSDL file and creates the Java stub files for you. JCreator lists these methods, such as the `manufacturerSearchRequest()` method shown in the example, when you type the name of the `Port` object. Because Amazon can change the interface, you need to exercise care in checking for changes to these method names or input values.

The code now has access to a `ProductInfo` data structure. It begins processing the data by obtaining the `Details` array from the `ProductInfo` data structure and extracting a single `Detail` structure. The code stores this information in `ProdData`. A `for` loop processes each `Detail` array member in turn and places the data in `tblResp`. Figure 8.5 shows typical output from this application.

> **NOTE**
>
> Some manufacturers, such as Microsoft, can appear in more than one product category or mode. This means that the mode entry that has remained somewhat useless for other examples in the book now has a new meaning. You can find a list of modes in the "Common Modes and Browse IDs" help topic of the Amazon Web Services Toolkit at `/AmazonWebServices/API Guide/common_modes.htm`.

Writing a Java Application with Database Support

Anyone who intends to use Amazon Web Services extensively in a multiuser environment will likely want to improve application performance by storing common query results locally. For example, you might own a music store and want to look up data regarding specific CDs on Amazon. Some CDs will receive multiple hits, making it possible to improve search speed by storing the UPC for

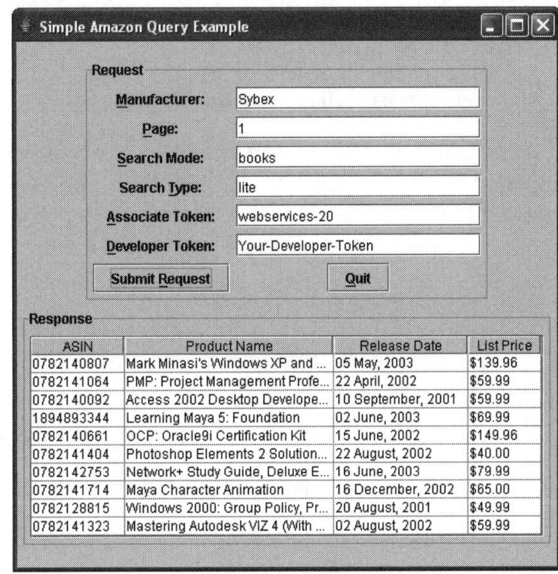

FIGURE 8.5: Manufacturer searches can retrieve different data depending on the product category selected.

that CD locally. The example in this section requires some type of database support. Because a Database Management System (DBMS) is platform specific, you might need to change the database portion of the code to match your database setup. I'm using Windows and SQL Server as the platform and DBMS for this example.

You'll need to work with this example in two parts. The first part handles the request from the database if possible. The second part makes the request from Amazon if the database doesn't contain the requested information or the information in the database is too old. Listing 8.3 shows the essential code for the first part of this example—the listing isn't complete. You'll find the complete code for this example in the `\Chapter 08\DatabaseStore` folder of the source code located on the Sybex Web site.

Listing 8.3 Handling the Initial Request

```
// This class handles button click events.
private class ButtonHandler implements ActionListener
{
   public void actionPerformed(ActionEvent AE)
   {
      SimpleDateFormat  ConvDate;    // Converts the date.
      java.util.Date    Now;         // Scanned date.
      java.util.Date    Released;    // Released date.
      java.util.Date    Scanned;     // Data scanning date.
      long              TimeComp;    // Date comparison.
      SimpleDateFormat  FormDate;    // Formats the date.
```

```
String            LPConv;     // Converts list price.

// End the program.
if (AE.getSource() == btnQuit)
   System.exit(0);

// Issue a request and receive a response.
if (AE.getSource() == btnTest)
{
   // Clear the output.
   txtASIN.setText("");
   ... Other Fields ...
   txtReleaseDate.setText("");

   // Create an instance of the JDBC-ODBC Bridge Driver.
   try
   {
      Class.forName("sun.jdbc.odbc.JdbcOdbcDriver");
   }
   catch (java.lang.ClassNotFoundException e)
   {
      System.out.println("Java didn't find the ODBC driver.");
      System.out.println(e);
   }

   try
   {
      // Make a connection to the database.
      Con =
         DriverManager.getConnection("jdbc:odbc:StoreAmazon");

      // Define an executable statement.
      Stmnt = Con.createStatement();

      // Get a result set.
      RS = Stmnt.executeQuery("SELECT * FROM DataStore " +
                              "WHERE UPC=" +
                              txtUPC.getText());

      // Verify the data exists.
      if (!RS.next())
      {

         // Make the request.
         GenerateRequest();

         // Exit the routine.
         return;
      }

      else
```

```
{
   // Display the current data.
   txtASIN.setText(RS.getString("ASIN"));
   ... Other Fields ...
}

// The received date requires special handling. First,
// convert from a string to a date.
ConvDate =
   new SimpleDateFormat("yyyy-MM-dd HH:mm:ss.SSS");
Released = new java.util.Date();
try
{
   Released =
      ConvDate.parse(RS.getString("Release_Date"));
}
catch (java.text.ParseException e)
{
   System.out.println("Released Date Parsing Error");
   System.out.println(e);
}

// Second, convert from date to formatted string.
FormDate = new SimpleDateFormat("dd MMMM, yyyy");
txtReleaseDate.setText(FormDate.format(Released));

// Update the picture.
ProdPict = new ImageIcon(RS.getBytes("Picture"));
lblProdPict.setIcon(ProdPict);

// Verify that the data is good or update it as needed.
// Convert the scanned date.
ConvDate =
   new SimpleDateFormat("yyyy-MM-dd HH:mm:ss.SSS");
Scanned = new java.util.Date();
try
{
   Scanned = ConvDate.parse(RS.getString("Scanned"));
}
catch (java.text.ParseException e)
{
   System.out.println("Scanned Date Parsing Error");
   System.out.println(e);
}

// Add 24 hours to the scan date.
TimeComp = Scanned.getTime();
TimeComp = TimeComp + 86400000;
Scanned.setTime(TimeComp);

// Get the current date.
```

```
                    Now = new java.util.Date();

                    // If the data is too old.
                    if (Now.after(Scanned))
                    {
                       // Remove the old record.
                       Stmnt.executeUpdate(
                          "DELETE FROM DataStore WHERE UPC=" +
                          txtUPC.getText());

                       // Make the request.
                       GenerateRequest();
                    }
                 }
                 catch (java.sql.SQLException e)
                 {
                    System.out.println("SQL Error");
                    System.out.println(e);
                 }
              }
           }
        }
```

The code begins with an essential housekeeping detail—clearing the fields. In some cases, a product won't include some information. For example, a product might not include an availability value.

The next step is to establish a connection with the database. As previously mentioned, this example relies on the JDBC-ODBC Bridge Driver to perform the required linkage between Java and SQL Server. The example shows a typical setup for this kind of database connection. Once the driver is instantiated, the code can use it to make the actual connection. The code also creates a standard statement—one that it can use for queries made up of executable SQL statements. The first statement returns a recordset, `RS`, when the database contains the information needed. If the `RS.next()` method fails, the code knows the data doesn't exist in the database and calls the `GenerateRequest()` method to request the information from Amazon.

The recordset is a forward-only cursor, which means you need to handle data queries carefully. The code optimizes the database connection by requesting each field value in turn and using it immediately as shown. Notice that the `Release_Date` field requires special handling. Amazon and SQL Server store dates differently. If you want a consistent look on screen, you need to perform data translation as needed. The example code shows how to perform this task using a minimum of steps. The use of `SimpleDateFormat` objects greatly reduces the amount of code.

The ProdPict object also requires special handling. SQL Server stores the picture as a series of bytes. Use the RS.getBytes() method to ensure you get the picture from the database and into the picture object without any problem. As always, you must store the picture within a label or similar object before you place it on screen.

At this point, the code needs to determine whether the information is up to date. It could have performed this step first, but the forward-only cursor makes it more efficient to perform the step last. The code places the numeric value of time within TimeComp, adds 24 hours to this value (which is 86,400,000 milliseconds—milliseconds is the standard unit of time measure for Java), and then stores the updated value back into Scanned using the setTime() method. (The reason the code adds 24 hours is so Scanned reflects a 24-hour time differential.) If the Now.after() method check fails, then the code deletes the existing record from the database and uses the GenerateRequest() method to perform an update. Listing 8.4 shows the code for the GenerateRequest() method.

Listing 8.4 Creating a UPC Request and Database Update

```
// This method generates a request if the local database doesn't
// have the required data.
private void GenerateRequest()
{
   String[]               Output;      // The output data.
   SimpleDateFormat       ConvDate;    // Converts the date.
   SimpleDateFormat       FormDate;    // Formats the date.
   java.util.Date         Now;         // Scanned date.
   String                 NowStr;      // Today's date as a string.
   java.util.Date         Released;    // Released date.
   String                 RelStr;      // Released date as string.
   String                 ConvLP;      // List price conversion.
   byte[]                 PictByte;    // Byte array for storage.
   URL                    AmazonImg;   // Product picture location.
   InputStream            PictIn;      // Amazon data read stream.
   ByteArrayOutputStream  PictOut;     // Picture output stream.
   PreparedStatement      PState;      // A prepared statement.

   try
   {
      // Create the required SOAP objects.
      Service = new AmazonSearchServiceLocator();
      Port = Service.getAmazonSearchPort(
         new URL("http://soap.amazon.com/onca/soap"));
      DataReq = new UpcRequest();

      // Insert the request data.
      DataReq.setUpc(txtUPC.getText());
```

```
      ... Other Request Data ...

      // Get the result.
      DataResult =
         (ProductInfo)Port.upcSearchRequest(DataReq);
   }
   catch(java.net.MalformedURLException e)
   {
      System.out.println("A MalformedURLException error occurred.");
      System.out.println(e);
   }
   catch(javax.xml.rpc.ServiceException e)
   {
      System.out.println("A ServiceException error occurred.");
      System.out.println(e);
   }
   catch(java.rmi.RemoteException e)
   {
      System.out.println("A RemoteException error occurred.");
      System.out.println(e);
   }

   // Retrieve the data for an individual product.
   ProdData = (Details)DataResult.getDetails()[0];

   // Convert the date by creating a custom date formatter
   // and using it to parse the string provided by Amazon.
   ConvDate = new SimpleDateFormat("dd MMMM, yyyy");
   Released = new java.util.Date();
   try
   {
      Released = ConvDate.parse(ProdData.getReleaseDate());
   }
   catch (java.text.ParseException e)
   {
      System.out.println("Date Parsing Error");
      System.out.println(e);
   }

   // Format the released date for use with SQL Server.
   FormDate = new SimpleDateFormat("yyyy/MM/dd HH:mm:ss");
   RelStr = FormDate.format(Released);

   // Create the scanned date.
   Now = new java.util.Date();
   NowStr = FormDate.format(Now);

   // Create a list price without the dollar sign.
   ConvLP = ProdData.getListPrice();
```

```
ConvLP = ConvLP.substring(1);

// Initialize the picture output data stream.
PictOut = new ByteArrayOutputStream();

// Update the picture.
try
{
   // Create an URL for the image.
   AmazonImg = new URL(ProdData.getImageUrlMedium());

   // Open an input data stream.
   PictIn = new BufferedInputStream(AmazonImg.openStream());

   // Create an intermediate buffer.
   PictByte = new byte[4096];

   // Use this odd looking code to read the data from
   // the Amazon online source into the local buffer.
   for (int Read=0;
        (Read=PictIn.read(PictByte))!=-1;
        PictOut.write(PictByte, 0, Read));

   // Place the resulting image into the picture object.
   ProdPict = new ImageIcon(PictOut.toByteArray());
}
catch (java.net.MalformedURLException e)
{
   System.out.println("Bad URL from Amazon.");
   System.out.println(e);
}
catch (java.io.IOException e)
{
   System.out.println("Input or Output Exception");
   System.out.println(e);
}

// Place the picture within a label for display.
lblProdPict.setIcon(ProdPict);

// Update the database using a prepared statement,
// rather than the usual SQL text. The only reason to
// use this technique is to assist in transferring binary
// data such as the image and reduce numeric errors.
try
{
   // Create a prepared statement with variables for
   // value entries. You must include one variable for
   // each database column.
```

```
         PState =
            Con.prepareStatement("INSERT INTO DataStore " +
                                 "VALUES (?, ?, ?, ?, ?, ?, ?, ?, ?, ?)");

         // The database entries are 1-based, not 0-based. Use
         // the correct set method for each entry.
         PState.setString(1, ProdData.getAsin());
         ... Other Update Fields ...
         PState.setFloat(7, Float.parseFloat(ConvLP));
         PState.setString(8, RelStr);
         PState.setBytes(9, PictOut.toByteArray());
         PState.setString(10, NowStr);
         PState.executeUpdate();
      }
      catch (java.sql.SQLException e)
      {
         System.out.println("Database Update Error");
         System.out.println(e);
      }


      // Display the output.
      txtASIN.setText(ProdData.getAsin());
      ... Other Output Values ...
   }
```

The `GenerateRequest()` method begins with a query to Amazon. The request code for this example is similar to the code shown in Listing 8.2. The main differences are that you don't supply a page value and the main input value is the UPC, rather than some other value such as a manufacturer or author name. Once the code successfully queries Amazon, it begins processing the data.

In this case, part of the data processing involves converting the release date from the Amazon format to something SQL Server can understand. This means creating a date by parsing the string provided by Amazon. You must use a `SimpleDateFormat` object as shown in the example because a standard `DateFormat` object won't understand the Amazon string. The code uses a different `SimpleDateFormat` object to convert both the release date and the scan date into strings. Notice that the list price requires similar conversion because Amazon sends it to you with a $ (dollar sign) attached.

The product picture presents a few problems in this case. You must download the image from the Amazon Web site. Normally, all you'd need to do is create an `URL` object and use it as input to the `ImageIcon` constructor. However, that technique leaves you without a method to obtain access to the bytes that make up the image. The technique shown in the example helps overcome this issue by placing the image in a `ByteArrayOutputStream` object. You still supply the image data to the `ImageIcon` constructor, but as a byte array, rather than an URL.

The last little oddity to consider for this example is the database update. Notice that the `GenerateRequest()` method relies on a `PreparedStatement` object, rather than the standard `Statement` object. The technique shown in this listing helps you overcome data transfer problems with SQL Server. You can store the image directly within the database, rather than in an external source. Figure 8.6 shows typical output from this application.

Your Call to Action

This chapter has helped you understand how to use Java to build an Amazon Web Services application. In fact, the chapter discusses how to build several application types so you get a better idea of just how flexible Java is. The chapter has also pointed out some of the hurdles you might encounter when building the application. Java is an outstanding language with amazing flexibility, but it also has significant problems that you can't overcome with ease. The important issue is to determine whether the benefits of using Java outweigh potential problems when you decide whether to use this language.

Begin your preparation for using Java by using the Web site URLs in the "Resources for Learning Java" section of the chapter. Once you know Java well enough, you're ready to look at the requirements for your application. Make sure you spend enough time considering the issue of whether the intelligence for your application will reside on the client or the server (or something in between). You also need to consider the server setup you want to use and decide what kind of functionality to build into your application. You might decide to start with something as simple as a search site so you can see how Amazon Web Services performs, as well as how you need to configure your setup for a more advanced application.

> **NOTE**
>
> Using SQL Server with Java means using the Java DataBase Connectivity (JDBC) to Open DataBase Connectivity (ODBC) adapter. The JDBC-ODBC Bridge driver supplied with the latest JDK complicates matters slightly, but not to the point of making a connection impossible. The example uses an ODBC Data Source Name (DSN) of StoreAmazon. You set up the DSN using the Data Sources (ODBC) applet of the Control Panel. You can learn how to use the ODBC Data Source Administrator online. The best place to start is the TechRepublic article at `http://techrepublic.com.com/5100-6268-5030474.html`. Another good source is the MSDN article at `http://msdn.microsoft.com/library/en-us/odbc/htm/sdkodbcadminoverview.asp`.

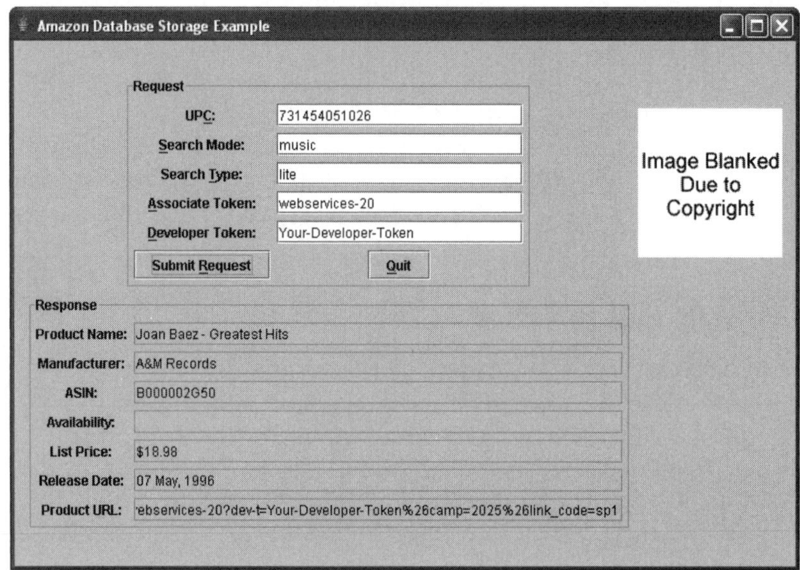

FIGURE 8.6: Performing a UPC search can help you find many specific products on Amazon.

Chapter 9 moves development from desktop, laptop, notebook, and other large devices to the small, mobile devices that many people use today. These devices are lightweight, easy to carry, and generally allow the user to communicate everywhere. As great as these devices are for the general user, they're a problematic platform at best for the developer because you need to consider the limitations of such devices. Most mobile devices have small displays, lack of full keyboard functionality, limited memory, reduced processing power, and significant operating system limits. However, even with these problems, mobile devices can serve as an important platform for your Amazon Web Services application and Amazon certainly makes it easy to use these devices.

Chapter 9

Considering the Limitations of Mobile Devices
Designing Applications Using Emulators
Developing Applications for Local or Remote Data Management

Writing Applications for Mobile Devices

Creating a Pocket PC Application
Creating a Cellular Telephone or Palm Application

People use Amazon Web Services for more than just desktop applications. It's true that desktop machines will probably host the majority of Amazon Web Services applications for the present, but some of the most interesting applications actually appear on mobile devices. For example, one Amazon Web Services application downloads a shopping list to a cellular telephone that the person then uses to make purchases at the store. Amazon doesn't necessarily miss a sale, in this case, because the Amazon price is often lower and the person buys from Amazon. You can read the details about this application at `http://www.businessweek.com/technology/content/jun2003/tc20030624_9735_tc113.htm`.

Mobile devices do present special problems for the developer, especially a developer using Amazon Web Services. The biggest problem is what to do with all the data Amazon returns with every request. Trying to fit all that information on a small screen isn't going to work, so you need to create prioritized displays. The request information presents a smaller problem, but is still something you need to consider. The first section of the chapter discusses the limitations you need to consider in light of the physical and operational characteristics of a mobile device.

It isn't always possible to test your Amazon Web Services application on the actual machine. Although you should test the application on an actual machine before you give it to anyone, using an emulator can greatly decrease development time and make the development process easier. The second section of the chapter discusses emulators.

Data management is also an issue. Many of the previous chapters of the book discussed scenarios where you can store data locally to improve performance. However, a mobile device doesn't stay in the same place, so using this technique can prove problematic. The third section of the chapter discusses techniques for local and remote data management options.

The remaining sections of the chapter discuss application development techniques for various devices. This chapter uses products such as Visual Studio .NET to show how to access Amazon Web Services using a mobile device. The mobile device you choose greatly affects the kind of development you perform. For example, a Pocket PC is perfectly capable of running an application locally. On the other hand, smaller devices might require some form of Web access through a custom server setup.

Understanding Mobile Device Limitations

Every device has limitations that you must consider. Whether those limits become a burden depends on what you plan to do with the device. The technique you use to perform a task is also a factor. Modern PCs have few limitations because vendors have increased their capabilities over the years. However, early PCs were so limited that developers worried about every byte of data. Mobile devices today are almost in the same position as early PCs—vendors simply haven't created ways to overcome problems with these small devices yet. Some of these problems might never go away because they have more to do with the limits of the humans using the device than the device itself. For example, you can place entire books on the head of a pin, but who can read them? Likewise, make the display of a mobile device too small and you encounter usage problems. The following sections discuss mobile device limitations of all types as they relate to Amazon Web Services.

Special Add-ons

Most vendors design PDAs as electronic versions of the calendar, address book, and personal note taker. Early versions of these products didn't include the mini-word processors and spreadsheets you'll find in modern versions. In fact, you can extend many PDAs to double as cameras, scanners, and other devices now with special add-ons. Other mobile devices, such as cellular telephones, have followed suit, but to a lesser degree.

The PDA isn't exactly a standard device to begin with. There are many hardware implementations, more than a few operating systems, and even different capabilities to consider. When users start adding features to their PDA, you may find that it's nearly impossible to determine what features you can rely on finding. In short, when you create an Amazon Web Services application for your company, try to standardize the device configuration. On the other hand, when you create an application that users outside the company can access, you need to provide a list of specific device requirements to reduce the potential for compatibility problems.

These special add-ons can also work to your advantage. For example, it's relatively easy to find a UPC reader for many PDAs today. Mating a UPC reader with a UPC request to Amazon means the user doesn't have to type anything to learn more about a product. A user could walk through a store, find an interesting product, scan the UPC, wait for the request to return, and then learn what other people think about the product by reading the reviews. This kind of application is impossible with a desktop machine and represents a unique use of the Amazon Web Services.

Networking

Distributed application development relies on a connection between the client and the server. Because most mobile devices have limited processing capability, distributed applications are especially important in this situation. It's easy to create a connection when you're working with a desktop machine. If you can't create a direct connection using a LAN, there are always alternatives such as using dial-up support. However, networking with a mobile can prove problematic.

> **NOTE**
>
> This chapter uses very specific terms for the various devices. A mobile device refers to any type of device the reader can move from one place to another (including PDAs and cellular telephones). A cellular telephone refers to a standard version of this device without built-in intelligence. A SmartPhone is a special kind of cellular telephone that includes built-in intelligence that a developer can program using a product such as Visual Studio .NET. A PDA is any kind of non-cellular telephone handheld device. For this book, the term PDA includes both Palm and Pocket PC devices. A Palm device specifically uses the Palm OS. A Pocket PC specifically uses some form of Windows. I won't discuss other PDA OS in this book.

The networking problem falls into three categories that can affect your Amazon Web Services session. The first problem is the limited networking potential of devices such as cellular telephones. These devices have good connectivity, but you'll find it difficult to run custom Web applications using them because it's tough to add any form of security. You can't reliably determine the identity of the caller, secure the application, or ensure the integrity of the connection. Consequently, cellular telephones are good for downloading noncritical information or performing nonsecure queries.

Newer PDAs have much better processing capability than any cellular telephone and include good connectivity through a wireless connection. It's possible to provide some form of reliable identity check with higher end systems such as the Pocket PC. In addition, you can provide some level of application security. Unfortunately, you still can't secure the communication path between server and Pocket PC easily, so critical data could become compromised. You can perform most Amazon Web Services tasks, but might not want to perform online ordering because there's a possibility that someone could intercept the credit card numbers and identifying information.

Older PDAs are far less capable than the newer products on the market. In some cases, you might not even have good networking capability. Some of these older models rely on an internal modem for communication. A few models I've see use an add-in card to provide a wired connection to the network. Although the wired connections of some older models are inconvenient for the user, they actually make it possible to create a very secure connection. A physical connection lets you secure the wire, the application, and provide full user credentials, but at the cost of user productivity. In general, you won't ever need to use one of these solutions with Amazon Web Services unless you plan to manage your company's product entries using a mobile device.

Operating System

The operating system you use for a mobile device affects the device functionality and your ability to interact with Amazon Web Services. Generally, you don't have a choice of operating system when it comes to your cellular telephone. Even the SmartPhone comes with a single operating system choice and that operating system really isn't capable of providing more than Web application access. (You can create certain classes of local application using Visual Studio .NET with the SmartPhone and we'll explore the Amazon Web Services perspective in this chapter.)

PDA users do have some choices to make, especially if you have a Pocket PC device at your disposal. Early versions of the Pocket PC used Windows CE. However, you can now find devices that come loaded with compact versions of Windows 2000 or Windows XP. No, you can't create a full desktop application for these devices, but the newer the operating system and the greater the device functionality, the better your chances are of creating an application that can perform most (perhaps all) tasks locally. Even Windows CE users can rely on local applications that use SOAP to communicate with Amazon Web Services using JavaScript (one of the options considered in this chapter).

Early versions of the Palm are extremely limited and any hopes you have of creating a local application are dim (unless you want to do the equivalent of assembly language programming). These early versions require that you use a Web application to communicate with Amazon Web Services. Newer versions of the Palm offer greater functionality and you'll probably find a strong third party market for development tools as these versions gain support. In

> **▶ TIP**
>
> Make sure you keep up-to-date with mobile device technologies by checking vendor sites often. For example, you can learn about updated capabilities for the Pocket PC and SmartPhone devices by visiting Microsoft's site at `http://www.microsoft.com/windowsmobile/default.mspx`. Visit the Web site for your particular cellular telephone vendor to obtain cellular telephone updates. Finally, make sure you visit the Palm site at `http://www.palm.com/home.html`.

the meantime, you can use the developer resources provided directly by Palm at `http://www.palmone.com/us/developers/` or rely on Web applications to access Amazon Web Services.

Screen Size

Many users have 17″ or 19″ monitors capable of a minimum of 1,280 × 1,024 resolution today. Developers have taken advantage of the screen real estate to create better applications that display more data at one time. Even Microsoft uses higher resolutions as a baseline for applications—many of their application screens won't fit on an 800 × 600 display anymore.

Everything you want to do with your PDA has to fit within a small screen space (320 × 200 pixels if you're using a Pocket PC model like the Casio Cassiopeia). That's a lot smaller than the typical computer screen. Developers working on cellular telephone applications have even less screen real estate—some models display just a few lines of information. In addition, some PDAs and most cellular telephones use black and white displays in place of color, so you can't even use the modern tricks to make the display look nicer. In short, mobile device screens tend to look a bit plain, and developers normally find themselves feverishly cutting their application screens down to size. However, with careful data sizing and information layout, you can create a perfectly acceptable display for Amazon Web Services requests and responses. The examples in this chapter demonstrate techniques for each device type.

Make sure you consider eXtensible Hypertext Markup Language (XHTML) for complex applications with many elements (`http://www.w3.org/TR/xhtml1/`). It helps you to display your application in segments with relative ease. Other options include using the Handheld Device Markup Language (HDML) (`http://www.w3.org/TR/NOTE-Submission-HDML-spec.html`) or Wireless Markup Language (WML) (`http://www.oasis-open.org/cover/wap-wml.html`). Both of these technologies use the concept of cards and decks to break up information into easily managed pieces. Of course, the mobile device you use has to provide support for these standards (most do) before you can use the tags within a document. Unfortunately, using any of these solutions normally prevents your Web application from appearing properly on a desktop machine.

Color

Developers have gotten used to seeing colors on their applications. Color dresses up a drab display and makes the application more fun to use. In addition, using color presents cues to the user. For example, many users associate green with a good condition and red with something bad. In short, most applications rely heavily on color today and with good reason.

Depending on the mobile device you use, you may not have any color at all. For example, many Palm models present the world in shades of gray. Most cellular telephones also represent all data using either black or white (and don't even provide for shades of gray). Even if a mobile device does provide color support akin to the Pocket PC, the developer still has to use color carefully.

The problem for mobile device users is that the screen is already small. If a user gets into an area with bright sunlight, seeing the screen might become impossible, especially if the screen contains colors that don't work well in such an environment. Amazon tends to use a lot of color—making its Web site less useful for some mobile device applications. One of the features your application can provide is a way to present the Amazon data without the use of color (or at least much color).

Using color to display icons or to convey a message is still a good idea, even in the world of the mobile device. For example, a red icon could signal danger or tell the user to wait without using up screen real estate for words. Of course, you need to explain the meaning of the color changes within a manual or help file (preferably both). Make sure the users of your application actually have a device capable of displaying color before you use color to signify anything in the application (some devices display only shades of gray). In addition, you must exercise care in using color because colorblind users might not be able to interpret the application correctly.

User Interface

Cellular telephone users commonly have just a keypad as an interface device. In some cases, the vendor will also supply some control keys, including an arrow keypad, but that's about it. If you want to create an Amazon Web Services application for a cellular telephone, you need to consider these limitations.

Most PDA users rely on a pointer to do all of their work. Sure, a few PDAs do offer a keyboard and mouse as separate items, but most of these offerings are bulky and difficult to use. Pointer use is one of the reasons that you want to keep your application on one screen, or use multiple screens when necessary. Scrolling on a PDA screen is less than intuitive and requires some level of skill to master.

No matter what type of mobile device development you do, be sure to include some pointer friendly features. For example, try to make as many tasks use a single pointer option or numeric keypad input as possible. The user should be able to point to what they want and allow the mobile device to complete the input for them.

Pointer friendly programs also make tasks yes or no propositions. Again, this allows the user to accomplish the task with a single click, rather than writing something down. The point is to make the PDA as efficient as possible so the user doesn't get frustrated trying to do something easy.

Working with Emulators

An important consideration for this chapter is that Amazon is offering data in response to a request. Handling the input and output is up to you. One of the problems that developers must solve when working with mobile devices is testing for multiple models. Unlike desktop systems, it's not always easy to determine whether an application will provide the correct presentation on a mobile setup. Each mobile device has different capabilities, installed software, and a host of other problem areas for the developer to consider.

> **▶ TIP**
>
> Keep apprised of the latest Microsoft mobility and embedded system developments at `http://msdn.microsoft.com/mobility/`. This Web site includes many of the links you'll need to download the latest Microsoft products to make your Amazon Web Services mobile application development easier.

Most developers turn to emulation software to help test their applications. An emulator provides the equivalent environment of the mobile device that it's supposed to model. I stress the word equivalent, because most of these emulators don't provide a complete picture of the mobile device environment. You can rely on an emulator to tell you whether the application fits within the screen area that the mobile device provides, but you can't rely on it to tell you about memory issues or whether a particular device has a piece of support software you need. These other issues require testing on an actual device—something you should do for at least a subset of the mobile devices you want to support.

The following sections describe four emulation software options. The first option is the built-in support that Visual Studio .NET 2003 provides. If you don't plan to use this IDE, you can skip the first section.

I chose these options because they provide a broad range of support, and you can download at least evaluation units of all three emulators. Here are the download locations so that you can get your copies of the products before you begin this section. The following sections assume that you've downloaded the software required for the installation.

- Microsoft eMbedded Visual Tools 3.0 (2002 edition): `http://www.microsoft.com/downloads/details.aspx?FamilyId=F663BF48-31EE-4CBE-AAC5-0AFFD5FB27DD` (full development package) or `http://www.microsoft.com/downloads/details.aspx?FamilyId=25F4DE97-AE80-477A-9DF1-496B85B3D3E3` (emulators only) or `http://www.microsoft.com/downloads/details.aspx?FamilyID=2dbee84a-bd94-4167-b817-2b2e548b2e92` (older full development version)
- Openwave SDK: `http://developer.Openwave.com/download/`
- SmartPhone: `http://www.yospace.com/spe.html`

Visual Studio .NET Built-In Emulator

Visual Studio .NET 2003 comes with a built-in emulator you can use for various kinds of development. When you create a mobile project, the IDE automatically sets up the required emulator support as well. After you develop the application, use the Debug ➢ Start command to display the Deploy PocketPC dialog box shown in Figure 9.1.

To use the emulator, simply select the Pocket PC 2002 Emulator (Default) option and click Deploy. The IDE will copy the application to the emulator folder, start the emulator, and load your application. At this point, you can begin testing the application as you would any another .NET application.

The emulator is configurable. Use the Tools ➢ Options command to display the Options dialog box. Select the Device Tools ➢ Devices option to display the list of devices available for this project. Select the device you want to configure and click Configure. You'll see a Configure Emulator Settings dialog box similar to the one shown in Figure 9.2.

You can change features such as the display size and color depth. More importantly, you can set memory restrictions on the System tab so that the application can model the memory restrictions of the target device to an extent. Note that the default Visual Studio .NET setup has a number of emulators including the Pocket PC and Windows CE devices.

FIGURE 9.1: Use the options in this dialog box to choose a deployment option.

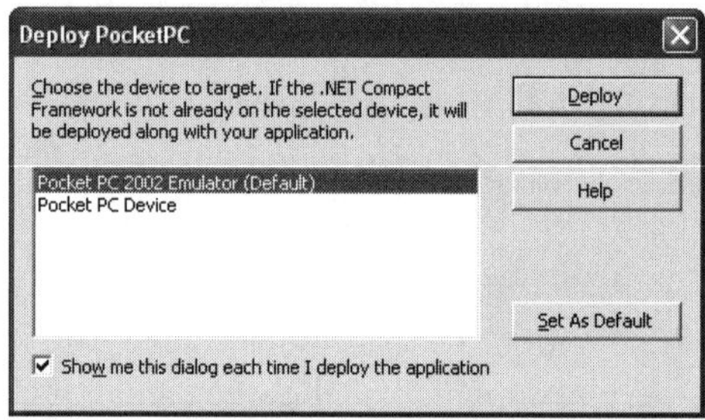

FIGURE 9.2: Configure the emulator to better model the mobile device you want to use.

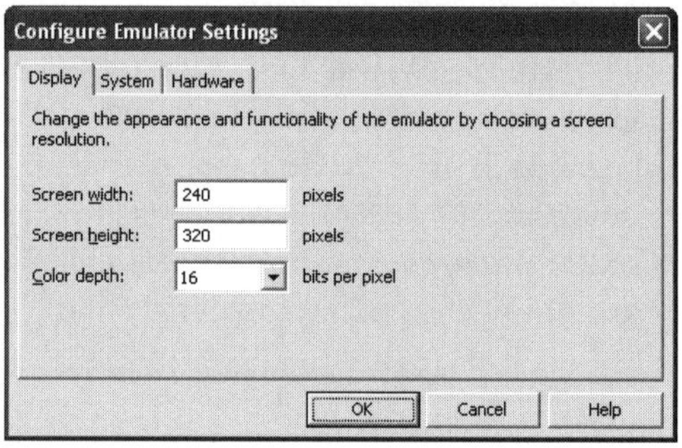

Microsoft eMbedded Visual Tools

The Microsoft eMbedded Visual Tools option is free. All you need to do is download the product and unpack it into an installation directory. You have a choice of two versions on the Internet right now, but the URL at the beginning of this section points to the latest version of the product. Developers have reported fewer problems with the newer version of the emulators and they do model the device more accurately.

Earlier versions of the product create two folders: one named `Disk1` and a second named Disk2. If you have an earlier version of the product, the `Disk2` folder contains the three emulators and you can install them individually if desired by using the Setup program found in the individual emulation product folder. For example, if you want to install just the Pocket PC emulation, you can double-click the Setup program in the `\Mobile Development Tools\DISK2\PPC12SDK` folder. If you're using Visual Studio .NET 2003 or a language such as PHP for development purposes, you only need to install these emulators. You also need the Microsoft Mobile Internet Toolkit (`http://www.microsoft.com/downloads/details.aspx?familyid=ae597f21-b8e4-416e-a28f-b124f41f9768`) when you use an older version of Visual Studio .NET. Users of older versions of Visual Studio will need to install the whole package, including the supplied language products.

> **▶ TIP**
>
> You can also download the Microsoft SmartPhone 2003 emulator at `http://www.microsoft.com/downloads/details.aspx?familyid=8fe677fa-3a6a-4265-b8eb-61a628ecd462`. This emulator requires eMbedded Visual C++ 4.0. The Microsoft eMbedded Visual Tools 3.0 (2002 edition) package does contain the SmartPhone 2002 emulator. Likewise, you can find the Microsoft Pocket PC 2003 emulator for eMbedded Visual C++ 4.0 at `http://www.microsoft.com/downloads/details.aspx?FamilyId=9996B314-0364-4623-9EDE-0B5FBB133652`.

The latest version of Microsoft eMbedded Visual Tools uses a self-extracting executable. When you start the application, it unpacks the contents of the executable into a temporary folder. It then displays a series of dialog boxes that help you install eMbedded Visual Tools 3.0, Microsoft Windows SDK for Pocket PC 2002, and Microsoft Windows SDK for SmartPhone 2002. The newer version only includes the Pocket PC and SmartPhone emulators—you can separately download SDKs for the handheld and palm size emulators found in the older version of Microsoft eMbedded Visual Tools at `http://msdn.microsoft.com/downloads/list/handheldpc.asp`. The SmartPhone SDK is only available for eMbedded Visual C++, so make sure you install this language if you want to create a SmartPhone application.

When you finish installing everything, it's important to test each of the emulators to ensure you received a good installation. Open one of the sample projects to test the emulator when using the newest version of Microsoft eMbedded Visual Tools. If one of these emulators fails, rerun the setup program and select just that emulator for a reinstall. You need to run each emulator separately when using the older product. If one of the emulators fails to work, you can always uninstall just that emulator using the appropriate entry in the Add/Remove Programs applet. Reinstall the emulator using the required Setup program for that emulator in the `Disk2` folder. Figure 9.3 shows a typical SmartPhone emulation.

Openwave SDK

Like the Microsoft emulators, the Openwave SDK is also a free download, but the Openwave Web site offers plenty of opportunity to purchase paid products as well. The Openwave file you download is an executable, so double-clicking it starts the installation process. Simply follow the prompts to install the product. Most versions of the product require yes or no answers to each question.

The Openwave Web site offers a number of versions of the product. I suggest you download the latest version of the product to ensure you get the latest features. However, the 5.1 version is also very capable and it includes a number of features not found in the 6.2.2 version used for this chapter. Figure 9.4 shows some of the optional features you can install with the 5.1 version. If you want to use Openwave as your development platform, you might want to download the 5.1 version (or both versions). The 6.2.2 version is most useful as an emulator only.

> **▶ TIP**
>
> Microsoft recently released the Visual Basic .NET Resource Kit, a must have addition for mobile development. The kit offers additional samples and makes it much easier to create robust mobile applications. Learn more about this kit at `http://www.microsoft.com/downloads/details.aspx?FamilyId=EF4289B4-FFCB-40BD-9BFE-95256ABD0E13`.

Once you get Openwave installed and have restarted your machine, you'll want to test this product. If you installed the 6.2.2 version, all you get is the emulator. To start the emulator, select the Start ➢ Programs ➢ Openwave SDK 6.2.2 ➢ Openwave SDK 6.2.2 HTTP option. You'll see an emulator similar to the one shown in Figure 9.5. The emulator automatically goes to the Openwave test site on first use, but you can change that location by opening the SDK Configuration dialog box using the Tools ➢ Options menu. Select the Browse tab and change the Homepage field.

As previously mentioned, Openwave SDK 5.1 has more to offer than other versions of the product. Unlike some of the other emulators you'll use, this one is actually part of a development IDE. Select the Start ➢ Programs ➢ Openwave SDK 5.1 ➢ Openwave SDK 5.1 option to open an IDE similar to other IDEs you may have used in the past. However, for this book, the important feature is the emulator that appears in the right side pane. To use this feature, you'll need to use the Simulator ➢ Go to Address command, enter an URL in the Go To Address dialog box, and then click OK. Figure 9.6 shows a typical example of the Openwave emulator within the IDE.

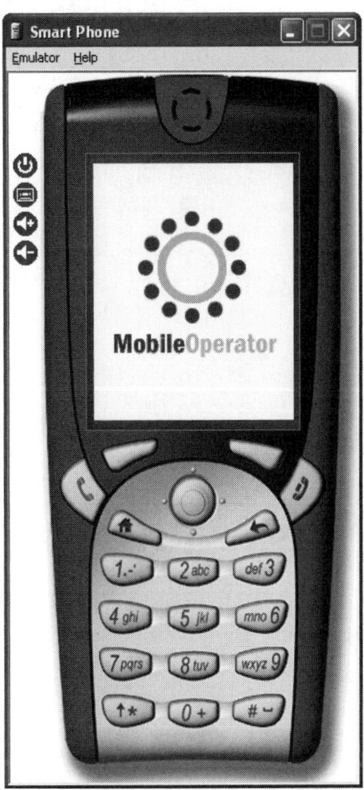

FIGURE 9.3:
Test each of the emulators to ensure they work.

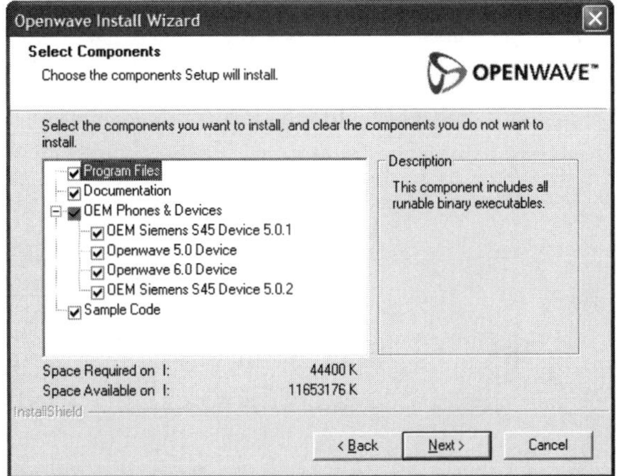

FIGURE 9.4:
Select custom options as needed for your emulator setup.

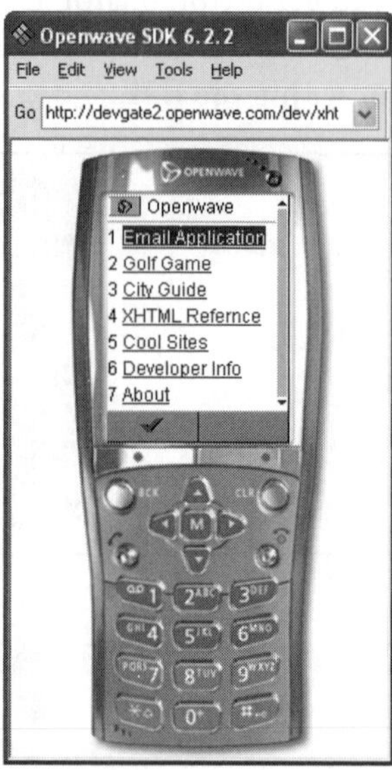

FIGURE 9.5:

Using the Openwave emulator means starting the associated IDE and entering an URL using a menu command. Image courtesy Openwave Systems Inc.

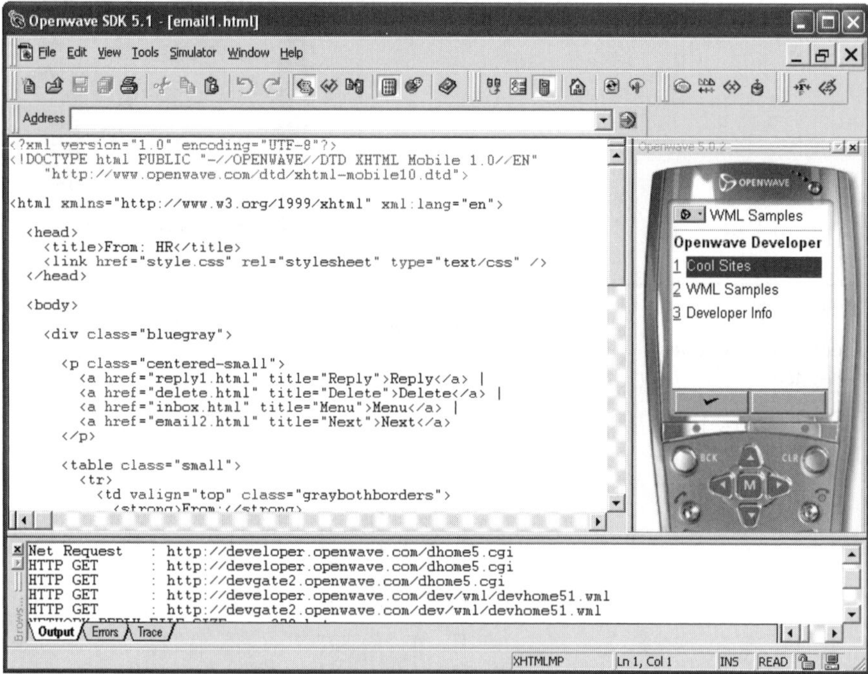

FIGURE 9.6:

Use the 5.1 version if you need an IDE in addition to the emulator. Image courtesy Openwave Systems Inc.

SmartPhone

The SmartPhone emulator is one of the timed usage options you can try. After you download the product, you can try it for anywhere from 5 to 15 days free (depending on the version you download), at which time your license will expire and the product will cease working. The SmartPhone emulator is in a Zip that you download and unpack to a temporary folder. To start the installation process, double-click the setup application that appears in the Zip file (the actual name varies by SmartPhone version number). Follow the prompts to install the product.

Now that you have the product installed, you can test it to see if it works. The first time you start this product, you'll see a dialog that requests your licensing details. This dialog box accepts your name, email address, and the key that you were sent in your email. (The company sends this key after you download the product from their Web site.) Make sure you use the information from the email because this step is quite picky.

You also have a choice of starting the product in Development or Display mode. The Development mode opens an IDE you can use to create applications. This mode also shows multiple forms of the emulation, as shown in Figure 9.7. These aren't the only emulators available. The number of emulation options provided surprised me—they're all available on the Workspace ➢ Add Emulator menu. This product also uses the concept of an emulator group. Figure 9.7 shows the default emulator group. A single test sends the same input to all of the emulators in a group—greatly reducing the time required for testing.

> **NOTE**
>
> The older versions of the emulators have a few problems. For example, the handheld PC emulation will sit in the upper left corner of your display and not move. However, it does provide a good environment in which to test your mobile application. Another potential problem with these emulators is that you can only run one of them at a time. Make sure you close an existing emulator before you start a new one. Generally, the new emulator will check for this problem and tell you to close the existing emulator. We'll discuss other emulator issues as the chapter progresses.

The Display mode opens a single emulator, as shown in Figure 9.8. Use this option when you want to fine-tune the display details of your application. Most of the emulators have a full view and several zoomed views. Figure 9.8 shows a full view.

Designing for Local or Remote Data Management

Most programming chapters of this book have mentioned the need to store commonly used Amazon data locally to improve performance and provide a backup should the main connection to Amazon fail. A desktop application can rely on any of a number of Database

Management Systems (DBMS) to perform the task of storing this data for future use. Given the static connection a desktop system enjoys, you can assume the user will always have access to the data. Unfortunately, it's not possible to say the same thing about mobile devices. Mobile devices have dynamic connections that might not be available when you need them.

The lack of connectivity means you have to make some hard choices about how to make your Amazon Web Services application get good performance. You could still rely on a server-based DBMS to perform this task for you. For the purposes of discussion, you can consider this a remote solution. It's remote because you can't count on a connection, and the mobile device might actually need to rely on a nonstandard connection to obtain the data (as when you're on the road).

An alternative for some devices is to use a product such as Microsoft SQL CE or Sybase iAnywhere. These DBMS let you build a local connectivity solution that stores data short term on the local device. This solution tends to solve the problem of remote connectivity—the user can always count on the local data store. However, this solution also has problems. For one thing, you might not see as great a performance gain as you might anticipate—the limited memory and processing capacity device is now running your application and a DBMS.

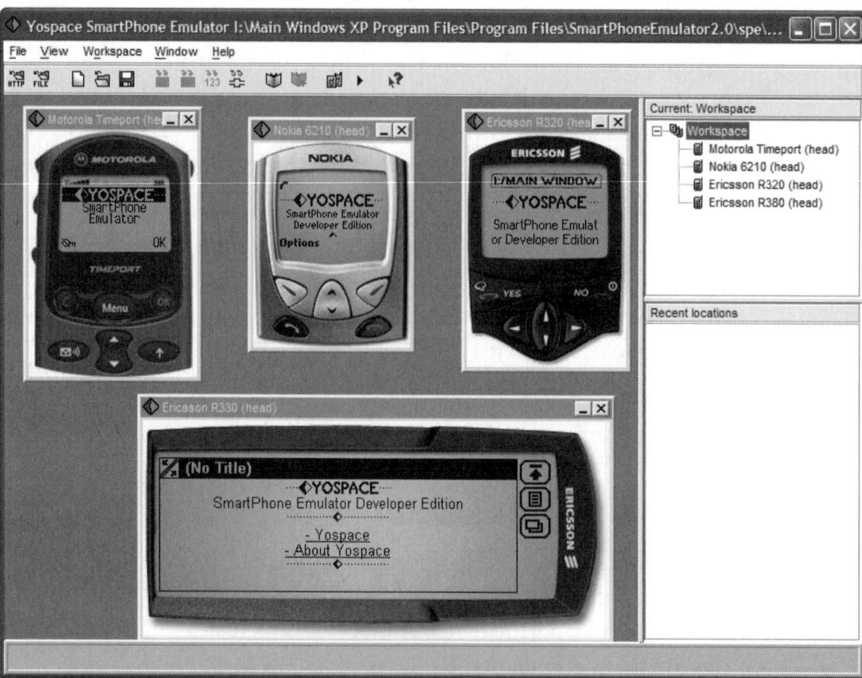

FIGURE 9.7: Create a complex emulator environment using the SmartPhone Development mode.

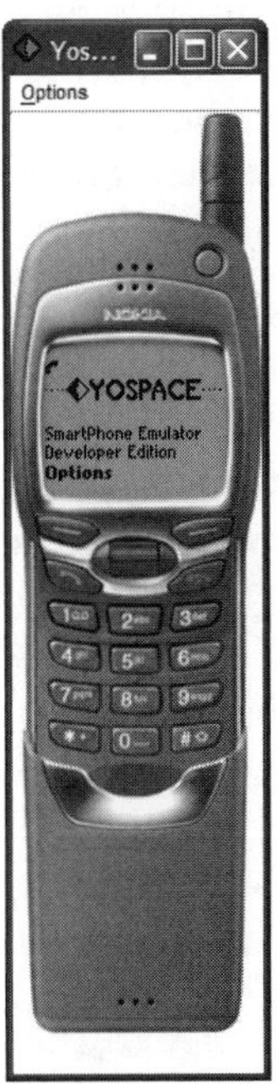

FIGURE 9.8:
Fine-tune the display details and perform final testing using the Display mode.

It might sound as if there aren't any good solutions for offline data storage for mobile devices. To some extent, that perception is true. However, you can make use of storage technology and improve both the functionality and performance of your mobile application incrementally. The best solution is to use local storage when the processing power and storage capability of the mobile device is up to the task. When you can't rely on the resources provided by the mobile device, use a Web application with server-based storage instead.

Developing for a Pocket PC

The Pocket PC is the most capable of the mobile devices you can use for an Amazon Web Services application. You can use local storage with this device and perform a multitude of tasks that some mobile devices can't perform, such as limited data analysis using the copy of Pocket Excel provided with the operating system. This platform even helps you create reports using Pocket Word. In sum, you can use a Pocket PC for most Amazon Web Services tasks—at least in a limited way.

> **▶ TIP**
>
> You may have to search the Internet for some Pocket PC resources. However, you can find many Microsoft-supplied developer tools at `http://www.microsoft.com/windowsmobile/resources/downloads/developer/default.mspx`.

The following sections discuss three methods you can use to create applications for the Pocket PC: eMbedded Visual Tools, Visual Studio .NET, and third party tools (emphasizing PocketSOAP). Each of these methods has advantages and disadvantages that make it useful for a particular kind of application. For example, eMbedded Visual Tools provides the best compatibility. Even earlier versions of the Pocket PC can easily use the eMbedded Visual Tools option.

Using Older Microsoft Products

Many developers have used the eMbedded Visual Tools product provided by Microsoft to create applications for the Pocket PC over the years. You have a choice of using either Visual Basic or Visual C++ for the application. As previously mentioned, the main advantage to using eMbedded Visual Tools is compatibility. You don't need anything special to use this solution and it's likely that the resulting application will run on all versions of the Pocket PC as native code (rather than as a Web application). The biggest disadvantage of this solution is that Microsoft created it at a time when SOAP wasn't part of the development strategy. Consequently, you'll find that writing the application requires a little more work than other solutions do. Listing 9.1 shows a typical solution using eMbedded Visual C++. Note that the listing isn't complete (some error trapping is missing for the sake of clarity). You'll find the complete source code for this example in the `\Chapter 09\WinCE` folder of the source code located on the Sybex Web site.

Listing 9.1 Creating an Amazon Request Using Visual C++

```
void CWinCEDlg::OnTest()
{
   HINTERNET          hInt = NULL;        // Internet handle.
   LPCTSTR            ReqUrl;             // Request URL.
   URL_COMPONENTS     CUrl;               // URL broken into parts.
   TCHAR              Server[1024];       // Remote server name.
   TCHAR              Path[1024];         // Remote data path.
   HINTERNET          hSession = NULL;    // Session handle.
   HINTERNET          hRequest = NULL;    // Request handle.
   char               DataReturn[1025];   // Original Response Buffer.
   CString            DataBuffer;         // Response buffer.
   CString            OutputBuffer;       // Output to application.
   DWORD              DataReturned;       // Bytes returned.
   HRESULT            Result;             // Result of operation.
   IXMLDOMDocument*   XMLDoc = NULL;      // Holds Amazon Data.
   VARIANT_BOOL       IsSuccessful;       // No data.
   IXMLDOMElement*    RpcElement;         // Holds entire RPC result.
   IXMLDOMNodeList*   List;               // Contains the 3 RPC nodes.
   IXMLDOMNode*       DataElement;        // Holds the data node of List.
   IXMLDOMNodeList*   Details;            // Contains up to 10 nodes.
```

```
IXMLDOMNode*      BookItem;         // An individual book detail.

// Open the Internet connection.
hInt = InternetOpen(_T("WinCE"),
                    INTERNET_OPEN_TYPE_DIRECT,
                    NULL,
                    NULL,
                    0);

// Initialize the URL variables.
ReqUrl = _T(... The long search string from Chapter 2 ...);
memset(&CUrl, 0, sizeof(CUrl));
CUrl.dwStructSize = sizeof(CUrl);
CUrl.lpszHostName = Server;
CUrl.dwHostNameLength = 1024;
CUrl.lpszUrlPath = Path;
CUrl.dwUrlPathLength = 1024;

// Break the URL into its components.
if (!InternetCrackUrl(ReqUrl, 0, 0, &CUrl))
{
   AfxMessageBox(_T("Invalid Request URL"));
   InternetCloseHandle(hInt);
   return;
}

// Create a session with Amazon.
hSession = InternetConnect(hInt,
                           CUrl.lpszHostName,
                           INTERNET_DEFAULT_HTTP_PORT,
                           NULL,
                           NULL,
                           INTERNET_SERVICE_HTTP,
                           0,
                           0);

// Create the request.
hRequest = HttpOpenRequest(hSession,
                           NULL,
                           CUrl.lpszUrlPath,
                           NULL,
                           NULL,
                           NULL,
                           0,
                           0);

// Send the request.
if (!HttpSendRequest(hRequest, NULL, 0, 0, 0))
{
   AfxMessageBox(_T("Request not sent correctly."));
```

```
      InternetCloseHandle(hRequest);
      InternetCloseHandle(hSession);
      InternetCloseHandle(hInt);
      return;
   }

   // Get the result.
   DataBuffer = "";
   do
   {
      InternetReadFile(hRequest,
                       DataReturn,
                       1024,
                       &DataReturned);
      DataReturn[DataReturned] = '\0';
      DataBuffer = DataBuffer + DataReturn;
   }
   while (DataReturned > 0);

   // Close the Internet handles.
   if (!InternetCloseHandle(hRequest) ||
       !InternetCloseHandle(hSession) ||
       !InternetCloseHandle(hInt))
      AfxMessageBox(_T("A resource handle failed to close!"));

   // Initialize the COM environment.
   Result = CoInitializeEx(NULL,COINIT_MULTITHREADED);
   if(!SUCCEEDED(Result))
   {
      AfxMessageBox(_T("Couldn't initialize COM environment"));
      return;
   }

   // Create an XML document.
   Result = CoCreateInstance(CLSID_DOMDocument,
                             NULL,
                             CLSCTX_INPROC_SERVER |
                             CLSCTX_LOCAL_SERVER,
                             IID_IXMLDOMDocument,
                             (LPVOID *)&XMLDoc);

   // Remove the XML header.
   DataBuffer.Delete(0, DataBuffer.Find(_T("<ProductInfo")));

   // Load the data obtained from Amazon.
   XMLDoc->loadXML(DataBuffer.AllocSysString(), &IsSuccessful);

   // Get all the child nodes.
   XMLDoc->get_documentElement(&RpcElement);
   RpcElement->get_childNodes(&List);
```

```
    // Process just the Details nodes.
    OutputBuffer = "";
    for (int Counter = 3; Counter < 13; Counter ++)
    {
       List->get_item(Counter, &DataElement);
       DataElement->get_childNodes(&Details);

       // Process each detail item in turn.
       Details->get_item(1, &BookItem);

       BSTR bStr;
       BookItem->get_text(&bStr);
       OutputBuffer = OutputBuffer + bStr + "\r\n";
    }

    // Display the results on screen.
    m_DataOutput.SetWindowText(OutputBuffer);

    // Uninitialize the COM environment.
    CoUninitialize();
}
```

The code begins by obtaining the data from Amazon Web Services. To perform this task, the code creates an Internet connection using the `InternetOpen()` function. The connection creates a path from the device to the software and hardware that manages an Internet connection. The next task is to create a request URL and break it into parts so that the code can use each part as it makes other calls. These preliminary steps always precede any Internet communication.

At this point, the code can create a connection to the host computer on the Internet using the `InternetConnect()` function. The next step is to tell the server to listen for a request using the `HttpOpenRequest()` function. Once the server is ready to receive the request, the code sends it using the `HttpSendRequest()` function.

Now it's time for the server to respond. You might think that you can simply create a huge buffer and receive the whole response in one call to the `InternetReadFile()` function. The problem that you'll encounter is that the buffer will truncate the data. The code uses a 1,025-byte buffer that receives 1,024-bytes of data and a 1-byte null to end the string. The loop continues until the application receives the whole response from the server, which is a complete XML document.

A string form of the response isn't very helpful, so the code creates an `IXMLDOMDocument` object. The only problem is that this object doesn't like the `<?XML?>` header that Amazon supplies as part of the response, so the code has to eliminate the header from the string. At this point, the code can load the data into the `IXMLDOMDocument` object. Notice how using a `CString` to hold the data reduces the effort required to load the string. The Microsoft examples don't emphasize the need to check the success of the loading process, but you can receive a bad document from Amazon Web Services, so you need to perform the check using the `IsSuccessful` return value.

The example performs some simple data parsing. All it retrieves is the book name, but you could easily retrieve other values using the techniques shown in other examples in the book (see Listing 9.2 for such an example). Figure 9.9 shows typical output from this application.

Using the .NET Compact Framework

The .NET Compact Framework offers a lot in the way of SOAP functionality. Using this product helps you create elegant Amazon Web Services applications with a minimum of fuss and without the need for third party solutions. However, the system you choose to support this application must have the .NET Compact Framework installed, which could result in memory problems for some older Pocket PCs. The example in this section performs an author search; however, the output provides a few surprises in that it uses a table, rather than the standard text elements. You'll find this example in the `\Chapter 09\PocketPC` folder of the source code located on the Sybex Web site.

FIGURE 9.9: Typical output using eMbedded Visual Tools

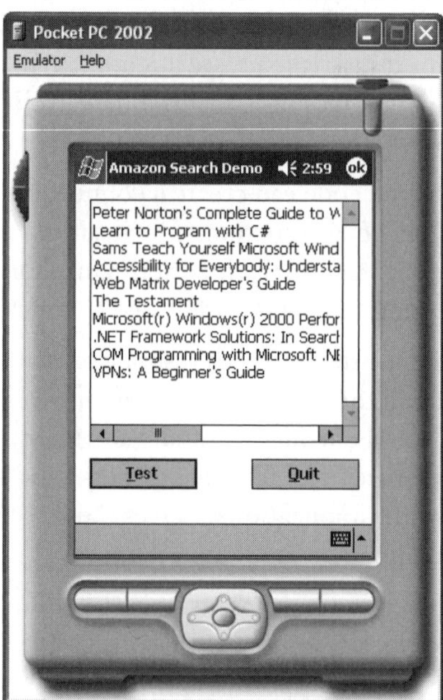

Listing 9.2 Creating an Amazon Request Using the .NET Framework

```
private void ApplicationTest_Click(object sender, System.EventArgs e)
{
   AuthorRequest          AR;        // The author request.
   ProductInfo            PI;        // Data returned from request.
   AmazonSearchService    Service;   // Connection to the service.
   DataRow                DR;        // Output data.
   Int32                  Counter;   // Loop counting variable.
   FrmDetail              Details;   // Detail form.

   // Instantiate the objects.
   AR = new AuthorRequest();
   PI = new ProductInfo();
   Service = new AmazonSearchService();

   // Create the author request.
   AR.author = txtAuthor.Text;
   AR.devtag = txtTag.Text;
   AR.mode = txtMode.Text;
   AR.page = txtPage.Text;
   AR.type = txtType.Text;

   // Make the request.
   PI = Service.AuthorSearchRequest(AR);

   // Create the details form.
   Details = new FrmDetail();

   // Create a data set to store the data and associate
   // it with the grid.
   Details.DS = new DataSet("dsAmazon");
   Details.DS.Tables.Add("AuthorOut");
   Details.DS.Tables["AuthorOut"].Columns.Add("Book Title");
   Details.DS.Tables["AuthorOut"].Columns.Add("ISBN");
   Details.DS.Tables["AuthorOut"].Columns.Add("Release Date");
   Details.DS.Tables["AuthorOut"].Columns.Add("Publisher");
   Details.dgOutput.DataSource = Details.DS.Tables["AuthorOut"];

   // Display the results on screen.
   for (Counter = 0; Counter < PI.Details.Length; Counter++)
   {
      // Create a new row to hold the data.
      DR = Details.DS.Tables["AuthorOut"].NewRow();

      // Add the data to the row.
      DR["Book Title"] = PI.Details[Counter].ProductName;
      DR["ISBN"] = PI.Details[Counter].Asin;
      DR["Release Date"] = PI.Details[Counter].ReleaseDate;
      DR["Publisher"] = PI.Details[Counter].Manufacturer;
```

```
            // Display the row on screen.
            Details.DS.Tables["AuthorOut"].Rows.Add(DR);
        }

        // Show the details form.
        Details.Show();
    }
```

The code begins by creating the three main objects for this example: `AR` (holds the request data), `PI` (holds the return data), and `Service` (sends and receives requests). The code fills `AR` with data from the text boxes displayed on the main form. At this point, the code makes the request and returns the result in `PI`.

Given that a Pocket PC doesn't provide enough screen real estate to hold both the input and the output data on one form, the example includes a `Details` form. The code creates the form immediately after it receives the results from Amazon Web Services. It uses the technique shown in the code to create a `DataSet` object, `DS`, dynamically and populate it with data.

The code associates the `DataGrid` object on the `Details` form with `DS`. Once `DS` contains all of the data from `PI`, the code displays the `Details` form on screen. Figure 9.10 shows typical return values for the `Details` form.

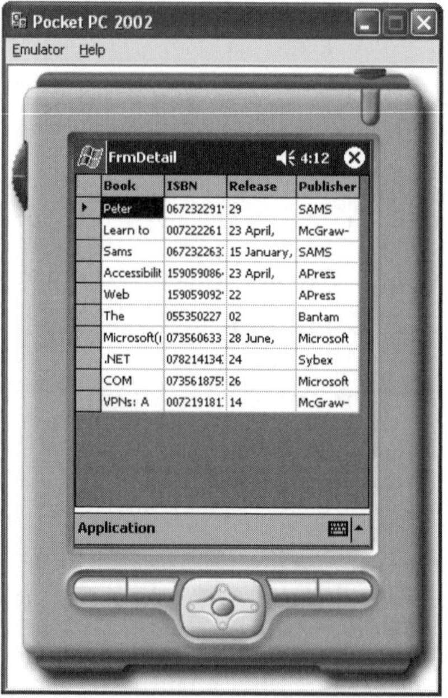

FIGURE 9.10: Typical output using the .NET Compact Framework

Using Third Party Development Products

You don't have to use a Microsoft solution for your Pocket PC. It's relatively easy to build a fully functional application using just a Web page and some JavaScript when you combine it with a third party SOAP solution. One of the better solutions on the market is PocketSOAP (`http://www.pocketsoap.com/`). This example relies on PocketSOAP, so you'll need to download a copy to use it. Listing 9.3 shows a typical solution using JavaScript. You'll find this example in the `\Chapter 09\PocketPC` folder of the source code located on the Sybex Web site.

Listing 9.3 Creating an Amazon Request Using PocketSOAP

```
<SCRIPT LANGUAGE="JScript">
function btnRequest_Click()
{
    var SOAPEnv;     // SOAP envelope
    var Transport;   // SOAP transport
    var Param;       // Parameter list
    var Details;     // Details array holder

    // Create the envelope.
    SOAPEnv = new ActiveXObject("pocketSOAP.Envelope.2");
    SOAPEnv.SetMethod("AuthorSearchRequest", "urn:PI/DevCentral/SoapService");

    // Create a parameter to place within the envelope.
    Param = SOAPEnv.Parameters.Create("AuthorSearchRequest", null);
    Param.Nodes.Create("author", "John Mueller");
    Param.Nodes.Create("mode", "books");
    Param.Nodes.Create("page", "1");
    Param.Nodes.Create("tag", "webservices-20");
    Param.Nodes.Create("type", "lite");
    Param.Nodes.Create("devtag", "Your-Developer-Token");

    // Send the request and receive the data.
    Transport = new ActiveXObject("pocketSOAP.HTTPTransport.2");
    Transport.SOAPAction = "http://soap.amazon.com";
    Transport.Send("http://soap.amazon.com/onca/soap3", SOAPEnv.Serialize());
    SOAPEnv.Parse(Transport, "UTF-8");

    // Get the Details.
    RecData = new VBArray(SOAPEnv.Parameters.Item(0).Nodes.Item(2).Value);

    // Process each book in turn.
    Output = "";
    for (Counter = RecData.lbound(); Counter <= RecData.ubound(); Counter++)
```

```
         {
            Output = Output +
                     RecData.getItem(Counter).Nodes.ItemByName("ProductName").Value +
                     "\r\n";
         }
         window.document.SampleForm1.Results.value =  Output;
      }
```

> **TIP**
>
> Many developers wrongly assume that cellular telephones will remain limited devices. However, many companies are working on advanced versions that will let users perform some advanced tasks. For example, Cisco recently released an IP cellular telephone with XML support. This device could allow a user full access to Amazon from any location. Read more about this new cellular telephone at `http://www.eweek.com/article2/0,4149,1259848,00.asp`. In addition, at least one company is working with Microsoft to include the Windows Mobile 2003 operating system in a cellular telephone (see the Computerworld story at `http://www.computerworld.com/mobiletopics/mobile/story/0,10801,84923,00.html`).

Because of the JavaScript environment and the number of environments where PocketSOAP works (you can use almost the same application on any of the platforms that PocketSOAP supports), the method of creating the request is a little different. The code begins by creating an object—the method varies by platform, but all of the Windows derivatives seem to work well with the `new ActiveXObject()` constructor.

You can obtain the particulars of a search by looking through the SOAP examples in the `\AmazonWebServices\SoapRequestSamples` folder. The example shows typical entries. Always set the method to include the Amazon namespace and the correct request method. The code creates the complex data structure used to form a request with relative ease. All you need to provide are the essentials—PocketSOAP appears to take care of the details of constructing the envelope for you.

After the code creates the request, it creates the `Transport` object. This object sends and receives data from the Amazon Web Services. Notice that you must include a value for the `SOAPAction` property or the code will fail. The return value appears in `Transport` and the code uses the `SOAPEnv.Parse()` method to retrieve it.

At this point, the code uses a combination of `Nodes` and `Items` properties to access the `Details` nodes. The details appear in `RecData` as an array, not as a list of nodes. Consequently, you access the data within the array. Each array element is a node, so you use the `Nodes` property and `ItemByName()` method to retrieve specific values. The output of this example is similar to the output shown in Figure 9.9.

Developing for a Cellular Telephone or Palm Device

Older versions of the Palm and most cellular telephones are so limited in processing capacity and memory that you really won't want to try to create a local Amazon Web Services application for them. The best alternative is to create a Web application that retrieves and formats the data for the device before passing it along. This example relies on a special ASP.NET application specifically designed for mobile devices. The server detects the device type and pages forms as needed to ensure each form appears correctly on the device.

Listing 9.4 shows the essential code you need for this example. Make sure you look at the form setup for this example in the source code. You'll find this example in the `\Chapter 09\WebApp` folder of the source code located on the Sybex Web site.

Listing 9.4 Creating Web-based Amazon Web Services Application

```
private void btnSubmit_Click(object sender, System.EventArgs e)
{
   ManufacturerRequest  MR;       // The manufacturer request.
   ProductInfo          PI;       // Data returned from request.
   AmazonSearchService  Service;  // Connection to the service.
   Int32                Counter;  // Loop counting variable.
   StringBuilder        SB;       // Contains the output data.

   // Instantiate the objects.
   MR = new ManufacturerRequest();
   PI = new ProductInfo();
   Service = new AmazonSearchService();

   // Create the author request.
   MR.manufacturer = txtManufacturer.Text;
   MR.devtag = "Your-Developer-Token";
   MR.mode = txtMode.Text;
   MR.page = txtPage.Text;
   MR.type = "lite";
   MR.tag = "webservices-20";

   // Make the request.
   PI = Service.ManufacturerSearchRequest(MR);

   // Display the results on screen.
   for (Counter = 0; Counter < PI.Details.Length; Counter++)
   {
      // Blank the StringBuilder.
      SB = new StringBuilder();

      // Create the Product Name input.
      SB.Append(PI.Details[Counter].ProductName);
```

```
            // Create the List Price input.
            SB.Append("     (");
            SB.Append(PI.Details[Counter].ListPrice);
            SB.Append(")");

            // Add the data to the list.
            lstOutput.Items.Add(SB.ToString());
        }

        // Show the form.
        this.ActiveForm = Results;
    }
```

The code begins by creating the objects used for a manufacturer search. Notice that the code assumes the value of some entries. For example, most users don't care about the developer or associate tokens. Keeping the entries on screen to a minimum helps users enter data quickly (possibly more accurately) and with a minimum of frustration. Imagine having to type **webservices-20** every time you want to access Amazon with a cellular telephone.

The output for this example is also relatively simple. Depending on the device, the output list can include bullets. However, as shown in Figure 9.11, some devices won't display the bullets, making it difficult to determine where one entry ends and another begins in the list. The example also uses other visual cues such as the parenthesis to display the data. Notice that the example only outputs product name and price to keep the amount of display clutter to a minimum.

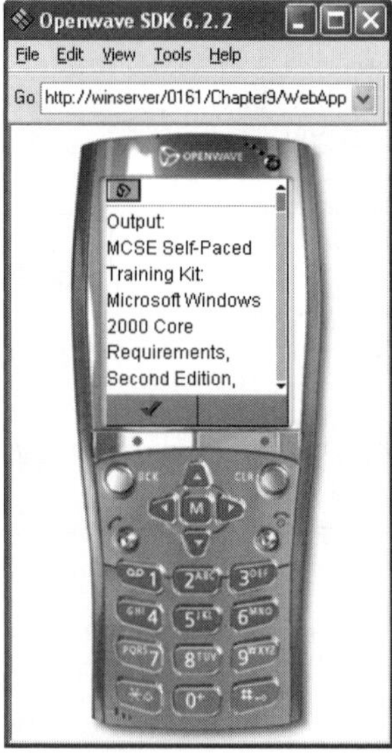

FIGURE 9.11: Typical output when working with a Web-based application. Image courtesy Openwave Systems Inc.

Your Call to Action

This chapter has helped you understand some of the mobile device options at your disposal. You shouldn't consider this chapter complete or comprehensive—mobile device development kits abound. This chapter only discussed some of the more popular options. However, the concepts in this chapter apply equally well to other kinds of mobile development and you can apply the lessons learned to other language products discussed in the book. For example, it's perfectly acceptable to create a mobile device solution using PHP or Java—all you need is a little inspiration.

Now that you have a little better perspective of what's possible, it's time to consider what types of mobile device you want to provide for your Amazon Web Services application. One mistake that developers make is to assume they must include support for every available device and that's simply not possible—at least not without a major investment in time and resources. A better path is to choose one or two devices to begin development and add additional devices as needed.

Chapters 4 through 9 introduced you to various language options. In each of these chapters, you learned how to access Amazon Web Services using various techniques. Now it's time to refine those examples and explore other ways to use Amazon Web Services. Chapter 10 takes you beyond simple database applications into refined database development. You also learn other techniques for creating a finely crafted application that helps users get the information they need faster.

Part III

Refining Your Amazon Web Services Program

Chapter 10

Addressing Performance Concerns
Addressing Reliability Concerns
Meeting the Data Refresh Requirements

Crafting Your Application

Implementing an Offline Storage Strategy
Developing Power Search Applications
Developing Blended Search Applications
Developing Browse Node Applications

All of the chapters so far have considered various ways to obtain data from Amazon. However, great applications do more than just get data—a developer crafts them to get the data efficiently, reliably, and quickly. For example, you could use multiple searches to get all the products a vendor produces, or you can use a single power search, or a blended search. Using the correct search to obtain multiple results makes your application more efficient, but not necessarily more reliable. Sometimes a power search will fail to obtain every result. Crafting an application means knowing what kind of interaction to perform with Amazon based on your specific needs.

This chapter assumes that you have read one or more of the preceding language-specific chapters (Chapters 5 through 9) and understand the concepts discussed in Chapters 1 through 4. This chapter answers the question of what comes next. You'll discover some of the concerns you need to address to move your application from *functional* to *usable*. In most cases, this means making your application efficient, reliable, and fast.

One of the major performance and reliability concerns you have to address is the use of databases in your application. Many of the examples in previous chapters showed how to create a database interface for your application so you can store information offline and therefore improve performance. However, the previous chapters left some questions unanswered, such as when to use database storage techniques to improve overall application performance. Sometimes, offline storage is more of a hindrance than a help.

You'll also learn about some new Amazon search techniques in this chapter. The reason these searches are important is that they help you look for data on Amazon in new ways. These three searches can make your application more efficient or faster (or, sometimes, both). However, you need to consider what you lose in the process. Sometimes the losses will add up to an effective performance loss and the search specific sections discuss this issue too.

Considering Performance Issues

Some developers confuse the concept of performance with the idea of speed. An application that performs well (has good performance) isn't necessarily fast. Performance is a measure of how well an application accomplishes the task that you set before it. Speed is only one aspect of performance. You also have to consider factors such as resource usage and user access speed (efficiency). The following sections discuss performance concerns for Amazon applications.

Addressing Speed Concerns

Speed measures how fast an application can perform a task. Many developers concentrate on this factor when developing an application because it's relatively easy to quantify. You can easily demonstrate that a particular coding change or technique improvement provides a corresponding increase in speed. Making changes that result in a speed increase is important when using a Web service such as Amazon Web Services because your application incurs a performance penalty when it requests the data.

> ▶ **NOTE**
>
> This book doesn't even begin to address local application speed issues because the language you choose, application environment, and platform affect the speed of your application. Look in the language-specific chapters of the book for suggestions on third party resources you can use for that language. Writing code that executes quickly takes time, effort, and planning, so make sure you begin with a good application specification.

Quantifying speed is relatively easy for most applications because the developer has control over the environment. On the other hand, getting, proving, and quantifying a speed increase with Amazon Web Services can prove elusive. For example, your application will always slow during peak activity periods on Amazon—you can't control this factor and it always affects the overall performance of your application. Consequently, long-term speed measurement is essential when working with Amazon Web Services. You need to consider whether a change actually provides a performance boost or the Amazon Web Services just happened to provide faster results during the initial test. In addition, make one change at a time because you can't accurately measure the effects of multiple changes.

It's also important to consider the state of Amazon Web Services at the time of your test. Monitor the state of changes by visiting the developer forum at `http://forums.prospero.com/am-assocdevxml/start/`. This newsgroup helps you keep up-to-date on changes that Amazon is making that could affect your application. (Amazon will also send you a newsletter with probable changes to Amazon Web Services.)

Initially, you might get the idea that you have to perform all kinds of weird programming to gain much of a speed increase. However, you can reduce all Amazon Web Services application speed improvements into five main areas.

Use the Fewest Possible Calls A combination of optimized searches, explicit input, and data ordering usually serves to reduce the number of calls your application has to make to Amazon. Every call costs time, so even reducing the number of calls by one round-trip helps. It's important to remember that Amazon returns data in 10 record chunks, so you should optimize your searches around this number.

Request Only Required Data Some developers have a habit of requesting all possible data with the idea that they might need the information later. When working with Amazon Web Services, request only the data you actually need. A lite search is far more efficient than a heavy search. Requesting only the bestselling products when that's what you need could reduce the amount of data you have to request as well. You also need to consider the effect of reduced data requests on user efficiency—less data means fewer decisions and improved user performance. Of course, you can easily carry efficiency too far—make sure you don't end up making multiple requests because you don't request enough information at the outset.

Use Offline Storage Effectively Don't assume that every application has to use offline storage or that you need to store everything offline. An application used to perform research might not benefit from offline storage as most requests are unique and data input is unlikely to repeat. In addition, an application that requires a source of constant updates might not benefit much from complete offline storage—you might want to store just the essentials for locating the data such as a UPC. (See the "Using Offline Storage Effectively" section of this chapter for details.)

Improve the Local Application Speed It's easy to become fixated on the speed of Amazon Web Services communication and forget local application requirements. The local application has a large effect on application speed. Consider items such as how fast the application makes a request. Using SOAP usually results in better application performance because you don't have to build a request string. Consider special programming needs as well. For example, don't rely on Amazon to sort the data if none of the default sort criteria completely meet your needs—sort the data locally instead.

Define the Best Possible User Experience Many developers assume that fast code always results in a fast application. When a user spends considerable time trying to figure out your application, code execution speed becomes a nonissue. Always check user performance when you consider the speed of your application because the user is going to be the main choke point. Whenever you make the user fast, you gain a significant improvement in application speed (not to mention reducing support costs). Chapter 11 discusses this concept in detail.

Addressing Efficiency Concerns

Efficiency affects performance by modifying the resource requirements for the application. An efficient application uses resources to their fullest and therefore reduces the cost of using the application. Making an application efficient can improve application speed as well. For example, an application that uses memory efficiently won't have to rely on swap files or other memory enhancements as much, which usually results in a speed boost. However, an efficient application can just as easily slow performance. An application that uses disk storage rather than memory to improve overall system efficiency by freeing memory for other applications is almost certain to work slower than an application that relies exclusively on memory.

You'll also find that efficiency affects reliability. An application that uses resources conservatively is less likely to run out of resources to process the incoming Amazon data. Resource deprivation is a major cause of application crashes, so using resources carefully means your application is likely to crash less often.

An Amazon Web Services application developer only considers the client side of the data exchange because Amazon takes care of the server side. When a user makes a request, you must consider the efficiency of that request. Inefficient requests can cause Amazon to return more results than needed and reduces overall system performance. As a side effect, consider how inefficient requests will add to the load the Amazon Web Services servers must handle. When multiple developers create applications that perform requests inefficiently, server load increases, and could increase the time the user waits for responses.

> **TIP**
>
> Always use the current version of Amazon Web Services to get speed, efficiency, reliability, and request features. For example, only version 3 and above provide availability data as part of a lite request. Remember that a lite request takes less time and consumes fewer resources than a heavy request, so getting this extra data in a lite request could prove helpful.

One of the most important efficiency considerations is the effect of false starts on application efficiency. For example, Amazon commonly lists new products before those products are available for sale. When a user requests one of these new products, you'll find that the order will normally go through Amazon without difficulty as a pre-order. However, using this technique might not be efficient because the user might never see the product if the release is cancelled for some reason. Some developers handle this problem by looking for a blank list price on the assumption that a product that isn't available for sale will have a blank list price. However, this technique isn't reliable. What you need to look for is the

`Availability` field of the `ProductInfo` data structure. Look for the words, "Usually ships" (or the equivalent in your language) in the `Availability` field to ensure the user can actually obtain the product.

Considering Reliability Issues

Reliable application performance is essential if you plan to use Amazon Web Services for any type of business purpose. Most people associate reliability with availability, but that's only part of the picture. When working with Amazon Web Services, you need to consider four reliability factors.

Availability of Data Unless a user can access the Amazon data, the application you create is useless. Fortunately, Amazon Web Services has a high availability rate, so most desktop applications will run fine even if you don't include backup data through a database. However, you need some form of local and/or remote database support for mobile applications where high availability is a requirement and a connection isn't always available.

> **▶ NOTE**
>
> It's important to understand that most performance tuning relies on assumptions that might not be true on the production system. The more control you exercise over the host machine, the better you can control the assumptions you make about performance tuning. Real systems run multiple applications, including background applications such as virus checkers. In addition, applications can experience problems such as memory leaks. Consequently, you need to make the best assumptions you can about the application environment and use those assumptions when tuning your application.

Consistency of Results Providing consistent results to application users is important. Consistency means including all data (or a standard response to all data outputs). Sometimes, Amazon won't provide an output that you need. For example, some products don't have pictures, so you have to provide something in the place of the picture so the user knows the application is operating correctly. (Amazon currently provides a small blank picture when it can't supply a real product picture.) Consistency also means providing similar response times (when possible) and standard notifications when errors do occur.

Accessibility of Amazon Site You have to decide, at some point, whether you can tolerate any availability problems with Amazon Web Services because they'll occur at some point. To provide maximum reliability, you must provide a cache of some sort. This doesn't mean creating a database to hold the data, although that is one option. You can also use memory caches or disk-based browser caches. For that matter, your application can rely on the cache provided by a proxy server. The point is to provide some alternative, if you need it, for the few times that the Amazon Web Services don't respond.

Availability of the Local Application Strange things can happen to an application between the time it leaves your development machine and appears on the user's machine. In general, you need to perform complete application testing on several (more is better) user machines that don't include all the features of your development machine. Make sure you test obscure as well as common features. For example, test every search time that your application supports. It's also important to test features such as the use of shopping carts. Make a few real world purchases from the test machine to ensure the entire process works as planned on that machine.

Considering the Data Refresh Requirements

Refreshing data you receive from Amazon is a requirement of your developer license (see Appendix B for details). However, Amazon doesn't state how to refresh the data. All of the examples in this book take a dynamic approach. The application checks the date that it last retrieved any data in the database when a user requested data from Amazon Web Services. If the data is too old, the application requests the information from Amazon Web Services. Unfortunately, this means that some users will observe an inconsistent delay in responses. You could also build a database of ASINs and refresh those ASINs every night at a convenient time—when no one is likely to need the information. The idea is to refresh the data every 24 hours using the technique that best suits your organization.

Make sure you keep up with current Amazon policy regarding offline data storage. For example, the license agreement you signed probably says that you have to refresh all data every 24 hours. However, Amazon Web Services Newsletter #3 states that you can store ASINs permanently provided you check the viability of the ASIN regularly. (You can find older copies of the Amazon Web Services Newsletter at `http://www.jungledeveloper.com/index.php`.) When a product is no longer available, Amazon usually retires the ASIN, so updating your database regularly to reflect retired ASINs is essential.

Sometimes you need to consider the source of Amazon data. For example, a UPC isn't Amazon data even if you get the UPC from Amazon. An association assigns the UPC number to the product manufacturer for that product and the UPC won't change for the life of the product. (See a list of UPC associations at `http://www.iddba.org/upcresce.htm`.) In short, storing a UPC permanently is safe because this value won't change. The same concepts hold true for various aspects of the product, such as the product name and the name of the vendor—these descriptive elements are unlikely to change.

You can't extend permanent storage to volatile information such as price. Always meet or exceed the Amazon Web Services requirements for volatile data or you might find that users get outdated information. In fact, the need to ensure the user gets current (and correct) information is the main reason that Amazon requires that you provide a refresh cycle for your application.

Using Offline Storage Effectively

Many of the performance enhancements you can add to your Amazon Web Services application revolve around some type of offline storage. How your application uses offline storage makes a big difference in performance enhancement. In most cases, the vendor and product you choose determines factors such as reliability and availability. The following sections describe a few of the issues you need to consider as part of your offline storage strategy.

Choosing the Correct Offline Storage Strategy

All of the examples so far in the book have considered offline storage from the perspective of storing the Amazon data that an application needs to handle multiple requests for the same information. This technique is the most important strategy to learn from a speed and reliability perspective. However, it's not the only strategy to consider because some applications simply don't benefit from this approach.

Another offline storage technique to consider is the use of a database containing ASINs or UPCs. You can associate the ASIN or UPC with specific non-changing data such as a manufacturer or product name. This database can help users quickly identify previously researched products that Amazon sells. Even if you can't save other information from Amazon Web Services, saving these values can improve user efficiency by reducing the number of research requests the user has to make.

Don't become fixated on output data when working with Amazon Web Services. All of the requests you make have value too. For example, you might create a database of recent request data to provide hints to the user. As the user fills in request data, your application can make suggestions for the next input value and reduce the chance the user will make an invalid request. Likewise, you can store requests that didn't work. Making a quick check for these requests before you send the data to Amazon will save a round-trip over the Internet and improve application speed. The application can also alert the user to the fact that the request won't work and make suggestions on how to change the request.

Selecting a Database that Suits Your Needs

The database-related examples in the book rely on one of three database managers: SQL Server, Microsoft Access, or MySQL. You can find many other alternatives—these are just a sampling of what's available. I chose these three database managers because they represent several steps in functionality, performance, ease of use, and cost. It's important to get a database manager that you can afford, that will perform the tasks you need it to do, and is easy enough to manage, so you might choose any of the myriad alternatives on the market.

SQL Server is the most expensive of the three, but it also provides the best functionality. Microsoft constantly touts the speed of SQL server, but it's a memory hog and can consume copious amounts of hard drive space. Given the complex tasks that SQL Server can perform, you might not find it as easy to use as Access, but the GUI-based tools do make it easier to use than the command line interface of MySQL.

> **▶ NOTE**
>
> You can use the Microsoft Data Engine (MSDE) as a substitute for SQL Server in some cases. It always works as a good alternative to SQL Server for local development. In some cases, you can also use MSDE as an alternative to SQL Server for groups of up to 5 people. Make sure that MSDE actually meets your needs before you spend time installing it—this product doesn't include all the features of SQL Server. Because MSDE relies on the same DLLs as SQL Server in many cases, you'll also want to apply any required patches to ensure the integrity of your system. Learn more about MSDE at `http://www.microsoft.com/sql/msde/default.asp`.

Microsoft Access is probably the easiest of the database managers to use because it provides a single GUI interface where you manage everything. Some developers feel that Access is only useful for local databases, but many small businesses rely on Access as their only multiuser database manager. From a speed perspective, Access is probably the slowest of the three database managers. However, it's very easy on hard drive usage and relatively light on memory use as well.

MySQL is the least expensive of the three database managers—you simply download your copy from a Web site. You'll find that this database manager is the hardest of the three to use because almost everything happens at the command line. Some middle-sized companies use MySQL because it has the speed required to handle larger applications. It's also relatively easy on memory use, but about equal with SQL Server when it comes to hard drive space requirements.

Considering Database Storage Alternatives

Don't assume that you need a database to provide the benefits of local storage. It's true that you need a database when the usage requirements are high or you need long-term storage of information. However, storing the Amazon data isn't exactly rocket science—you can use any of a number of alternatives. For example, the "Using a Script to Call an XSLT Page" section of Chapter 3 discusses a technique where you rely on the capabilities of a browser to process the Amazon data. In this case, the simple fact that the browser caches pages it downloads from the Internet is enough to improve performance for multiple calls for the same data—at least for the local user. Obviously, the browser caching solution won't work for multiple sessions if the user sets the browser to clear the cache after each session.

Sometimes you need something a little more substantial than the cache provided by a browser, but still don't need permanent storage. In these situations, you can use an in-memory solution. The simplest solution is an array or other memory structure. However, many languages also provide actual caches you can use and some vendors provide caches as part of their third party product.

It's possible to get by without using a database even when you need some form of permanent storage. For example, you could store a list of ASINs in an XML file. In fact, you can easily extend XML storage to entire requests or other types of permanent data. At some point, the performance of such a system is going to become problematic, but it works for small amounts of data for one user and could even work for a few users if you use a central storage location for the XML files.

Using Power Searches Effectively

Power searches can help you find books more efficiently than just about any search because you control precisely how the search engine looks for entries. This search only works on books at the moment, but eventually it could work with other products as well. The benefit of using a power search is that you describe every element of the search using Boolean statements. For example, if you want to locate all of the books I've written for Sybex, you would use a statement like this:

```
Author:John Mueller and Publisher:Sybex
```

You add this string to the `PowerRequest.power` structure member. Make sure you check out the `/AmazonWebServices/API Guide/search_power.htm` help topic in the kit to ensure you know which keywords to use for a particular search.

You can run into a number of problems using a power search. For example, the complex search criteria can make it difficult to build a database of search responses. A user could build the previous search string as `Publisher:Sybex and Author:John Mueller` and get the

> **▶ TIP**
>
> You can find a great article on caching techniques for PHP and Web services ("Caching With PHP Cache_Lite") at `http://www.devshed.com/Server_Side/PHP/PHP_Cache_Lite/page1.html`. This article considers important issues, such as using the browser cache and implementing server-based caching.

same results from Amazon. In addition, you'll normally need to rely on the user providing the correct search string unless you want to build a complex form that contains all of the required keywords. Listing 10.1 shows a typical example of a SOAP power search. You'll find the complete source code for this example in the `\Chapter 10\PowerSearch` folder of the source code located on the Sybex Web site.

Listing 10.1 Defining a Power Search Using SOAP

```
private void btnTest_Click(object sender, System.EventArgs e)
{
   PowerRequest         PR;      // The power search request.
   ProductInfo          PI;      // Data returned from request.
   AmazonSearchService  Service; // Connection to the service.
   DataRow              DR;      // Output data.
   Int32                Counter; // Loop counting variable.

   // Instantiate the objects.
   PR = new PowerRequest();
   PI = new ProductInfo();
   Service = new AmazonSearchService();

   // Create the power search request.
   PR.devtag = txtTag.Text;
   PR.mode = txtMode.Text;
   PR.page = txtPage.Text;
   PR.power = txtPowerSearch.Text;
   if (txtSort.Text.Length > 0)
      PR.sort = txtSort.Text;
   PR.type = txtType.Text;

   // Make the request.
   PI = Service.PowerSearchRequest(PR);

   // Display the results on screen.
   ... Display Code ...
}
```

As with all SOAP searches, this one places the various inputs into an object that you pass to Amazon using a search request. The difference for a power search is the power search string—the use of values separated by or, not, or and. For example, you can build a complex search string that looks for two specific authors such as:

```
Author:John Mueller or Author:Richard Mansfield and Publisher:Sybex and not
Keywords:Hacker
```

In this case, the search will include all books written by John Mueller or Richard Mansfield and published by Sybex unless the book contains the keyword hacker. It's possible to create strings of any complexity, making this technique suitable for directed searches. Consequently, these searches tend to improve overall application performance and user satisfaction. However, the introduction of the complex string also makes the searches less reliable because it's easy to create a string with incorrect information that returns a bad search error.

Notice the use of the `PR.sort` field in this example. Using a sort in other kinds of searches is optional because you might not even know how the user wants to view the data. However, given the highly targeted use of this search, you'll usually want to include a sort value to ensure the user sees the needed data quickly.

Performing Blended Searches

You might use a blended search more often than you think as an application input, rather than a user output. The concept is simple. Given a keyword, find how many Amazon modes (product lines) contain that keyword and return at most three values for each mode. Although, the average user is going to want more than three return values for a particular search, your application can gain access to every mode value for a particular keyword. It's possible to use this list of modes to perform a more extensive search across all product lines that contain the keyword in question. In short, rather than guess where Amazon might hide a particular product, you can ensure you'll find it. Listing 10.2 shows a SOAP application that relies on a blended search. You'll find the complete source code for this example in the `\Chapter 10\BlendedSearch` folder of the source code located on the Sybex Web site.

Listing 10.2 Defining a Blended Search

```
private void btnTest_Click(object sender, System.EventArgs e)
{
   BlendedRequest       BR;       // The power search request.
   ProductLine          []PL;     // List of product lines.
   ProductInfo          PI;       // Data returned from request.
   AmazonSearchService  Service;  // Connection to the service.
   DataRow              DR;       // Output data.
   Int32                PLCount;  // Product line counter.
   Int32                Counter;  // Loop counting variable.

   // Instantiate the objects.
   BR = new BlendedRequest();
   Service = new AmazonSearchService();

   // Create the power search request.
   BR.blended = txtBlended.Text;
   BR.devtag = txtTag.Text;
   BR.type = "lite";
   BR.tag = "webservices-20";

   // Make the request.
```

```
      PL = Service.BlendedSearchRequest(BR);

      // Display the results on screen.
      dsAmazon.Tables["ProductsOut"].Rows.Clear();
      for (PLCount = 0; PLCount < PL.Length; PLCount++)
      {
         // Get the current product information.
         PI = PL[PLCount].ProductInfo;

         // Process this particular product information.
         for (Counter = 0; Counter < PI.Details.Length; Counter++)
         {
            // Create a new row to hold the data.
            DR = dsAmazon.Tables["ProductsOut"].NewRow();

            // Add the data to the row.
            DR["Product Name"] = PI.Details[Counter].ProductName;
            ... Other Fields ...
            DR["Mode"] = PL[PLCount].Mode;

            // Display the row on screen.
            dsAmazon.Tables["ProductsOut"].Rows.Add(DR);
         }
      }
   }
```

The request process for a blended search is different from other search types. You don't provide a `mode` or a `page` field value. In addition, unless you really do plan to provide user output, anything other than the "lite" `type` field value is a waste of resources because all search types return the modes you need.

Should you decide to process the information returned by this call, you need to use a double loop. The outer loop counts through each of the `ProductLine` values returned by the call. Each `ProductLine` array element reflects a different mode and contains a `ProductInfo` object. After you retrieve the `ProductInfo` object, you can process the data as normal.

Notice that the code contains a `PL[PLCount].Mode` property. You enumerate these property values to obtain a list of modes for the current keyword. The keyword could be anything, including a vendor or product name element.

Performing Browse Node Searches

Amazon uses browse nodes to organize data. By accessing a specific browse node, you can run through a list of related products using the same organization that Amazon uses. This particular search is handy when you want to create a list of product types, such as a list of computer science books. See the Common Product Modes and Browse IDs help topic in the kit at `/AmazonWebServices/API Guide/common_modes.htm` for a list of common browse node numbers. Listing 10.3 shows how to create a SOAP browse node request. You'll find the complete source code for this example in the `\Chapter 10\BlendedSearch` folder of the source code located on the Sybex Web site.

Listing 10.3 Performing a Browse Node Search

```
private void btnTest_Click(object sender, System.EventArgs e)
{
   BrowseNodeRequest    BNR;      // The browse node search request.
   ProductInfo          PI;       // Data returned from request.
   AmazonSearchService  Service; // Connection to the service.
   DataRow              DR;       // Output data.
   Int32                Counter; // Loop counting variable.

   // Instantiate the objects.
   BNR = new BrowseNodeRequest();
   PI = new ProductInfo();
   Service = new AmazonSearchService();

   // Create the power search request.
   BNR.browse_node = txtBrowseNode.Text;
   BNR.devtag = txtTag.Text;
   BNR.mode = txtMode.Text;
   BNR.page = txtPage.Text;
   if (txtSort.Text.Length > 0)
      BNR.sort = txtSort.Text;
   BNR.tag = "webservices-20";
   BNR.type = txtType.Text;

   // Make the request.
   PI = Service.BrowseNodeSearchRequest(BNR);

   // Display the results on screen.
   ... Display Code ...
}
```

As you can see, a browse node search works much like the other searches examined in the book. The major difference is that you use a browse node number instead of a keyword, ASIN, or other tangible search criteria. The most reliable way to use a browse node search is to browse Amazon. The browse nodes appear on the left side of the display near the bottom. When you click a browse link, you'll see an URL similar to this one:

```
http://www.amazon.com/exec/obidos/tg/browse/-/283155/
```

The key here is the word *browse* and the number at the end. The 283155 browse node is books in general. This brings up a potential error that you'll encounter. Some resources discuss browse node 1000 (the top level browse node for all books). Amazon is working to make this browse node work, but hasn't so far, so you should avoid using it.

A browse node search is so general that your application should include filtering and the request should include sorting. Otherwise, you could end up with results that you'll never need or use. In general, a browse node search is most helpful when you have some idea of what you want, but don't have specifics like an author or manufacturer in mind.

Your Call to Action

This chapter has helped you consider some of the fit and finish items for your Amazon Web Services application. Making your application reliable, efficient, and fast is important if you want to get the most out of the features Amazon Web Services provides. However, it's also important to remember that some choices are mutually exclusive—you might have to give up a little performance to obtain better application reliability.

While reading this chapter you considered options, not absolutes. The only absolute is your application needs. You need to use the information presented in this chapter to address your specific application needs. Consider elements such as the application platform and user environment as part of the option selection process. For example, a mobile device will probably give up a little reliability to ensure the application operates fast enough, but this isn't always a hard and fast rule. You might find that your particular mobile application manipulates the company offerings on Amazon and therefore requires superior reliability.

Chapter 11 continues the process of honing your application. However, instead of considering the application requirements, Chapter 11 considers user requirements. Making an application faster can net you an overall gain in performance, but making the user faster always nets an overall gain in performance because user task speed is usually the critical performance factor for an application.

Chapter 11

Working with Specific Types of Users

Creating Flexible Interfaces

Developing for Users with Special Needs

Considering User Needs

Considering Privacy Issues

Designing a Wishlists Application

Designing a Listmania! Application

No matter what kind of application you write, you must consider the user's needs to ensure someone will actually use the application. Most developers realize that a Graphical User Interface (GUI) is better than a character mode interface and a few even realize that help is a requirement—not a nicety. A few developers understand that tooltips are also important and speed keys (shortcut keys) help users keep their hands on the keyboard so they can remain efficient. All of these elements, along with layout and design, are common to any application you might create. The market already has a number of good User Interface (UI) design books, so I won't replicate their information here (you'll find some of them listed in the "Selecting User Interface Design Resources" sidebar in the "Targeting a Specific User Type" section). This chapter helps you decide how to create a great interface for your Amazon Web Services application using a combination of general and specific coding techniques.

Along with specific interface requirements for your application, this chapter also considers helpful design decisions. For example, although no one requires you to address privacy issues, many users are beginning to request this functionality and might not visit your site more than once if you don't provide a privacy policy. In addition, it's important to personalize the user's experience with your site so you don't have to ask the same questions every time the user visits. A user might like to use a specific stylesheet with your Web site or request a specific setup for your application. Personalization helps users have a better experience and improves user efficiency.

Finally, this chapter helps you discover two personalization features that Amazon provides: Listmania! and Wish Lists. You can use Listmania! to determine how users group various products or provide alternative suggestions to users of your application. The Listmania! feature relies on user-generated lists on topics such as "World's scariest movie." Wish Lists contain a list of items that an individual would like to own. You can use these lists for everything from birthday shopping to weddings. The idea behind Wishlist searches is that you can help users determine what to buy without the embarrassment of asking the person what they want. The user simply accesses the person's list and locates a product they can afford.

Targeting a Specific User Type

You'll invest a lot of time honing your Amazon Web Services application if you plan to present it to other people. For that matter, it doesn't hurt to hone your application even if you only plan to use it to meet your own needs. No matter who uses your application, you have to consider their needs or the user will quickly tire of the application and not use it. Targeting specific user types helps you design an interface that works well, meets the user's needs, and requires less maintenance time.

Many books and Web sites on application design target generic applications—the type that anyone could use. However, this book considers a more specific application type—the one that relies on Amazon Web Services. Even so, the number of uses for applications in this group is quite large, so you need to consider your specific application. It's essential to consider how the user will interact with the application and the user's skill level. In fact, you should consider the following elements when targeting your application to meet a specific user's needs.

- The environment in which the application executes—Web applications often have different requirements than desktop applications.
- The device the user will use to access your application—mobile devices have strict limitations that will affect your user interface design.
- The user's skill level—advanced users require less help and will quickly tire of repetitive help offers.
- The input and output requirements for the application—complex applications (those with more input or output) could require multiple screens.
- The request parameters of the application—simple Amazon searches that don't use sorting are the easiest to accommodate.
- The user's expectations for the application—a user who simply wants to browse will have fewer expectations than one making a purchase.
- The kind of Amazon searches performed—browse node searches are inherently more complex and require more explanation than an author search.
- The availability of localized help—users of Web applications typically receive less help than users of desktop application.

It's relatively easy to use these criteria to build a profile of an individual user, but assessing the needs of multiple user types can become more difficult. In this case, you need to build a profile of each user type and then organize the users by priority. This exercise lets you determine how much weight to give each requirement. An advanced user who only uses the application once a month can easily turn off the extra help you provide to novice users (assuming that you provide a switch for turning the help off).

Sometimes several user types will conflict, making prioritization essential. For example, if most of your users will employ a cellular telephone to access the site, you might need to provide alternatives for the few desktop users who visit. In many cases, careful development will allow both groups to access the site—the desktop users might notice that the site is a little plain, but that's about it. The goal is to accommodate the needs of each group based on their level of access to your site—don't accommodate the needs of a small group to the detriment of the users who normally support your site.

> **NOTE**
>
> The Listmania! and Wishlist IDs used in this chapter come from the Amazon Web Services Kit. I used these IDs to ensure I didn't inadvertently reveal anyone's personal information. In addition, because these IDs appear as part of the Amazon Web Services Kit, they should remain useful (a personal ID could become unusable after a while if Amazon removes it from the list).

Designing Flexible Interfaces

No matter how well you design your application, someone will complain that some feature doesn't work as expected. During my years of programming, I've personally seen arguments between users about order of fields on a form. One discussion about a screen degenerated into an intense argument about the order of name elements on the form (one user wanted last name first—the other wanted the first name to appear first). Users will grumble about every aspect of your application given a chance and you'll never satisfy all the users. Some developers solve the problem by giving up and creating the application they want. However, this solution probably works least often because the user's immediate reaction is that the developer isn't listening and lacks any form of human interaction skills.

Flexible user interfaces resolve the user problem by letting each user design the interface that meets their specific needs. Just how flexible you can make the interface depends on a number of factors including the application environment and the programming language you use. Making Web applications flexible is somewhat harder than for most desktop applications because many browsers lack the support required to move visual elements around and perform other manipulations the user would like. Depending on your programming skill, schedule, programming language, and patience, you can make some desktop applications so flexible that the user has control over every display element and the application will remember its configuration between sessions.

Let's start with something a little more reasonable than complete application configuration. Even the most mundane Web page allows configuration. For example, you can use Cascading Style Sheets (CSS) to format the Web page. Some browsers let the user substitute

Selecting User Interface Design Resources

Getting great user interface design references helps you get started faster and ensures you won't make as many mistakes during the design process. Typically, you'll find that books are better than Web sites for this kind of information because books have more space to cover contingencies that articles or other online resources can't discuss. However, don't discount Web sites—you might find something that meets a specific need. Newsgroups can help, but you need to state the design issues you want to overcome very clearly and take any advice with a grain of salt because the developer helping you might not have a clear picture of the issues.

You can find a number of good books online. The trick is to find a book that is either completely generic or meets the need of a specific environment. For example, if you want to design a Web application, then you might consider reading *Designing Web Usability: The Practice of Simplicity* by Jakob Nielsen (New Riders, 1999). Although Web developers could rely on this book, desktop developers can benefit most from *The Humane Interface: New Directions for Designing Interactive Systems* by Jef Raskin (Addison-Wesley, 2000) and *About Face 2.0: The Essentials of Interaction Design* by Alan Cooper and Robert Reimann (John Wiley & Sons, 2003). A good generic book that addresses interface design as a component of total application design is *Designing Highly Usable Software* by Jeff Cogswell (Sybex, 2004).

It's possible to find good help online. For example, the Microsoft User Interface site at `http://msdn.microsoft.com/nhp/default.asp?contentid=28000443` provides a wealth of information on topics as diverse as accessibility and Microsoft Agent. Dr. Jakob Nielsen presents a number of usability articles at `http://www.useit.com/alertbox/`. This monthly column provides continuing help with your application as user needs and expectations change. In some cases, you can even find online books such as *Task-Centered User Interface Design* by Clayton Lewis and John Rieman at `http://www.hcibib.org/tcuid/`. The authors offer this book as shareware, so make sure you support them if you use it.

Locating a newsgroup that offers advice on user interfaces isn't hard—it's hard to find good advice. Generally, you'll need to find a newsgroup that caters to your language and choice of device (such as the .NET Compact Framework for mobile devices at `microsoft.public.dotnet.framework.compactframework`). Some newsgroups, such as `comp.human-factors` provide limited generic help should you need it. After many hours of searching, I couldn't find a suitable newsgroup devoted to the topic of user interfaces. Contact me at `JMueller@mwt.net` if you know of such a newsgroup and I'll post it on my Web site with the updates for this book.

their CSS file for the default that you provide on your Web site—making it possible for the user to have complete control over the presentation of information even if you don't provide any other form of programming with the Web page. Some sites extend this principle by providing multiple CSS files. A simple cookie entry controls which CSS file the Web site uses when presenting information to the user. Desktop applications are even easier to control in this area. All you need is an Options dialog box containing the display element settings so the user can change them to meet specific needs. Most desktop applications already provide this feature. Make sure you save the user options in a file or other central location (such as the Windows Registry) if you offer this feature.

The next level of application configuration is component selection. For example, not every Amazon Web Services user will want to sort the output results. It might seem that simply ignoring the sort field would work, but unnecessary fields are annoying to some users. Again, Web pages can use a cookie to store a list of fields or controls the user doesn't want to see. You'll likely have to provide a configuration page to support this form of configuration—adding a simple link to the page to allow configuration usually works fine. Desktop applications can use an Options dialog box. Most desktop applications don't offer this feature—likely because the developer didn't think to offer the feature or assumed that everyone would want access to every field.

Web applications don't commonly use toolbars or special menus in the same way that desktop applications use them. However, both environments can benefit from some level of customization for both items. Quite a few desktop applications offer this feature. Generally, the user selects a special menu command that allows them to move menu or toolbar elements around, add new menu or toolbar options, or delete options the user feels aren't important. Trying to implement this feature on a Web site would be very hard, but doable if you use some technologies such as ASP.NET. Make sure you offer a feature that returns everything to its default state in case the user makes a few too many changes.

> **NOTE**
>
> Don't make every field on a form optional. A user will have to make some entries to perform even basic tasks. For example, a user can't perform an author search without entering an author name, so the author name field isn't optional. However, hiding optional fields can make the application faster and easier to use. You might even find that you want to include some developer-only fields in the list that you control with special entries in the configuration file.

The ultimate level of interface flexibility lets the user move controls around on screen. This feature lets one user place names in last name order and another user place them in first name order. Complete interface control is difficult to implement on a desktop application and likely impossible for a Web application. Applications that allow complete interface configuration are extremely

> **NOTE**
>
> If you plan to provide complete interface flexibility for your application, you should go all the way by allowing the user to change even mundane features such a font size and typeface. It's even possible to let the user add graphics and perform other odd configuration changes given the right programming language, a platform that supports the changes, and enough time.

rare. However, an Amazon Web Services application doesn't suffer from the level of complexity that some applications do, so this might be a viable solution in some cases. At least you can provide the user with enough flexibility to define precisely how the display appears so that your application works as efficiently for that user as possible.

Addressing Users with Special Needs

This section of the chapter considers some of the features that make an application easier to use for those with special needs. Don't automatically equate special needs with physical challenges faced by some people. As users age, they need better screens because their eyesight begins to fail. Older hands often suffer from arthritis and require more options for executing commands. Even someone who is very young can require help at the end of the day when a day full of eye fatiguing research means using a display with larger type. With this in mind, the following sections describe some things you can do to make your Amazon Web Services application more usable without a large investment in time or effort.

> **NOTE**
>
> A section of a chapter can't possibly address every accessibility requirement. In addition, if you work for an organization that provides services to the government, you have certain legal requirements you must meet to address accessibility concerns. See my book, *Accessibility for Everybody: Understanding the Section 508 Accessibility Requirements* (Apress, 2003) for a complete treatment of this topic.

Adding Hints for Desktop Applications

Desktop applications commonly rely on hints to help a user understand its operation. For example, when you see a letter of a field underlined, you realize that pressing Alt+Letter selects that field. If the developer has wisely selected a different letter for each field, every field is a single key combination away. The use of speed keys helps touch typists work faster by allowing them to keep their hands on the keyboard, rather than use a mouse. However, speed keys also help those who can't use a mouse at all. In this case, the user has a choice of pressing Tab multiple times to locate the field or using a speed key to access it—the speed key is preferable because it's faster and requires fewer key presses. Adding speed keys to your application takes moments—all you need to do is type an ampersand in front of the letter you want to use for the speed key for most Windows languages.

Another common hint that also serves an accessibility need is the tooltip. Adding a tooltip for each control lets you explain the purpose of that control using a single sentence. If the user needs additional information, they can refer to the online help, but this feature usually provides enough information so that a trip to the help file isn't necessary. From an accessibility perspective, a screen reader or other piece of accessibility software normally reads the information in the tooltip to the user. Consequently, the tooltip helps users with vision needs build an image of the application and its functionality in their mind. The technique used to add a tooltip to an application depends on the language product used. For example, Visual Studio .NET developers can rely on the simple addition of a `ToolTip` control to make the tooltip addition. The `ToolTip` control adds a new ToolTip property to each of the other controls—just type the text you want to appear in the tooltip. The desktop applications in this book contain both speed keys and tooltips to ensure anyone can use them.

Platforms such as Windows include a number of operating system–specific accessibility features as well. Windows includes a high contrast setting that displays images in just a few colors using large fonts. The display makes it a lot easier for people with less than perfect vision to see the display. However, many people with normal vision also use the setting at the end of a hard day when a standard display is apt to give them a headache. The problem for developers is that the high contrast setting tends to make labels and other text elements on a form difficult or impossible to see because the element consumes too much space. Figure 11.1 shows a typical example of this problem.

I chose this particular dialog box because it demonstrates two common problems. First, the information in the middle of the display is garbled—unreadable for the most part. Second, the application-specific text didn't size with the change in high contrast setting, so the application user receives minimum benefit. Generally, you can avoid problems with the high contrast display by testing this setting with your application. All you need to do is open the Accessibility Options applet in the Control Panel, select the Display tab, and click Use High Contrast. Click OK and you'll see your display change to a high contrast representation. Note that Windows supports a number of high contrast configurations, so you might want to try several out with your application.

> **NOTE**
>
> Always try to support the accessibility features provided by the operating system. For example, Windows supports a number of accessibility features, including the use of high contrast displays for users with special visual needs. Some of these features, such as support for a screen reader, are so easy to implement that there's never a good reason not to implement them. Other features, such as the use of the Windows ShowSounds, can incur a higher cost in programming time because most programming languages don't support the feature.

FIGURE 11.1: High contrast displays can make some information unreadable.

Amazon Web Services returns some data that you might need to modify to make it accessible. For example, most products have an associated image. Several examples in the book show how to download and display this image using various languages. The problem with the images is that they assume you can see well. You might need to download a large version of an image for some users or create a dynamic description of the image for other users. Fortunately, most products include descriptions as part of the `ProductDescription` field returned in the `ProductInfo` structure you can use in place of the image. All you need to do is ask users whether they prefer the image or description. You could also automatically detect the presence of software such as JAWS (`http://www.freedomscientific.com/fs_downloads/jaws.asp`) or the high contrast setting and use the description automatically in those situations.

Another problem with Amazon Web Services is that it provides a wealth of data—too much in some cases. It's easy to overwhelm someone with special needs with data they'll never use. The problem isn't quite as noticeable with many Web applications because the Web presentation format can reduce the problem. However, desktop applications can suffer significant information overload problems. In some cases, you'll need to present details one at a time or on separate displays to keep the display focused on the essentials.

Adding Hints for Web Applications

Web applications use many of the same hints used by desktop applications, but the techniques for creating the hint differ. As with desktop applications, one of the more important hints is the use of speed keys. You implement a speed key using a combination of special text formatting and HTML tag attributes as shown in the following code for a label (not all tag attributes will work with all browsers).

```
<label id="Input">
   <span style="TEXT-DECORATION: underline">I</span>nput:
</label>
<input id="InputVal"
       type=text
       value="Hello World"
       name="InputVal"
       accesskey="I"
       title="Type the input string."
       autocomplete=on/>
```

The user needs to know which Alt+<key> combination to use to access the field, so the `style` attribute for the label is important—it underlines the target key. The `accesskey` attribute defines the speed key for the field associated with the label. The `title` attribute defines the tooltip text. When the user hovers the mouse over the input, the browser displays a tooltip, just like a desktop application. Use the `autocomplete` attribute to control the use of automatic completion for the field. Some fields benefit from this setting because the user is likely to type the same text more than one time, but for other fields automatic completion is a nuisance because the user will never type the same text twice.

Images require a little special handling because you can't easily determine whether the user can see the image or not. In this case, you don't use the `title` attribute because that would display a tooltip. In most cases, you'll use the `alt` attribute, as shown here, to provide a description of the image.

```
<img align="middle"
     src="OddImage.gif"
     alt="This image contains the words, 'An Odd Image'."
     height=130
     width=130/>
```

It's easy to use the `ProductDescription` field returned in the `ProductInfo` structure for the `alt` attribute text in most cases. You'll find an example of an accessible Web page in the `\Chapter 11\AccessibleWeb` folder of the source code found on the Sybex Web site. Try this page out in a browser to see how your browser reacts to it. In most cases, browsers do provide support for accessibility features—at least the basic features described in this section.

The example is a little plain. Generally, you should avoid adding too much formatting to your Web page if you can help it, but most of us like a little color and some formatting to make the page interesting. You can follow some basic guidelines to avoid causing accessibility problems while you dress up the page. For example, use CSS to avoid formatting problems.

Someone with special needs can substitute a CSS file of their choosing that makes the page easier to read and you still get the formatting you want. Make sure you page is compliant by testing it with any of a number of online testers such as Bobby (`http://bobby.watchfire.com/bobby/html/en/index.jsp`).

Designing for Privacy Issues

Privacy has become a major concern for most people because the news contains numerous stories of personal information misuse. One of the major misuses of personal information is identity theft, but that's by no means the largest misuse. Many users also feel that gathering personal information for marketing purposes without permission and full disclosure of how the requestor will use the information is also a major misuse of personal information. People don't want to suffer through a barrage of unwanted sales calls as witnessed by the

Considering Color-Blind Users

Before you read any further, it's important to understand that color-blind doesn't mean the viewer can't see color. What a color-blind viewer sees is the wrong color. A red or green dot might appear brown or some other color. Generally, the viewer can still see the object so long as you don't surround it with the color their eyes substitute for the real color of the object. In addition, not everyone has the same kind of color blindness. Most doctors agree there are three main forms of color blindness to consider (read the explanation of the types of color blindness at `http://webexhibits.org/causesofcolor/2.html` for details).

Because Amazon returns raw data and not color (at least until you display images), you have a choice about the color content of your desktop application or Web site. Even so, you might want to add a little pizzazz to your presentation and that usually means adding color. You can find information about working around color-blindness issues on a number of Web sites, but here are three exceptional sources.

- Can Color-Blind Users See Your Site? (`http://msdn.microsoft.com/voices/hess10092000.asp`)
- Color Vision Color Deficiency (`http://www.firelily.com/opinions/color.html`)
- Visicheck (`http://www.vischeck.com/vischeck/vischeckImage.php`)

The first two sites tell you about color blindness and provide example images that show how things appear to someone with a particular kind of color blindness. The third site lets you check your image for color blindness—all you need is a Web site URL. You can use this site to check an entire Web page by grabbing a screenshot of the Web site and uploading it to your site. The same technique works for desktop applications.

proliferation of "No Call" lists both locally and nationally. In fact, many people are taking positive steps to take back their personal information or at least block further attempts to acquire new information.

Personal information covers a range of topics today. Most developers recognize that name, address, telephone number, and other personally identifying information is private. However, users don't want developers to know a lot of other information that some developers see as belonging to the public domain. For example, some developers will try to get the `Referrer` (the previous Web page), `User-Agent` (the browser type, version, and host operating system), and `From` (the user's email address) headers of the user's browser. Brisk sales of products such as Norton Internet Security demonstrate that users don't want developers to collect this information. An interesting side effect of this battle between user and developer is that even though the user is using a new version of products such as Internet Explorer and Netscape, the Web site often reports the user has an outdated version of the product.

Given that the Amazon Web Services handles the details of shopping cart transactions for you (see the "Developing a Shopping Cart Application" section of Chapter 12 for details), you can easily create a Web application that doesn't require any personal information. You can also avoid collecting browser information through careful design and by following standards. The Webmonkey chart at `http://hotwired.lycos.com/webmonkey/reference/browser_chart/index.html` helps you understand which design features to avoid based on browser compatibility.

Even with the best design, however, you'll eventually encounter a situation where you want to use cookies (assuming the user has their browser set to accept cookies). Many users realize that cookies aren't inherently evil, but they also realize that a Web site could use cookies for nefarious purposes. All the pop-up ads that you see floating around on your favorite Web site are one reason that people are suspicious. Some of these vendors follow people around to the various sites they visit and keep track of their movements. However, you can overcome the fears of most users by maintaining a privacy policy and including special tags for that policy on your Web site. The most common way to publish and use a privacy policy is Platform for Privacy Preferences (P3P). The World

> **▶ NOTE**
>
> The example in this section uses the IBM P3P generator (`http://www.alphaworks.ibm.com/tech/p3peditor`). The W3C site lists several other generators—I chose this particular generator because it comes with a 90-day free trial. Your code might turn out different from mine if you use another generator for your code. For some reason, the IBM P3P generator doesn't work with the current version of the Java Runtime Environment (JRE)—version 1.4.2. IBM recommends using the 1.3.1 version of the JRE that you can download at `http://java.sun.com/j2se/1.3/`.

Wide Web Consortium (W3C) sponsors this technique and you can read about the six easy steps for implementing P3P on your Web site at http://www.w3.org/P3P/details.html. The P3P standard (http://www.w3.org/TR/P3P/) also contains a wealth of information you should review.

Your privacy statement will consist of several files, including at least one P3P file that you create using the P3P generator and an XML reference file. A good generator will also help you create a generic privacy summary that you can use for queries from the user and a compact policy statement you can use in the response headers of pages that contain cookies. If you own the server you use for the Web page, you can place the privacy information in the \w3c folder of the Web site. It's also possible to create linkage between the privacy information and your Web page using a <link> tag similar to the one shown here.

```
<link rel="P3Pv1" href="http://www.mwt.net/~jmueller/p3p.xml">
```

The problem comes in when you don't own the server that hosts your Web page—the situation for many people, including small business owners. Internet Explorer 6 has several levels of cookie protection built in. The highest level will likely reject your privacy information because Internet Explorer relies exclusively on the compact policy statement supplied as part of the response headers. Adding the compact policy statement is relatively easy if you own the server. Listing 11.1 shows an alternative you can try when you don't own the server, plus some test code you can use to verify the results. You'll find the complete source code for this example in the \Chapter 11\Privacy folder of the source code located on the Sybex Web site.

Listing 11.1 Adding a Compact Policy to a Web Page

```
<html>
<head>
<meta http-equiv='P3P'
      content='policyref="http://www.mwt.net/~jmueller/p3p.xml",
      CP="NOI DSP COR NID CURa OUR NOR NAV INT TST"'>
<title>Privacy Demonstration</title>
<script>
function SetCookie()
{
    var  UserCookie; // Stores the user name.

    // Create the username cookie.
    UserCookie = "UserName=" + escape(InputVal.value);

    // Add the cookie to the document.
    document.cookie = UserCookie;
```

```
        // Tell the user the cookie was saved.
        alert("The cookies were saved.");
    }

    function ReadCookie()
    {
        var  ACookie; // Holds the document cookie.
        var  Parsed;  // Holds the split cookies.
        var  Name;    // The user name.

        // Get the cookie.
        ACookie = unescape(document.cookie);

        // Split the cookie elements.
        Parsed = ACookie.split("=");

        // Get the user name.
        Name = Parsed[1];

        // Display the name.
        alert("Your name is: " + Name);
    }
```

The `<meta>` tag at the beginning of the code is the essential addition to your application. The `http-equiv` attribute tells the server what kind of response header to add. Some servers don't honor this attribute, so this solution might not work completely in all cases. The `content` attribute tells the client where to locate the privacy policy for your Web site—it works much the same as the `<link>` tag discussed earlier in this section. Finally, the `CP` attribute defines the compact policy for your server. Most tools, such as the IBM P3P Policy Editor shown in Figure 11.2, tell you what these codes mean and generate a text file containing them for you.

The test code consists of two functions attached to buttons on the example form. The first creates a cookie and attaches it to the document. The second retrieves the cookie stored in the document and displays the results on screen. Neither function is that exciting, but this is enough code to create an error with Internet Explorer 6 if the compact policy isn't accepted. You must have a compact policy in place and Internet Explorer 6 must accept it if you want users to use the high privacy setting. However, even if Internet Explorer 6 decides that it won't accept the compact policy, having a privacy policy in place and set up using the information provided in this section lets the user rely on the medium high privacy setting. Although, the medium high setting isn't quite as comfortable as the high setting, it's much better than the low setting your Web site would require if it didn't have a privacy policy.

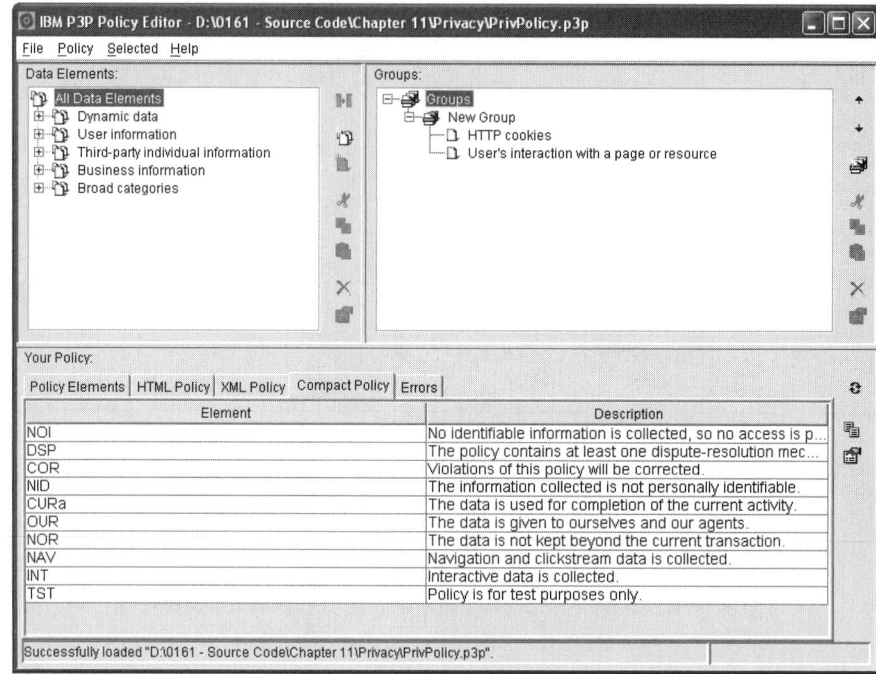

FIGURE 11.2: Make sure you generate a compact policy for Web pages that have cookies.

Working with Wishlists

Amazon maintains wish lists of users who want to express their product preferences. Essentially, a wish list tells the user's friends what they can get for gifts or special occasions. From a personalization perspective, a wish list can help you build a community of users for your Web site or business. It would be easy to think of a wish list as something that only Web users could use, but a wish list can work easily in any setting, including as a kiosk for a business. Some businesses tend to attract groups of faithful buyers and a kiosk where they can look up the desires of friends who also shop at the business only adds to the sense of community. Listing 11.2 shows a typical example of wish list access using a `WishlistRequest`. The Amazon Web Services kit help file refers to this as a Wishlist search (see `/AmazonWebServices/API Guide/search_wishlist.htm` for details.) You'll find the complete source code for this example in the `\Chapter 11\WishList` folder of the source code located on the Sybex Web site.

Listing 11.2 Accessing a Wishlist Entry on Amazon

```
private void btnTest_Click(object sender, System.EventArgs e)
{
   WishlistRequest      WLR;     // The WishList search request.
   ProductInfo          PI;      // Data returned from request.
   AmazonSearchService  Service; // Connection to the service.
   DataRow              DR;      // Output data.
   Int32                Counter; // Loop counting variable.

   // Instantiate the objects.
   WLR = new WishlistRequest();
   PI = new ProductInfo();
   Service = new AmazonSearchService();

   // Create the power search request.
   WLR.devtag = txtTag.Text;
   WLR.page = txtPage.Text;
   WLR.tag = "webservices-20";
   WLR.type = txtType.Text;
   WLR.wishlist_id = txtWishList.Text;

   // Make the request.
   PI = Service.WishlistSearchRequest(WLR);

   // Display the results on screen.
   dsAmazon.Tables["WishListOut"].Rows.Clear();
   for (Counter = 0; Counter < PI.Details.Length; Counter++)
   {
      // Determine whether the product is available.
      if (PI.Details[Counter].Availability.StartsWith("Usually ships"))
      {
         // Create a new row to hold the data.
         DR = dsAmazon.Tables["WishListOut"].NewRow();

         // Add the data to the row.
         DR["Product Name"] = PI.Details[Counter].ProductName;
         DR["ASIN"] = PI.Details[Counter].Asin;
         DR["Manufacturer"] = PI.Details[Counter].Manufacturer;
         DR["List Price"] = PI.Details[Counter].ListPrice;
         DR["Availability"] = PI.Details[Counter].Availability;

         // Display the row on screen.
         dsAmazon.Tables["WishListOut"].Rows.Add(DR);
      }
   }
}
```

After spending so much time learning about the various modes that Amazon supplies, it's interesting to note that a Wishlist search doesn't require a mode. The lack of a mode makes sense because you'll want to view all of the person's Wishlist entries, regardless of product line, in most cases. Making the request follows the usual pattern of using the correct method call for the `Service` object (`WishlistSearchRequest()` in this case).

Notice that this example makes use of the `Availability` field of the `ProductInfo` structure to determine whether a product is available. A Wishlist search is one time that you might want to keep unavailable items out of the return set because if the product isn't available, then the person checking the list can't get it. The "Discovering Product Availability" section of Chapter 12 discusses this issue in detail. You might find other occasions to remove unavailable items from a list or even filter a list so it contains only used items. The output table for this example also includes the `Availability` field so that you can verify the filtering really does work.

Using Listmania!

The world is filled with top 10 or 20 lists. We track the best of everything, with best defined by our own tastes. It's not too amazing that Amazon decided to let people upload their favorites in list form so other people could use the lists as a basis for making buying decisions. Sometimes it's nice to have a second opinion. No matter what reason you have for creating a list, the Listmania! feature can also act as a point of sales for an organization. For example, you might come up with a recommended reading list from which members of the organization can choose reading material (the same holds true for music or movies).

Listmania! presents an interesting challenge that you won't run into with other searches. Most of the Amazon searches return a maximum of 10 results—the exception is the browse node search, which returns three results for each product line. When you work with most searches, such as an author search, Amazon provides the `<TotalResults>` and `<TotalPages>` elements so you know how many pages to check for results when you want to retrieve everything. Unlike most searches, the Listmania! search doesn't return these two elements, so you have no way to know how long to make the list. Trying to obtain more than the number of pages that the list actually supports results in an error and if you use the standard method to detect the error, it appears as a bad request. The actual error message is "There are no exact matches for the search." but you won't know that unless you know where to look. Listing 11.3 shows how to correct both issues. You'll find the complete source code for this example in the `\Chapter 11\ListMania` folder of the source code located on the Sybex Web site.

Listing 11.3 Creating a Listmania! Search

```
private void btnTest_Click(object sender, System.EventArgs e)
{
   ListManiaRequest     LMR;     // The ListMania! search request.
   ProductInfo          PI;      // Data returned from request.
   AmazonSearchService  Service; // Connection to the service.
   DataRow              DR;      // Output data.
   Int32                Counter; // Loop counting variable.

   // Instantiate the objects.
   LMR = new ListManiaRequest();
   PI = new ProductInfo();
   Service = new AmazonSearchService();

   // Create the power search request.
   LMR.devtag = txtTag.Text;
   LMR.lm_id = txtListManiaID.Text;
   LMR.page = txtPage.Text;
   LMR.tag = "webservices-20";
   LMR.type = txtType.Text;

   // Clear the table.
   dsAmazon.Tables["ListManiaOut"].Rows.Clear();

   // Keep requesting pages until the list is complete.
   do
   {
      try
      {
         // Make the request.
         PI = Service.ListManiaSearchRequest(LMR);
      }
      catch (SoapException SE)
      {
         // Display the actual error from the server.
         MessageBox.Show(SE.Detail.InnerText);
         return;
      }

      // Display the results on screen.
      for (Counter = 0; Counter < PI.Details.Length; Counter++)
      {
         // Create a new row to hold the data.
         DR = dsAmazon.Tables["ListManiaOut"].NewRow();

         // Add the data to the row.
         DR["Product Name"] = PI.Details[Counter].ProductName;
```

```
                DR["ASIN"] = PI.Details[Counter].Asin;
                DR["Manufacturer"] = PI.Details[Counter].Manufacturer;
                DR["Catalog"] = PI.Details[Counter].Catalog;
                DR["List Price"] = PI.Details[Counter].ListPrice;

                // Display the row on screen.
                dsAmazon.Tables["ListManiaOut"].Rows.Add(DR);
            }

            // Increment the page count.
            LMR.page = Convert.ToString(Int32.Parse(LMR.page) + 1);

        } while (PI.Details.Length > 0);
    }
```

The initial request process is the same as usual—you fill in a request object and send it to Amazon using the `ListManiaSearchRequest()` method. Notice that this method appears in a `try...catch` block and that the catch portion detects the `SoapException` exception. This example works by attempting page after page of requests until the system generates an error—then it stops by returning to the calling function. The example shows how you can detect the "There are no exact matches for the search." error mentioned earlier. Using this technique lets you handle other kinds of errors that result from bad input on the part of the user or server errors.

Theoretically, Listmania! provides lists of like items. However, it's interesting to return the `Catalog` field in this example because the items in the list aren't always part of the same product line.

The code ends with two important statements. The first statement increments the page number in the request so that the example moves from page to page. The second statement is a check of the `Details` node length. If a situation occurs where the call doesn't return any details, yet doesn't generate an error, you need the `while` statement to end the loop.

Your Call to Action

Chapter 10 discusses enhancement issues for your application and this chapter discusses enhancement issues for the user. Depending on your development goals, it's easy to miss opportunities to address one or both issues, but you must address both to create the best possible Amazon Web Services application. The main point of this chapter is that you can address user needs without incurring an undue burden in terms of development time or effort. In fact, addressing user needs at the outset always reduces long-term application costs, so the little extra effort you apply today will pay dividends tomorrow. This chapter also addresses some special Amazon user features in the form of Listmania! and Wish Lists.

Now it's time for you to decide how to address user issues. You need to consider the kind of user who will use your application—advanced users require less help than novice users. It's also important to address special needs your users might have to ensure they can derive maximum benefit from the application. For example, the addition of a simple tooltip for every control is essential for users with vision needs. The same tooltip can help all users by providing a little more information about the control so they doesn't have to access help constantly. Finally, you need to consider whether the special Amazon features, Listmania! and Wish Lists, can help your users. Any time you develop a community of users, you need some way to keep members in personal contact. These features can make the community stronger by helping individual members address personal needs.

Chapter 12 discusses some final enhancements—the optional types of application additions that you might consider. No, these additions won't make your application faster or more efficient. However, they do help you interact more easily with the users of your application. The chapter considers three issues: learning more about the user through feedback forms, assisting users with purchases through special search techniques, and setting up a shopping cart for your users. Of course, this chapter isn't completely about the user—you'll also gain compensation for your efforts in routing sales to Amazon.

Chapter 12

Letting the User Tell You about Your Application

Using the Amazon Honor System Payment Method

Other Refinements You Should Consider

Defining Sales-Oriented Searches

Creating a Shopping Cart Application

This chapter addresses the needs of a serious Amazon Web Services developer—one who wants to go the extra step to provide superior service. Not everyone can or even should implement the features of this chapter. For example, if you plan to build an application that runs only in-house, you might forgo adding feedback to your application because you have some other feedback mechanism in place. Likewise, not everyone will want to implement the Amazon Honor System payment method—perhaps you want to simply provide a referral and let Amazon take care of the details. Some Web sites might not even benefit from the sales-oriented searches described in this chapter. In short, this chapter has extra features—additional refinements—that you should consider, but might not need to implement.

Feedback is the most common feature that you'll use in this chapter because even a Web site that performs simple searches should include some type of user feedback form. Desktop applications also benefit from feedback, although far too few applications include this feature. The idea is to provide a means for a user to make a comment about your application immediately during use—when an idea, concern, or other comment is fresh and they're most likely to send it to you.

Amazon provides a number of sales-oriented searches that you won't find on every Web site because they're not appropriate. For example, a developer who writes a product review application might want to include the seller profile search as part of the application. This search won't necessarily accomplish much on a regular sales site because there's only one seller to consider. Likewise, a kiosk application could make good use of a similarities search to help the user find the best product at the lowest cost. Again, this might not be a very good search to provide if you're the manufacturer providing a product because you want the user to see your product—not someone else's product.

You might want to use Amazon Web Services for more than just searches or personal use. Your business use of Amazon Web Services can extend beyond mere referrals to using shopping carts. Maintaining a shopping cart supplied by Amazon lets you create a more complete user shopping experience. For example, you might use this approach if you run a boutique store and want to provide your expert opinion on products you recommend to clients. The client is used to obtaining advice from you regarding sales, so this approach is natural. Obviously, you can use the shopping cart technique for a vast array of other purposes, but this gives you an idea of how to use it.

Adding Feedback to Your Application

Most people have an opinion. The opinion doesn't have a right or wrong value—it's simply how they feel about a particular topic. Getting an honest opinion from people can be difficult, but you can do it. When the topic concerns your application or Web site, the need to get an honest opinion is essential. Otherwise, changes you make to an application or Web site as the result of user feedback are going to be off target—you want to target the users of your site to ensure they have a great experience.

> ▶ **TIP**
>
> Don't assume that every positive feedback message you receive means that you're doing everything right with your application. Some people will tell you positive things to obtain benefits they might not normally receive or simply because they don't want to hurt your feelings. Likewise, not every negative message is an indictment against your programming practices. Sometimes a user will have a bad day and decide to take it out on you because you're the nearest target that can't attack back. Deciphering feedback often means reading the message several times and deciding just how it affects your application (or whether it affects your application at all).

When you mix interaction with another application, Amazon Web Services in this case, the problems of getting honest feedback intensify. You need to consider whether the feedback relates to your application, a connectivity issue caused by an ISP, the user's environment, or Amazon Web Services (among other things). It's not always easy to sort even a good opinion into the right area.

The following sections discuss user feedback. This information reflects issues you need to consider when working with Amazon Web Services. For example, it discusses some of the problems of sorting information into the right area for consideration.

Designing User Feedback

One of the problems in getting good user feedback is designing the form so that it elicits a response, even from users who don't normally express themselves well. A nebulous question, such as, "How do you feel about this search?" won't net you a very good response. You need to direct the user to the kind of input you want, without contaminating the user's response. For example, "Does the author search help you find the book you need, or does a vendor search work better?" offers the user a choice and makes them think about alternatives. The question is still specific enough that even a shy user can provide an answer. Offering yes, no, and other (with a comment field) lets the shy user off the hook, but also lets vocal users state their answers in precise terms.

The simplest method for obtaining user feedback on a Web page is to create a form and send it to your email (or other location). Although this method does require a little interpretation, it has the advantage of allowing you to get feedback almost free. If you use a programmable email reader such as Microsoft Outlook, you can write a macro to interpret and save the results for you. Otherwise, the careful use of form values will let you read the report with a little effort. Listing 12.1 contains an example of a simple form that works with almost all browsers even if the user has turned off scripting support and cookies. You'll find the complete source code for this example in the `\Chapter 12\SimpleRespForm` folder of the source code located on the Sybex Web site.

Listing 12.1 A Simple, Low-cost Feedback Form

```
<!DOCTYPE HTML PUBLIC "-//W3C//DTD HTML 4.0 Transitional//EN">
<html>
<head>
<title>Simple Response Form</title>
</head>
<body>

<!-- Display a heading. -->
<h1 align=center>Simple Response Form</h1>

<!-- Define the form and anticipated action. -->
<form action="mailto:JMueller@mwt.net?subject=Test Message"
      method=post
      name=SimpleRespForm
      enctype="text/plain">

<!-- Ask about product selection. -->
<label>Did you find every product you needed?</label>
<input type=hidden
       name="Q1"
       value="Product Available"/><br/>
<label>Yes</label>
<input type=radio name="1A" value="Y"/><br/>
<label>No</label>
<input type=radio name="1A" value="N"/><br/>
<label>Other</label>
<input type=radio name="1A" value="O"/><br/>
<label>Additional comment (40 characters max):</label><br/>
```

```
<input type=text name="1E" maxlength=40/><p/>

<!-- Ask about product description. -->
... Required Inputs ...

<!-- Submit the form to email. -->
<input type=submit value="Send" accesskey="S"/>
</form>
</body>
</html>
```

For anyone who has spent considerable time working with Web pages, this might look like old technology crying for a makeover. However, this technique works quite well. I didn't include the accessibility information in this example for the sake of clarity. You could also dress it up a bit using Cascading Style Sheets (CSS). The underlying example, however, is easy to understand.

The focus of this example is the `<form>` tag. Notice that the `action="mailto:JMueller@mwt.net?subject=Test Message"` attribute defines my email address as the destination for the data in the form. In addition, the email subject is Test Message. By giving each survey a different name, you know precisely where the user took the survey and what to expect as input. Most developers would stop here and complain about the results received in their email (a rather unattractive attachment). By adding the `enctype="text/plain"` attribute, you can change the output to something that is easy to parse using any script and not all that hard to read using the email application's preview pane as shown in Figure 12.1.

FIGURE 12.1: Encoding your survey form correctly lets you read it directly in email.

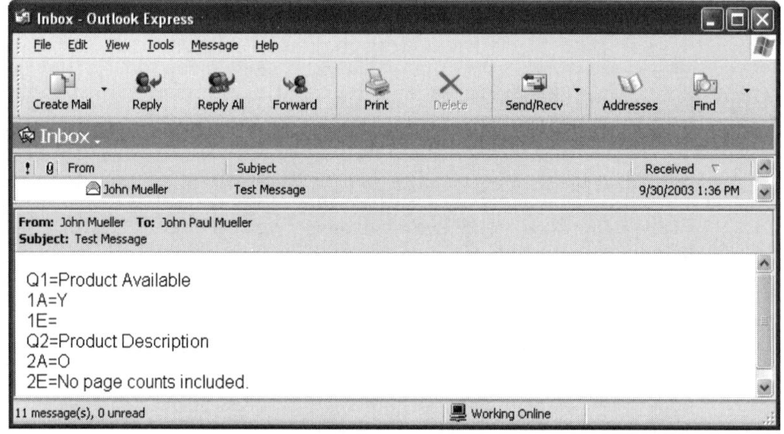

Each of the entries in the email has a corresponding tag in the form that has the name attribute shown. Notice how the example separates the questions using a hidden `<input>` tag like this:

```
<input type=hidden name="Q1" value="Product Available"/>
```

The value you provide should include a reminder about the question content. In this case, I provided a reminder that the question asks whether the user found every product needed.

The main problem with using this technique is content size. Forms can have a 255-character limit on the amount of data they can send; although, this limit is apparently uncommon. (Make sure you also check for potential limits with the Web server that you use.) This means you have to provide limits on the size of comment fields using the `maxlength` attribute as shown in Listing 12.1. You also need to design your form carefully and make answers terse whenever possible.

> **TIP**
>
> Many developers don't understand the `mailto:` URL very well. The problem is that the protocol doesn't appear very often on Web pages and most Web pages don't use the full potential of the `mailto:` URL. You can use most of the same fields with a `mailto:` that you use with an email program including such features a cc and bcc. You can find several good resources about the `mailto:` URL on the Internet. One of the better places to look is the Web Design Guides site at `http://www.ssi-developer.net/design/mailto.shtml`. Another good place to look for tips of this sort is the Ezine-Tips.com site at `http://ezine-tips.com/articles/format/20001020.shtml`.

Developing Automated Feedback

This chapter doesn't delve into automated feedback systems because there are a number of resources you can use for this type of programming. Here are a couple of resources you should consider.

User Feedback HTML Form `http://www.bytesworth.com/learn/html00009.asp`

Creating Feedback Forms for WAP Sites `http://www.aspfree.com/articles/1137,1/articles.aspx`

However, given that many Amazon Web Services developers want to provide a research or buyer resource, making the feedback page friendly is critical. In general, the more you automate the feedback to make things easier for your company, the fewer users will be able to use the feedback system. This issue is especially true of form-based Web feedback because many users now turn off scripting, cookies, applets, and plug-ins for fear their systems will download viruses or experience other problems. Automation usually requires some level of client and server scripting, along with cookies and even plug-ins.

The problem even occurs with desktop applications. Some vendors make feedback available as part of a Help menu option. In most cases, the feedback form works and sends the information to the vendor (usually over the Internet). However, problems arise when the vendor assumes the user has a permanent connection to the Internet—many users use dial-up connections. Fortunately, Amazon Web Services developers can assume that the user has some kind of Internet connection (even if it's through a proxy server) because otherwise their application won't work at all.

Using the Amazon Honor System Payments

The Amazon Honor System is a great way for small businesses to get started on the Internet. To make this system work, you create linkage between your site and Amazon. When a user wants to buy your product, they click on a special link on your site. This link transfers the user to Amazon and relies on the standard Amazon payment setup. When Amazon receives the payment for the product, they pay you. The fees that Amazon charges for this service will vary, so make sure you read the agreement you sign to ensure your business can handle the increased costs.

> **▶ TIP**
>
> Some ISPs consider user feedback forms so important they make it part of the documentation for their service. For example, check out the AT&T site at `http://www.att.com/style/wc_feedback.html`. This site tells how to create a user feedback for using the special features of the AT&T servers. Your ISP might provide similar services that you can use to make development of automated pages easier.

The only problem with the Amazon Honor System is that it doesn't really exist in solid form. Yes, you can sign up for it and become a member of the system, but the Application Programming Interface (API) for the service is still in beta. You'll find a brief description of the Amazon Honor System in the Amazon Web Services Kit at `/AmazonWebServices/API Guide/honor_system_payments.htm`. A visit to the Amazon Honor System Web site (`https://s1.amazon.com/exec/varzea/subst/fx/help/payee-faq.html/058-1439525-1884037`) sheds a little more information on the topic. The fact is that as of the time of writing, the Amazon Honor System is under beta test.

Fortunately, you can get involved with the beta test of the Amazon Honor System by sending a message to `webservices@amazon.com` with a subject "HS API." This information only appears in the Amazon Web Services Newsletters (you can get previous editions at `http://www.jungledeveloper.com/index.php`). Make sure you read and understand the participation agreement found at `https://s1.amazon.com/exec/varzea/subst/fx/help/participation-agreement.html` before you proceed with the program.

Using Sales-Oriented Searches

Amazon provides a number of sales-oriented searches you can use. These searches help you perform a number of special tasks. For example, you can search for products within a particular price range or check the comments received about a seller. You won't use these special searches for every application and might only need them for internal application needs (such as making a vendor recommendation). The following sections describe each sales-oriented search.

Performing Exchange Searches

Every third party product on Amazon has an exchange identifier. This identifier often appears in addition to the Amazon Standard Item Number (ASIN) in the product description. For example, Wherehouse Music offers Dvorak: Piano Concerto in G minor/Symphony No.9 using an exchange ID of Y01Y4863202Y3792886. Amazon also offers this product using an ASIN of B000005VZJ. Use the exchange ID when you want the third party product and the ASIN when you want the Amazon product. You can see this product using the exchange ID or ASIN with these URLs.

```
http://s1.amazon.com/exec/varzea/ts/exchange-glance/Y01Y4863202Y3792886/
http://www.amazon.com/exec/obidos/ASIN/B000005VZJ/
```

The exchange ID is unique for a particular store. For example, if you wanted to buy Pink Floyd's *Dark Side of the Moon* paperback, you could use exchange IDs for SubeeBooks (Y01Y1881326Y5770009), rross316 (Y01Y6146318Y7996698), and kaitech (Y01Y6176926Y9802594). The exchange IDs are only valid so long as the third party store carries the product, so it pays to use mainstream sellers whenever possible for an application. Listing 12.2 shows a typical example of an exchange ID search. You'll find the complete source code for this example in the `\Chapter 12\ExchangeSearch` folder of the source code located on the Sybex Web site.

Listing 12.2 Performing an Exchange Search

```
private void btnTest_Click(object sender, System.EventArgs e)
{
   ExchangeRequest        ER;      // The exchange search request.
   ListingProductDetails  PI;      // Data returned from request.
   AmazonSearchService    Service; // Connection to the service.

   // Instantiate the objects.
   ER = new ExchangeRequest();
   PI = new ListingProductDetails();
   Service = new AmazonSearchService();
```

```
        // Create the exchange search request.
        ER.devtag = txtTag.Text;
        ER.exchange_id = txtExchangeID.Text;
        ER.tag = "webservices-20";
        ER.type = txtType.Text;

        // Make the request.
        PI = Service.ExchangeSearchRequest(ER);

        // Display the product details.
        txtProductName.Text = PI.ExchangeTitle;
        ... Other Details ...
    }
```

The process for creating the request is the same as normal in this example. You fill out the `ExchangeRequest` object and send it to Amazon using the `ExchangeSearchRequest()` method. Notice that this request doesn't require a mode because you're requesting a specific item. In addition, you don't supply a page because the results contain only one item. The return type is special—you receive a `ListingProductDetails` structure in place of the normal `ProductInfo` structure. The `ListingProductDetails` structure requires special handling as shown in the code. Figure 12.2 shows typical output from this application.

FIGURE 12.2: Exchange searches return third party vendor information.

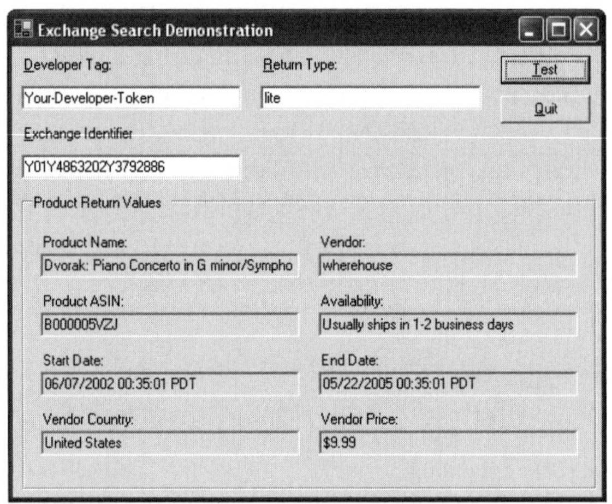

The `ListingProductDetails` structure contains some special information, such as the start and end of the sale. It also tells you the vendor's seller identification number so you can learn more about the seller. The structure normally includes an ASIN, which might seem frivolous. However, you need the ASIN to retrieve product details such as the customer comments because the `ListingProductDetails` structure doesn't return this information. Consequently, you'll find that you need to perform an ASIN search in many cases to find the additional information needed to create a display on your Web site. (See Listing 6.10 in Chapter 6 for an example of how to perform an ASIN search.)

Performing Marketplace Searches

The keyword searches found in other chapters of the book return Amazon products and services. However, when you want to learn about third party vendors who provide a product and the products they sell, you need to perform a marketplace search. It's important to keep the keyword search and the marketplace search separate because they provide different kinds of information. A marketplace search always returns third party products and associated information.

A marketplace search can perform more than one search task. For example, you can use the listing identifier version to get product details for items that Amazon doesn't stock. You can retrieve a listing identifier in a number of ways—the easiest of which is to perform an exchange search (see Listing 12.1). You can also perform a keyword search that includes all of the same sort criteria as an Amazon search, plus a few other items such as ZIP code and product sale dates. Listing 12.3 shows a typical example of a marketplace search. You'll find the complete source code for this example in the `\Chapter 12\MarketSearch` folder of the source code located on the Sybex Web site.

Listing 12.3 Performing a Marketplace Search

```
private void btnTest_Click(object sender, System.EventArgs e)
{
   StringBuilder  Query;      // Query string for Amazon.
   XmlDocument    Doc;        // Complete document
   XmlNode        ProdInfo;   // All product listings returned.
   XmlNode        Details;    // A single product.
   Int32          Counter;    // Loop counter;
   DataRow        DR;         // Output data.

   // Build the common query elements.
   Query = new StringBuilder();
   Query.Append("http://xml.amazon.com/onca/xml3?");
   Query.Append("t=webservices-20");
   Query.Append("&dev-t=" + txtTag.Text);
   Query.Append("&type=" + txtType.Text);
   Query.Append("&f=xml");

   // Determine the search type.
   if (cbSearchType.SelectedIndex == 0)
   {
      // Set the search type.
      Query.Append("&MarketplaceSearch=listing-id");

      // Obtain the Listing ID search items.
```

```
            Query.Append("&listing-id=" + txtListingID.Text);
         }
         else
         {
            // Set the search type.
            Query.Append("&MarketplaceSearch=keyword");

            // Obtain the Keyword search items.
            Query.Append("&keyword=" + txtKeyword.Text.Replace(" ", "%20"));
            Query.Append("&page=" + txtPage.Text);
            if (txtSort.Text.Length > 0)
               Query.Append("&sort=" + txtSort.Text);
         }

         // Make the query from Amazon.
         Doc = new XmlDocument();
         Doc.Load(Query.ToString());

         // Extract all the product information nodes.
         ProdInfo = Doc.ChildNodes[1]
                                 ["MarketplaceSearchDetails"]
                                 ["ListingProductInfo"];

         // Process each of the product information nodes.
         dsAmazon.Tables["ProductOut"].Rows.Clear();
         for (Counter = 0; Counter < ProdInfo.ChildNodes.Count; Counter++)
         {
            // Get an individual product.
            Details = ProdInfo.ChildNodes[Counter];

            // Create a new row to hold the data.
            DR = dsAmazon.Tables["ProductOut"].NewRow();

            // Add the data to the row.
            DR["Product Name"] = Details["ExchangeTitle"].InnerText;
            ... Other Columns ...

            // Check the search type and handle the vendor field
            // accordingly.
            if (txtType.Text.ToLower() == "lite")
               DR["Vendor"] = "N/A";
            else
               DR["Vendor"] = Details["ExchangeSellerNickname"].InnerText;

            // Display the row on screen.
            dsAmazon.Tables["ProductOut"].Rows.Add(DR);
         }
      }
```

The code begins by building the common elements of the request string. It's important to remember that the marketplace search can perform multiple tasks. The form associated with this example includes a search type list box that contains the two main search types. The code uses the `cbSearchType` setting to determine which kind of specific string to build. When building a listing ID string, the code sets the `MarketplaceSearch` argument to `listing-id` and adds the contents of `txtListingID`. When building a keyword string, the code sets the `MarketplaceSearch` argument to `keyword` and adds the search criteria.

The example shows only a few of the search criteria you can use. You can also add an `index` argument that defines the source of findings (marketplace or zshops), a `zipcode` argument that defines the location of the stores, and an `area-id` that defines the country. You can find a complete list of area IDs in Appendix C. Look at the Marketplace Searches help topic in the kit at `\AmazonWebServices\API Guide\search_marketplace.htm` to discover other search criteria. Note that one of the search criteria listed in the help topic is wrong. You need to replace the `rank` argument with the `sort` argument as shown in the listing.

After the code builds the query string, it uses it to load the query result from Amazon into an `XmlDocument` object, `Doc`. The data return structure for a marketplace search is different from the other searches in the book—it doesn't rely on a `ProductInfo` data structure. Figure 12.3 shows typical XML document results for a marketplace search. Notice that this call ultimately relies on the same `ListingProductDetails` data structure used for an exchange search, but that this structure appears several layers below the top level to accommodate multiple return values. Fortunately, .NET makes it very easy to locate the information needed.

> **▶ NOTE**
>
> The example in this section uses the XML over HTTP technique to obtain the data from Amazon Web Services. The reason for using this unusual technique is that the WSDL file for a marketplace search is incorrect as of the time of this writing. Consequently, no matter how well you write your application, the call will fail when using the SOAP technique. You can find an example showing the error in the `\Chapter 12\Old MarketSearch` folder of the source code located on the Sybex Web site. You can also use this example to verify Amazon's fix once it arrives. Simply update the WSDL by right-clicking the `Web References\com.amazon.soap` entry in Solution Explorer and selecting Update Web Reference from the context menu. The example will run without error when Amazon fixes the problem. Amazon is aware of the problem and promises to provide a solution. The point is that you have multiple access methods available, so if one technique fails, try another.

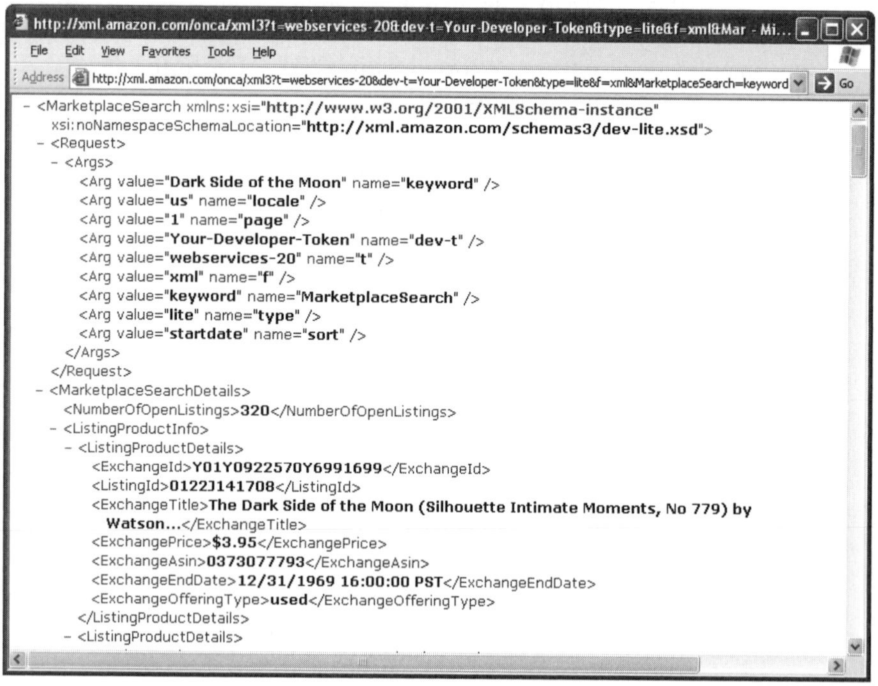

FIGURE 12.3: The marketplace search returns a unique data structure.

http://xml.amazon.com/onca/xml3?t=webservices-20&dev-t=Your-Developer-Token&type=lite&f=xml&Mar - Mi...

File Edit View Favorites Tools Help

Address http://xml.amazon.com/onca/xml3?t=webservices-20&dev-t=Your-Developer-Token&type=lite&f=xml&MarketplaceSearch=keyword Go


```
- <MarketplaceSearch xmlns:xsi="http://www.w3.org/2001/XMLSchema-instance"
   xsi:noNamespaceSchemaLocation="http://xml.amazon.com/schemas3/dev-lite.xsd">
 - <Request>
  - <Args>
     <Arg value="Dark Side of the Moon" name="keyword" />
     <Arg value="us" name="locale" />
     <Arg value="1" name="page" />
     <Arg value="Your-Developer-Token" name="dev-t" />
     <Arg value="webservices-20" name="t" />
     <Arg value="xml" name="f" />
     <Arg value="keyword" name="MarketplaceSearch" />
     <Arg value="lite" name="type" />
     <Arg value="startdate" name="sort" />
    </Args>
   </Request>
 - <MarketplaceSearchDetails>
    <NumberOfOpenListings>320</NumberOfOpenListings>
  - <ListingProductInfo>
   - <ListingProductDetails>
      <ExchangeId>Y01Y0922570Y6991699</ExchangeId>
      <ListingId>0122J141708</ListingId>
      <ExchangeTitle>The Dark Side of the Moon (Silhouette Intimate Moments, No 779) by
        Watson...</ExchangeTitle>
      <ExchangePrice>$3.95</ExchangePrice>
      <ExchangeAsin>0373077793</ExchangeAsin>
      <ExchangeEndDate>12/31/1969 16:00:00 PST</ExchangeEndDate>
      <ExchangeOfferingType>used</ExchangeOfferingType>
     </ListingProductDetails>
   - <ListingProductDetails>
```


Now that the code has the return values from the request, it can display them in a table on the form using approximately the same technique used for other .NET examples in the book. However, you should notice that the method of retrieving the data differs from the usual example—you need to use the `InnerText` property for each element you want to retrieve from the data structure.

The marketplace search breaks the rules in one other important way. Your application won't necessarily receive 10 results for each keyword search request. (A listing ID request always returns one result.) For example, the test application routinely returned 19 to 27 results depending on the input arguments used. This example points out the need to provide flexibility in your application to handle an uncertain number of return values.

Performing Price Range Searches

Sometimes you not only need to find a particular product type, but the product must fall within a specific price range. For example, the world is full of very nice toasters, but not every toaster is the same price. Finding the toaster you want in the price range you can afford could prove difficult. As a product becomes more of a commodity and the range of differentiation increases, the need for a price range search also increases. A refrigerator with built-in icemaker and in-door dispenser is likely to cost more than a similar model lacking these features.

You couple a price range check with other searches that support it. The Amazon Web Services Kit help file states that only the browse node search supports this feature. However, viewing the WSDL and performing a few experiments shows that you can use the price range search with these search requests.

- Actor
- Artist
- Author
- Browse node
- Director
- Keyword
- Manufacturer
- Text stream (see Appendix D for details)

> **NOTE**
>
> To use this technique, you must rely on Amazon Web Services version 3. This means using the `http://xml.amazon.com/onca/xml3` URL when using the XML over HTTP technique. Use schema 3 (as in `http://soap.amazon.com/schemas3/AmazonWebServices.wsdl`) for the SOAP technique.

The example in this section shows how to perform a price range search as part of a browse node search. Listing 12.4 shows a typical price range search. You'll find the complete source code for this example in the `\Chapter 12\PriceRange` folder of the source code located on the Sybex Web site.

Listing 12.4 Performing a Price Range Search

```
private void btnTest_Click(object sender, System.EventArgs e)
{
   BrowseNodeRequest    BNR;     // The browse node search request.
   ProductInfo          PI;      // Data returned from request.
   AmazonSearchService  Service; // Connection to the service.
   DataRow              DR;      // Output data.
   Int32                Counter; // Loop counting variable.

   // Instantiate the objects.
   ... Required Objects ...

   // Create the browse node search request.
   BNR.browse_node = txtBrowseNode.Text;
   ... Other Property Settings ...

   // Perform the required price range checks.
   if (txtPriceRange.Text.Length > 0)
      if (txtPriceRange.Text.IndexOf("$") == -1)
         if (txtPriceRange.Text.IndexOf("-") == -1)
         {
            MessageBox.Show("Please enter a price range using " +
```

```
                                    "the form: 2000-3000 for $20.00 to " +
                                    "$30.00.");
                 return;
              }
              else
                 BNR.price = txtPriceRange.Text;
           else
           {
              MessageBox.Show("Please enter the price in pennies " +
                              "using the form: 2000-3000 for " +
                              "$20.00 to $30.00.");
              return;
           }

        // Make the request.
        PI = Service.BrowseNodeSearchRequest(BNR);

        // Display the results on screen.
        dsAmazon.Tables["AuthorOut"].Rows.Clear();
        for (Counter = 0; Counter < PI.Details.Length; Counter++)
        {
           // Create a new row to hold the data.
           DR = dsAmazon.Tables["AuthorOut"].NewRow();

           // Add the data to the row.
           DR["Amazon Price"] = PI.Details[Counter].OurPrice;
           ... Other Columns ...

           // Display the row on screen.
           dsAmazon.Tables["AuthorOut"].Rows.Add(DR);
        }
     }
```

This example works much like the browse node search example shown in Listing 10.3. However, this newer version includes much of the logic that you would need to add for a price range search. The critical piece of information, in this case, is how you handle the price range. Depending on your Web site and the expectations of the users visiting it, you might have to add quite a few checks. A price range always uses pennies (not dollars) and includes a dash (-) for the range. The range can be the same number if you're looking for a specific price such as 2995-2995 (or simply 2995) for $29.95.

The results reflect the Amazon price for a product, not the list or third party prices. That's why the Amazon Price column of the output grid relies on the `PI.Details[Counter].OurPrice` property. If you use other properties for output, you'll find that the prices won't match the price range you selected. You'll also find that sorting relies on the Amazon price when you use the `+pricerank` sort order (used for the example). Consequently, when you want to implement price filtering or sorting based on list price, you need to implement it in your own code.

Performing Seller Profile Searches

Seller profile searches are important when you want to buy a product and need to determine whether the vendor has worked well for other people in the past. The seller profile search returns the overall vendor rating, as well as individual comments. It's important to remember that a seller profile is largely a matter of opinion—not concrete fact, so your experience can differ from the experiences of people who provided an opinion online. In addition, vendors can receive negative feedback for reasons other than poor service—a competitor could seek to ruin the vendor's reputation or the person uploading the review might have had a bad day. Even the best vendors will receive negative comments because not every shopping experience is a good one. Because Amazon doesn't provide a means for filtering unwarranted criticism, you have to read these reports with a grain of salt. With these caveats in mind, Listing 12.5 shows how to perform a seller profile search. You'll find the complete source code for this example in the `\Chapter 12\SellerProfile` folder of the source code located on the Sybex Web site.

Listing 12.5 Performing a Seller Profile Search

```
private void btnTest_Click(object sender, System.EventArgs e)
{
   SellerProfileRequest SPR;     // Seller profile search request.
   SellerProfile        PI;      // Data returned from request.
   AmazonSearchService  Service; // Connection to the service.
   SellerFeedback       SF;      // All buyer feedback.
   DataRow              DR;      // Output data.
   Int32                Counter; // Loop counting variable.

   // Instantiate the objects.
   SPR = new SellerProfileRequest();
   PI = new SellerProfile();
   Service = new AmazonSearchService();

   // Create the power search request.
   SPR.devtag = txtTag.Text;
   SPR.page = txtPage.Text;
   SPR.seller_id = txtSellerID.Text;
   SPR.tag = "webservices-20";
   SPR.type = txtType.Text;

   // Make the request.
   PI = Service.SellerProfileSearchRequest(SPR);

   // Clear the dataset.
   dsAmazon.Tables["CommentOut"].Rows.Clear();

   // Display the store data.
   txtStoreID.Text = PI.SellerProfileDetails[0].StoreId;
```

```
        ... Other Store Data ...

        // Display the customer comments.
        SF = PI.SellerProfileDetails[0].SellerFeedback;
        for (Counter = 0; Counter < SF.Feedback.Length; Counter++)
        {
            // Create a new row to hold the data.
            DR = dsAmazon.Tables["CommentOut"].NewRow();

            // Add the data to the row.
            DR["Rating"] = SF.Feedback[Counter].FeedbackRating;
            ... Other Columns ...

            // Display the row on screen.
            dsAmazon.Tables["CommentOut"].Rows.Add(DR);
        }
    }
```

The code begins by creating the usual request. Notice that a seller profile search returns a `SellerProfile` data structure, rather than the usual `ProductInfo` data structure. You must provide a `seller_id` field value for the call to succeed.

Once the code makes the call, `PI` contains the `SellerProfile` data structure. This data structure actually contains two levels of information. The first level contains general information about the seller, such as the seller name and the store identifier. This level also contains the number of feedback entries for the seller.

> **▶ NOTE**
>
> It's important to differentiate the seller ID from the store ID. You'll see the store ID when you look up a store online—using this number won't retrieve the seller profile. To get the seller profile, use one of the third party searches, such as an exchange search, to locate the product you want. The `ListingProductDetails` data structure contains the `ExchangeSellerId` property that holds the seller ID.

The second level contains a `SellerFeedback` data structure. Unlike the `Details` portion of a `ProductInfo` data structure, the `SellerFeedback` data structure will only contain up to 5 entries. To obtain the number of pages of feedback comments, you divide the `NumberOfFeedback` field by 5, not 10. Each of the `Feedback` entries contains a `FeedbackRating`, `FeedbackComments`, `FeedbackDate`, and `FeedbackRater` field.

As previously mentioned, each of these entries is an opinion, so you need to consider the source. For example, unsigned entries could be suspect because the contributor didn't feel comfortable enough to sign their comment—you'll need to decide for yourself whether the comment has merit. Another issue you need to consider is that some large sites can have a horrendous number of entries. For example, Wherehouse Music had 60,241 comments at the time of this writing. The only way to get anything out of that many comments is to use data mining techniques. For example, you could filter entries based on a certain keyword in the comment, or you might choose to throw out all five and one star comments and view only those that chose the middle ground. Again, the technique you use depends on what you want to get out of the data.

Performing Similarities Searches

The similarities search can be quite useful or quite misleading, depending on the kind of item you want and your expectations for that product. Amazon tracks similarities based on people's shopping habits and the product features. For example, you might see several C# books grouped together because they all discuss C#. The search might group refrigerators together because they all have built-in icemakers. Amazon might base clothing groups on style and the sequence of clicks made by a visitor to look for like items. The problem with a similarity search is that the similarity might be superficial or might not exist at all. A book designed for novice C# developers won't have the same content as a book designed for experts, yet you might see them grouped together as similar items. The search is automated—you must decide whether the results of the search actually reflect a similarity from your perspective and the needs of the user.

Similarities searches can also prove extremely helpful. Two refrigerators with precisely the same features might have different prices. You can provide a service for discerning users by letting them decide whether two items are similar enough to make a cost comparison worthwhile. Listing 12.6 shows how to perform a similarities search. You'll find the complete source code for this example in the `\Chapter 12\SimilaritySearch` folder of the source code located on the Sybex Web site.

Listing 12.6 Performing a Similarities Search

```
private void btnTest_Click(object sender, System.EventArgs e)
{
   SimilarityRequest    SR;      // The similarities search request.
   ProductInfo          PI;      // Data returned from request.
   AmazonSearchService  Service; // Connection to the service.
   DataRow              DR;      // Output data.
   Int32                Counter; // Loop counting variable.

   // Instantiate the objects.
   SR = new SimilarityRequest();
   PI = new ProductInfo();
   Service = new AmazonSearchService();

   // Create the similarities search request.
   SR.asin = txtASIN.Text;
   SR.devtag = txtTag.Text;
```

```
        SR.tag = "webservices-20";
        SR.type = txtType.Text;

        try
        {
           // Make the request.
           PI = Service.SimilaritySearchRequest(SR);
        }
        catch (SoapException SE)
        {
           // There is a good chance that no similarities exist,
           // so catch the error.
           MessageBox.Show(SE.Detail.InnerText);
           return;
        }

        // Display the results on screen.
        ... Display Data Statements ...
    }
```

This example works much like the other examples in the book that rely on the `ProductInfo` data structure. However, you don't provide as many arguments for the request because most of them don't make sense in this case. For example, the mode is superfluous because the ASIN defines the mode.

In general, you'll want to use a heavy search to ensure you have the maximum data. Most important, you must know the availability of a particular item because the vendor might not even have it in stock. In addition, you must provide `SoapException` handling for this example, even if you provide exceptional input checking because there's a good chance that new products won't have similar products associated with them. The `SE.Detail.InnerText` property will contain a message similar to "SimilaritySearchRequest: No similarities were found for asin(s): 0782142664" when a product has no similar products associated with it.

Developing a Shopping Cart Application

Amazon has a built-in shopping cart system, so the question for many developers is why they should consider building a shopping cart application for an Amazon Web Services setup. In many cases, it doesn't make sense for you to build such an application. You can receive credit for sales by providing an associate tag as part of a request, so the potential to make money is there. However, you need to consider why people visit your Web site. If you provide a Web site as a subject matter expert or because you have special knowledge that the Amazon Web site might not provide, a shopping cart application that helps you maintain control over the shopping experience might make sense. This option will make even more sense when you can offer your products alongside the Amazon and other third party offerings using the Amazon Honor System because you can create a total shopping experience at an extremely low cost. The following sections discuss the essentials of using the Amazon Shopping Cart setup.

Becoming an Associate

You can perform many of the tasks in this book without getting anything more than a developer token. Using the default webservices-20 entry for the associate tag works fine for most tasks. You can set up a Web site that includes complete Amazon search capability without doing much more than that. However, when you start working with Amazon as a third party seller, you need an associate tag. To get credit for a sale made from your site, every transaction must include the associate tag. Begin the process of becoming an associate by going to the Amazon Associate site at `http://www.amazon.com/gp/browse.html/ref=sd_str_as_dir/103-6173590-8512617?node=3435371`.

When you arrive at this site, you can either go to the area for existing associates or click the link to become an associate. Use the second option to go to the secure Amazon site. You'll need to provide a customer account on Amazon as a starting point. If you don't have a customer account, you'll need to create one. After you log into the system, you'll need to provide personal information such as your address (so they know where to send the check), telephone number, and Social Security number (for tax purposes). The questionnaire also requests information about your Web site.

The next step is to agree to the terms of the Operating Agreement. Make sure you read the agreement completely, print out or save a copy for future use, and agree to all of the terms. This book doesn't discuss the Operating Agreement terms because these terms can change at any time and reflect your personal associate agreement with Amazon. The agreement does spell out uses for the associate program, discusses your responsibilities, and defines what Amazon offers in return.

At some point, you'll receive your associate tag in email. You can also access Associates Central, which provides the latest information about the Amazon Associates program. Make sure you check out Associates Central before you begin adding Amazon links to your site so you can incorporate any recent changes to the program.

Discovering Product Availability

Amazon has information on many products, but not every product is available from Amazon. Sometimes a user will have to buy a product from a third party source. In other cases, Amazon has to special order the product. You'll also find that Amazon lists products long before they become available. Consequently, it's important to know when Amazon actually has a product available and what to do when it doesn't.

You might think that Amazon would make a single availability indicator accessible in the ProductInfo data structure returned by a search request. However, this approach probably won't provide sufficient information to most developers because it provides limited information. Instead, you need to look in several areas and use code to make an availability decision. The biggest indicator of availability is the words, "Usually ships" in the Availability field of the ProductInfo structure. When this field is blank or contains some other value, Amazon normally doesn't have the product on hand.

When Amazon will stock an item in the near future, but doesn't have it available yet, you'll normally find a special string in the Availability field such as "Not yet published." Make sure you scan for these values if you want to tell the user that they won't receive the product any time soon, but that the product will be available in the future. For example, if you're running a library application, a book that's available in the future isn't going to be much use to a reader who needs information today.

> **NOTE**
>
> This section assumes you've read the shopping cart sections of the Amazon Web Services Kit. You can find essentials, such as a definition of shopping cart terms used in this section in the /AmazonWebServices/API Guide/remote_shopping_cart.htm folder. You can also use the techniques shown in this section to affect Amazon services such as wish lists and wedding registries. The big difference is the URL that you use to make the request. Check the information in the kit at /AmazonWebServices/API Guide/add_to_cart.htm for details.

A third party item won't have an entry in the Availability field. However, the ThirdPartyNewPrice, CollectiblePrice, or UsedPrice fields will have a value. Depending on which fields have a value, you can tell the user whether the product is new or used. Always assume that a price in the CollectiblePrice field means the product is used. Used products could incur some type of liability to you depending on the laws in your state. Make sure you understand liability issues before you reference used products.

The final option is that you won't find a value in any of the fields. This means that Amazon has to special order the product. It's important to tell the user that special orders might never arrive and you might consider not displaying the item if you want to make your potential sales easier to manage. However, special orders can be quite lucrative, especially for collectors. Most collectors understand that finding a product is half the fun—that truly collectible items are often difficult to locate.

Unfortunately, none of this information appears in the kit now. Amazon promises that some future version of the kit will contain this information. In the meantime, it's best to remember that you need to use multiple fields to determine the availability of a product and discover whether you want to offer that product on your site.

Creating the Shopping Cart Application

Once you have the required tokens and you know that a product is available for sale, you can begin building a shopping cart for the user. Amazon takes care of the shopping cart, but your code sends and retrieves the items as needed. When the user finishes adding or removing items, you can transfer the shopping cart to Amazon. At this point, you can't make changes to the shopping cart—Amazon takes care of the purchasing details. Here are the six tasks that a shopping cart application for Amazon Web Services normally performs:

- Create a shopping cart.
- Add items to a shopping cart.
- Modify items in a shopping cart.
- Retrieve the shopping cart contents.
- Clear a shopping cart.
- Transfer the shopping cart to Amazon.

The code in Listing 12.7 shows how to perform the six essential shopping cart tasks. The listing lacks several important features, such as the error trapping found in the actual source code. You'll find the complete source code for this example in the `\Chapter 12\ShoppingCartDemo` folder of the source code located on the Sybex Web site.

Listing 12.7 Working with Shopping Carts

```
// Holds the shopping cart.
ShoppingCart   SC;

private void btnAdd_Create_Click(object sender, System.EventArgs e)
{
   AddShoppingCartItemsRequest   ASCIR;   // Add cart item request.
   AddItem                       []Items; // Items to add.
   AmazonSearchService           Service; // Service connection.

   // Instantiate the objects.
   ASCIR = new AddShoppingCartItemsRequest();
   Service = new AmazonSearchService();

   // Create the basic shopping cart request.
   ASCIR.devtag = txtTag.Text;
   ASCIR.tag = "webservices-20";

   // Add Items to the request.
   Items = new AddItem[1];
   Items[0] = new AddItem();
```

```
        Items[0].Asin = txtASIN.Text;
        Items[0].Quantity = txtQuantity.Text;
        ASCIR.Items = Items;

        // Add a cart identifier and HMAC string if necessary.
        if (SC != null)
        {
            ASCIR.HMAC = SC.HMAC;
            ASCIR.CartId = SC.CartId;
        }

        try
        {
            // Make the request.
            SC = Service.AddShoppingCartItemsRequest(ASCIR);
        }
        ... Trap Errors ...

        // Enable the other buttons when the first call is successful.
        ... Work with Buttons ...

        // Display the list of items.
        DisplayCart();
    }

    private void btnModify_Click(object sender, System.EventArgs e)
    {
        ModifyShoppingCartItemsRequest   MSCIR;   // Modify cart request.
        AmazonSearchService              Service; // Service connection.
        Int32                            Counter; // Loop counter.

        // Instantiate the objects.
        MSCIR = new ModifyShoppingCartItemsRequest();
        Service = new AmazonSearchService();

        // Create the shopping cart request.
        MSCIR.CartId = SC.CartId;
        MSCIR.devtag = txtTag.Text;
        MSCIR.HMAC = SC.HMAC;
        MSCIR.tag = "webservices-20";

        // Build a list of items.
        MSCIR.Items = new ItemQuantity[SC.Items.Length];
        for (Counter = 0; Counter < SC.Items.Length; Counter++)
        {
            // Add the individual item.
            MSCIR.Items[Counter] = new ItemQuantity();

            // Move the values.
            MSCIR.Items[Counter].ItemId = SC.Items[Counter].ItemId;
            MSCIR.Items[Counter].Quantity = SC.Items[Counter].Quantity;
        }
```

```
   // Modify the quantity for each item.
   for (Counter = 0; Counter < MSCIR.Items.Length; Counter++)
      MSCIR.Items[0].Quantity =
         dsAmazon.Tables["ProductOut"].Rows[0].ItemArray[2].ToString();

   try
   {
      // Make the request.
      SC = Service.ModifyShoppingCartItemsRequest(MSCIR);
   }
   ... Trap Errors ...

   // Display the list of items.
   DisplayCart();
}

private void btnClear_Click(object sender, System.EventArgs e)
{
   ClearShoppingCartRequest   CSCR;    // Clear cart request.
   AmazonSearchService        Service; // Connection to the service.

   // Instantiate the objects.
   CSCR = new ClearShoppingCartRequest();
   Service = new AmazonSearchService();

   // Create the shopping cart request.
   CSCR.CartId = SC.CartId;
   CSCR.devtag = txtTag.Text;
   CSCR.HMAC = SC.HMAC;
   CSCR.tag = "webservices-20";

   try
   {
      // Make the request.
      SC = Service.ClearShoppingCartRequest(CSCR);
   }
   ... Trap Errors ...

   // Disable the Delete and Clear buttons.
   ... Work with Buttons ...

   // Display the list of items.
   DisplayCart();
}

private void btnPurchase_Click(object sender, System.EventArgs e)
{
   // Start the default browser and go to the purchase Web site.
   System.Diagnostics.Process.Start(SC.PurchaseUrl);
}
```

```
private void DisplayCart()
{
   DataRow              DR;       // Output data.
   Int32                Counter; // Loop counting variable.

   // Clear the current table content.
   dsAmazon.Tables["ProductOut"].Rows.Clear();

   // Verify that SC has items to process.
   if (SC.Items == null)
      return;

   // Process the items.
   for (Counter = 0; Counter < SC.Items.Length; Counter++)
   {
      // Create a new row to hold the data.
      DR = dsAmazon.Tables["ProductOut"].NewRow();

      // Add the data to the row.
      DR["Product Name"] = SC.Items[Counter].ProductName;
      ... Other Columns ...

      // Display the row on screen.
      dsAmazon.Tables["ProductOut"].Rows.Add(DR);
   }
}
```

The code begins with a seemingly innocent variable declaration that can cause all kinds of problems. The `ShoppingCart` object `SC` is unique for each Amazon user, but the `ShoppingCart` object is also persistent. The example uses a global variable, but this technique won't work in situations where multiple users could visit the same application at the same time (as in a Web application). Make sure you consider thread safety in your application—a global variable could become contaminated with data from multiple users in a multiuser setting.

The request process for the three request methods (`btnAdd_Create_Click()`, `btnModify_Click()`, and `btnClear_Click`) isn't much different from the requests you've seen in other parts of the book. You still need to provide request arguments and make a query. However, now you're working with a shopping cart, which means you have to track the cart during each request. The code does this by using a `SC.CartId` argument. The Hashed Message Authentication Code (HMAC) found in the SC.HMAC argument helps Amazon track the shopping cart.

The process of creating a cart is the same as adding an item to a cart except for one small detail. When the code sends the request with a `HMAC` and a `CartId`, Amazon adds a new item. Requests without these two field values create a new cart.

The modify process means creating a copy of the items in the shopping cart in an `ItemQuantity` object contained within the `ModifyShoppingCartItemsRequest` object. The only element you can modify is the quantity. Setting a quantity to 0 won't delete it from the list. To delete an element, you'd have to clear the shopping cart and then add the items you wanted back into the shopping cart.

Every call requires error trapping because you can run into a number of error scenarios. For example, if you request a product that Amazon doesn't have in stock, you'll receive a server error 500 in many cases. In other cases, you'll receive a specially formatted SOAP error. Amazon could simply tell you that the product isn't available, but you'll receive one of these two errors instead.

The Amazon Web Services Kit talks about the purchase URL in several places, but never does mention where this URL resides. The `btnPurchase_Click()` method shows that this URL resides in the `SC.PurchaseUrl` field. This value is unique for each user, so don't make the mistake of hard coding the URL.

The `DisplayCart()` method shows how to display the items in the shopping cart. If you follow the techniques used in this example, you'll never have to retrieve the shopping cart items from Amazon—the `ShoppingCart` object maintains a perfect inventory of the items for you.

Your Call to Action

This chapter is all about additional steps—features you can add to your application to make it better in some way. Unlike the material found in Chapters 10 and 11, most of the information in this chapter is nice to have, but not essential. You can write a perfectly acceptable application without these features, but some of them could make your application special. The best way to approach this chapter is to consider whether the technique described actually helps present your application message in some way. Anything that helps the message is a bonus to the user and makes the user more likely to enjoy your work.

The question you need to consider for this chapter is whether the cost of implementing a feature is likely to provide a benefit of equal value. Some features such as user feedback always garner some benefit to you and the user. A few of the best ideas I've had for my applications came from user feedback that I implemented to ensure the user has a good experience. However, you might find some features, such as managing a shopping cart, are more trouble than they're worth. The consideration is always whether the value of the implementation is worth the cost of adding the required software, with value as anything you consider valuable—including customer support.

Congratulations! You've reached the last chapter of the book. However, your journey should also include the appendices for this book. Appendix A helps you locate useful third party utilities. Use Appendix B to ensure your application meets all of the Amazon licensing requirements. Finally, use Appendix D to learn about breaking Amazon Web Services news—new technologies made available as this book went to press. If you've read from the beginning to the end of the book, you know that it covers a lot of ground. I encourage you to continue to use the book as a reference. Amazon Web Services is a truly remarkable undertaking and I'd love to hear about your experiences with it. Make sure you contact me at `JMueller@mwt.net` if you have any questions about this book. Also, look on my Web site at `http://www.mwt.net/~jmueller/` for updates and additional information.

Appendix A

Helpful Third Party Resource Sites

Thoughout the book, you discovered a number of resources that would help you perform some tasks with less effort or faster. In some cases, a product added the special functionality required to make Amazon Web Services access possible. I usually placed the special products in a separate section or used them to demonstrate a particular type of Amazon Web Services access. The book also contains a number of Web sites that feature special information—these helpful Web sites normally appear as part of notes or tips. This appendix is an extension of all those special sections, notes, and tips—it contains a number of helpful third party resources that will make your Amazon Web Services experience better.

Of course, this appendix begs the question of why these third party products and sites don't appear in the main part of the book somewhere. In many cases, these products fulfill a special need that I didn't demonstrate in the book or they duplicate functionality that you'll already find in the book. This appendix contains additional information that I thought you would find helpful, but didn't find a place in the main part of the book for whatever reason.

I'm always on the lookout for great third party products, and I like to know about Web sites with helpful information. These sites often appear in my newsletter (sign up at `http://www.freeenewsletters.com/`). I also provide them as updates to the book on my Web site at `http://www.mwt.net/~jmueller/`. If you know of a special third party product or Web site that has special information that would help users of this book, please let me know by writing to me at `JMueller@mwt.net`.

Amazon Web Services-Specific Web Sites

Amazon Web Services has been so successful that many language vendors are beginning to take notice, as well as a number of third parties. The following list presents a few of the most interesting places to find Amazon Web Services information. However, you should also check with the vendor that creates your programming language product and look around at other third party solutions too. For example, the "Microsoft Office 2003 Add-on" section describes how Microsoft is adding Amazon Web Services support to their Office product.

Sun Web Services `http://developer.java.sun.com/developer/technicalArticles/WebServices/`

Amazon Web Services Frequently Asked Questions `http://cybaea.com/faq/AWS/`

Dev Shed Articles on Amazon Web Services `http://www.devshed.com/Search.php?search=Amazon%20Web%20Services`

Amazon Web Services Developer's Forum `http://www.mallasch.com/amazon-newsletter/aws-dev.php`

Amazon Web Services Support `http://www.rexx.com/~dkuhlman/amazon_ws_support.html`

Simon Willison's Amazon Web Services Weblog `http://simon.incutio.com/archive/2002/07/17/amazonWebServices`

Demonstration Web Sites

Sometimes a demonstration is better than any amount of descriptive text. Most of the demonstrations I've seen on the Internet are simple at this point, but the potential for creating some very interesting Web applications is definitely there. The following Web sites provide demonstrations you can try online.

IBM developerWorks Web Services Demo `http://www-106.ibm.com/developerworks/webservices/demos/amazon/`

Cape Science Amazon Web Services Demonstration `http://www.capescience.com/webservices/amazon/index.shtml`

Systinet Developer's Corner `http://dev.systinet.com/code_samples/toolkits/index`

Scott Loftesness' Amazon Web Services Test Page `http://www.loftesness.com/radio/stories/2003/04/22/scottLoftesnessAmazoncomWebServices.html`

One Web site deserves a special mention because the developer has created a production quality Amazon Web Services application. However, this application doesn't stop at providing Amazon information—it also uses the Google Web Services API, which makes this site quite interesting. You can learn more about the developer at `http://blog.outer-court.com/archive/2003_06_21_index.html`. The application appears at `http://www.authorama.com/`. Figure A.1 shows typical output from this Web site—the Google output appears on the left and the Amazon output on the right.

Web Sites That Provide Other Facts You Should Know About

You'll find helpful Web sites in every chapter of the book. However, some useful Web sites didn't quite fit in any of the chapters, yet they supply useful information for your Amazon Web Services experience. For example, the "Sending Special Characters Using URL Encoding" section of Chapter 3 discusses the need to URL encode special characters before you send a request to Amazon Web Services. Equally important is the need to *escape* special characters in some types of HTML and XML output by converting them to numeric sequences. The quote (') and double quote (") often cause problems, as do the angle brackets (<>). You can escape these characters as ', ", <, and >. The HTML Character Codes site at `http://home.online.no/~pethesse/charcodes.html` contains a good list of these codes.

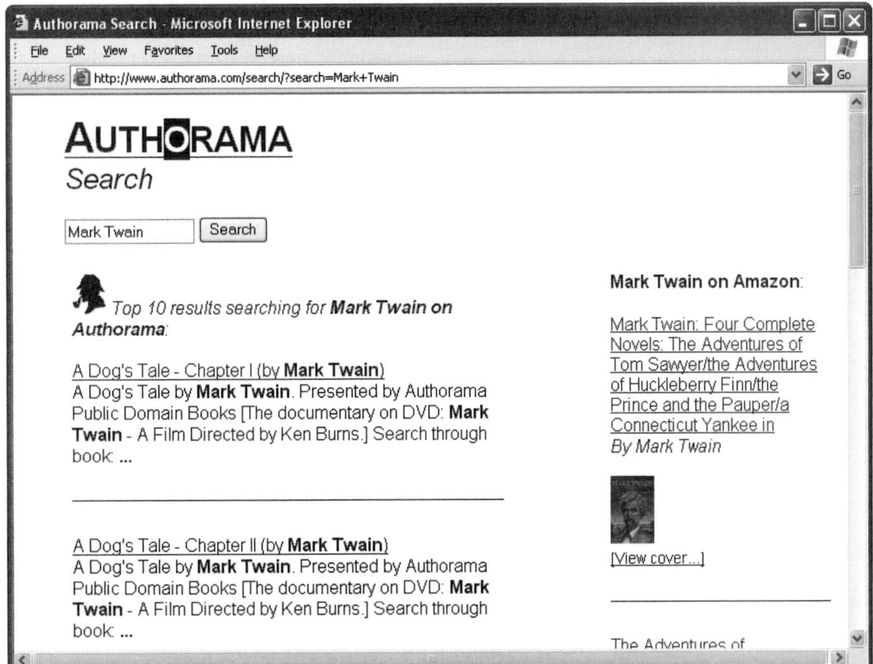

FIGURE A.1: This production Web site relies on output from two Web services.

Web accessibility is an extremely important topic and I hope that you take it as seriously as I do. You can find multitudes of statistics on Web sites that specialize in accessibility such as `http://www.w3.org/1999/05/WCAG-REC-fact`. An ExtremeTech article entitled "The State of Web Accessibility" (`http://www.extremetech.com/article2/0,3973,11774,00.asp`) says it all by stating that accessibility is for everyone—the 180 posts for this article provide some interesting insights as well. These additional Web sites provide some pointers you can use to make your site accessible and yet keep development costs to a minimum.

Policies Relating to Web Accessibility `http://www.w3.org/WAI/Policy/`

Safe Web Colors for Color-Deficient Vision `http://more.btexact.com/people/rigdence/colours/`

Usability and Accessibility—Everyone Learning `http://www.cdlr.tamu.edu/dec_2002/Proceedings/david_peter.pdf`

Once you learn about Web services and understand how valuable they can be, you'll want to try out other Web services to learn whether they can help you with your application. One of the most interesting places to learn about new Web services is the Macromedia Flash site at `http://www.flash-db.com/services/`.

Sometimes you can find individual sites that include some Amazon Web Services material. I like browsing these sites because many of them include insights and perspectives you won't find on mainstream sites. Of course, some of them just repeat material you find elsewhere. Here are a few of the more interesting selections.

Charon Internet Tutorials `http://www.charon.co.uk/content.aspx?CategoryID=4`

Windley's Enterprise Computing Weblog `http://www.windley.com/2002/07/18.html`

Steve Sharrock's AspAlliance Contributions `http://authors.aspalliance.com/shark/`

Integrating Amazon Web Services with Your Notes Databases `http://www-10.lotus.com/ldd/today.nsf/lookup/AWSintegration_pt3`

Microsoft Office 2003 Add-on

Most Microsoft Office users will need to use the VBA programming techniques found in Chapter 5 to access Amazon Web Services. However, Office 2003 users have an alternative solution that works in some cases. Microsoft is creating a new add-on for the Research Task Pane that should be available when you read this. This add-on lets you locate products on Amazon and purchase them without ever leaving the Office environment. You can find the add-on at `http://www.office.microsoft.com/marketplace`.

After researching this add-on a bit more, it appears that it won't provide a customizable interface. You'll interact with this add-on much as you interact with the Amazon Web site, so even with this add-on, you might find yourself creating a custom application to define the interface you want. Unfortunately, Microsoft didn't release all of the details about this add-on immediately, but you can find additional details at `http://www.infoworld.com/article/03/10/07/HNmsamazon_1.html` and `http://www.computerworld.com/managementtopics/ebusiness/story/0,10801,85822,00.html?nas=PM-85822`.

Appendix B

▶ Amazon License Checklist

This appendix discusses some of the requirements you must fulfill to use Amazon Web Services. The purpose of this appendix is to help you create a checklist to ensure you meet the legal requirements—the appendix doesn't tell you about your legal rights, act as a legal guide, or provide anything that would normally require a lawyer. I often create checklists of this sort for my own use and find that many other people find them useful too. The main reason I create these checklists for myself is that they make it easier for me to determine whether an application I create fulfills the basic requirements of the license. If you do have questions about the legal requirements, make sure you contact Amazon (`webservices@amazon.com`) to ensure you understand your role completely. In addition, although this appendix is current as of the date of writing, Amazon could change the licensing agreement at any time—you must make sure you that you keep current on all of the requirements.

General Requirements

The following topics discuss requirements found in Section 1.A. of the licensing agreement. This section discusses general issues, such as what you can do with the Amazon Web Services. Each section roughly corresponds to a section in the license agreement. I've assumed that you know that you can write an application that interfaces with Amazon Web Services, so you won't find provision 1) listed, but most of the other provisions do appear in the list.

Making Calls that Don't Exceed Limits

Amazon notes that you can make calls using any method that it supports—as you see in the book, that list is very long. You can make calls to Amazon Web Services any time day or night, 7 days a week. Those are the good things you should simply file somewhere.

However, Amazon is a business and its customers come first. When you use Amazon Web Services for development, you're a developer, not a customer. It's not too surprising that Amazon places some limits on the resources you can use. These limits ensure customers can access the Web site and get good service. In addition, it means that all developers get a fair share of the available resources. Amazon asks that you not exceed 1 call per second. This limitation is the reason that I manually execute each request, rather than perform the task through code. You also have a limit of 20 KB per upload—that's not 20 KB of data, but the entire size of the file.

Keeping the Information You Receive Private

Amazon knows that you'll display the information you receive from Amazon Web Services in your application—they're counting on it. The underlying reason for making this Web service available is to generate sales using your contacts. However, you can't give the raw information you receive to someone else. If Amazon sees that you have a duplicate of its database on your Web site, and that you're selling that information to someone else, you'll probably hear a representative knocking at your door. Make sure you process the information you receive in some way that adds value for the people using your application—otherwise, they might just as well use the Amazon Web site directly.

This requirement ties directly into the requirement of Section 1.D.5). Make sure that any database you create to store the Amazon information remains private too.

Always Observe the Requirements of the Law

Most people realize that you can't use information you receive from Amazon as a bludgeon to hurt someone else. Amazon doesn't want to get involved in the long running feud between you and your neighbor. They're being nice enough to let you use the data on their site for any of a number of useful purposes. All they ask in return is that you don't violate the law—whatever the law is in your country.

It's also important to consider Amazon's rights when you create your application. An application that violates Amazon's proprietary rights is going to attract the wrong kind of attention. In short, don't do things like claim you created the information displayed by your application when Amazon obviously provided it to you.

Maintaining a Problem-Free Relationship with Amazon

Developers are finding that Amazon Web Services can offer substantial functionality for their applications. Consequently, when someone interferes with the operating of Amazon Web Services, they're not only causing problems for Amazon, but for every developer who relies on Amazon Web Services. To ensure you maintain a good relationship with Amazon, make sure you test applications thoroughly before releasing them. Also, if you have a question, ask someone about it rather than assume your little kludge won't do any harm.

Following the Rules Listed in the Amazon Associates Agreement

This is one of those hidden clauses that checklists make easier to follow. You can find a copy of the Amazon Associates Operating Agreement at `http://associates.amazon.com/exec/panama/associates/join/operating-agreement.html`. The essential point is that you don't want to inhibit Amazon sales or steal them away with your application. As previously noted, Amazon is sharing its database with you in hope of receiving additional sales, so the agreement probably doesn't allow anything that works contrary to that goal.

Display Requirements

The following topics discuss requirements found in Section 1.B. of the licensing agreement. This section discusses display issues, such as how you can present Amazon Web Services information in your application. The important consideration in this section is that Amazon realizes that you want to add value to the content, but they also have to maintain the integrity of the content they supply to you.

Selecting a Formatting Method

You can display the data in any format you choose so long as you don't break one of the rules in this agreement. For example, you can display text in bold or in an odd font if you want, but you have to follow the rules for using text.

Altering the Text

Some Amazon content gets rather long and you might not be able to display all of the text on one page of your Web site. You can shorten the text as needed to make it easier to display. However, you can't change the text. For example, if a reviewer uses poor grammar, you can't make editorial changes to it. The only cure is to avoid using the review.

You also need to keep your content separate from Amazon's content. For example, you might be tempted to add your commentary to a review, but you can't display the commentary as part of the review. Displaying the commentary as a separate item from the review is acceptable. The same caution holds true for other items, such as a Listmania! list. Adding your own items to the list would break the rules, but you can participate in the list or you can provide your items separately.

Leaving Proprietary Information in Place

Amazon will provide the copyright and trademark symbols with their content as needed. You must leave these symbols in place. The same holds true for any notices or other identifying information. There really isn't a good reason to modify any of this information.

Using Quick-Click Correctly

Amazon provides the Quick-Click feature to let people buy products without a lot of effort. This feature actually makes it easier for you too because you don't have to maintain as much information about the user. However, you can't misrepresent the product the user is buying or alter its price when you use this feature. Actually, this rule makes sense whether the user relies on Quick-Click or not. Anything you do that modifies the price or the product description will only cause problems for you when the user receives the product.

Linking and Diversion Requirements

The following topics discuss requirements found in Section 1.C. of the licensing agreement. This section discusses linking and diversion issues, such as how to create a link between your application and the Amazon Web site. It also describes some forms of diversion you can't perform, such as directing sales away from the Amazon Web Site.

Creating the Proper Linkage

Whenever you display products or product information in your application, you must create some type of link back to Amazon. It's easy to meet this requirement because Amazon always provides the correct link as part of the query response. However, if you don't want to go through all the work of create a unique link for each product, you can still link people to the main Amazon site and meet this requirement.

Directing Sales to Amazon

You might not realize it yet, but you're actually in a partnership with Amazon. In fact, if you become a member of the Amazon Associates program, you can earn money for your efforts. Creating an application that works with Amazon Web Services might seem interesting, but that doesn't have to be the end of the process. The application can help you earn additional money by directing sales to Amazon. Of course, you won't want to divert sales from your partner.

Storage and Obligation to Refresh Requirements

The following topics discuss requirements found in Section 1.D. of the licensing agreement. This section discusses storage and obligation issues, such as how long you can store Amazon Web Services data. It also describes your obligations to Amazon when you use Amazon's data (but not necessarily your obligations to the user of your application).

Using Correct Data Storage Methods

Amazon lets you store any information you download from its database for up to 24 hours. Several of the applications in this book show techniques that ensure you follow this requirement. Old data doesn't help anyone—Amazon misses a potential sale, you lose potential visitors, and the user receives the wrong impression about both the product and your site.

> **NOTE**
>
> This requirement doesn't affect someone using your application. If they store the information from your application locally, Amazon doesn't expect you to locate the user and force them to update the information.

The only exception to the 24-hour rule is price information. You must refresh prices every hour. To ensure that your user receives the best possible information, you might want to request new prices with each call. Most users will tolerate a little error that doesn't affect their purchasing decision, but I've seen people almost come to blows over a few cents' difference.

Ridding Yourself of Old Products

Some developers leave an abundance of old data in the database. I've personally had to clean up some of these nightmares and know that the task is anything but fun. In some cases, a database can get so filled with old data, that the only way to clean it is to start from scratch. Amazon expects that you'll write a great application—one that maintains the database used to store the information they have lent you in good shape. Consequently, when Amazon no longer stocks a product, they expect that you'll also remove this product from your database.

> **NOTE**
>
> Amazon will make some storage requirement concessions on a case-by-case basis. If you have a question about the storage requirements, contact Amazon at `webservices@amazon.com`.

Intellectual Property Issues

The checklist portion of this appendix discusses development issues. However, you need to consider the entire licensing agreement before you make your application public. For example, you have to consider ownership rights. While you do own the rights to any application you create, you need to consider the data you obtain from Amazon as part of the application picture. Amazon doesn't give up any rights to its intellectual property. Because intellectual property rights are figuring in a number of legal cases right now, it's important to keep track of how you use Amazon property in your application. Amazon grants you certain rights, but those rights could change at any time. Amazon spells out ownership rights in Section 2 of the licensing agreement.

Amazon also provides you with access to some of its trademarked material in order to promote the Amazon connection to your application. Obviously, Amazon doesn't want you to use its trademarked material in a way that would cause problems. For example, you couldn't use the trademarked material on a Web site that disparages other people based on sex, religion, or ethnic origin (among other things). Although the usage requirements in Sections 3 and 4 of the agreement don't spell out every good use of the trademarked material, they do spell out a few of the ways that you can't use the material. As usual, make sure you contact Amazon if you have any questions about how to use the trademarked material.

You also can't modify trademarked material in any way. Some people are going to be tempted to make some type of a change to the graphics because the colors don't match their site or they don't find the current material aesthetically pleasing. The important thing to remember is that Amazon provides this material for optional display. If you don't want to use it, you don't have to. Sections 3 and 4 of the agreement tell you how you can use the images and other trademarked material, with an emphasis on not changing the material in any way.

You'll find that Amazon, like most large companies, is very conscious of its public appearance. This means you have to exercise care in spelling out your relationship with Amazon. Saying that you're Amazon's main representative, when you're just using their Web service, isn't a good idea. Generally, it's best to keep a low profile and simply say that some information presented with your application comes from Amazon Web Services.

Section 5 presents some information you really do want to read. It's a blanket agreement that states anything you send to Amazon becomes their property. Many people don't understand the ramifications of this statement. For example, you might write a book review and upload it to Amazon. The book review now belongs to Amazon. The same thing holds true for other kinds of content, including images. The right is non-exclusive, which means that you can upload the content somewhere else. However, Amazon can use the material you provide for any of a number of purposes and you need to consider that aspect of ownership. You might not want them to use your picture for promotional purposes, but they can if you upload that picture to them as content. If you don't want Amazon to use your material, don't send it to them.

Appendix C

Amazon Area ID List

You can use Amazon Web Services to search for products and services by area. To perform this kind of search, you must specify an Area ID as part of the search criteria (along with other information in some cases). The only problem is that finding the Area ID can be difficult because Amazon requires you to read the source code of a special Web page to locate the information. The following is a complete list of the Area ID values as of the time of writing.

Area ID	Country Name	Area ID	Country Name
4000000	Afghanistan	4000122	Lesotho
4000001	Albania	4000123	Liberia
4000002	Algeria	4000125	Liechtenstein
4000003	American Samoa	4000126	Lithuania
4000004	Andorra	4000127	Luxembourg
4000005	Angola	4000128	Macau
4000006	Anguilla	4000129	Macedonia
4000007	Antarctica	4000130	Madagascar
4000008	Antigua and Barbuda	4000131	Malawi
4000009	Argentina	4000132	Malaysia
4000010	Armenia	4000133	Maldives
4000011	Aruba	4000134	Mali
4000012	Australia	4000135	Malta

Area ID	Country Name	Area ID	Country Name
4000013	Austria	4000136	Marshall Islands
4000014	Azerbaijan	4000137	Martinique
4000015	Bahamas	4000138	Mauritania
4000016	Bahrain	4000139	Mauritius
4000017	Bangladesh	4000140	Mayotte
4000018	Barbados	4000141	Mexico
4000019	Belarus	4000142	Micronesia, Federated States of
4000020	Belgium	4000143	Moldova, Republic of
4000021	Belize	4000144	Monaco
4000022	Benin	4000145	Mongolia
4000023	Bermuda	4000146	Montserrat
4000024	Bhutan	4000147	Morocco
4000025	Bolivia	4000148	Mozambique
4000026	Bosnia and Herzegovina	4000149	Namibia
4000027	Botswana	4000150	Nauru
4000028	Bouvet Island	4000151	Nepal
4000029	Brazil	4000152	Netherlands
4000030	British Indian Ocean Territory	4000153	Netherlands Antilles
4000031	Brunei Darussalam	4000154	New Caledonia
4000032	Bulgaria	4000155	New Zealand
4000033	Burkina Faso	4000156	Nicaragua
4000034	Burma	4000157	Niger
4000035	Burundi	4000158	Nigeria
4000036	Cambodia	4000159	Niue
4000037	Cameroon	4000160	Norfolk Island
4000038	Canada	4000161	Northern Ireland
4000039	Cape Verde	4000162	Northern Mariana Islands

Area ID	Country Name	Area ID	Country Name
4000040	Cayman Islands	4000163	Norway
4000041	Central African Republic	4000164	Oman
4000042	Chad	4000165	Pakistan
4000043	Chile	4000166	Palau
4000044	China	4000167	Panama
4000045	Christmas Island	4000168	Papua New Guinea
4000046	Cocos (Keeling) Islands	4000169	Paraguay
4000047	Colombia	4000170	Peru
4000048	Comoros	4000171	Philippines
4000049	Congo	4000172	Pitcairn
4000050	Congo, Democratic Republic of the	4000173	Poland
4000051	Cook Islands	4000174	Portugal
4000052	Costa Rica	4000175	Puerto Rico
4000053	Cote d'Ivoire	4000176	Qatar
4000054	Croatia	4000177	Reunion
4000056	Cyprus	4000178	Romania
4000057	Czech Republic	4000179	Russian Federation
4000058	Denmark	4000180	Rwanda
4000059	Djibouti	4000181	Saint Kitts and Nevis
4000060	Dominica	4000182	Saint Lucia
4000061	Dominican Republic	4000183	Saint Vincent and the Grenadines
4000062	East Timor	4000184	Samoa (Independent)
4000063	Ecuador	4000185	San Marino
4000064	Egypt	4000186	Sao Tome and Principe
4000065	El Salvador	4000187	Saudi Arabia
4000066	England	4000188	Scotland
4000067	Equatorial Guinea	4000189	Senegal

Area ID	Country Name	Area ID	Country Name
4000068	Eritrea	4000190	Seychelles
4000069	Estonia	4000191	Sierra Leone
4000070	Ethiopia	4000192	Singapore
4000071	Falkland Islands	4000193	Slovakia
4000072	Faroe Islands	4000194	Slovenia
4000073	Fiji	4000195	Solomon Islands
4000074	Finland	4000196	Somalia
4000075	France	4000197	South Africa
4000076	French Guiana	4000198	South Georgia and the South Sandwich Islands
4000077	French Polynesia	4000199	Spain
4000078	French Southern Territories	4000200	Sri Lanka
4000079	Gabon	4000201	St. Helena
4000080	Gambia	4000202	St. Pierre and Miquelon
4000081	Georgia	4000204	Suriname
4000082	Germany	4000205	Svalbard and Jan Mayen Islands
4000083	Ghana	4000206	Swaziland
4000084	Gibraltar	4000207	Sweden
4000085	Great Britain	4000208	Switzerland
4000086	Greece	4000210	Taiwan
4000087	Greenland	4000211	Tajikistan
4000088	Grenada	4000212	Tanzania
4000089	Guadeloupe	4000213	Thailand
4000090	Guam	4000214	Togo
4000091	Guatemala	4000215	Tokelau
4000092	Guinea	4000216	Tonga
4000093	Guinea-Bissau	4000217	Trinidad and Tobago

Area ID	Country Name	Area ID	Country Name
4000094	Guyana	4000218	Tunisia
4000095	Haiti	4000219	Turkey
4000096	Heard and McDonald Islands	4000220	Turkmenistan
4000097	Holy See (Vatican City State)	4000221	Turks and Caicos Islands
4000098	Honduras	4000222	Tuvalu
4000099	Hong Kong	4000223	Uganda
4000100	Hungary	4000224	Ukraine
4000101	Iceland	4000225	United Arab Emirates
4000102	India	4000226	United Kingdom
4000103	Indonesia	4000227	United States
4000106	Ireland	4000228	United States Minor Outlying Islands
4000107	Israel	4000229	Uruguay
4000108	Italy	4000230	Uzbekistan
4000109	Jamaica	4000231	Vanuatu
4000110	Japan	4000232	Venezuela
4000111	Jordan	4000233	Vietnam
4000112	Kazakhstan	4000234	Virgin Islands (British)
4000113	Kenya	4000235	Virgin Islands (U.S.)
4000114	Kiribati	4000236	Wales
4000116	Korea (South)	4000237	Wallis and Futuna Islands
4000117	Kuwait	4000238	Western Sahara
4000118	Kyrgyzstan	4000239	Yemen
4000119	Lao People's Democratic Republic	4000241	Zambia
4000120	Latvia	4000242	Zimbabwe
4000121	Lebanon		

Appendix D

▶ Late Breaking Amazon Web Services News

This appendix brings you late breaking news about Amazon Web Services as of the time of this writing. With many products, there are definite breaks in the development cycle so you can say one version is complete and another is beginning. The Web makes it easy to create products that have a continuous development cycle—there aren't any real versions to consider. Amazon Web Services falls into this category. Every new release of the newsletter tells of new features and functionality you can access in Amazon Web Services. Consequently, you'll want to review every newsletter you receive. Remember that you can always retrieve older newsletters from the Jungle Developer site at `http://www.jungledeveloper.com/index.php`.

The following sections describe some of the latest Amazon Web Services features. These new features add to an already useful product by letting you do more with less code in most cases. You'll also find that these new features make it easier for you to create robust applications that fulfill more user needs.

Additional Mobile Device Search Techniques

One of the features I wanted to discuss in Chapter 9 was the use of special URLs to deliver content to mobile device users without a lot of work on your part. You'd perform the required Amazon Standard Item Number (ASIN) search on the server, add the ASIN to the URL, and send the URL to the mobile device. The Amazon Web site takes care of the details from that point on. Here is an example of a typical mobile device URL.

```
http://www.amazon.com/exec/obidos/redirect?tag=your_assoc_tag%26creative=your_
developer_token%26camp=2025%26link_code=xm2%26path=ct/text/vnd.wap.wml/-/tg/aa/
xml/glance-xml/-/0782142664
```

All of these URLs use the same Web site, `http://www.amazon.com/exec/obidos/redirect`. Notice that the URL includes the associate tag and the developer token so that you still receive credit for the applications you create. The arguments are different in this URL from the arguments used for other URLs in the book. The `dev-t` argument now appears as a `creative` argument. For now, all the URLs use the same `camp` and `link_code` arguments, but make sure you check for changes in the newsletter. The product ASIN appears at the end of the URL in all cases. The big difference between URLs appears in the `path` argument. Each device has a different path you must use as listed here.

Standard PDA `dt/upda-1.0-anywhere/tg/aa/upda/item/-/`

Research In Motion (RIM) Blackberry Device `dt/upda-1.0-i/tg/aa/upda/item/-/`

Handheld Device Markup Language (HDML) Enabled Cellular Telephone or Browser `ct/text/x-hdml/-/tg/aa/hdml/item/-/`

Wireless Application Protocol (WAP) Enabled Cellular Telephone or Browser `ct/text/vnd.wap.wml/-/tg/aa/xml/glance-xml/-/`

Figure D.1 shows typical output in a WAP enabled cellular telephone. As you can see, Amazon formats the data to fit within a very small space. The page includes links for moving to other pages and ordering the product. The user receives specially formatted pages during the entire process—making it easier to promote and sell products using a mobile device.

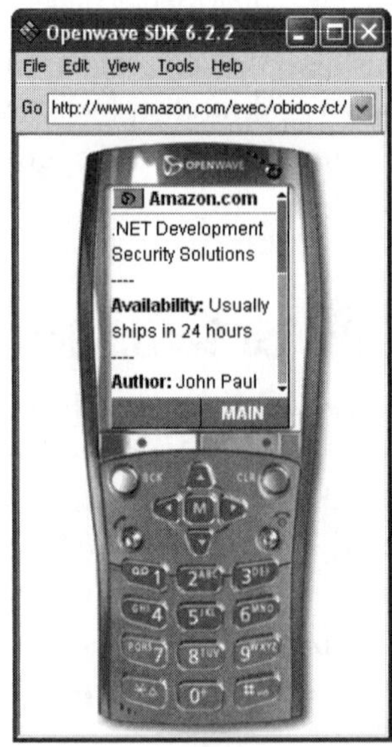

FIGURE D.1: Using the specially formatted Amazon Web Services pages means you don't have to write special mobile code. Image courtesy Openwave Systems Inc.

This technology is still young and riddled with potential problems. For example, Amazon also provides methods for performing a keyword search, but the results are disappointing on smaller devices (you have to move the cursor keys a lot to locate the information you want). You can also provide VoiceXML support, but these features are also somewhat difficult to use and limited to just two vendors—Tellme (`http://www.tellme.com/`) and Bevocal (`http://bevocal.com/corporateweb/`). However, the biggest problem is that the information handling is out of your hands. Amazon now decides who sees what information, rather than the application you created. Consequently, you can't tailor the presentation to meet specific needs easily. You can learn more about this feature by viewing the Mobile Access to AWS topic in the kit at `/AmazonWebServices/API Guide/search_marketplace.htm` and the various newsletters.

> **NOTE**
>
> As of the time of writing, the text stream search only works with the books, electronics, toys, photo, video games, or music modes. In addition, you can only use this search with the United States Web site and it accepts only English input. In addition, the page field seems nonfunctional, so this search is only good for receiving the first page of results. Amazon is working on making this search more usable.

Developing a Text Stream Search

Amazon recently introduced the text stream search as a way to work with human language—at least to a point. When you execute a keyword search, Amazon Web Services looks for every word you provide in the database and provides matching results. Using a keyword search strategy normally works well, but might not always succeed. For example, you might want to perform a search based on spoken input or the text of an article. In these cases, you should use a text stream search. A text stream search won't look for every word you provide. Instead, it looks for keywords in the text and then uses the keywords as the basis for the search. Consequently, you could provide "I want all video produced by people named George" and Amazon could process the request for you because it would look for words such as video and George.

Listing D.1 shows a typical example of a text stream search. You'll find the complete source code for this example in the `\Appendix D\TextSearch` folder of the source code located on the Sybex Web site.

Listing D.1 Performing a Text Steam Search

```
private void btnTest_Click(object sender, System.EventArgs e)
{
   TextStreamRequest    TSR;      // The text stream request.
   ProductInfo          PI;       // Data returned from request.
```

```
   AmazonSearchService  Service; // Connection to the service.
   DataRow              DR;      // Output data.
   Int32                Counter; // Loop counting variable.

   // Instantiate the objects.
   TSR = new TextStreamRequest();
   PI = new ProductInfo();
   Service = new AmazonSearchService();

   // Create the text stream search request.
   TSR.devtag = txtTag.Text;
   TSR.mode = txtMode.Text;
   TSR.page = txtPage.Text;
   TSR.textStream = txtTextStream.Text;
   if (txtSort.Text.Length > 0)
      TSR.sort = txtSort.Text;
   TSR.type = txtType.Text;

   // Make the request.
   PI = Service.TextStreamSearchRequest(TSR);

   // Display the results on screen.
   ... Display Code ...
}
```

As the listing shows, the text stream search works very much like other searches in the book, such as the author search. However, unlike other searches in the book, this search doesn't return a total number of results. Consequently, you don't have any way to check the number of possible pages. The only way to detect the last page is to check for an error condition where the response doesn't contain any results. Because the **page** field doesn't work now, the example doesn't show how to perform the last page check.

The `TextStreamRequest` data structure is very flexible. As previously mentioned, the search helps you perform searches based on common text input such as recommendations. Not shown in the code is the `price` field of the `TextStreamRequest` data structure. This field lets you further filter the results by specifying a price range. See Listing 12.4 in Chapter 12 for an example of how to use the price range feature.

Developing a SKU Search

Sometimes you'll want to buy a product from a particular third party vendor on Amazon, but you don't know much more than the vendor's Stock Keeping Unit (SKU) for the product. (Interestingly enough, Amazon actually displays the SKUs for products from some third party vendors such as Wherehouse Music.) Amazon developed a special search for this situation that lets you specify a manufacturer identifier and a SKU for the product. Using these two numbers lets you sidestep the whole issue of learning a new Amazon number for a product.

You can also use a combination of the SKU and some keywords, normally the product name or title. This second approach is more reliable and I recommend you use it whenever possible. The keywords portion of the search can return multiple results for the same SKU—it depends on the popularity of the topic. Amazon Web Services attempts to match both the SKU and the keywords. However, in many cases, the search returns just one product and not any related products.

Listing D.2 shows how to perform a SKU search. You'll find the complete source code for this example in the `\Appendix D\SKUSearchDemo` folder of the source code located on the Sybex Web site.

Listing D.2 Performing a SKU Search

```
private void btnTest_Click(object sender, System.EventArgs e)
{
   SkuRequest           SR;      // The SKU search request.
   ProductInfo          PI;      // Data returned from request.
   AmazonSearchService  Service; // Connection to the service.
   DataRow              DR;      // Output data.
   Int32                Counter; // Loop counting variable.

   // Instantiate the objects.
   SR = new SkuRequest();
   PI = new ProductInfo();
   Service = new AmazonSearchService();

   // Create the SKU search request.
   SR.devtag = txtTag.Text;
   SR.keywords = txtKeywords.Text;
   SR.mode = txtMode.Text;
   SR.sku = txtSKU.Text;
   SR.tag = "webservices-20";
   SR.type = txtType.Text;
   if (txtSort.Text.Length > 0)
      SR.sort = txtSort.Text;

   // Make the request.
   PI = Service.SkuSearchRequest(SR);

   // Display the results on screen.
   ... Display Code ...
}
```

This search works like many others in the book, but you'll find that it's quite fussy about the input you provide. Make sure you provide a SKU and a manufacturer identifier or a SKU and some keywords. Although the service indicated that the search should work with just `devtag`, `mode`, `sku`, `tag`, and `type` field entries, I was never able to get this combination to work. Your results will vary as Amazon continues to work on the Amazon Web Services.

Writing Applications that Rely on Variation Data

Amazon is currently testing a new method of providing data for products that don't quite fit within the usual data structure. For example, clothing can have color and size. Not every piece of clothing will have the same colors or the same sizes, however, so creating a consistent data structure is impossible. The variation data helps you retrieve an indeterminate amount of data about a product that could improve the product description. Here's the example Amazon uses for variation data.

```
<Variations>
  <Variation>
    <Asin>B00007BA9N</Asin>
    <ClothingSize>0X</ClothingSize>
    <ClothingColor>BLACK</ClothingColor>
    <Price>$35.00</Price>
    <ShipDate>09/19/2003</ShipDate>
    <Availability>Usually ships in 1-2 business days</Availability>
  </Variation>
  <Variation>
    <Asin>B00007BA9R</Asin>
    <ClothingSize>1X</ClothingSize>
    <ClothingColor>BLACK</ClothingColor>
    <Price>$35.00</Price>
    <ShipDate>09/19/2003</ShipDate>
    <Availability>Usually ships in 1-2 business days</Availability>
    <MultiMerchant>0</MultiMerchant>
  </Variation>
</Variations>
```

Notice that each entry refers to the same product (an article of clothing in this case), but that the details vary. To avoid confusion, each product variation has a separate ASIN. To order the size 0X item, you'd use the B00007BA9N ASIN, but you'd need to use the B00007BA9R ASIN if you needed the 1X size.

The current WSDL file contains the information needed for the variation data, but tests show that the data isn't available yet. You'll need to use a heavy, rather than a lite, request to obtain this data. Spend some time testing the variation data in your application so that you know it can handle this new data type. Besides adding code to handle situations where a particular piece of variation data isn't available, you might have to consider the order of the data and overcoming situations where the variation data includes unexpected entries.

An Overview of RSS Feeds

A Rich Site Summary (RSS) feed is a kind of publishing service. A Web site that wants to make all or part of its content generally available to the public finds an RSS publisher. Users subscribe to this RSS publisher when they want to receive certain types of information. The information often appears on Web sites as part of a headline news feature. Most vendors use this kind of information publication for news, events, headlines, project updates, discussion group excerpts, and even corporate news. Amazon uses RSS feeds to make people aware of the status of certain browse nodes.

You would subscribe to an RSS feed if you wanted to keep people aware of certain product categories. For example, you would subscribe to an RSS feed for browse node 25 if you want to keep people updated on science fiction and fantasy books. Amazon uses a combination of a browse node search and a special XSLT page to provide the RSS feedback. For example, the following URL will display the RSS feed for browse node 25.

```
http://xml.amazon.com/onca/xml3?t=onfocus&dev-t=amznRss&BrowseNodeSearch=
25&mode=books&bcm=&type=heavy&page=1&ct=text/xml&sort=+salesrank&f=http://
xml.amazon.com/xsl/xml-rss091.xsl
```

Notice that this is a typical browse node search with two exceptions. First, you need to provide a special `dev-t` field entry—`amznRss`. Second, notice that the `f` field no longer equals `xml`, but uses the special `http://xml.amazon.com/xsl/xml-rss091.xsl` page instead. The result of these changes is the XML shown in Figure D.2 that you could add to a Web site or an application.

It's also possible to use other searches to create an RSS feed. For example, you could use a keyword or an author search if you wanted to produce a feed for a specific kind of book. The point is that the XSL page specially formats the XML output to provide information to an RSS reader so that a user gets news pushed to them, rather than digging the information out. The concept is much the same as watching the news on television or picking up a newspaper. The publisher provides content to the information user.

The problem with RSS feeds is that it normally requires special software to use or at least an understanding of XML to create your own RSS reader software. However, you can access two Web sites that have the required software (`http://www.onfocus.com/bookwatch/AmazonRSS.asp` and `http://www.neopoleon.com/blog/chooseFeedGroup.aspx`) and get the RSS feeds that way. These RSS builder sites can reduce the work required to create an RSS feed.

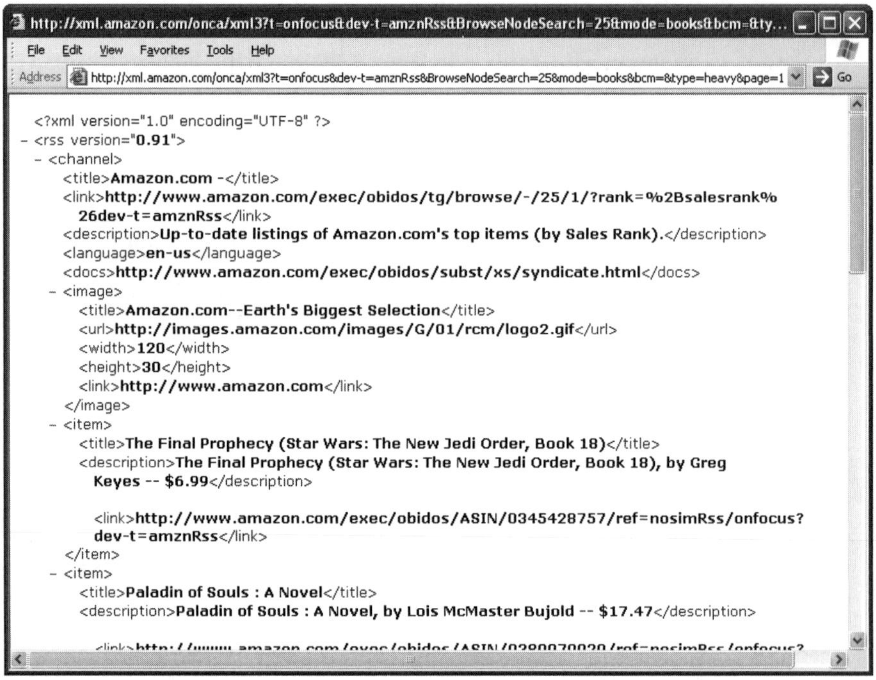

FIGURE D.2:

RSS feeds rely on specially formatted XML.


```
http://xml.amazon.com/onca/xml3?t=onfocus&dev-t=amznRss&BrowseNodeSearch=25&mode=books&bcm=&ty...
File Edit View Favorites Tools Help
Address http://xml.amazon.com/onca/xml3?t=onfocus&dev-t=amznRss&BrowseNodeSearch=25&mode=books&bcm=&type=heavy&page=1  Go

  <?xml version="1.0" encoding="UTF-8" ?>
- <rss version="0.91">
  - <channel>
      <title>Amazon.com -</title>
      <link>http://www.amazon.com/exec/obidos/tg/browse/-/25/1/?rank=%2Bsalesrank%
        26dev-t=amznRss</link>
      <description>Up-to-date listings of Amazon.com's top items (by Sales Rank).</description>
      <language>en-us</language>
      <docs>http://www.amazon.com/exec/obidos/subst/xs/syndicate.html</docs>
    - <image>
        <title>Amazon.com--Earth's Biggest Selection</title>
        <url>http://images.amazon.com/images/G/01/rcm/logo2.gif</url>
        <width>120</width>
        <height>30</height>
        <link>http://www.amazon.com</link>
      </image>
    - <item>
        <title>The Final Prophecy (Star Wars: The New Jedi Order, Book 18)</title>
        <description>The Final Prophecy (Star Wars: The New Jedi Order, Book 18), by Greg
          Keyes -- $6.99</description>

          <link>http://www.amazon.com/exec/obidos/ASIN/0345428757/ref=nosimRss/onfocus?
          dev-t=amznRss</link>
      </item>
    - <item>
        <title>Paladin of Souls : A Novel</title>
        <description>Paladin of Souls : A Novel, by Lois McMaster Bujold -- $17.47</description>
```


You can obtain more information about Amazon's RSS feed program at `http://www.amazon.com/exec/obidos/subst/xs/syndicate.html/002-3718369-4641611`. The Code101.com site at `http://www.code101.com/Code101/DisplayArticle.aspx?cid=41` provides a simple tutorial on RSS feeds.

Glossary

This book includes a glossary so that you can find terms and acronyms easily. It has several important features you need to know about. First, every acronym in the entire book appears here—even if there's a better than even chance you already know what the acronym stands for. (The book does exclude common acronyms such as units of measure and most file extensions because these terms are easy to find in other sources and most people know what they mean.) This way, there isn't any doubt that you'll always find everything you need to use the book properly.

Second, these definitions are specific to the book. In other words, when you look through this glossary, you're seeing the words defined in the context in which they're used in this book. This might or might not always coincide with current industry usage since the computer industry changes the meaning of words so often.

Finally, I've used a conversational tone for the definitions here in most cases. This means that the definitions might sacrifice a bit of puritanical accuracy for the sake of better understanding. The purpose of this glossary is to define the terms in such a way that there's less room for misunderstanding the intent of the book as a whole.

What to Do If You Don't Find It Here

While this glossary is a complete view of the words and acronyms in the book, you'll run into situations when you need to know more. No matter how closely I look at terms throughout the book, there's always a chance I'll miss the one acronym or term that you really need to know. In addition to the technical information found in the book, I've directed your attention to numerous online sources of information throughout the book and few of the terms the Web site owners use will appear here unless I also chose to use them in the book. Fortunately, many sites on the Internet provide partial or complete glossaries to fill in the gaps:

Acronym Finder `http://www.acronymfinder.com/`

Free Online Dictionary Of Computing (FOLDOC) `http://nightflight.com/foldoc/`

Microsoft Encarta `http://encarta.msn.com/`

TechDis Accessibility Database `http://www.niad.sussex.ac.uk/glossary.cfm`

Webopedia `http://webopedia.internet.com/`

yourDictionary.com `http://www.yourdictionary.com/`

Let's talk about these Web sites a little more. Web sites normally provide acronyms or glossary entries—not both. An acronym site only tells you what the letters in the acronym stand for, it doesn't provide definitions to explain what the acronym means in everyday computer use. The two extremes in this list are Acronym Finder (acronyms only) and Webopedia (full-fledged glossary entries).

Acronym Finder has the advantage of providing an extremely large list of acronyms from which to choose. At the time of this writing, the Acronym Finder sported 164,000 acronyms. Many of the acronyms have nothing to do with computers—making Acronym Finder an excellent resource for acronyms of all types.

Most of the Web sites that you'll find for computer terms are free. In some cases, such as Microsoft's Encarta, you have to pay for the support provided. However, these locations are still worth the effort because they ensure you understand the terms used in the jargon-filled world of computing.

Webopedia has become one of my favorite places to visit because it provides encyclopedic coverage of many computer terms and includes links to other Web sites. I like the fact that if I don't find a word I need, I can submit it to the Webopedia staff for addition to their dictionary, making Webopedia a community-supported dictionary of the highest quality.

One of the interesting features of the yourDictionary.com Web site is that it provides access to more than one dictionary and in more than one language. If English isn't your native tongue, then this is the Web site of choice.

A

Accessibility A measure of a user's ability to interact with an application. For example, applications should provide both mouse and keyboard access to every control to ensure the user can reach the control for use. In addition to direct user support, an application should support all devices without providing specialized support for a particular device unless necessary. A Braille input device should receive no special treatment beyond that required for a keyboard.

Active Server Pages (ASP) A special type of scripting language environment used by Windows servers equipped with Internet Information Server (IIS). This specialized scripting language environment helps the developer create flexible Web applications that include server scripts written in a number of languages such as VBScript, JavaScript, JScript, and PerlScript. The use of variables and other features, such as access to server variables, helps the developer create scripts that can compensate for user and environmental needs as well as security concerns. ASP uses HTML to display content to the user. Recent extensions to ASP in the form of Active Server Pages eXtended (ASPX) provide a broader range of application support functionality, improved debugging, new features such as "code behind," and improved performance.

Amazon Standard Item Number (ASIN) A unique identifier that Amazon assigns to every product offered on its Web site. The ASIN makes it easier for buyers to locate products and developers to ensure an application user is seeing the intended product details. In some cases, the ASIN is the same as the general product identification. For example, the ASIN is the same as the ISBN for a book.

Amazon Web Services (AWS) A set of methods and properties that enables a developer to access the Amazon database using technologies such as Simple Object Access Protocol (SOAP) and eXtensible Markup Language (XML) over HyperText Transfer Protocol (HTTP). Amazon publishes the services using the Amazon Web Services Kit and through programmatic interfaces such as Web Services Description Language (WSDL). A few people use AWS as an acronym for Amazon Web Services.

Amazon Web Services Kit A special product from Amazon that helps developers create Amazon Web Services applications. The kit consists of a help system and several examples using languages such as Java and PHP.

API See Application Programming Interface

Applet A helper or utility application that normally performs a task within a specialized environment such as a browser or as part of an operating system. Java is one of the most commonly used languages for creating applets for browser applications. Another example is the Control Panel applications used to configure Windows. In both cases, the applications perform a limited task within a specialized environment.

Application The complete program or group of programs. An application is a complete environment for performing one or more related tasks.

Application Programming Interface (API) A method of defining a standard set of function calls and other interface elements. It usually defines the interface between a high-level language and the lower-level elements used by a device driver or operating system. The ultimate goal is to provide some type of service to an application that requires access to the operating system or device feature set.

Area Identifier A special number representing a particular country or geographic on Amazon. A developer could use the area identifier to locate products or services associated with a particular country.

Array A structure that acts like an in-memory database. An array provides random or sequential access to each element by number (also called a subscript). Arrays normally contain a single dimension. In some cases, arrays provide multidimensional access to data. A multidimensional array has the same number of elements in each sub-array in a given dimension. Jagged arrays treat each dimension as a separate sub-array, which means that each sub-array can contain a different number of elements.

ASIN See Amazon Standard Item Number

ASP See Active Server Pages

Associate Tag A special number issued by Amazon to individuals or companies selling products offered for sale on the Amazon Web site. The individual or company uses the number to receive credit for sales generated by an associated Web site.

AT&T American Telephone and Telegraph

AWS See Amazon Web Services

B

Bandwidth A measure of the amount of data a device can transfer in a given time. For example, the amount of data a processor can send to memory every second. In many cases, bandwidth also considers software limitations, such as the estimated bandwidth of an Internet connection.

BBB Better Business Bureau

Binary 1. A numbering system that only uses two digits: 0 and 1. 2. A method used to store worksheets, graphic files, and other non-text information. The data store can appear in memory, but most often appears in a file on disk. While you can use the DOS TYPE command to send these files to the display, the contents of the file remain unreadable. Other binary files include programs with extensions of EXE, DLL, or COM.

Browse Identifier A special identifier used to categorize items in the Amazon database. Using this identifier helps a developer locate product groups based on their type, such as computer books. The browser identifier list is hierarchical, with product categories becoming more specific.

Browser A special application, such as Internet Explorer, Opera, or Netscape, normally used to display data downloaded from the Internet. The most common form of Internet data is the HTML (HyperText Markup Language) page. However, modern browsers can also display various types of graphics and even standard desktop application files such as Word for Windows documents directly. The actual capabilities provided by a browser vary widely depending on the software vendor and platform.

Browser Plug-in An external application that a browser calls to help it perform certain tasks. For example, the browser could call upon the application to display a specific file type such as a PDF. The browser plug-in can take the form of a library or a standalone application. In many cases, browser documentation will also refer to them as helper applications.

C

CAD See Computer-Aided Drafting

Cascading Style Sheets (CSS) A method for defining a standard Web page template. This may include headings, standard icons, backgrounds, and other features that would tend to give each page at a particular Web site the same appearance. The reason for using CSS includes speed of creating a Web site (it takes less time if the developer doesn't have to create an overall design for each page) and consistency. Changing the overall appearance of a Web site also becomes as easy as changing the style sheet instead of each page alone. CSS is also a standards supported technology, so it represents an easy method for developers to create Web pages that will work in standards compliant browsers.

CD Compact disk

CGI See Common Gateway Interface

Client The requestor and recipient of data, services, or other resources from a file or other server type. This term can refer to a workstation or an application. Often used in conjunction with the term *server*, this is usually another PC or an application.

CLR See Common Language Runtime

Common Gateway Interface (CGI) One of the more common methods of transferring data from a client machine to a Web server on the Internet. CGI is a specification that defines how a Web server can launch EXEs and communicate with them. A developer normally writes a GCI application using a low-level language such as C. CGI receives input through the standard input device and output data through the standard output device. There are two basic data transfer types. The user can send new information to the server or can query data already existing on the server. A data entry form asking for the user's name and address is an example of the first type of transaction. A search engine page on the Internet (a page that helps the user find information on other sites) is an example of the second type of transaction. The Web server normally provides some type of feedback for the user by transmitting a new page of information once the CGI application is complete. This could be as simple as an acknowledgment for data entry or a list of Internet sites for a data query.

Common Language Runtime (CLR) The engine used to interpret managed applications within the .NET Framework. All Visual Studio .NET languages that produce managed applications can use the same runtime engine. The major advantages of this approach include extensibility (you can add other languages) and reduced code size (you don't need a separate runtime for each language).

Compiler A program that converts English-like statements into machine instructions in an executable or intermediate form. In some cases, the executable code can run without assistance on the host machine (called a native executable). In other cases, the intermediate code requires compilation into an executable form. This secondary form can rely on an interpreter (BASIC) or runtime engine (Java), or it can use a secondary compiler or linker to change an object format into a standard native executable (C).

Computer-Aided Drafting (CAD) A special type of graphics program used for creating, printing, storing, and editing architectural, electrical, mechanical, or other forms of engineering drawings. CAD programs normally provide precise measuring capabilities and libraries of predefined objects, such as sinks, desks, resistors, and gears.

Connectivity A measure of the interactions between clients and servers. In many cases, connectivity begins with the local machine and the interactions between applications and components. Local Area Networks (LANs) introduce another level of connectivity with machine-to-machine communications. Finally, Wide Area Networks (WANs), Metro Area Networks (MANs), intranets, and the Internet all introduce further levels of connectivity concerns.

Cookie One or more special files used by an Internet browser to store site-specific settings or other information specific to Web pages. The purpose of this file is to store the value of one or more variables so that the Web page can restore them the next time the user visits a site. A Webmaster always saves and restores the cookie as part of some Web page programming task using a programming language such as JavaScript, Java, VBScript, or CGI. In most cases, this is the only file that a Webmaster can access on the client site's hard drive. The cookie could appear in one or more files anywhere on the hard drive, depending on the browser currently in use. Microsoft Internet Explorer uses one file for each site storing a cookie and places them in the Cookies folder that normally appears under the main Windows directory or within a user specific directory (such as the `\Documents and Settings` folder). Netscape Navigator uses a single file named `COOKIE.TXT` to store all of the cookies from all sites. This file normally appears in the main Navigator folder.

Cracker A hacker (computer expert) who uses their skills for misdeeds on computer systems where they have little or no authorized access. A cracker normally possesses specialty software that allows easier access to the target network. In most cases, crackers require extensive amounts of time to break the security for a system before they can enter it. Some sources call a cracker a black hat hacker.

CSS See Cascading Style Sheets

D

Data Source Name (DSN) A name assigned to an Open Database Connectivity (ODBC) connection. Applications use the DSN to make the connection to the database and gain access to specific database resources such as tables. The DSN always contains the name of the database server, the database, and (optionally) a resource like a query or table. Many database technologies such as OLE-DB rely on the use of DSN connection information.

Database Management System (DBMS) A method for storing and retrieving data based on tables, forms, queries, reports, fields, and other data elements. Each field represents a specific piece of data, such as an employee's last name. Records are made up of one or more fields. Each record is one complete entry in a table. A table contains one type of data, such as the names and addresses of all the employees in a company. It's composed of records (rows) and fields (columns), just like the tables you see in books. A database may contain one or more related tables. It may include a list of employees in one table, for example, and the pay records for each of those employees in a second table. Sometimes also referred to as a Relational Database Management System (RDBMS) that includes products such as SQL Server and Oracle.

DBMS See Database Management System

DCOM See Distributed Component Object Model

Delimiter 1. A special symbol or symbols used to separate text. For example, many programming languages use the single (') or double (") quote to separate text elements. 2. A boundary between two different objects. The boundary normally consists of a special symbol or group of symbols. A delimited file contains variable length records. Each field normally uses a comma as a delimiter. Each record normally uses a carriage return as a delimiter.

Developer Token A special identifier issued by Amazon to Amazon Web Services developers. The developer uses this token for identification purposes when creating an Amazon Web Services application.

Digital Video Disk (DVD) A high capacity optical storage media with capacities of 4.7 GB to 17 GB and data transfer rates of 600 KBps to 1.3 GBps. A single DVD can hold the contents of an entire movie or approximately 7.4 CD-ROMs. DVDs come in several formats that allow read-only or read-write access. All DVD drives include a second laser assembly used to read existing CD-ROMs. Some magazines will also use the term digital versatile disk for this storage media.

Distributed Component Object Model (DCOM) A transport protocol that works with the component object model (COM), and is used for distributed application development. This protocol enables data transfers across the Internet or other non-local sources, but is usually limited to a Local Area Network (LAN) or Wide Area Network (WAN) environment. DCOM adds the capability to perform asynchronous, as well as synchronous, data transfers between machines. The use of asynchronous transfers prevents the client application from becoming blocked as it waits for the server to respond.

DLL See Dynamic Link Library

DSN See Data Source Name

DVD See Digital Video Disk

Dynamic Data Information that changes regularly due to internal or external events, as a result of the nature of the data, or consistent with a systematic or mathematical progression. For example, an application can provide automatic updates as it detects changes in the underlying data used for presentation. Many research sources, such as the Internet, now rely on dynamic data to reduce the effects of data aging.

Dynamic Link Library (DLL) A specific form of application code loaded into memory by request. It's not executable by itself like an EXE is. A DLL does contain one or more discrete routines that an application may use to provide specific features. For example, a DLL could provide a common set of file dialogs used to access information on the hard drive. More than one application can use the functions provided by a DLL, reducing overall memory requirements when more than one application is running. DLLs have a number of purposes. For example, they can contain device specific code in the form of a device driver. Some types of COM objects also rely on DLLs.

E

Error Trapping The additional code required to detect, analyze, repair, report, and overcome errors in an application. An error trapping routine normally locates the precise origin of the error, determines the error type, and defines a course of action for repairing the error when possible. If the application can't recover, the error trapping routine helps the application fail gracefully after reporting the source and cause of the error to the application user.

Escaped Character A technique for representing a character when using the actual character would present interpretation problems. This technique is most commonly used in Web applications. For example, the quote (') and double quote (") often cause problems, as do the angle brackets (<>). The character escaping technique would replace these charaters with ', ", <, and > respectively.

Exchange Identifier A special number representing a third party vendor on Amazon. Every third party vendor has a unique number. A developer can use the exchange identifier to location products the vendor sells, as well as information about the vendor.

eXtensible Markup Language (XML) 1. A method used to store information in an organized manner. The storage technique relies on hierarchical organization and uses special statements called tags to separate each storage element. Each tag defines a data attribute and can contain properties that further define each data element. 2. A standardized Web page design language used to incorporate data structuring within standard HTML documents. For example, you could use XML to display database information using something other than forms or tables. It's actually a lightweight version of Standardized Generalized Markup Language (SGML) and is supported by the SGML community. XML also supports tag extensions that allow various parts of a Web-based application to exchange information. For example, once a user makes a choice within a catalog, that information could be added to an order entry form with a minimum of effort on the part of the developer. Since XML is easy to extend, some developers look at it as more of a base specification for other languages, rather than a complete language.

eXtensible Style Language (XSL) This term is also listed as eXtensible Stylesheet Language by some sources. XSL is a technology that separates the method of presentation from the actual content of either an eXtensible Markup Language (XML) or HyperText Markup Language (HTML) page. The XSL document contains all of the required formatting information so that the content remains in pure form. This is the second style language submitted to the World Wide Web Consortium (W3C) for consideration. The first specification was for Cascading Style Sheets (CSS). XSL documents use an XML-like format.

eXtensible Style Language Transformation (XSLT) The language used within the eXtensible Style Language (XSL) to transform the content provided in an eXtensible Markup Language (XML) file into a form for display on screen or printing. An XSL processor combines XML content with the formatting instructions provided by XSLT and outputs a new document or document fragment. XSLT is a World Wide Web Consortium (W3C) standard.

F

Fault Tolerance The ability of an object (application, device, or other entity) to recover from an error. For example, the fault tolerance provided by a transaction server allows a network to recover from potential data loss induced by a system or use failure. Another example of fault tolerance is the ability of a Redundant Array of Inexpensive Disks (RAID) system to recover from a hard drive failure.

G

Graphical User Interface (GUI) 1. A method of displaying information that depends on both hardware capabilities and software instructions. A GUI uses the graphics capability of a display adapter to improve communication between the computer and its user. Using a GUI involves a large investment in both programming and hardware resources. 2. A system of icons and graphic images that replace the character-mode menu system used by many older machines including "green screen" terminals that are connected to mainframes and sometimes to cash registers. The GUI can ride on top of another operating system (such as DOS, Linux, and UNIX) or reside as part of the operating system itself (such as the Macintosh and Windows). Advantages of a GUI are ease of use and high-resolution graphics. Disadvantages include cost, higher workstation hardware requirements, and lower performance over a similar system using a character mode interface.

GUI See Graphical User Interface

H

Hacker An individual who works with computers at a low level (hardware or software), especially in the area of security. A hacker normally possesses specialty software or other tools that allows easier access to the target hardware or software application or network. The media defines two types of hackers that include those that break into systems for ethical purposes and those that do it to damage the system in some way. The proper term for the second group is crackers (see *Cracker* for details). Some people have started to call the first group "ethical hackers" or "white hat hackers" to prevent confusion. Ethical hackers normally work for security firms that specialize in finding holes in a company's security. However, hackers work in a wide range of computer arenas. For example, a person who writes low-level code (like that found in a device driver) after reverse engineering an existing driver is technically a hacker. The main emphasis of a hacker is to work for the benefit of others in the computer industry.

Handheld Device Markup Language (HDML) A technology that predates most standardized efforts, such as the Wireless Access Protocol (WAP), for transmitting Internet content to cellular telephones. It is a proprietary language that users can only view using OpenWave browsers. The associated transport protocol is the Handheld Device Transport Protocol (HDTP). A user types a request into the phone, which is transferred to a gateway server using HDTP. The gateway server translates the request to HTTP, which it sends to the Web server. The Web server provides specialized HDML content, which the gateway server transfers to the cellular telephone using HDTP. To use this protocol, the Web server must understand the text/x-hdml Multipurpose Internet Mail Extensions (MIME) type.

Hashed Message Authentication Code (HMAC) A technique for identifying a particular sender by creating a code based on all or part of the original message or message stream. The resulting number uniquely identifies the sender. The technique is secure because only the original sender can generate the HMAC number, which means only the original sender can authenticate using the number. Many developers rely on the techniques presented in standards such as Request for Comment (RFC) 3537 for creating secure transactions based on HMAC.

HDML See Handheld Device Markup Language

Hierarchical 1. A method of arranging data within a database that relies on a tree-like node structure, rather than a relational structure. 2. A method of displaying information on screen that relies on an indeterminate number of nodes connected to a root node. 3. A chart or graph in which the elements are arranged in ranks. The ranks usually follow an order of simple to complex or higher to lower.

HMAC See Hashed Message Authentication Code

HTML See HyperText Markup Language

HTTP See HyperText Transfer Protocol

HyperText Markup Language (HTML) 1. A data presentation and description (markup) language for the Internet that depends on the use of tags (keywords within angle brackets <>) to display formatted information on screen in a non-platform-specific manner. The non-platform-specific nature of this markup language makes it difficult to perform some basic tasks such as placement of a screen element at a specific location. However, the language does provide for the use of fonts, color, and various other enhancements onscreen. There are also tags for displaying graphic images. Scripting tags for using scripting languages such as VBScript and JavaScript are available, although not all browsers support this addition. The <OBJECT> tag addition allows the use of ActiveX controls. 2. One method of displaying text, graphics, and sound on the Internet. HTML provides an ASCII-formatted page of information read by a special application called a browser. Depending on the browser's capabilities, some key words are translated into graphics elements, sounds, or text with special characteristics, such as color, font, or other attributes. Most browsers discard any keywords they don't understand, allowing browsers of various capabilities to explore the same page without problem. Obviously, there's a loss of capability if a browser doesn't support a specific keyword.

HyperText Transfer Protocol (HTTP) One of several common data transfer protocols for the Internet. HTTP normally transfers textual data of some type. For example, the HyperText Markup Language (HTML) relies on HTTP to transfer the Web pages it defines from the server to the client. The eXtensible Markup Language and Simple Object Access Protocol (SOAP) also commonly rely on HTTP to transfer data between client and server. It's important to note that HTTP is separate from the data it transfers. For example, it's possible for SOAP to use the Simple Mail Transfer Protocol (SMTP) to perform data transfers between client and server.

I

IDE See Integrated Development Environment

IETF See Internet Engineering Task Force

IIS See Internet Information Server

Integrated Development Environment (IDE) A programming language front end that provides all the tools you need to write an application through a single editor. The IDE normally includes support for development language help, access to any tools required to support the language, a compiler, and a debugger. Some IDEs include support for advanced features such as automatic completion of language statements and balloon help showing the syntax for functions and other language elements. Many IDEs also use color or highlighting to emphasize specific language elements or constructs. Older DOS programming language products provided several utilities—one for each of the main programming tasks. Most (if not all) Windows programming languages provide some kind of IDE support.

International Standard Book Number (ISBN) A unique 10-digit identifier assigned to a book. Every book has a different identifier. In fact, different book formats (such as hard cover and paperback) will have different ISBNs, even if the content is the same. The ISBN contains four groups of numbers: the group identifier (first number), the publisher identifier (next four numbers), the title identifier (next four numbers), and the check digit (last number).

Internet Engineering Task Force (IETF) The standards group tasked with finding solutions to pressing technology problems on the Internet. This group can approve standards created both within the organization itself and outside the organization as part of other group efforts. For example, Microsoft has requested the approval of several new Internet technologies through this group. If approved, the technologies would become an Internet-wide standard performing data transfer and other specific kinds of tasks.

Internet Information Server (IIS) Microsoft's full-fledged Web server that normally runs under the Windows Server operating system. IIS includes all the features that you'd normally expect with a Web server: FTP and HTTP protocols along with both mail and news services. Older versions of IIS also support the Gopher protocol; newer versions don't provide this support because most Web sites no longer need it.

Internet Server Application Programming Interface (ISAPI) A set of function calls and interface elements designed to make using Microsoft's Internet Information Server (IIS) easier. Essentially, this set of API calls provides the programmer with access to the server itself. This technology makes it easier to provide full server access to the Internet server through a series of ActiveX controls, without the use of a scripting language. There are two forms of ISAPI: filters and extensions. An extension replaces script-based technologies like CGI. Its main purpose is to provide dynamic content to the user. A filter can extend the server itself by monitoring various events like user requests for access in the background. You can use a filter to create various types of new services like extended logging or specialized security schemes. Most developers use technologies such as Active Server Pages (ASP) in place of ISAPI because these technologies are easier to use. For example, ASP makes it easy to modify a file without the need to recompile it. However, ISAPI is still used for speed critical applications such as the Simple Object Access Protocol (SOAP) listener used by some SOAP implementations.

Internet Service Provider (ISP) A vendor that provides one or more Internet-related services through a dial-up, Digital Subscriber Line (DSL), Integrated Services Digital Network (ISDN), or other outside connection. Normal services include email, newsgroup access, full Internet Web site access, and personal Web page hosting.

ISAPI See Internet Server Application Programming Interface

ISBN See International Standard Book Number

ISP See Internet Service Provider

J

Java DataBase Connectivity (JDBC) A method of providing database interoperability similar to Open Database Connectivity (ODBC). This form of connectivity is Java specific and other applications require a JDBC-ODBC bridge to provide the necessary interoperability between the two systems. JDBC always uses SQL statements to request data from the database manager. Although ODBC is language independent, it has limited platform support. JDBC is language specific, but runs on any platform that supports Java.

Java Development Kit (JDK) A special set of application development tools, resources, example code, help files, and other resources designed to help a programmer create Java applications. The JDK normally contains a full set of development tools and a copy of the Java Runtime Environment (JRE). However, most developers will require one or more third party solutions to create a complex Java application. For example, unlike many languages today, Java doesn't provide SOAP support, so the developer would require a third party library to create an application that relies on SOAP.

Java Runtime Environment (JRE) Another name for the Java Virtual Machine (JVM). This set of files provides Java support on the host machine allowing it to run Java applications.

Java Virtual Machine (JVM) The application used to interpret the Java language originally developed by Sun Microsystems. This includes both text and byte code .CLASS files containing common routines. Java is similar to C++, but eliminates many of the complex programming constructs and uses a more restrictive security scheme. Many operating systems have a Java Virtual Machine including most versions of Windows, Mac OS, and Unix. The use of text files means that Java applets can run on any number of operating system platforms without modifications, but the use of an interpreter implies slower execution speed.

JDBC See Java DataBase Connectivity

JDK See Java Development Kit

JRE See Java Runtime Environment

JVM See Java Virtual Machine

L

LCID See Locale Identifier

Listmania! Identifier A special number representing a unique list of items on Amazon. For example, a group could create a Listmania! category for scary movies. The list would have a unique identifier that a developer could use to locate movies of this type.

Locale Identifier (LCID) A number that uniquely identifies a country, language, or other nationalistic information. An application, online resource, or data manager uses the LCID to provide specific information, services, or resources in a form that the user can understand. For example, many applications support more than one language and the application would use the LCID to change the prompts to match the user's language.

Loop A method of running repetitive instructions. Most languages implement several kinds of loop instructions that include specific counts or Boolean terminations. An example of a specific count loop is a structure supported by most languages, which processes a set of instructions a specific number of times and then stops. An example of a Boolean termination is the while structure that continues processing instructions until the terminating condition meets a specific requirement such as variable equality.

M

Marshal The act of making data created by one object accessible and acceptable to another object. The process of marshaling usually includes moving the data from one memory space to another memory space. The marshaling process could also include some type of data conversion. The type of data conversion depends on the requirements of both objects and the data types that they support.

N

Node 1. A single element in a file that might contain a number of leaf elements. The file normally couples nodes into a hierarchical structure, such as the structure used by the eXtensible Markup Language (XML). Some database systems also use the hierarchical structure of nodes and leaves to make data easier or faster to locate. 2. A single element in a network. In most cases, the term *node* refers to a single workstation connected to the network. It can also refer to a bridge, router, or file server. It doesn't refer to cabling, passive, or active elements that don't directly interface with the network at the logical level.

O

ODBC See Open Database Connectivity

Open Database Connectivity (ODBC) One of several methods for exchanging data between DBMSs. In most cases, this involves three steps: installing an appropriate driver, adding a source to the ODBC applet in the Control Panel, and using specialized statements, such as Structured Query Language (SQL), to access the database.

P

P3P See Platform for Privacy Preferences

Parse The act of reducing a string or other data structure to its constituent parts. For example, spreadsheets normally break words and numbers apart using the spaces between them as the break point. Developers use a multitude of application programming techniques to perform data element parsing and some object technology even includes a Parse() method.

PDA See Personal Digital Assistant

Personal Digital Assistant (PDA) A small handheld device such as a Palm Pilot or Pocket PC. These devices are normally used for personal tasks such as taking notes and maintaining an itinerary during business trips. Some PDAs rely on special operating systems and lack any standard application support. However, newer PDAs include some level of standard application support, because vendors are supplying specialized compilers for them. In addition, you'll find common applications included, such as browsers and application office suites that include word processing and spreadsheet support.

Personal Web Server (PWS) A less capable version of Internet Information Server (IIS) that's designed to provided limited Web access on an intranet. PWS isn't designed to provide the same level of services as IIS, but it does provide enough capability for a small company intranet or for a developer's test setup.

PHP PHP Hypertext Processor

Platform A description of the combination of software and hardware used to create a computing system. For example, many users use a combination of the Windows operating system and an Intel processor. The combination often appears as the Wintel platform. In some cases, a discussion will only use the operating system as the basis for a platform. A developer might create applications only for the Windows platform. The use of the term *platform* is often ambiguous and requires the actual platform type to make the meaning clear.

Platform for Privacy Preferences (P3P) A World-wide Web Consortium (W3C) sponsored technique for ensuring privacy through specialized programming techniques. The specification defines methods of communicating information requests, use, storage technique, and requirements to the requestor. The requestor then decides whether the requirements are acceptable and optionally transfers the necessary information.

Pocket PC A mobile, handheld device used to perform any of a number of computing tasks. A Pocket PC normally runs some form of advanced mobile operating system such as Windows CE or Windows XP. Most developers differentiate a Pocket PC from a Palm handheld device by the enhanced processing power, greater number of features, and larger display of the Pocket PC. A Pocket PC is also bulkier than a Palm, making it less suitable for some applications.

PWS See Personal Web Server

R

Remote Procedure Call (RPC) One of several methods for accessing data within another application. RPC is designed to look for the application first on the local workstation, and then across the network at the applications stored on other workstations.

Rich Site Summary (RSS) A technology that enables a content creator to register content with a publisher using specially formatted eXtensible Markup Language (XML) data. Subscribers access the content through the publisher. Content creators use this technology, originally developed by Netscape, to output information such a news feeds, product announcements, events, and other items of general or specific interest. Also known as Resource Description Framework (RDF) Site Summary.

RIM Research in Motion

RPC See Remote Procedure Call

RSS See Rich Site Summary

S

Schema A formal method for describing the structure of a database, storage technology, or data transfer technique such as XML. The schema defines the requirements for constructing the object in question. For example, a schema for a relational database would include information on the structure of tables, fields, and relations within the database.

Script Usually associated with an interpreted macro language used to create simple applications, productivity enhancers, or automated data manipulators. Most operating systems support at least one scripting language. You'll also find scripting capability in many higher end applications such as Web browsers and word processors. Scripts are normally used to write small utility type applications rather than large-scale applications that require the use of a compiled language. In addition, many script languages are limited in their access of the full set of operating system features.

SDK See Software Development Kit

Secure Socket Layer (SSL) A digital signature technology used for exchanging information between a client and a server. Essentially an SSL-compliant server will request a digital certificate from the client machine. The client can likewise request a digital certificate from the server. Companies or individuals obtain these digital certificates from a third party vendor like VeriSign or other trusted source that can vouch for the identity of both parties.

Security Token A number or other unique symbol used to identify a requestor (user or other entity). The security token acts as a key that allows a requestor to obtain resources from a secure location.

Seller Identifier A special number that identifies a particular seller on Amazon. A third party seller might not be associated with a particular company and some companies have more than one seller. A developer can use the seller identifier to learn more about the products and services the seller offers. In addition, the seller identifier helps the developer locate information about the seller, such as customer comments.

Simple Mail Transfer Protocol (SMTP) One of the most commonly used protocols to transfer text (commonly mail) messages between clients and servers. This is a stream-based protocol designed to allow query, retrieval, posting, and distribution of mail messages. Normally, this protocol is used in conjunction with other mail retrieval protocols like point of presence (POP). However, not all uses of SMTP involve email data transfer. Some Simple Object Access Protocol (SOAP) applications have also relied on SMTP to transfer application data.

Simple Object Access Protocol (SOAP) A Microsoft-sponsored protocol that provides the means for exchanging data between COM and foreign component technologies like Common Object Request Broker Architecture (CORBA) using XML as an intermediary. SOAP is often used as the basis for Web services communication. However, a developer could also use SOAP on a LAN or in any other environment where machine-to-machine communication is required and the two target machines provide the required infrastructure.

SKU Stock Keeping Unit

SLN See Solution File

SmartPhone A special form of the cellular telephone that normally includes a larger display, better processing capabilities, and more memory. The SmartPhone makes some types of advanced development possible. However, a SmartPhone doesn't possess the same capabilities of some handheld devices such as the Pocket PC or Palm. Some programming environments, such as Visual Studio .NET, provide special support for the SmartPhone.

SMTP See Simple Mail Transfer Protocol

SOAP See Simple Object Access Protocol

Software Development Kit (SDK) A special add-on to an operating system or an application that describes how to access its internal features. For example, an SDK for Windows would show how to create a File Open dialog box. Programmers use an SDK to learn how to access special Windows components such as the Component Object Model (COM) or the Media Player.

Solution File (SLN) The file used by Visual Studio and other development environments to store application settings such as special file views and a list of the files contained within the application. The solution file is the central storage location for application-specific information that doesn't affect the actual application code.

SSL See Secure Socket Layer

Static Data Information that doesn't change. For example, many Web sites provide static data output; the information remains the same from visit to visit.

Store Identifier A unique identifier that Amazon assigns to a store that lists products or services. This identifier often appears on the Amazon Web site listing; don't confuse it with the seller identifier.

T

TCP/IP See Transmission Control Protocol/Internet Protocol

Transaction Identifier A number or other indicator used to identify a data exchange between client and server. The transaction identifier serves to maintain the link between individual transactions.

Transmission Control Protocol/Internet Protocol (TCP/IP) A standard communication line protocol (set of rules) developed by the United States Department of Defense. The protocol defines how two devices talk to each other. TCP defines a communication methodology where it guarantees packet delivery and also ensures the packets appear at the recipient in the same order they were sent. IP defines the packet characteristics.

U

Uniform Resource Locator (URL) A text representation of a specific location on the Internet. URLs normally include the protocol (http:// for example), the target location (World Wide Web or www), the domain or server name (mycompany), and a domain type (com for commercial). It can also include a hierarchical location within that Web site. The URL usually specifies a particular file on the Web server, although in some situations a Web server will use a default filename. For example, asking the browser to find `http://www.mycompany.com`, would probably display the `DEFAULT.HTM` or `INDEX.HTM` file at that location. The actual default filename depends on the Web server used. In some cases, the default filename is configurable and could be any of a number of files. For example, Internet Information Server (IIS) offers this feature, so the developer can use anything from an HTM, to an ASP, to an XML file as the default.

Universal Product Code (UPC) A 12-digit numbering system used to uniquely identify products of all types. The UPC is normally accompanied by a bar code that makes the number computer readable using scanning technology. A central agency manages the number list and each country has one agency that manages the pool of numbers assigned to that country. For example, the Uniform Code Council (UCC) manages the 12-digit numbers for North America. A UPC contains three groups of numbers: company prefix (6 digits), item reference number (5 digits), and check digit (1 digit). The 13-digit European Article Numbering (EAN) system is compatible with UPC to a point; all systems that read EAN can also read UPC, but the reverse isn't always true.

UPC See Universal Product Code

URL See Uniform Resource Locator

V

Variation Data Specialized information associated with an Amazon search, such as clothing size or color. In most cases, variation data describes the product in a way that the standard data structures, such as ProductInfo, won't allow. The amount of variation data depends on the product; some products won't include any variation data, while other products will include a large quantity of variation data.

VBA See Visual Basic for Applications

VISA Visa International Service Association

Visual Basic for Applications (VBA) A true subset of the Visual Basic language. This form of Visual Basic is normally used within applications in place of a standard macro language. Normally, you can't create stand-alone applications using this language in its native environment; however, you could move a VBA program to Visual Basic and compile it there.

Voice eXtensible Markup Language (VoiceXML) A speech Application Programming Interface (API) based on the eXtensible Markup Language (XML). The main vendors supporting this standard are AT&T, IBM, Lucent Technologies, and Motorola. VoiceXML relies on a series of elements (specially formatted tags) to perform speech input, output, configuration, and control.

VoiceXML See Voice eXtensible Markup Language

W

W3C See World Wide Web Consortium

WAP See Wireless Access Protocol

Web Services Description Language (WSDL) A method for describing a Web-based application that is accessible through an Internet connection, also known as a service. The file associated with this description contains the service description, port type, interface description, individual method names, and parameter types. A WSDL relies on namespace support to provide descriptions of common elements such as data types. Most WSDL files include references to two or more resources maintained by standards organizations to ensure compatibility across implementations.

Wireless Access Protocol (WAP) A method of providing secure access for mobile devices of all types to Web-based application content through a gateway. The underlying technology works much like Handheld Device Markup Language (HDML), but using standardized and secure access techniques. This technology supports most mobile networks including Cellular Digital Packet Data (CDPD), Code-Division Multiple Access (CDMA), Global System for Mobile Communications (GSM), and Time Division Multiple Access (TDMA). Supported mobile device operating systems include PalmOS, EPOC, Windows CE, FLEXOS, OS/9, and JavaOS. The technology can support pages in either Wireless Markup Language (WML) or HyperText Markup Language (HTML) format; although, WML is preferred because it better supports mobile device requirements.

World Wide Web Consortium (W3C) A standards organization essentially devoted to Internet security issues, but also involved in other issues such as the special <OBJECT> tag required by Microsoft to implement ActiveX technology. The W3C also defines a wealth of other HTML and XML standards. The W3C first appeared on the scene in December 1994, when it endorsed SSL (Secure Sockets Layer). In February 1995, it also endorsed application-level security for the Internet. Its current project is the Digital Signatures Initiative—W3C presented it in May 1996 in Paris.

WSDL See Web Services Description Language

X

XML See eXtensible Markup Language

XSL See eXtensible Style Language

XSLT See eXtensible Style Language Transformation

Z

Zip A file that acts as a container for other files. The Zip normally provides some level of data compression to make the resulting package smaller than the individual files. Some operating systems such as Windows XP provide built-in support for the Zip file. However, in many cases you need to buy or download an application that provides the Zip file functionality.

Index

Note to the Reader: Page numbers in bold indicate the principle discussion of a topic or the definition of a term. Page numbers in *italic* indicate illustrations.

A

B

N

O

P

Q

R

S

W

X

Y

Z

Official DevX Books from SYBEX®

.NET PROGRAMMING 10-MINUTE SOLUTIONS

by A. Russell Jones and Mike Gunderloy

ISBN: 0-7821-4253-2 • US $29.99

Based on the popular question-and-answer feature of the DevX website, these ten-minute solutions fill the gaps in your knowledge. From them, you'll learn a lot about the realities of programming with .NET technologies, whether you're writing database applications, web applications, or desktop applications.

JAVA™ PROGRAMMING 10-MINUTE SOLUTIONS

by Mark Watson

ISBN: 0-7821-4285-0 • US $34.99

Java Programming 10-Minute Solutions provides direct solutions to the thorny problems you're most likely to run up against in your work. Especially when a project entails new techniques or draws you into a realm outside your immediate expertise, potential headaches abound. With this book, a veteran Java programmer saves you both aggravation and—just as important—time.

.NET DEVELOPMENT SECURITY SOLUTIONS

by John Paul Mueller

ISBN: 0-7821-4266-4 • US $39.99

.NET Development Security Solutions uses detailed, code-intensive examples—lots of them—to teach you the right techniques for most scenarios you're likely to encounter. This is not an introduction to security; it's an advanced cookbook that shows experienced programmers how to meet tough security challenges.

DEVELOPING KILLER WEB APPS WITH DREAMWEAVER MX® AND C#™

by Chuck White

ISBN: 0-7821-4254-0 • US $39.99

Written for both web page designers and Internet programmers, this unique book guides your transition from using Dreamweaver as a designer's tool to a developer's tool and IDE. Find out how Dreamweaver MX, when combined with Visual C#, becomes a rapid application development tool.

devX SYBEX®